THE ANATOMY OF
MADNESS

Essays in the History of Psychiatry

VOLUME II

THE ANATOMY OF MADNESS

Essays in the History of Psychiatry

VOLUME II

Institutions and Society

EDITED BY
W.F. Bynum, Roy Porter,
and Michael Shepherd

Tavistock Publications
LONDON AND NEW YORK

First published in 1985 by
Tavistock Publications Ltd
11 New Fetter Lane, London EC4P 4EE
Published in the USA by
Tavistock Publications
in association with Methuen, Inc.
29 West 35th Street, New York, NY 10001

Typeset by Graphicraft Typesetters Ltd, Hong Kong
Printed in Great Britain at
the University Press, Cambridge

British Library Cataloguing in Publication Data

The Anatomy of madness: essays in the history of psychiatry.
1. Psychiatry—History
I. Title II. Porter, Roy, 1946– III. Bynum,
W.F. 1943– IV. Shepherd, Michael, 1923–
616.89'009   RC438

ISBN 0–422–79430–9 (V. 1)
ISBN 0–422–79440–6 (V. 2)
ISBN 0–422–60350–3 (Set)

Library of Congress Cataloging in Publication Data

Main entry under title:
The Anatomy of madness.

'Most of the papers in these volumes arose from a seminar series
on the history of psychiatry and a one-day seminar on the same
theme held at the Wellcome Institute for the History of
Medicine, London, during the academic year 1982–83'—
Acknowledgements.
Includes bibliographies and indexes.
Contents: v. 1. People and ideas   v. 2. Institutions and society.
1. Psychiatry—Europe—History—Addresses, essays,
lectures. 2. Psychiatric hospitals—Europe—History—Addresses,
essays, lectures. I. Bynum, W.F.
(William F.), 1943– II. Porter, Roy,
1946– III. Shepherd, Michael, 1923–
IV. Wellcome Institute for the History of Medicine.
RC450.A1A53   1985   362.2'094   85–9824

ISBN 0–422–79430–9 (V. 1)
ISBN 0–422–79440–6 (V. 2)
ISBN 0–422–60350–3 (Set)

Contents

Contents

Contents of companion volume
Volume I
People and Ideas

Contributors

Patricia Allderidge, MA (Cambridge), has been archivist to The Bethlem Royal Hospital and The Maudsley Hospital since 1967. Her publications include *The Late Richard Dadd* (catalogue of an exhibition at the Tate Gallery). She has also published articles on the history of Bethlem Hospital, and the history of institutional care of the insane.

W.F. Bynum is Head of the joint Academic Unit for the History of Medicine at the Wellcome Institute for the History of Medicine and University College London. He is the editor (with Roy Porter and E.J. Browne) of *A Dictionary of the History of Science*, and the author of a number of articles on the history of psychiatry. His study of the relationship between basic science and clinical medicine in the nineteenth century will be published by Cambridge University Press.

Anne Digby is a Research Fellow at the Institute for Research in the Social Sciences at the University of York, and was formerly Senior Lecturer in History at Homerton College, Cambridge. She read economics and history at New Hall, Cambridge and received her PhD from the University of East Anglia. She has written extensively on modern British social history. She is the author of *Pauper Palaces*, and, with Peter Searby, of *Children, School and Society in Nineteenth-Century England*. Her book on the Retreat – *Madness, Morality and Medicine* – is soon to be published. Currently, she is working on doctor–patient relationships in the eighteenth and nineteenth centuries.

Joel Peter Eigen is Associate Professor and Chair of the Department of Sociology at Franklin and Marshall College in Lancaster, Pennsylvania. His BS is from Ohio University and his MA and PhD are from the University of Pennsylvania. Affiliated in the past with the Center for Studies in Criminal Justice at the University of Chicago Law School and the Center for Studies in Criminology and Criminal Law at the University of Pennsylvavia, his research has appeared in the *Journal of Criminal Law and Criminology*, *The American Sociologist*, and *The University of Chicago Law Review*. During the years 1982 and 1983, he was appointed Visiting Fellow at the Institute of Criminology, University of Cambridge, where he engaged in historical research on the jurisprudence of intent, reported on in this volume. In the summer of 1984, he received a Legal History Fellowship from the American Bar Foundation and returned to Cambridge to continue work on the evolution of forensic testimony in early English insanity trials.

FIONA GODLEE studied the history of medicine at University College London and the Wellcome Institute (BSc First Class Honours), and is at present in her final year as a medical student at the University of Cambridge.

RUTH HARRIS graduated from the University of Pennsylvania in 1979. She began her graduate work as a Thouron Scholar at St Anthony's College, Oxford and held Wellcome studentships for two years. Currently a Junior Research Fellow at St John's College, Oxford, she has completed her PhD in the history of criminal insanity and has particular interests in the history of law, psychiatry and the social aspects of criminality in nineteenth-century France.

NICHOLAS HERVEY is currently a psychiatric social worker at The Bethlem Royal Hospital and The Maudsley Hospital. A history graduate from Bristol University, he is also completing a PhD at that University, on the role of the Lunacy Commission in the formulation and implementation of lunacy legislation in the mid-nineteenth century. He has published a monograph, *Bowhill House: St Thomas's Hospital for Lunatics, Asylum for the Four Western Counties 1801–1896*. He is also the author of a forthcoming paper on the Alleged Lunatic's Friends Society, and has a special interest in the private care of single patients in the nineteenth century.

CHARLOTTE MACKENZIE read history at New Hall, Cambridge. She is currently completing a PhD on the history of Ticehurst Asylum at the Wellcome Institute in London. Her other interests include women's history and the history of psychoanalysis.

ROY PORTER is Senior Lecturer at the Wellcome Institute for the History of Medicine, London. After working early on the history of the earth sciences, and writing *The Making of Geology*, he has subsequently researched in parallel into social history, (*English Society in the Eighteenth Century*) and the social dimensions of the history of medicine. He is currently working on the early history of psychiatry in Britain, on quackery and on the lay experience of illness and doctors.

ROGER QVARSELL is a PhD and lecturer at the Department of History of Science and Ideas at the University of Umeå, Sweden. He has written a book and several articles (in Swedish) about the history of psychiatry and the treatment of the mentally ill in Sweden during the nineteenth century. He has also written a book about the cultural milieu and the conditions for the spreading of ideas in the little town of Härnöand in the northern part of Sweden around the middle of the nineteenth century. He is presently working on an essay on the history of child psychiatry in Sweden and planning a research project about the history of forensic psychiatry.

MICHAEL SHEPHERD is Professor of Epidemiological Psychiatry and Honorary Director, General Practice Research Unit at the Institute of Psychiatry, University of London. He is the author of several monographs and many research papers; a bibliography of his publications may be found in a volume of his selected papers, *The Psychosocial Matrix of Psychiatry*. In 1970 he founded the distinguished journal *Psychological Medicine*, which he still edits. He is also general editor of the multivolume *Handbook of Psychiatry*.

MARTIN STONE studied biology and social and political science at the University of Cambridge and has recently completed a PhD thesis at the London School of Economics on the industrial and military roots of clinical psychology in Britain. He has researched several aspects of the development of modern mental medicine and psychology and is interested in the politics of current mental health questions.

ANNAMARIA TAGLIAVINI graduated in philosophy in 1978 with a thesis on the psychological themes in the work of Charles Darwin, particularly in his Notebooks of 1837–38. As a collaborator of the Institute of Philosophy of the University of Bologna, she has since studied the history of Italian psychiatry in the second half of the nineteenth century, publishing several articles. In collaboration with other colleagues she edited a book (V.P. Babini, M. Cotti, F. Minuz, A. Tagliavini), *Tra sapere e potere. La psichiatria italiana nella seconda metà dell'Ottocento*. Her section therein was particularly concerned with theoretical aspects of the psychiatric profession in the period influenced by the cultural climate of Positivism. In the context of Italian science, she studied the Congresses of Italian scientists (F. Minuz, A. Tagliavini), 'Identikit degli scienziati a congresso', in G. Pancaldi (ed.), *I congressi degli scienziati italiani nell'età del positivismo* and the naturalistic expeditions (A. Tagliavini, 'Alla scoperta della natura', in M. Bossi (ed.), *Notizie di viaggi lontani. L'esplorazione extraeuropea nei periodici del primo Ottocento, 1815–1845*. During the academic year 1983–84 she had a Nato-CNR Fellowship at the Wellcome Institute for the History of Medicine, London, doing research on the influence of evolutionism on British psychiatry.

JOHN K. WALTON is a Lecturer in History at the University of Lancaster, teaching courses on English social history since the seventeenth century with special reference to Lancashire and the Lake District. His publications include *The Blackpool Landlady: A Social History*; *The Lake Counties from 1830 to the Mid-twentieth Century* (with J.D. Marshall); *The English Seaside Resort: A Social History, 1750–1914*; and *Leisure in Britain 1790–1939* (edited with James Walvin). He is currently working on a social history of Lancashire between the mid-sixteenth century and the Second World War.

Acknowledgements

MOST OF THE papers in these volumes arose from a seminar series on the history of psychiatry and a one-day seminar on the same theme held at the Wellcome Institute for the History of Medicine, London, during the academic year 1982–83. The editors wish to express their gratitude to the Wellcome Trustees for providing facilities for these meetings and for providing funds to meet research expenses. We also wish to put on record our deep thanks to the staff of Tavistock Publications, in particular its chief editor, Gill Davies, for the exemplary interest and courtesy, enthusiasm, and efficiency which we have received from them during the putting of these volumes through the press.

Introduction

THROUGHOUT EUROPE AND North America, the past century and a half has seen the gradual development of what has been called the 'therapeutic state'. Governments have assumed increasing responsibility for a vast array of functions which in earlier times were either unrecognized or fell within the domain of individual charity or co-operative philanthropy. Whether the process be subsumed under the guise of the 'Welfare State', or 'social security', or *assistance publique*, or *Sozialeinrichtungen*, the phenomenon itself (at least until the fiscal crises of the past decade) has seemed inexorable.[1]

There were, of course, problems. Not everyone has always subscribed to the philosophy of 'you never had it so good', but until the early 1960s or so, most commentators assumed things *were* getting better and better, and that the problems could be solved by more rational planning and increased public spending. The development of an increasing number of professions with their own areas of expertise; the increasing influence of science and science-based technology; the perceptible augmentation of human control over nature: these and many other facets of 'modernity' seemed to guarantee that difficulties could be surmounted, given sufficient allocation of man-power and resources.[2]

The psychiatric profession and psychiatric services have been a touchstone for this aspect of modern western history. Although psychiatry has never been a particular darling of politicians (chronic schizophrenics or old people with senile dementia are less newsworthy than homeless orphans or young victims of cancer), the issues central to the status of contemporary psychiatry are also fundamental to debates about the modern therapeutic state. Many of these can be encapsulated through a series of polarities: individual v. state; hospital v. asylum; freedom v. coercion; localism v. bureaucracy; private v. public. These dichotomies are not the exclusive province of psychiatry, as attested by the appearance in recent dictionaries not just of the ugly word 'psychiatrization', but of the more euphonious 'medicalization' as well.[3] But the 'antipsychiatry' movement has been more sharply defined than the 'antimedical' movement, and for many people, psychiatry symbolizes more than any other discipline the intrusiveness of contemporary welfare services. In many western societies, the number of psychiatric beds borders on 50 per cent of the total for all 'sick' people, yet many of the occupants are there not by choice but by certification.[4]

The writing of the *history* of psychiatry seems to have been growing proportionally even faster than the presumed explosion of psychiatric services implied by the word 'psychiatrization'. From being the almost exclusive preserve of elderly psychiatrists, the history of psychiatry has become an arena for medical, legal, and social historians, sociologists, and philosophers. Much of this literature has reflected the more general disquiet with the psychiatric scene, and has concentrated on institutional aspects of the subject: not surprisingly, because the antipsychiatry movement itself has been rooted in history and tends to view psychiatric hospitalization after certification as the 'natural' culmination of the contemporary psychiatrist acting as agent for the therapeutic state intent on imposing conformity and social order.

This can be seen clearly in the late Peter Sedgwick's recent analysis of the antipsychiatry movement, *Psychopolitics*.[5] For Sedgwick, four apocalyptic individuals stand out: Erving Goffman, Michel Foucault, Thomas Szasz, and R.D. Laing. It was Goffman who etched the concept of the 'total institution' on to modern consciousness, and although he insisted that prisons, sanitaria, boarding schools, and ships at sea were also instances of total institutions, it was at a psychiatric hospital – St Elizabeth's in Washington DC – where he conducted his research.[6] And through novels such as *One Flew Over the Cuckoo's Nest* and attention by the media, the psychiatric hospital itself has come most vividly to represent the total institution.

For the historiography of psychiatry, the late Michel Foucault remains the most important of Sedgwick's four horsemen. Although many would see him as a philosopher rather than a historian (he once described himself as a 'contented positivist'), Foucault has written with such graphic power on 'the ship of fools', 'the great confinement', the Salpêtrière under Pinel, or the York Retreat under the Tukes, that it is these images above all that the reader takes away from *Madness and Civilisation*.[7] The empirical accuracy of his work has been challenged, as has the more widespread applicability of his account, based largely on French sources, but he inevitably remains a point of departure even for psychiatric historians who are dubious about the ultimate coherence of his vast, but sadly uncompleted, philosophico-historical enterprise.[8]

For Thomas Szasz, too, psychiatric institutions embody physically all that is wrong with contemporary psychiatry. His critiques of diagnosis and 'therapy' make polemical use of historical instances (for example, the presumed similarity between labelling a person a witch in the Renaissance and labelling a person 'insane' in the present century). For Szasz the only legitimate psychiatry is contractual, and the use of psychiatric diagnosis to 'explain' the behaviour of deviants or non-conformists is not only a misuse of proper medical diagnosis (which can be done only for physical disease) but also results in more pernicious consequences for the offender himself than would have accrued from any sentencing in ordinary courts of law. Better prison than a psychiatric hospital without consent: in hospitals, one should go in voluntarily and be able to leave at will.[9]

Szasz argues from the individualistic philosophical standpoint elaborated in the nineteenth century by John Stuart Mill, but his own position requires the assumption of a rigorous mind/body dualism at odds with contemporary neuroscience, and a notion of the conscious goal-directedness of all behaviour which discounts much modern psychological, psychiatric, and psychoanalytical work. Although Szasz and Laing have been politically at odds, they are often yoked together since each has criticized the extent to which psychiatry judges its 'therapeutic' success in terms of social functioning, which in practical terms may mean behavioural conformity. When psychiatrists talk of 'insight', both would argue, they too often mean that the patients are simply beginning to come round to the psychiatrist's way of thinking.

There are, of course, thousands of psychiatrists quietly engaged in practice and research without much direct reference to the antipsychiatry movement. But Szasz and Laing, Foucault and Goffman remain far more visible than workaday psychiatrists (although in England, Anthony Clare, a contributor to Volume I, the companion to this volume, seems set fair to become the man in the street's psychiatrist for the next decade). And in these matters, historians and sociologists have moved with the times. The old meliorism is gone. Although the word 'reform' is still used, its meaning is no longer unambiguous. 'More' no longer has to equal 'better'.

This newer historiographical stance is perhaps best seen in the work of Andrew Scull (whose study of John Conolly also appears in Volume I). In a series of articles, and in two books – *Museums of Madness* and *Decarceration* – he has examined both historical and contemporary dimensions of psychiatric institutions.[10] He is sensitive to the social, legal, and professional ramifications of the faith pinned by the Victorians on the capacity of large, well-run asylums to deal with the problem of 'madness' within the context of a rational, industrial and increasingly anonymous society. Although using the perspective of sociology, Scull writes primarily as a historian with a fine ear for striking quotations and the nuances of historical meanings. His analysis may be stimulating, but it is also depressing, with its sprawling architectural monstrosities, its regimentation and monotony, its chemical restraint replacing mechanical, its medical superintendents becoming managerial bureaucrats. His work on contemporary critiques of the asylum (or 'psychiatric hospital' in preferred parlance) has alerted him to the deep-rootedness of the issues, for he can find remarkable continuities between the insights of Victorians who, from the 1860s, became increasingly disaffected with the asylum, and Californian descendants a century later who legislated hospitalizable insanity out of existence. Scull has been accused of wanting it both ways: of castigating both psychiatrists who advocated asylums and legislators (and psychiatrists) who tried to create 'community psychiatry'. Kathleen Jones, a historian of social policy who has continued to adhere largely to the older, meliorist approach, has characterized this as 'Scull's Dilemma'.[11] Scull's tone may be strident, but *pace* Jones, the dilemma is not Scull's. It is society's. Chronic schizophrenia, psychopathy, and senile dementia may not be best dealt with in a total institution, but neither can they be legislated away.

Scull has been concerned primarily with the asylum phenomenon itself: for his purposes it was irrelevant what was 'really' wrong with those individuals who inhabited the Victorian asylums. The figures themselves bespeak a dramatic increase – both in total numbers and in percentages – of the population who inhabited lunatic asylums. Until recently, he has been reluctant to engage in much debate on whether mental disorders *actually* increased during the course of the nineteenth century, but his analysis suggests that the very existence of asylum beds generated the individuals to fill them, as unwanted misfits – the demented, the old, the awkward – were dumped by relatives no longer willing or able to care for their own.[12]

Scull's work has not included any in-depth analysis of an individual asylum; seeking, for instance, to use diagnostic criteria or case records to test his implications. This is not so easy as it sounds, for although nineteenth-century asylum records survive, sometimes in abundance, as J.N. Walton points out in his essay below, they are often too patchy to permit systematic analysis of why Victorians 'cast out' or 'brought back' the insane. Neverthe-less, his work, based largely on the Lancashire County Asylum, does portray vividly the range of circumstances surrounding admission to asylums, and, incidentally, gives the lie to the caricature of them as largely silted up, geriatric institutions with little movement out except via the morgue. One other study of a single asylum – that of Richard Hunter and Ida Macalpine on Colney Hatch, in North London – has suggested that Victorian asylums were filled with unfortunates suffering from physical (mainly neurological) disorders – general paresis, epilepsy, ataxias, and the like.[13] Such an analysis, if confirmed by more systematic investigations, would not necessarily blur the contours of Scull's figures, but it might shift their social implications. It might also make nineteenth-century asylum doctors not so much conscious agents of social control and professional aggrandizement as medical men trying to cope with difficult circumstances. As Walton suggests, however, the evidence fits no single or simple explana-tory model.

Historical circumstances are often flexible enough to accommodate, without snapping, a variety of interpretive glosses. Recent historical research has uncovered a vast number of new 'facts' relating to the history of asylums. However, it is not simply these new facts but their evaluation which has given post-Foucaultian psychiatric history its bite. Thus, for instance, the work of Fears, Mellett, and Donnelly has examined aspects of what Mellett has called 'the prerogative of asylumdom'. Fears has been interested in the ideological dimensions of moral therapy, Donnelly has retraced many of Scull's steps in looking at the early nineteenth-century institutional management of the mad, and Mellett has paid particular attention to the bureaucracy (especially in the form of the Commissioners of Lunacy) which the asylum movement spawned.[14] While the latter work in particular is finely textured, and does not carry the flavour of historical inevitability sometimes characteristic of Fears's and Donnelly's analyses, across all these studies Foucault casts a long shadow.

And it is not simply his *Madness and Civilization*. His subsequent book on the French penal system, *Discipline and Punish*, has been viewed as a parallel investigation. The historical interplay between prisons (aiming at both reformation of character and chastisement of transgression) and asylums has been seen as far richer (and more ominous) than the older psychiatric history allowed. Historians of English asylums can now be expected to be familiar with Michael Ignatieff's *A Just Measure of Pain*.[15] This examination of the English prison between about 1780 and 1850 makes only occasional sideways glances at contemporary psychiatric developments, but such explicit comparisons no longer need to be drawn, so 'obvious' have they become. Likewise, Robin Evans's fine study of English prison architecture between 1750 and 1840 will have many resonances for historians of psychiatry.[16]

Some, though by no means all, of this literature has been produced using the concept of 'social control'. Like 'by and by', 'social control' is easily said, though less easily defined. Who is controlling whom, and why? Some indication of the complexity of the concept can be gleaned from the recent volume edited by Scull and Stanley Cohen, *Social Control and the State*.[17] Although it may to a certain extent simply reflect the interests of the editors, almost half the essays deal with psychiatry. The volume makes it clear that there is no monolithic 'strong programme' among the contributors. For example, one of the essayists is David Rothman, whose book *Discovery of the Asylum* (1971) was one of the first to examine the varieties of institutional experience in Jacksonian America. The subtitle of Rothman's book is 'social order and disorder in the New Republic', and the fact that he examines penitentiaries, lunatic asylums, and almshouses between the covers of a single volume suggests common elements in early American perceptions of crime, insanity, and poverty.[18]

Rothman's book is now more than a decade old, and though much praised when it appeared (and still much used), it has been seriously faulted by Scull, among others, on both factual and interpretive grounds. The former concerns Rothman's 'account of the discovery of the asylum that emphasizes its sudden eruption on to the nineteenth-century scene, and its uniquely American origins'. Scull himself stresses the earlier European origins of the idea and ideal of the asylum. More consequential, however, is Scull's charge that Rothman fails adequately to integrate 'changing social practices with underlying structures'. For Scull, Rothman's account remains too little concerned with the collectivities of class and profession, and too much rooted in the 'perceptions of society's individual members'.[19]

Although Rothman's work has been much cited by those who accept a labelling theory of deviance, Rothman himself seems less than happy about the current state of historical scholarship in the whole area of social control. In his essay in the Cohen and Scull volume ('Social Control: The Uses and Abuses of the Concept in the History of Incarceration'), he argues that the 'reform/social control' polarity is too sharp: neither perspective has a monopoly on historical (or contemporary) truth. The world, after all, is not black and white; it is probably black and grey.

The 'probably' in the last sentence is of course a giveaway, an identifying feature of the middle ground. Certainly the social control approach has been enriching for the history of psychiatry, and the now-related field of history of criminology. Many younger historians (and a few not so young) are more likely to study the history of deviance than the history of psychiatry *per se*. But as several of the contributors to the Cohen-Scull volume insist, there are limitations to the applicability of the social control model. It sometimes seems to impute completely cynical and hypocritical motives to individuals whom an earlier tradition counted as humanitarian reformers. Literary critics are taught that imputing motives – good or bad – to an artist or writer is a transgression: an instance of the 'intentional fallacy'. Like thoughts, motives are essentially private and historians need to beware of straying beyond the evidence. In practice, however, historical actors are generally endowed with motives in the very act of historical reconstruction, and the social control literature is no more value-free than the liberal historiography it has sought to replace. But the question of motive is still often unresolved, even when a strategy is employed to replace individual motives with collective (class or professional group) ones, thus making individuals automatic mouthpieces for the interests of their class or profession.

It has been remarked recently that, despite 'differences in approach and methodology, such scholars as Michel Foucault, David J. Rothman, Andrew Scull, Richard T. Fox, Michael B. Katz and Christopher Lasch all have one element in common: a critical if not hostile view of psychiatry and mental hospitals'. Such a statement may take us back to the unfruitful *ad hominem* arguments, and the problem of motive (in this case, the motives of historians), but it reminds us that the 'new' history of psychiatry has not commanded universal assent, even among historians. It was penned by Gerald Grob, a historian whose initial excursion (along with Norman Dain) into the field some two decades ago was in fact a signal that American historians were at last taking the history of psychiatry seriously.[20] Both scholars have remained productive, Grob primarily as a chronicler of the asylum in America, Dain operating more within the sphere of ideas and people. Both have recently produced books on twentieth-century topics, and the gap that has widened between the traditional style and the 'new' style history of psychiatry may be seen by comparing Dain's biography of Clifford Beers, or Grob's *Mental Illness and American Society, 1875–1940*, with *The Psychiatric Society*, by Castel, Castel, and Lovell.[21] All three books are concerned with the eclipse of the asylum in twentieth-century America. Dain charts the rise and fall of the Mental Hygiene Movement, the brainchild of the ex-patient Clifford Beers. Although the Movement was dedicated to both community action and asylum reform, it was hardly the success its founder dreamed of: something more than a noble failure, perhaps, but certainly more capable of raising money than of improving 'mental hygiene' or fundamentally changing the structure of American psychiatry. Grob's account stops shy of the disaffection with psychiatry of the past two decades, but he accepts psychiatry's golden period in America on its own terms. Although psychoanalysis gets short shrift in his account, he sees the gradual abandonment of the asylum as a positive step, part of psychiatrists' 'dream of a transforming social redemption'.[22] But Grob's dream is the Castels' nightmare (ironically, François Castel is herself a psychiatrist): an explosion of what they call the 'psy services' (psychiatry, psychoanalysis, psychology, psychiatric social work, psychotherapy, etc.). The Castels are French, and *The Psychiatric Society* was originally published in French, as a possible warning to their countrymen about what to expect as France becomes as 'advanced' psychiatrically as the United States. Their gaze is at 'a padded world watched over night and day by guards of skilled specialists, many of them well-meaning. Skilled at what? At manipulating people to accept the constraints of society.'[23]

Although the heyday of the asylum may be past, it continues to occupy the centre stage in much historical writing, because of its crucial links with the development of the psychiatric profession in the nineteenth century. Throughout Europe and North America, asylums were public institutions, funded by public money and thereby fusing an alliance between the state and the profession from the latter's earliest formative period. The other major point of intersection has been between the profession and the law, and at this juncture, too, historical analysis has proved an important constituent of contemporary debate. The asylums of course had their own legal frame-works, relating both to finances and more crucially, perhaps, to the procedure whereby patients were admitted. As far as the history of criminology is concerned, David Philips has recently insisted that:

> 'Future impressive advances in this field are not going to come from people who keep their noses buried in dusty files in the Public Record Office – or County Record Offices or libraries – and lift them only to tell us that they find the detailed process of interaction between the various individuals involved too complex to yield any overall patterns.'[24]

Presumably the same thing could be said of dusty asylum records, and Philips is correct to assert that new theoretical stances often generate new historical questions. Quite frankly, however, it is easier to generalize from single instances, impressions, and secondary sources than it is from systematic analysis and we simply do not know enough about diagnostic criteria or admission procedures in nineteenth-century asylums either to substantiate or refute some of the sweeping claims in the historical literature. Nancy Tomes's study of Thomas Kirkbride and the Pennsylvania Hospital provides new understanding of the American scene, and Nicholas Hervey's forthcoming examination of the Surrey asylums should help with England.[25] But careful and cautious empirical research does not have to end in the 'one damn thing after another' camp.

About the other dimension to psychiatry and the law interaction – the courtroom and criminal insanity – we are beginning to know a bit more. For Szasz, of course, the courtroom is the site *par excellence* where madness is manufactured, and certainly early nineteenth-century formulations of categories like 'moral insanity', the monomanias (e.g. dipsomania, kleptomania, nymphomania), and affective disorders widened the boundaries of what counted as 'disease'.[26] This meant that some people formerly seen as sinful, or depraved, or even criminal were now judged, by at least some medical men, as being sick.

American and British forensic psychiatry have of course developed in their own separate ways, though for both societies the trial of Daniel McNaughten for murder was a crucial event.[27] As is so often the case, however, historical analysis has been coloured by contemporary concerns, and in America this has meant the challenge of Szasz and the more general preoccupation with medical ethics. Symptomatic, perhaps, is the recent volume edited by Brody and Engelhardt, *Mental Illness: Law and Public Policy*. The contributors are almost all philosophers or lawyers, and though the essays almost always pay attention to historical precedent, their concern is primarily with the present litigious American scene. Szasz is by far the single most cited author.[28] There are a couple of articles on the foremost nineteenth-century American psychiatric commentator on the legal status of the madman, Issac Ray, and Charles Rosenberg has written a fascinating account of the trial of Guiteau, who assassinated the President of the United States, James Garfield.[29] But much historical (as opposed to philosophical or legal) analysis still remains to be done.[30]

The American legal system was heavily influenced by the English, and English legal psychiatry is beginning to be investigated historically. The standard source remains Nigel Walker's two-volumed study of past and present, the first volume setting the historical framework.[31] More recently, Roger Smith has subjected the crucial formative period – the mid-nineteenth century – to rigorous scrutiny. He has looked at the status of psychiatrists and general physicians in the courtroom, and has elucidated the almost inevitable conflicts between psychiatry and the law: conflicts because the world of psychiatrists is (in theory, at least) deterministic, while that of lawyers is voluntaristic.[32] Disease exculpates whereas the law assumes criminals to be free agents. McNaughten and his trial have been subjected to two full-length analyses, that by two psychiatrists Walk and West, leaving one with the distinct impression that McNaughten would be diagnosed today as a paranoid schizophrenic.[33] More recently Richard Moran, an American sociologist, has subjected McNaughten to his most searching historical examination and has concluded that the question of 'real' insanity or normality is irrelevant. He was, Moran insists, guilty of a political crime and consequently denied a proper trial because of the political realities of his time. 'From a sociological standpoint, whether McNaughten was persecuted or paranoid is not critical', Moran writes.[34] If he meant by this that in the long run it was the rules which mattered, it is a reasonable statement. But what he seems to have meant is that, irrespective of McNaughten's mental state, the political circumstances were such that his action (shooting Edward Drummond, mistaking him for the Prime Minister Robert Peel) had an 'objective correlative'. Moran argues that McNaughten was pronounced insane because an uneasy Tory government could not face the adverse publicity of a political martyrdom for McNaughten, a possible result had he been tried and executed.

Whatever the cogency of Moran's account, it reminds us that legal precedents are established within definite socio-political environments, and that within the large grey area of 'criminal insanity' psychiatrists have become important actors in the drama that Herbert Spencer called Man v. the State. Far more than any other medical speciality, psychiatry has been bound up with the legal provisions attending asylums and illegal acts committed by those deemed incapable of knowing right from wrong.

Three of the papers in the present volume explore fairly specific dimensions of these issues. That of Joel Eigen investigates the interactions of judges, juries, and medical men at the Old Bailey in trials where the insanity plea was used between about 1760 and 1815. Based on a systematic examination of the Old Bailey Records, Eigen's essay throws much light on the situation a generation before McNaughten's trial and the 'McNaughten Rules', at a time when the criteria for determining criminal insanity were still flexible and before doctors were so commonly used as 'expert witnesses'. In such a context it is not surprising that the dominant figure was the judge, who could sum up the evidence and instruct the jury in such a way as to make the verdict virtually a foregone conclusion. The recent trial of Peter Sutcliffe, the 'Yorkshire Ripper', gives his study a particular topicality, but the present essay also provides an important baseline for his continued investigations into the later period, characterized not only by the guidelines (unsatisfactory as they have always been) supplied by the McNaughten Rules, but also by the changing relationships between doctors and the law after a more cohesive psychiatric profession began to form. Eigen's work represents a pioneering attempt to go beyond the history of forensic psychiatry as a series of famous trials and legal precedents by examining the ordinary day-to-day situation.

It has often been remarked that the McNaughten Rules governed Anglo-American thinking on the matter until well into the present century. Their emphasis was on cognitive aspects of insanity: on the *knowledge* of right and wrong which the responsible 'normal' person is supposed to possess. In other cultures, as Ruth Harris's essay suggests, the situation was different. Her analysis of the trial of Gabrielle Bompard, charged in 1890 with complicity in the murder and robbery of a Parisian bailiff, uncovers significant differences between French and Anglo-American legal psychiatry. In France, strong emotions were permitted greater sway in what counted as legitimate exculpatory evidence: crimes of passion (*crimes passionnels*) often made good new copy, and those who had murdered an unfaithful spouse or a faithless lover (or a faithless lover's lover) could be elevated to an exalted popular status. As Ian Dowbiggin has demonstrated in volume I, the concept of degenerationism was pervasive in French psychiatry, and though it would have profound consequences for the way bourgeois psychiatrists (and judges) viewed their lower class 'clients', it also increased the range of crimes and criminals which might come within the psychiatric ken. Although Gabrielle was a 'typical' degenerate – sexually promiscuous and frequenting the haunts of outcast Paris – her case was further complicated by her defence resting on the fact that she had been hypnotized into submission by her accomplice-lover. Her trial thus became an ideological battle-ground for the opposing psychiatric schools (that of Charcot at the Salpêtrière, and that of Bernheim at Nancy) with differing views about the possibility of people under the influence of hypnosis committing acts (crimes, sexual submission, etc.) which they would not normally do.[35] Harris thus uses the trial as a window to French society, law, and psychiatry in the *belle époque*.

At first sight, Martin Stone's study of the diagnosis and treatment of shell-shock in the First World War might appear to be more appropriately placed in Volume I. In fact, however, it is concerned not simply with the early use of explicitly psychoanalytical and psychotherapeutic techniques in the treatment of what came to be referred to as a kind of 'war neurosis'. At another level, it describes an important aspect – in the British context – of the final parting of the ways of neurology and psychiatry, of the recognition that the physicalist implications of the phrase 'shellshock' were misplaced. Recent studies of 'miner's nystagmus' and 'soldier's heart' have elucidated the extent to which doctors had achieved, by the early twentieth century, the power to act as the state's official representatives in the certification of illness now deemed worthy of pensionable status.[36] Shellshock – recognized by many by the end of the First World War as a 'mental' disorder – was another of these conditions. Although abreaction and other psychological techniques were only part of the story, and although many military authorities continued to see shellshock in terms of morale or plain cowardice, the very fact that some 200,000 soldiers and sailors developed symptoms severe enough to be relieved from active duty, and that Ministry of Pensions payments were still being made for shellshock by the time the Second World War broke out, testifies to the status of 'psychological medicine' by the early twentieth century. At one level, shellshock is a cautionary tale of 'psychiatrization'. But it can also remind us how complicated are the issues, for the alternatives in 1916 were stark: one could be invalided out, court-martialled for cowardice, or returned, disintegrated and debilitated, to the trenches.

The essays by Eigen, Harris, and Stone examine important aspects of the growing use by the modern state of the psychiatric profession and of the concepts on which the profession was based. Inevitably, though, the majority of the essays in this volume are concerned with the central feature of the nineteenth-century profession, the asylum. As remarked above, the profession and the institution were intimately intertwined historically. Despite the relative familiarity of the main outline of the story, however, in our knowledge there are still surprisingly large gaps.

Take Bedlam, for instance, arguably the most famous psychiatric hospital in the world. As Patricia Allderidge reminds us, we know precious little about Bethlem, and much of what we 'know' is myth. At point after point, she demonstrates that the Bedlam of historians is not the Bethlem of history. She examines layer after layer of the myth: about conditions, about 96,000 frolicking visitors coming to see the mad folk, about James Norris chained up for ten years or more. Of course, conditions were not as good as they might have been, to put it mildly; of course, it was possible (until about 1770; we are told by Foucault that it was still going on in 1815) for the man in the street to visit the institution; of course, Norris was chained. But the archives show that realities behind the myths were far more subtle, more ambiguous, than the cobwebs which have been spun. The Bethlem archives may or may not be dusty, but it is high time some historians started burying their noses in them.

After Bethlem, probably the second most famous psychiatric institution in Britain is the York Retreat. It shot into public consciousness around the time of the 1815 parliamentary enquiry into madhouses, when it appeared to represent all that an asylum ought to be. The testimony William and Samuel Tuke gave to the committee had simply reinforced the account in the first 'official' history of the Institution: Samuel Tuke's *Description of the Retreat* (1813). It remained our main source of information and interpretation until, following Foucault, historians like Scull and Fears have emphasized the more oppressive aspects of moral therapy. But Tuke has continued to be the primary source of basic information, despite the passage of 170 years. Tuke's own words are used either to praise or condemn, but, for historians, the institution itself seemed never to have changed after 1813.

Because of this, Anne Digby's full-scale history of the Retreat – based on rich and probably dusty archives – is to be doubly welcomed.[37] Her essay in the present volume uses these archives to examine the central issue of moral therapy at the Retreat – and not just for the period up to 1813. She is less concerned with exposing bourgeois mentalities than in finding out what happened in the Institution. Her careful research has revealed a number of interesting features of the later history of the Retreat, including the extent to which 'chemical restraint' was used, and her forthcoming book will help correct a number of myths – old and new – about this Quaker establishment.

Some selected aspects of the Retreat's Quaker background are examined in Fiona Godlee's sketch of the way an awareness of Quaker beliefs, practices, and values helps us 'read' Tuke's *Description*. In their transformation from seventeenth-century religious enthusiasts to nineteenth-century businessmen, this religious group was mirroring much that was happening to English society as a whole.[38] Quaker records tend to be relatively full and certainly deserve more systematic analysis for the light they shed on social perceptions of deviancy and insanity; Godlee's essay highlights the extent to which conformity to the group's norms was a feature of Quaker life during two centuries of change.

The essays by Walton, MacKenzie, and Harvey look at other aspects of nineteenth-century asylums. As we have noticed, Walton uses the Lancaster Asylum to examine the 'casting out' (admission) and 'bringing back' (discharge) of pauper lunatics. 'Social control' is a part of his framework, but by no means all. For as he points out, lunatic asylums were expensive alternatives to other available agencies – Poor Law workhouses, prisons, etc. Average ages of patients on admission of thirty-five to forty suggest that asylums were not geriatric dumping grounds. Rather, they seem to have been places of last resort, although the circumstances which led relatives or authorities to decide that the time had come for admission are often impossible to determine.

Fuller records exist for some of the private madhouses, catering for the well-to-do.[39] Of these, Ticehurst Asylum, in Sussex, was one of the most prominent. It was run as a successful family business by the Newingtons for almost two centuries, and case records survive from 1845. Charlotte MacKenzie's essay looks at the social matrix from which Ticehurst received its patients and at the hierarchical, largely patriarchal lines on which it was run. She notes that the patient records often contain rich psychological detail with a speculative organic gloss; and they may prove sufficiently textured to make diagnostic analysis feasible.[40] Equally significant is the fact that the social class to which patients at Ticehurst belonged makes it possible at times to supplement their hospital records with other sources – letters, diaries, published writings – and to begin to understand some of the social and familial circumstances surrounding admission and discharge: factors (as Walton has reminded us), generally elusive in the case of patients in the public sector. This in turn provides additional insight into the patients' experience of incarceration in Victorian Britain.[41]

Overseeing the asylums, of course, were the Commissioners of Lunacy, minutely analysed for the period 1845–60 by Nicholas Hervey. His essay provides much new information about the composition of the Commission, and about its relationship to the psychiatric profession, and to the bureaucracy which the 1845 Act accentuated. His study is particularly revealing about the piecemeal and gradual evolution of policy, and about the relative rigidity which came to characterize the Commissioners' attitudes in the late Victorian period. But by delving behind official reports – to diaries, correspondence, and private papers – he is also able to allow the Commissioners their individuality, even while being primarily concerned with their corporate activity.

On the Continent, too, the asylum loomed large during the nineteenth century, and the essays by Qvarsell and Tagliavini remind anglophonic readers that there was a world elsewhere. Qvarsell's study of Swedish psychiatry between 1800 and 1920 surveys developments in this country where social policy and medical science have their own rich histories. His essay is particularly useful in its demonstration of the impact which dynamic psychiatry had on Swedish asylums and points towards an important area of psychiatric history largely unexplored for any country: psychiatric education.[42] Tagliavini emphasizes the importance of evolutionary biology and positivism for Italian psychiatrists. She draws on a rich primary and secondary literature, the latter revealing the extent of Foucault's sway on Italian historians of psychiatry and the way in which Italian historiography has also been deeply influenced by the crisis of legitimation now facing psychiatry and psychiatric institutions in that country. Despite important differences, however, her analysis uncovers striking parallels with British developments, particularly in the way that psychiatrists became increasingly involved and identified with the state. Her essay, and that of Qvarsell, remind us that there is sufficient material available to make comparative historical studies feasible.

The value of the essays in this volume lies particularly in the variety of new empirical detail which they present. They offer no sweeping generalizations but demonstrate the profusion of sources touching on the history of psychiatry. As always, they uncover new questions in answering old ones, but they also show the value of patient historical enquiry in understanding the roots of psychiatry's contemporary dilemmas.

Notes

1 From the vast literature, cf. W.J. Mommsen (ed.), *The Emergence of the Welfare State in Britain and Germany* (London: Croom Helm, 1981); Jacques Donelot, *The Policing of Families* (London: Hutchinson, 1979); Robert Pinker, *The Idea of Welfare* (London: Heinemann, 1979); and, for psychiatry, Klaus Doerner, *Madmen and the Bourgeoisie* (Oxford: Blackwell, 1981).

2 The contrast between the attitudes of a generation or two ago and today can be seen from comparing A.M. Carr-Saunders and P.A. Wilson, *The Professions* (Oxford: Oxford University Press, 1933) with Ivan Illich (ed.), *Disabling Professions* (London: Marion Boyars, 1977).

3 The best-known work of the 'medicalization' literature is probably Ivan Illich, *Limits to Medicine* (Harmondsworth: Penguin, 1977).

4 For statistics for Britain, see Anthony Clare, *Psychiatry in Dissent*, 2nd edn (London: Tavistock, 1980), ch. 9.

5 Peter Sedgwick, *Psychopolitics* (London: Pluto Press, 1981).

6 Erving Goffman, *Asylums* (Harmondsworth: Penguin, 1968).

7 Michel Foucault, *Madness and Civilization* (London: Tavistock, 1965).

8 For a systematic critique of Foucault's book, see E. Midelfort, 'Madness and Civilization in Early Modern Europe', in B. Malament (ed.), *After the Reformation* (Philadelphia, Pa.: University of Pennsylvania Press, 1980), pp. 247–65; the best general exposition of Foucault's thought is A. Sheridan, *Michel Foucault, the Will to Truth* (London: Tavistock, 1980).

9 Szasz's books all develop similar themes. Among the most general of them is his *The Manufacture of Madness* (London: Paladin, 1973); also of particular

relevance is *Law, Liberty and Psychiatry* (London: Routledge and Kegan Paul, 1974).

10 A. Scull, *Museums of Madness* (London: Allen Lane, 1979); A. Scull, *Decarceration*, 2nd edn (Oxford: Polity Press, 1984).

11 Kathleen Jones, 'Scull's Dilemma', *British Journal of Psychiatry* 141 (1982): 221–26; Jones's earlier work on the subject includes *A History of the Mental Health Services* (London: Routledge and Kegan Paul, 1972).

12 For a recent airing of this issue, see Edward Hare, 'Was Insanity on the Increase?', *British Journal of Psychiatry* 142 (1983): 439–55; and A. Scull, 'Was Insanity Increasing? A Response to Edward Hare', *British Journal of Psychiatry* 144 (1984): 432–36.

13 R.A. Hunter and I. MacAlpine, *Psychiatry for the Poor. 1851 Colney Hatch Asylum, Friern Hospital 1973: A Medical and Social History* (London: Dawsons, 1974).

14 Michael Fears, 'The "Moral Treatment" of Insanity: A Study in the Social Construction of Human Nature' (PhD thesis, University of Edinburgh, 1978); D.J. Mellett, *The Prerogative of Asylumdon* (New York: Garland Press, 1983); M. Donnelly, *Managing the Mind* (London: Tavistock, 1983).

15 Michael Ignatieff, *A Just Measure of Pain* (London: Macmillan, 1978).

16 Robin Evans, *The Fabrication of Virtue. English Prison Architecture, 1750–1840* (Cambridge: Cambridge University Press, 1982); and A. Scull, 'A Convenient Place to Get Rid of Inconvenient People: the Victorian Lunatic Asylum', in Anthony O. King (ed.), *Buildings and Society* (London: Routledge and Kegan Paul, 1980), pp. 37–60.

17 S. Cohen and A. Scull (eds), *Social Control and the State* (Oxford: Martin Robertson, 1983).

18 D. Rothman, *The Discovery of the Asylum* (Boston, Mass.: Little, Brown, 1971). His more recent *Conscience and Convenience. The Asylum and Its Alternatives in Progressive America* (Boston, Mass.: Little, Brown, 1980) extends his analysis into the later period.

19 Cf. The essays by Rothman and Scull in Cohen and Scull, *Social Control and the State*.

20 Gerald Grob, *Mental Illness and American Society, 1875–1940* (Princeton, NJ: Princeton University Press, 1983), p. x; Grob's early works include *The State and the Mentally Ill: A History of Worcester State Hospital in Massachusetts, 1830–1920* (Chapel Hill, NC: University of North Carolina Press, 1966); and *Mental Institutions in America* (New York: Free Press, 1973). Dain's works include *Concepts of Insanity in the United States, 1789–1865* (New Brunswick, NJ: Rutgers University Press, 1964).

21 Grob, *Mental Illness and American Society*; R. Castel, F. Castel, and A. Lovell, *The Psychiatric Society* (New York: Columbia University Press, 1982).

22 Grob, *Mental Illness*, p. 109.

23 Castel, Castel, and Lovell, *The Psychiatric Society*, p. 320.

24 David Philips, '"A Just Measure of Crime, Authority, Hunters and Blue Locusts": The Revisionist Social History of Crime and the Law in Britain, 1780–1850', in Cohen and Scull (eds), *Social Control*, p. 68.

25 Nancy Tomes, *A Generous Confidence. Thomas Story Kirkbride and the Art of Asylum-keeping, 1840–1883* (New York and Cambridge: Cambridge University Press, 1984). Hervey's University of Bristol thesis should be finished shortly. His essay on the Commissioners of Lunacy appears in this volume.

26 A useful survey of the relevant conceptual dimensions is Henry Werlinder, *Psychopathy: A History of the Concepts* (Stockholm: Almqvist and Wiksell, 1978).

27 D.J. West and A. Walk (eds), *Daniel McNaughten: His Trial and the Aftermath* (Ashford: Gaskell Books, 1977).

28 B.A. Brody and H.T. Engelhardt, Jr (eds), *Mental Illness: Law and Public Policy* (Dordrecht and Boston, Mass.: Reidel, 1980).

29 J.M. Quen, 'Issac Ray and Mental Hygiene in America', *Annals of the New York Academy of Science* 291 (1977): 83–93; C.E. Rosenberg, *The Trial of the Assassin Guiteau: Psychiatry and Law in the Gilded Age* (Chicago: Chicago University Press, 1968).

30 On contemporary issues in forensic psychiatry in America, see Michael S. Moore, *Law and Psychiatry*. Rethinking the Relationships (Cambridge and New York: Cambridge University Press, 1984); Walter Bromberg, *The Uses of Psychiatry in the Law*: A Clinical View of Forensic Psychiatry (Westport, Conn.: Quorum Books, 1979); H. Fingarette, *The Meaning of Criminal Insanity* (Berkeley, Calif.: University of California Press, 1972).

31 Nigel Walker, *Crime and Insanity in England*, vol. 1, *The Historical Perspective* (Edinburgh: Edinburgh University Press, 1968).

32 Roger Smith, *Trial by Medicine. Insanity and Responsibility in Victorian Trials* (Edinburgh: Edinburgh University Press, 1981); Roger Smith, 'Defining Murder and Madness: An Introduction to Medicolegal Belief in the Case of Mary Ann Brough, 1854', *Knowledge and Society: Studies in the Sociology of Culture Past and Present* 4 (1982): 173–225.

33 West and Walk, *Daniel McNaughten* (note 27).

34 Richard Moran, *Knowing Right from Wrong. The Insanity Defense of Daniel McNaughtan* (New York: Free Press, 1983), p. 5. McNaughten's name has been spelled many different ways. We have followed West and Walk, although the spelling Moran uses has equal claims.

35 A general overview of these differences is provided by Henri F. Ellenberger, *The Discovery of the Unconscious* (New York: Basic Books, 1970).

36 Karl Figlio, 'How Does Illness Mediate Social Relations? Workman's Compensation and Medico-legal Practices, 1890–1940', in P. Wright and A. Treacher, *The Problem of Medical Knowledge* (Edinburgh: Edinburgh University Press, 1982), pp. 174–224; Joel Howell, 'From "Soldier's Heart" to the Cardiac Club: An Early British Speciality Group', in W. F. Bynum and C.J. Lawrence (eds), *The Emergence of Modern Cardiology, Medical History, Supplement* 5 (1985).

37 Anne Digby, *Madness, Morality and Medicine* (Cambridge and New York: Cambridge University Press, 1985).

38 Aspects of this transformation may be gleaned from Michael MacDonald, *Mystical Bedlam* (Cambridge and New York: Cambridge University Press, 1981); M. MacDonald, 'Religion, Social Change and Psychological Healing in England 1600–1800', in W. Sheils (ed.), *The Church and Healing* (Oxford: Basil Blackwell, 1982), pp. 101–26; Roy Porter, 'The Rage of Party: a Glorious Revolution in English Psychiatry?', *Medical History* 27 (1983): 35–50.

39 W.L. Parry-Jones, *The Trade in Lunacy* (London: Routledge and Kegan Paul, 1972), is a pioneering exploration of the private psychiatric sector in England.

40 Michael Clark, 'The Rejection of Psychological Approaches to Mental Disorder in Late Nineteenth-century British Psychiatry', in A. Scull (ed.), *Madhouses, Mad-doctors and Madmen* (London: Athlone Press, 1981), pp. 271–312, explores the paradox of the reluctance of late nineteenth-century psychiatrists in Britain to

put much weight on psychological definitions of mental disorders.

41 Cf. Peter McCandless, 'Liberty and Lunacy: the Victorians and Wrongful Confinement', in Scull, *Madhouses, Mad-doctors and Madmen.*

42 Although for France there is much useful material about the early nineteenth century in Jan Goldstein, 'French Psychiatry in Social and Political Context: The Formation of a New Profession, 1820–1860' (PhD thesis, Columbia University, 1978).

CHAPTER ONE

Bedlam: fact or fantasy?

Patricia Allderidge

THE ARCHIVES OF the Bethlem Royal Hospital have been open to the public for research since May 1967.[1] During the last seventeen years they have been consulted, in person and (more often) by letter and telephone, by local historians, architectural historians, heraldic historians, photographic historians, art historians, genealogists, poets, film makers, school children, training college students, novelists, picture researchers, and one historian of bagpipe music. They have also been used by a very small handful of people working in specific areas of psychiatric history which have led them, unavoidably, to these archives for information: two examples which come to mind both involved extensive use of the records of the nineteenth-century criminal lunatic department. But the most notable absentees have, in general, been those engaged in research in the history of psychiatry.

I have considered the possibility that nobody engaged in research in the history of psychiatry has ever heard of Bethlem or wishes to write about it, perhaps because it is too irrelevant: but that is not so. In every new book on the subject it appears faithfully in the index, and faithfully too it has its passing reference in the text. The reference usually sounds convincing and circumstantial, and has probably been introduced for the purpose of reinforcing some general point with evidence of pertinent historical fact.

This would seem to suggest, therefore, that Bethlem history has been very well researched, using all the resources of modern scholarship and up-to-date opinion, and published in great detail so that all the pertinent facts are already available in print. But there have actually been only two works published on the subject based on original research from primary sources: the practically unreadable *Story of Bethlehem Hospital* by E.G. O'Donoghue, published in 1914, and the practically unknown Bridewell and Bethlem section of the Charity Commissioners Report of 1837 by F.O. Martin. It is the former, where anything, that is cited: but there must be few subjects on which contemporary historians are prepared to accept unquestioningly, as their only source, the amateur and self-congratulatory work of a hospital chaplain with time on his hands, written nearly seventy years ago

in a style which manages to combine historical voyeurism with an unfortunate turn of whimsy (and, what is more, to accept it at second or third hand,
as is often undoubtedly the case).

Moreover, it is striking that the references to Bethlem which do appear in
print may vary in their degree of deviation from fact, but very little in the
subject matter and time span to which they confine themselves. They
generally refer – you could almost say invariably – to some aspect of the
absolute and utter awfulness of Bethlem, supported, if at all, by instances
which are used by implication to cover virtually any period you care to
mention, but which are actually drawn from the mid-eighteenth or early
nineteenth centuries. I have a theory that if there was not much time to go
into detail, the whole of history could probably by summarized as, 'Things
were pretty awful for most people most of the time'; but despite this, I
suspect that anyone who did not come up with more than two examples by
the end of the year would not get his research grant renewed: so I find it a
little surprising that it should even be supposed that in all its 737 years of
existence, only two or three things worth mentioning ever happened in
Bethlem.

I have therefore come to the conclusion that, on the whole, historians of
psychiatry actually do not want to know about Bethlem as a historical fact
because Bethlem as a reach-me-down historical cliché is far more useful. It
has, after all, fulfilled this role in the popular imagination throughout much
of its existence; and the instantly recognizable 'Bedlam' image can be used
on most occasions to fill in odd gaps in the picture, and add a touch of
verisimilitude to the whole. There are certain things 'everybody knows'
about Bethlem, which are fortunately not so closely defined that variations
cannot be worked on them to fit the required context; and they are all, of
course, irredeemably bad. Bethlem as the ultimate symbol of all that is evil is
far too useful a space-filler to be risked in the refining fires of academic
research: and it does not really matter too much what it symbolizes, so
long as it is sufficiently discreditable to be credible. The reading public
seems preconditioned to accept that if it is bad enough, it is bound to
be true.

The most striking illustration that I have come across lately is perhaps also
one of the most trivial: but its very triviality has some significance. In the
TLS review of Andrew Scull's *Madhouses, Mad-doctors and Madmen*,
Robert Brown writes (and he is here attemping to answer his own rhetorical
question, 'Who in Victorian psychiatry was curing what, and why?'):

'It is clear enough who was keeping watch on the mentally afflicted.
Throughout the eighteenth century, and well into the nineteenth, it was
clergymen, jailors, relatives, private mad-house proprietors, hospital
attendants unwillingly or unwittingly, and the keepers of borough
asylums and workhouses. Bethlem (Bedlam) Hospital, the oldest institution in England for the custody of the mentally ill, was noted for the
business enterprise of its custodians, but they did not pretend to offer

either refuge, good care, or cure. That was left to such people as William Battie . . .'[2]

and so on.

The throwaway nature of the Bethlem reference puts it firmly in the category of 'well known facts', not to be lingered over, but dropped in for good measure because, since everybody knows it, the scene will look more convincing if it is there: and I doubt whether many people would think it worthwhile even to question its accuracy. It is unfortunate, therefore, that the only identifiable 'fact' in that brief sentence is an exact reversal of the truth: and the rest is, to put it charitably, inconclusive.

Take the fact first: Bethlem – or rather, its custodians – did not pretend to offer either refuge, good care or cure. 'Good care' I shall leave aside, because we are talking about what the custodians pretended to offer, not what we think of what they did offer, and I do not myself know enough of what went on in their minds to speak for them. This is a perfectly serious point, because there is plenty of scope for research into what the governors of Bethlem, and others similarly placed at other institutions, really did think they were providing in the way of care. Unless we accept that they were all very uncomplicated sadistic monsters, which I see no reason to accept, then their doubtless multifarious views on what they thought they were doing must surely have some relevance in the history of psychiatry.

'Refuge' possibly comes in the same category, although the dictionary definition of 'refuge' which would seem most relevant here is 'asylum', which is almost certainly what the governors of Bethlem thought they were offering. But about 'cure' I can be positive. That is very precisely what the hospital did pretend to offer: so much so, that it had had quite specific rules and practices about it since long before the period about which Robert Brown is talking (whatever that period is, within his specification of 'throughout the eighteenth century and well into the nineteenth').

I shall return in more detail to the question of 'cure' later on. For the moment I will merely summarize from various scattered fragments of evidence: already by the mid-fifteenth century Bethlem was spoken of by an independent outside witness as being a place where the insane might be cured: in the early seventeenth century the master or keeper of the hospital was accused, in a Privy Council enquiry, of not fulfilling his obligation to attempt the cure of the patients: and during the late seventeenth and early eighteenth centuries there was evolving the system whereby only those patients who were thought to be curable were accepted in the first place, and all were discharged after twelve months if they had not been cured by that time. Moreover, the Bethlem authorities frequently produced complacent statistics showing the number of cures they had achieved: and, indeed, a glance through the admission and discharge registers (which run from 1683, though they do not start mentioning the state of the patients on discharge until around the 1730s), shows a substantial proportion being sent out 'well'. Whatever role one may think the hospital played in their recovery, there is no doubt that Bethlem has for most of its history been largely geared to the concept of curability, and has certainly pretended, in the most exact sense of the word, to offer cure.

It might well be asked whether it is worth making all this fuss about so ephemeral a remark: I would ask rather, whether anyone would have thought it worth making that very ephemeral remark at all, about any institution other than Bethlem? Its function appears to be to consolidate the impression that an improvement has taken place in the treatment of the insane, by contrasting it with the worst that has gone before: and if we are looking for the worst, then of course it must be Bethlem. Battie at St Luke's was offering cure, which is good: therefore Bethlem, which we all know was bad, cannot possible have done so. Well as it happens, it did.

Turning now to the first half of Robert Brown's *obiter dictum*, we find the well known fact that 'Bedlam ... was noted for the business enterprise of its custodians'; (and that, presumably, throughout the eighteenth century and well into the nineteenth). I really do not know precisely what axe is being ground here, but the statement is obviously intended to be discreditable to Bethlem. Taking it at its face value, therefore, the reply would be that Bethlem was a public charity, run exclusively for the reception and treatment of the poor. Poverty was one of the absolute criteria for admission. Certainly from the eighteenth century (and probably earlier) up to 1882, when the Charity Commissioners first gave permission for a handful of paying patients to be admitted, patients were not admitted to Bethlem if they had any money: and although parishes paid maintenance for their pauper patients, from 1702 onwards the rest were taken free except for clothes. The charity was financed entirely from current benefactions and from the management of its accumulated endowments: therefore business enterprise on the part of its custodians, had they had any, could only be to their credit.

In fact the governors, except for the treasurer, were so unbusinesslike that in 1835 their accountant and receiver absconded to the continent having systematically defrauded the hospital of £10,066. 6s. 9d, shortly to be followed by the treasurer himself who had managed to pass a further £14,473. 12s. 7d. of the hospital's money through his own accounts.[3] I think this is rather enterprising: but I don't think it is what Mr Brown had in mind. Nor, in fact, do I know which 'custodians' he had in mind, because Bethlem was administratively somewhat more complicated than the cardboard cut-out of the popular imagination.

Sharing with Bridewell Hospital, with which it was jointly administered from 1557 on, it had at the top a large court of governors, a fairly active president, and a highly active (as we have seen) treasurer, all of whom might be the custodians in question. But from the governors, most of whom were largely figureheads by the nineteenth century, was selected a general committee of forty-six, dating from 1737, which gradually took over the administration of the hospitals from the court of governors, and various sub-committees, including the Bethlem sub-committee which managed the day-to-day business of Bethlem, including the admission and discharge of patients. This sub-committee met weekly (twice a week for a time), and was more intimately concerned with Bethlem's affairs, so the particular governors serving on it at any time might perhaps be considered to be Bethlem's custodians. Then there was the steward, a resident officer who, from 1634, took over the practical management of the hospital from a previous succession of masters and keepers (which was the title of the former and usually sinecure post of governor of Bethlem): and from the 1630s there was the physician (or after 1816, the two physicians), who was not a resident officer but certainly believed himself to be at the head of the medical establishment: and from the 1750s an apothecary who, as the only resident medical officer, was *de facto* head of the medical department. There was, from sometime in the seventeenth century, a matron who was in charge of the women patients, a post which in its early days was filled by the porter's wife: and of course there were the keepers (known until the early nineteenth century as 'basket men' on the men's side, and 'maid-servants' or 'gallery-maids' on the female, then 'keepers', and later 'attendants'). Which, of all these, were the custodians who were noted for their business enterprise?

I suspect that what the remark really refers to, of course, is that well-known fact that Bethlem charged people to look at the patients. This is the one fact that everyone knows about Bethlem; it is so well known that a recent quiz in a nursing journal asked simply, 'How much did it cost to tease the patients in Bedlam?', giving rise to a spate of telephone calls to the Bethlem archives asking for the answer. Unfortunately it was impossible to help, for I appear to be the only person to whom the facts appear less than straightforward.

From the way this matter is usually referred to, it seems to be generally supposed that there was an official and fixed charge for admission, which was at some stage laid down by the authorities, and that the rate remained the same for several centuries. There is also the clear implication that someone was profiting from it, though who, among all the 'custodians', it would be difficult to say: and whether it is also envisaged that someone sat at a turnstile selling tickets, cashed up at the end of the day, and changed the programme if it proved unpopular I can't be certain, but there is a strong hint that things went some way along these lines.

The wilder speculations on this subject have certainly been based on very flimsy evidence, much misunderstanding and a fair amount of ignorance, but it has so far proved impossible to establish the facts with certainty. From what I have gathered so far, however, I think it more likely that the habit of taking money from visitors grew up by custom, rather than that a deliberate policy was worked out at any particular time: and that although there may have been a minimum amount solicited, many people almost certainly gave whatever they felt like. In 1632, for example, there is a reference to 'money given at the hospital door by persons that come to see the house',[4] and in 1677 a rule was made 'that no officer or servant . . . do move or speak to any person coming thither for any gift or gratuity till the Charity of such person be put into the Poor's box'.[5] And, of course, it should be remembered that visiting at Bethlem went on for a very long time, possibly 200 years or more, and it is most unlikely that proceedings were exactly the same thoughout that period: and of course also, at a still earlier period, it would have been considered a Christian duty to call at the door to give alms, whether visiting or not.

One certainty is that for a long time money was collected from visitors as they left the hospital, not as they came in: this was changed only in 1765, and in 1770 the admission of visitors was ended altogether.[6] It is also clear that this money was, whether hypocritically or not, regarded by the governors as being by way of almsgiving for the support of the charity, and was certainly treated as such. It is referred to as 'the money for the poor', which is just what it was. Doubtless some of it was diverted by corrupt members of the staff (although there was quite specifically a separate box for gratuities to the servants, the money from which was divided up according to strict rules), but no one was intended to benefit from the poor's money except the patients. The 'Poor's box', into which all the money given at the door was supposed to be put, was opened once a month at the Bethlem sub-committee, and the money was handed over direct to the steward to pay bills for the maintenance of the patients, and formed an important part of the hospital's income for this purpose.

This too may all seem very trivial, even though it would be nice to know the exact details sometime, but unfortunately a monstrous statistic has been erected on the shaky little foundation of partially understood and half-invented facts relating to this question of payment: that is, that in the eighteenth century Bethlem was visited by 96,000 people a year. This is actually about the number of people worldwide who were visiting the painted caves of Lascaux in the early 1960s, before they were closed, and I would have thought it just might have seemed so incredible, even in the context of Bethlem, that someone would have paused a moment and asked, 'Can it really be true?'. But of course when we are talking about people being charged to come and see the lunatics, the more the worse; and as this is Bethlem, the worse the better: so it seems to have been swallowed hook, line, and sinker, and is even escalating. It has been referred to in print recently at least twice as established fact,[7] and it has been mentioned in passing at one of the Wellcome seminars that Bethlem was visited by '100,000 people a year'. And why stop there: soon it will be rounded up to an equally credible 200,000 which will be casually referred to as 'about 1/4 million'. 'Incredible', people will murmur to themselves as they slip it into their latest work on the history of psychiatry, to show what a truly awful place Bethlem was in the fifteenth, seventeenth, nineteenth, or whichever century is under consideration.

The calculation goes as follows: visitors paid one penny each to visit Bethlem. In the eighteenth century the hospital made an income of at least £400 a year from visitors which, at one penny a head, gives 96,000 visitors a year. What could be simpler? Robert Reed, who in *Bedlam on the Jacobean*

Stage[8] has done most to propagate this myth, makes it sound even more convincing by mentioning that in 1657 there was an order banning visitors on Sunday. Therefore, on the basis of a six-day week, Bethlem entertained an average of 300 visitors a day. Reed, of course, relied on O'Donoghue, and did not actually consult the records, or he might have pursued the matter further and found that in fact most Sunday visiting was banned in 1650, when the porter was ordered to keep the gates shut and 'suffer none to come there but such as bring relief to the said poor lunatics or come to do them good'.[9] The 1657 ban was total, excluding everyone except the doctor, apothecary, and surgeon, and covered 'every Lords Day, days of public fasting and thanksgiving',[10] so he would have had to eliminate a few more days to get his calculation right. Another of the things that Reed did not know was that there were many more visitors in summer than winter, and most of all in Easter week, though the Christmas holiday period seems to have been quite popular too: so if he had taken his sums to their logical conclusion, he might have come up with a figure of something like 1800 people, say, on a single day in Easter week (which happens to be the same as for the busiest day at the Lascaux caves, so seems quite appropriate).

What Reed also did not know, however, was that the £400 was actually the whole of the money which came out of the poor's box, and so included anything given to the hospital by way of casual charity, as well as the hypothetical entrance charge: and what he refused to accept was that there is no real evidence for a 'charge' of one penny in the eighteenth century.

Few contemporary references do mention a precise sum, but one certainly does refer to a penny. Thomas Brown in his 'Amusements Serious and Comical', published in 1700 (which is incidentally at least fifty years earlier than when the income is known to have sometimes reached £400), refers to 'one penny, which is *Cerberus*'s fee at the entry'.[11] But we know anyway that at this time the money was taken on the way out, and I at least know that the porter didn't happen to be called Cerberus, so we are not going to accept the entire statement as one of incontrovertible fact in any case: and Ned Ward, at around the same time, writes of 'redeeming our *Liberties* from this *Piss-burn'd Prison*, at the Expence of two-pence'.[12] Reed points out that Ward went with a friend, so this must mean one penny each, and presumably, had he known it, he would have found an equally easy way round the account in *The World* for June 1753, which talks of '100 people at least who, having paid their two-pence apiece, were suffered unattended to run rioting up and down the wards' (note the hundred people, because this was in Easter week which is known to have been the busiest period). So even if one insists on believing that these somewhat facetious (in two cases) pieces of journalism do mean exactly what they say, and must be true because journalism is always totally reliable, the evidence is still two to one in favour of twopence: and we are down to 48,000 visitors already. But when we have allowed for everything else that went into the box, who knows what the figure might be reduced to? (And incidentally, the sums recorded when the poor box was opened are invariably in round pounds, shillings and sixpences, and mainly in pounds and shillings, with never the odd penny at any time. I regard this as a complete mystery: but what scope for speculation there!)

This may seem all very trivial. There is no doubt that a very large number of people did visit the hospital in the eighteenth century, that many of them abused the patients shamefully, that it was a most degrading spectacle, and that the governors were equally guilty for not ending it sooner than they did, and anyway there is no conceivable possibility of getting rid of those 96,000 visitors a year now that they have entered Bethlem folklore: but it does further demonstrate the point that even the best-known facts about Bethlem will stand up to very little examination. And a recent addition to the mythology indicates that new facts are still being conjured from the air, soon, doubtless, to become well known.

Andrew Scull in *Museums of Madness* makes this statement about Bethlem in 1814: 'Notwithstanding the occasional hints of scandal, it had remained a favourite upper-class charity. Its respectability was attested by the presence of a Board of Governors who were almost exclusively of aristocratic background.'[13] This is not, of course, really a reference to Bethlem's respectability, but a preliminary to saying how awful it was despite its aristocratic governors, and it sounds to the uninitiated like a very well-known fact indeed. Unfortunately, there does happen to be in the archives a list of the governors of Bridewell and Bethlem for 1818[14] (and they had not changed much in social class since 1814), and out of the 414 governors, only 21 were members of the aristocracy (helpfully placed at the beginning of the list, so not difficult to find). And the statement continues, 'despite its upper-class trappings Bethlem contained few patients from wealthy backgrounds'. Well, no, none at all actually: as already mentioned, it was quite specifically a charity for the poor. Moreover, it is difficult even to be sure what charge is being levelled here, unless it is that the upper classes should have better things to do than meddle in the welfare of the poor.

None of this is very important, of course: but why bother to make up such unimportant things about Bethlem, rather than try to find out whether there is anything worthwhile to be said, or thought, about it? Because, it would appear, where Bethlem is concerned anything goes so long as it scores the right point. What concerns me is that the instant availability of a few pieces of information or misinformation, which never do more than reinforce the pre-conceived stereotype, leads people to believe that every-thing important really has been said, and positively deters them from making the effort to investigate what might lie behind the stereotype.

Does it matter? Possibly not, but let us consider two further examples. Whenever the awfulness of Bethlem is being adduced in support of the awfulness of things in general for the insane in the early nineteenth century, the case of James Norris is cited. He is sometimes called William but that is neither here nor there, and he was actually James. Now we do indeed know how appalling the treatment of Norris was: and here I must make it clear, as I should have done before, that I am not for one moment trying to whitewash Bethlem. I am not trying to suggest that the treatment of many, perhaps most, of its patients was not, at many or perhaps most periods of its history, horrific; or that the hospital was not frequently grossly mismanaged, its staff often corrupt and brutal, and so forth. I am trying to suggest that when you have said that you have not said all there is to say, and that even if that is all you are going to say, it would be better to get the details right than wrong.

Norris was an American marine, admitted on 1 February, 1800 via the Office for Sick and Wounded Seamen, which was the government department responsible for all Bethlem's naval patients.[15] A year later he was transferred to the incurable department (of which, more later), having failed to recover. Norris seems to have been the most violent and dangerous patient that Bethlem had ever encountered. He made a number of murderous attacks on keepers and fellow patients. He was exceptionally strong and very cunning. He could not be restrained by manacles because of the peculiar conformation of his wrists and hands, the bones of the wrists being larger than those of the hands: he simply slipped them off, and used them as weapons. For four years he terrorized all who came in contact with him until finally, in June, 1804, it was decided that he should be permanently confined in an iron harness, with an iron collar and chain which prevented him from ever moving further from his bed than to stand beside it. Horrific is certainly the word to describe this apparatus and its use.

He remained thus for the next nine years, until his case was publicized to the outside world by Edward Wakefield and formed one of the central charges brought against Bethlem at the Committee on Madhouses enquiry of 1815.[16] There is, of course, far more to be said about Norris than this, but this is not the place for it: and anyway this, or considerably less, is all that usually is said about him – a mere reference to 'Norris in his iron cage' is often enough – because his role in history is to serve as a typical example of the extreme brutality of the treatment at Bethlem and elsewhere. One thing that could be said, incidentally, is that Norris was certainly not typical: there was little that Bethlem did not know about restraining people, with wristlocks, leglocks, belts, gloves, and chains, and they had all failed. Norris was quite literally unique in Bethlem history. However, it is true that his was a uniquely extreme form of restraint which was, in a lesser degree, commonly practised.

But Norris's case is cited by Andrew Scull in *Museums of Madness* as illustrative of the fact that the Bethlem governors still, in 1814, clung to the seventeenth- and eighteenth-century paradigm of insanity, which is defined thus: 'In seventeenth- and eighteenth-century practice, the madman in confinement was treated no better than a beast; for that was precisely what, according to the prevailing paradigm of insanity, he was.'[17] In the light of this, the most important fact about Norris seems to me to be the one which is least likely to be quoted, but which I find one of the most interesting of all: during his nine years of confinement, the way in which he occupied himself was by reading the books and newspapers which were given to him, and amusing himself with his pet cat.[18] It seems to me to be at least worth a mention that this man, who was certainly chained up 'no better than a beast', was at the same time encouraged to indulge in one of the least beast-like of all human activities, reading, not to mention playing with a cat. Can the picture really be quite so straightforward, or the Bethlem authorities' paradigm of insanity – perhaps even the seventeenth and eighteenth centuries' paradigm of insanity – really be quite so uncomplicated, as we are led to believe?

The second example of a Bethlem patient who does not quite fit the stereotype, and who therefore does not get mentioned at all even though his case is as accessible as Norris's, is James Tilly Matthews.[19] He was a contemporary of Norris, having been admitted in 1797 and transferred to the incurable department in 1798, and also became well known to the outside world though for different reasons. There is not room for much detail here, though his story is a fascinating one, but Matthews generated much documentation, as well as producing a good deal of his own, because his relatives made great efforts to prove that he was sane and to get him discharged. There seems little doubt that he was actually insane, if such a state exists at all (to beg a rather large question), though probably not very dangerous. But while Bethlem might well have been quite glad to get rid of him, since he and his family were really rather a nuisance (and anyway Bethlem had no vested interest in keeping *anyone* in the hospital), Matthews had been detained in the first place because he was thought to be a danger to the royal family, and also to members of the government. This was because he laboured under various endlessly intricate delusions, springing apparently from the central belief that he was emperor of the whole world – or 'Omni Imperias Arch-Grand Arch-Sovereign' as he sometimes expressed it – and that every other head of state or government was a usurper: so there was a fairly firm directive from the Home Secretary that he was not to be let out.

This is all rather by the way: the point that I want to make is that while in Bethlem, Matthews did a great deal of writing and drawing, including the production of designs for his own Omni-Imperias Palace; and when a competition was announced for the design of a new Bethlem Hospital in 1810 he submitted his plans for that, for which the governors made him an *ex-gratia* payment of £30. I suspect that this may have been an attempt to pacify his relatives, who were currently trying to get him out again: but whatever the reason, it was surely *not* because they regarded him, like all other madmen, as 'no better than a beast'. Eventually he was also allowed to fit up his own room with various extra comforts, and was allowed candles so that he could sit up late working. John Haslam, the apothecary, claimed at the 1815 enquiry that he brought in one of his friends to teach Matthews engraving for nothing.[20] Whether he did or not – and I see no reason to doubt it, though no one else has ever seen reason to mention it – Matthews certainly published from Bethlem in 1812 a set of designs entitled *Useful Architecture*, which he had engraved himself.[21]

There is, of course, a great deal more to be said about James Tilly

Matthews too. I only wish to make the point that he was in Bethlem at the same time as James Norris: and while neither is exactly typical, they do represent the extreme polarities of treatment which were to be found simultaneously in the hospital. Why then, do we hear always about Norris in his iron cage, though without the newspapers and the cat, and never about Matthews sitting up by candlelight working on his Omni-Imperias Palace and publishing folios on Useful Architecture? Because, of course, one fits the Bedlam stereotype and the other doesn't. But I think that a Bethlem which contains both, together with all the gradations in between, is likely to make a more rewarding subject for study, and to tell us more about, for example, attitudes to the insane, than a Bethlem dedicated to brutality and inhumanity as its sole policy. I think such a study might reveal, for example, that at least some of the inhumane treatment stemmed as much from the total inadequacy of everyone concerned when faced with the very real fact of violent and dangerous patients, as from any deeply held belief in the nature of insanity or the animality of the insane. Andrew Scull suggests that the governors saw nothing wrong with treating a lunatic as they treated Norris, because they saw him as no better than a beast. I suggest that we should at least consider the possibility that they simply could not think of anything else to do with him. I have often asked myself a question which would probably be most improper for historians to concern themselves with, but which seems to me to be only fair: given all the circumstances, and the resources then available to them, what could or should the various people involved have been expected to do about Norris? Obviously something better than they did – but what? Could they have done *anything* that we would not now castigate as inhumane? I doubt it.

These two cases are both available in contemporary print to the library-based researcher. There now follow some rather random examples of never-mentioned, because never-researched, facts which seem to me at the very least to modify the picture offered by the standard 'well-known' ones. We are usually given to understand for example, that the treatment of patients was universally brutal, and the implication is that this was actually the policy of those who were running the hospital. Yet if we look at the rules and other *dicta* of the governors, we will find them often quite startlingly at variance with this assumption. They are often, I may say, also startlingly at variance with what we do know was going on in the hospital, and it is necessary to make a clear distinction between the behaviour of the keepers and the declared intentions of the governors. But incompetence, mismanagement, and neglect should not be mistaken for deliberate policy, and particularly when it comes to deducing the attitudes to insanity which lay behind such policy.

I quote again from Andrew Scull:

'That madmen were chained and whipped in asylums in the eighteenth century was well known at the time. How could it be otherwise when, throughout the century, the doors of Bethlem were open to the public, and the inmates exhibited before the impertinent curiosity of sightseers at a mere penny a time, and when every treatise on the management of the mad advocated such treatment?'[22]

They were certainly chained: but leaving aside the thirty years at the end of the century when the doors of Bethlem were very firmly shut (and which is, incidentally, almost certainly when the worst practices developed, behind those locked doors), and of course the dubious value of the 'mere penny', this would seem to imply that throughout the eighteenth century wholesale whipping was a commonplace in Bethlem, and was meted out as a regular part of the treatment. But as early as 1677 the rules of the hospital (possibly the first formal set of rules to be drawn up) stated that 'None of the Officers or Servants shall at any time beat or abuse any of the Lunatics in the said hospital neither shall offer any force unto them but upon absolute Necessity for the better government of the said lunatics.'[23] Admittedly the last clause leaves the question of necessary force somewhat open-ended: but here is a clear indication that in 1677 the governors of Bethlem, if no one else, did not regard the beating of lunatics as being appropriate at any time, let alone as a regular treatment for all and sundry.

Again, in the 1720 edition of Stowe's *Survey of London*, updated by John Strype, Strype states that 'there is nothing of Violence suffered to be offered to any of the Patients, but they are treated with all the Care and Tenderness imaginable'.[24] Of course Strype obtained much of his information from the hospital itself, probably from the then physician Dr Edward Tyson, and of course we know that it wasn't all loving tender care for the patients in practice: but however sanctimonious they may be, these expressions do not seem to me to issue directly out of a belief that madmen are no better than beasts, and should therefore be treated by whipping and brutality. And for what it is worth, I do not think that the accounts left by visitors to Bethlem in the eighteenth century ever do mention whipping or deliberate physical abuse of that sort by the keepers: nor, indeed, was it a criticism levelled at Bethlem by the 1815 Committee on Madhouses enquiry. And again, for what it is worth, the Vagrancy Act of 1714 (which was the first statutory provision for the detention of dangerous lunatics, as opposed to the provisions under the common law which had existed for many hundreds of years previously) did specifically exclude lunatics from the whipping which was to be administered to all other vagrants, before they were returned to their own parishes. It is probably time that somebody took a closer look at when whipping did begin to be discounted as a regular treatment for lunatics: and I offer 1677 in Bethlem, as a starting point from which to work back.

There are other rules which seem to have been formulated in a rather more humane spirit than the governors are usually credited with possessing. Also as early as 1677, for example, the chaplain of Bridewell had been asked to compose some suitable prayers to be read to those of the Bethlem patients who were capable of receiving them.[25] In 1765 – and probably earlier, that just happens to be the reference which has come to light – it was one of the matron's duties to make sure that 'such of the [women] patients as are low spirited or inclinable to be mopish' should be made to get up, and be shut out of their cells 'so that they may not creep back again to their beds': also to employ such as were capable at needlework when they were not otherwise busy, 'rather than let them walk idle up and down the house showing it to strangers and begging money'.[26] She and the gallery maids were also enjoined to make sure that the patients were brought down to the room where there was a large stove in the winter, to keep warm. From the end of the seventeenth century, there was a fund from which clothes and other necessities could be provided for the completely destitute on discharge, and the governors sometimes also made *ad hoc* payments to enable discharged patients to get home and survive until they did so. The picture which emerges, even though it obviously needs a great deal of adjustment from other sources, is not a wholly unrelieved one of deliberate brutality and inhumanity.

As to the concept of curability in Bethlem, which I mentioned earlier, this is another subject which would seem relevant to some of the current preoccupations in the history of psychiatry. There is, for example, much interest in the question of whether, at any particular period, insanity was regarded as curable, whether it was considered susceptible to medical treatment, when 'moral treatment' and 'management' were first promulgated and/or practised, and so on. In all the discussions, I never see a reference to what was happening at Bethlem: but why not? Bethlem had been claiming to cure insanity since the fifteenth century: surely there is something here to be contributed to the argument? Again, it would seem that the Bedlam stereotype obscures the very possibility.

The first written reference to Bethlem as a place of cure is probably the one which is found in the same MS as William Gregory's 'Chronicle of London', dating from about 1450, in which the author writes of,

> 'A church of our Lady that is named Bedlam. And in that place be found many men that be fallen out of their wit. And full honestly they be kept in that place; and some be restored unto their wit and health again. And some be abiding therein for ever, for they be fallen so much out of themselves that it is incurable unto man.'[27]

Bethlem first employed a physician as such from some time in the 1630s, but Dr Hilkiah Crooke was appointed 'master' or 'keeper' of the hospital, at the King's instigation, in 1619.[28] He rarely came near the place except to take money from it, and used the position to exploit the patients and bleed the hospital of its resources, as had done most of his lay predecessors for many years before him. However, one of the charges brought against him in 1632, when retribution in the form of an investigation by the Privy Council finally caught up with him, was that he had made no attempt to cure the distracted persons: so it was clearly intended that he should do so. Crooke replied that when he first came to the hospital he had cured seventeen people, but hadn't tried since, because the governors would not pay his apothecaries' bills, which the commissioners found to be quite untrue, like nearly everything else that Crooke told them.[29] Unfortunately he did not say how he had cured the seventeen, but it was obviously by means of medicine of some kind.

References to the admission of patients, which occur in the minute books of the court of governors before the start of proper admission registers in 1683, fairly typically refer to the patient being 'taken and kept in the hospital for his cure': and the notion that Bethlem cured people was well known outside its walls, though it did occasion some surprise. In 1632 Donald Lupton, in *London and the Countrey Carbonadoed*,[30] wrote:

> 'It seems strange that any should recover here, the cryings, screechings, roarings, brawlings, shaking of chaines, swarings, frettings, chaffing, are so many, so hideous, so great, that they are more able to drive a man that hath his witts, rather out of them, than to help one that never had them, or hath lost them, to finde them againe.'

However, he also wrote that, 'Here Art strives to mend or cure Nature's imperfections and defects.'

And not just Art: God was on Bethlem's side too. At the end of the seventeenth century we find references to recovered patients of which this, in 1682, is typical:

> 'Whereas Priscilla Campbell about six months since was admitted into the hospital of Bethlem for cure of her lunacy And now the said Priscilla being by the blessing of God and the means that hath been used recovered and restored to her former senses It is ordered that she be discharged'.[31]

Sometimes the theological mechanics of such cures is still more explicitly spelled out, as with another case the same year: 'It having pleased God to give such a blessing in the means that hath been used for his recovery that he is now recovered to his former senses'.

Lupton also mentioned that many were probably kept there not so much in hope of recovery, as to keep them from 'further and more desperate inconveniences'. I do not know exactly when the hospital started its policy of deliberately discharging those who were regarded as incurable, but there was a clear-out in July, 1681 of 'several persons not distracted and others incurable and not fit to be kept in the said hospital',[32] and others followed in subsequent years. Throughout most of the eighteenth century and thereafter, patients were not kept for longer than a year unless there seemed a good chance of their recovery, and were not accepted in the first place unless deemed to be curable. It is not clear precisely what criteria were used, but there is, for example, an order in 1765 that, 'No patient be admitted who has been mad more than one year and when taken in to remain only six months unless there is a prospect of cure'.[33] Some time during the eighteenth century – again, it is not yet certain exactly when – there also began the practice of discharging those who had recovered, initially, for a month's leave of absence. If they kept well during that period they were supposed to come back to be seen by the committee before final discharge, though I would be surprised if most of them did come back in person. Former patients who relapsed were given priority for readmission, and quite a number are to be found flitting in and out of the admission and discharge registers at intervals over the years.

In the 1720s and 1730s a department for incurables was established, and two wings were added to the building to accommodate fifty each of men and women: but this was only for the readmission of Bethlem's own curable cases, after they had spent their year failing to be cured in the main hospital, and it was only for those who were considered dangerous to themselves or others. The opening of an incurable department might alone, perhaps, in any other institution than Bethlem, have alerted historians to the possibility that cure was at least being contemplated elsewhere in the hospital. And if so, presumably some means of effecting it was also being contemplated, the 'Art' to which Lupton referred. At the time of which he wrote, this was certainly medicine.

We have already seen that Hilkiah Crooke was criticized for not providing medicine to cure the patients in the early part of the seventeenth century. Bethlem had such a high regard for medicine as a means of cure at this time, that in 1700 there was set up a fund through which it could be supplied to discharged patients on an out-patient basis. A minute for 26 April reads:

> 'This Comittee being this day Informed by Dr Tyson the Phisitian ... That several of the patients who have been Cured of their Lunacyes in the Hospital of Bethlem being very poore are not able to procure themselves a little necessary phisick at the Spring and Fall of the yeare For want whereof many of them have relapsed into their former Lunacyes and become Patients again in the said Hospitall to the great Charge thereof And this Comittee having ... considered by what meanes the like Inconvenience may be prevented for the future consistant with the Charity of this Hospitall are of Opinion That such poor Lunaticks as have been Cured and discharged as aforesaid may upon their due Application to the weekly Comittee of the said Hospitall have Phisick at the Charge thereof in such measure as the said Comittee and Phisitian shall direct.'[34]

One might justly level a charge of optimism here, but the intention seems unexceptionable. The assumption that physic is only required in the spring and autumn is, however, difficult to reconcile with the views of one of the governors, Captain Clarke, who in 1682

> 'doth desire that his brother who hath been kept in the hospital of Bethlem for cure of his Lunacy and now recovered to his former senses may be continued in the said hospital until the season of the year is cooler for fear he should relapse into his distracted condition'.[35]

As to the introduction of anything that might be considered a prototype of 'moral treatment' or 'management', the field is wide open for research. So pervasive is the Bedlam image that I had myself assumed that this would not be a profitable area for enquiry, until coming across the matron's rule that she should chivvy the low-spirited patients out of bed and keep them occupied with needlework, and the still earlier request to the Bridewell chaplain to say prayers with them. I now wonder how much more the records might contain on this subject. It is just possible that in this as in many other areas, the historian of psychiatry who could break down his inhibitions about treating Bethlem as a serious subject for research might find that it repaid a little investigation. He might even find it as rewarding as do those school children and others who already find their way to its archives, having not yet learned the well-known fact about Bethlem that it has always been utterly and irredeemably awful, and that is all that needs to be said on the subject.

Notes

1 The minute books of the Court of Governors of Bridewell and Bethlem (beginning 1559) and of the General Committee of Bridewell and Bethlem (beginning 1737), which remain at Bridewell Hospital and are not accessible, are available on microfilm in the Bethlem archives.

2 *Times Literary Supplement* (8 January, 1982): 23.

3 *Report of the Commissioners for Enquiring Concerning Charities*, 32, Part VI (London: HMSO, 1840), pp. 445 ff.

4 Public Record Office, SP.16, 224, no. 21, findings of a Privy Council commission of enquiry into affairs at Bethlem Hospital, first report, 1632.

5 Bethlem Hospital archives, minutes of the Court of Governors of Bridewell and Bethlem, 30 March, 1677.

6 Minutes of the Court of Governors of Bridewell and Bethlem, 20 June, 1765, 21 November, 1770.

7 Michel Foucault, *Madness and Civilization* (London: Tavistock, 1965), p. 68; Michael Macdonald, *Mystical Bedlam* (Cambridge: Cambridge University Press, 1981), p. 122.

8 Robert R. Reed, *Bedlam on the Jacobean Stage* (Cambridge, Mass.: Harvard University Press, 1952), pp. 25–6.

9 Minutes of the Court of Governors of Bridewell and Bethlem, 12 September 1650.

10 Minutes of the Court of Governors of Bridewell and Bethlem, 12 June, 1657.

11 Thomas Brown, *Works*, 9th edn (London: 1760), vol. 3, p. 30.

12 Ned Ward, *The London-Spy Compleat* (London: The Casanova Society, 1924), reprint of 1700 edition, p. 67.

13 Andrew T. Scull, *Museums of Madness* (London: Allen Lane, 1979), p. 74.

14 *A List of the Governors of the Royal Hospitals of Bridewell and Bethlem* (London: Governors of Bridewell and Bethlem Hospitals, 1818).

15 Information about Norris is taken from the Bethlem Hospital archives, admission registers, Bethlem Sub-Committee minute books, minutes of the Court of Governors; and from the *Report from the Committee on Madhouses*, 1815.

16 *Report from the Committee on Madhouses in England*, (London: House of Commons, 1815), *passim*.

17 Scull, *Museums of Madness*, pp. 64–6.

18 *Report from the Committee on Madhouses*, p. 89, evidence of John Haslam.

19 Sources as for Norris, plus miscellaneous papers in the Bethlem Archives.

20 *Report from the Committee on Madhouses*, p. 91, evidence of John Haslam.

21 J.T. Matthews, *Useful Architecture* (London: 1812), Sir John Soanes's Museum, London.

22 Andrew Scull (ed.), *Madhouses, Mad-doctors, and Madmen. The Social History of Psychiatry in the Victorian Era* (London: Athlone Press, 1981), p. 107; and *Museums of Madness*, p. 63.

23 Minutes of the Court of Governors of Bridewell and Bethlem, 30 March, 1677.

24 John Strype, *A Survey of the Cities of London and Westminster ... Corrected, Improved, and very much Enlarged* (London: 1720), pp. 192 ff.

25 Minutes of the Court of Governors of Bridewell and Bethlem, 30 March, 1677.

26 Minutes of the Court of Governors of Bridewell and Bethlem, 20 June, 1765.

27 J. Gairdner (ed.), *The Historical Collections of a Citizen of London in the Fifteenth Century* (London: Camden Society, 1876), introduction, p. ix.

28 See Patricia Allderidge, 'Management and Mismanagement at Bedlam 1547–1633', in Charles Webster (ed.), *Health, Medicine and Mortality in the Sixteenth Century*, (Cambridge: Cambridge University Press, 1979).

29 Public Record Office, SP.16, 237, no. 5, findings of a Privy Council commission of enquiry into affairs at Bethlem Hospital, second report, 1633.

30 Donald Lupton, *London and the Countrey Carbonadoed and Quartered into severall Characters* (London: Nicholas Okes, 1632): also reprinted in *The Harleian Miscellany* (London: 1812), vol. 9, p. 322.

31 Minutes of the Court of Governors of Bridewell and Bethlem, 20 May, 1682.

32 Minutes of the Court of Governors of Bridewell and Bethlem, 1 July, 1681.

33 Minutes of the Court of Governors of Bridewell and Bethlem, 20 June, 1765.

34 Minutes of the Court of Governors of Bridewell and Bethlem, 26 April, 1700.

35 Minutes of the Court of Governors of Bridewell and Bethlem, 22 September, 1682.

CHAPTER TWO

Intentionality and insanity: what the eighteenth-century juror heard

Joel Peter Eigen

ALTHOUGH PURSUED FROM a variety of disciplinary vantage points, recent scholarship in the history of madness continues to point to one particular theme: the importance of social setting in the interpretation of madness and in decisons taken about its management.[1] The sharper focus on mental derangement as social deviance has helped historians of law and medicine, and medical sociologists to illuminate an array of cultural consequences attendant with the 'scientific' definition and isolation of the mad.[2] The social setting to be investigated in this paper concerns late eighteenth-century, early nineteenth-century felony trials in which defendants raised some form of mental derangement as an exculpatory defence. The trials were drawn from a survey of cases heard at London's central criminal court, the Old Bailey, between the years 1760 and 1815. This period precedes the introduction of a recognized 'insanity plea', and therefore affords a rare glimpse into the evolving jurisprudence of criminal intent in response to the introduction of medical testimony bearing on insanity in 1760. Because the authority of medical testimony had a potentially profound effect on the conceptualization of criminal intent, particular attention will be paid to the social setting in which medical opinion, judicial summations, and instructions to the jury cast the imagery of insanity against a central element of criminal culpability: intentionality.

The legal concept of intentionality refers to what the actor meant to do, in other words, his control of events. Control, in this sense, signifies the individual's capacity to make choices based on an understanding of the circumstances surrounding his actions. Intent carries a rather specialized meaning in this context because one assumes that purposeful, that is non-accidental, actions are intended by the actor; at the most basic level, actions are the simple product of physical movements. It would be absurd for the law to insist that in order for a crime to occur, physical actions had to be accompanied by a simultaneous intent in the actor's mind to do harm. Rather, the historical meaning of intent has been that the culpable individual has the capacity to choose between good and evil, and having this capacity, chooses to (intends to) do evil. In this particular sense, the individual has acted intentionally.

Stress is placed on acting intentionally, rather than 'having an intention' because, as Hyman Gross has written, the latter phrase is misleading in that it involves an element of anticipation, perhaps even commitment, and as such, brings one precariously close to the concept of motive.[3] Although intent and motive are often used interchangeably, they are considerably different in terms of their significance at law. For example, the desire to be wealthy may be the wellspring for an almost irresistible motive to do away with a rich and redundant uncle. But it is not the motive that makes one legally culpable. Motives, alone, won't convict the individual unless he acts, and unless he acts intentionally. One can kill an uncle with no motive at all, but if a jury were convinced that at the time, the actor comprehended the circumstances surrounding the action, that is, its probable consequences, and had the capacity to choose between pulling or not pulling the trigger, the greedy nephew would stand an excellent chance of being convicted. The fact that no motive could be found would keep few jury members up at night once they were satisfied that the actor simply and competently had control of his actions. Not fantasy, not desire, not even purpose; rather the ability to make a choice – to exercise will – this is the essence of intent. A choice can only be termed a choice when the actor is capable of pursuing a logical enquiry into the probable consequences of his behaviour and can appreciate the culpability of his actions.[4] Without this capacity, one cannot choose, that is, choose to obey the law. And without intent, the actor is not legally culpable.

England enjoys a rich history in the jurisprudence of mental derangement and criminal intent. Although the first recorded acquittal on the grounds of insanity dates to 1505, care taken to distinguish blameworthiness from unintentional behaviour goes back a good deal further.[5] Nigel Walker has traced legal concern with intention to tenth-century manuscripts which characterize acts as either voluntary or unintentional. 'And if it happens that a man commits a misdeed involuntarily, or unintentionally, the case is different from that of one who offends of his own free will, voluntarily and intentionally.'[6] Reflecting this attention to unintentional behaviour, the first acquittal in 1505 reads as follows: 'the felon was of unsound mind (*de non saine mémoire*). Wherefore it was decided that he should go free (*qu'il ira quite*)'.[7] One notes the interesting use of the criterion 'unsound mind'. The verdict could have just as easily listed madness, or lunacy, or idiocy as the basis for acquittal. Each term implies a condition in which one is unable to know what one is about, and each term was known to the court by the sixteenth century. Instead, the recorder preferred the term 'unsound mind', a point worth noting because this particular construction would come to bedevil nineteenth-century medical practitioners who offered testimony in specially convened commissions on lunacy in an effort to explain their reasons for finding the defendant to be either a lunatic or an idiot. Unfortunately for medical witnesses, the Lord Chancellor was in the habit of insisting that neither lunacy nor idiocy would, in and of itself, suffice as a 'finding' unless the jury inferred *from* the described condition that the defendant was of 'unsound mind'. It was a matter of no small irritation in the medical community that the judiciary provided few guidelines concerning what exactly 'unsound mind' consisted of.[8]

The wording of the 1505 acquittal may have set the groundwork for the clashes that have come to characterize relations between medicine and law. These clashes were to a certain extent inevitable because the practice of criminal law has been to recognize only a narrow and quite restrictive conception of madness, a 'total lack of discretion and understanding', as the standard which could render an individual incapable of forming intent. This was the opinion articulated by Bracton in the twelfth century and, with minor variations, remained essentially unchanged through the eighteenth century with which the present survey is concerned. In the sixteenth century, Dalton refined the conception of a total lack of rationality to include an evolving standard of juvenile culpability: the inability to distinguish good from evil. Thus, if one who is 'non compos mentis [not of sound mind] or an idiot kills a man, this is no felony for they have not knowledge of Good and Evil, nor can have a felonious intent, nor a will nor a mind to do harm'. A century later, in the *History of the Pleas of the Crown*, Hale continues the standard that only absolute madness, absolute deprivation of memory, could define the 'furious man'. Hale indicated in his writings that he was not unmindful of less severe states of mental derangement, but that persons suffering from these particular maladies 'had as great an understanding as ordinarily a child of 14 hath', and such persons may be found guilty of treason or felony.[9] Hale singled out melancholy distempers as just such a 'partial state' of insanity, and the separation of melancholia from other, more 'furious' diseases carried profound courtroom significance given the prevalence of melancholy distempers not only in medical literature of the early nineteenth century, but as one of the more frequent grounds for alleging insanity.[10]

How was this standard of total want of understanding, of intentionality, explained to the jury? Two celebrated decisions which preceded the period from which the present data are drawn will serve to set out the conception of intention and derangement operating in the late eighteenth-century courtroom. The first is the case of Arnold, on trial for his part in a plot to kill the king. Mr Justice Tracy, in addressing the jury, announced that,

> 'guilt arises from the mind, and the wicked will and intention of the man. If a man be deprived of his reason and consequently of his intention, he cannot be guilty: and if that be the case, though he had actually killed Lord Onslow, he is exempted from punishment ... [but] ... we must be very cautious; it is not every frantic and idle humour of a man that will exempt him from justice ... it must be a man that is totally deprived of his understanding and memory, and doth not know what he is doing, no more than an infant, than a brute or a wild beast'[11]

One sees in Tracy's summation the retention of Bracton's criterion: total deprivation. To this Justice Tracy added the imagery of the 'brute' conjuring up the sort of mental picture which animated the so-called 'wild beast test'. Nigel Walker has noted that the decision in the Arnold case (1723) was the earliest on record to couple the jurisprudence of insanity with infancy: 'not only does the insane not know what he is doing, but he is not able to distinguish good from evil'.[12]

The trial of Earl Ferrers in 1760 marks the first recorded instance of 'psychiatric' testimony offered in the criminal trial. 'The defence I mean is occasional insanity of mind; and I am convinced from recollecting within myself, that at the time of this action, I could not know what I was about.'[13] With these words, Earl Ferrers began a defence which was to include the testimony of no less a medical figure than Dr John Monro, physician superintendent of Bethlem. Monro, who testified on the subject of insanity in general – not actually on the defendant's condition *per se* – explained that the symptoms of insanity were often uncommon fury (not occasioned by liquor), jealousy, or suspicions without grounds. Ferrers questioned Monro himself, which, quite apart from being a tricky enterprise in a court where 'wild beast' imagery greeted a plea of insanity, was apparently a pretty sorry display of witness examination. Monro's testimony, and the general issue of insanity as an exculpatory condition, were the subjects of the Solicitor General's remarks to the jury. For an acquittal, there had to be either a total permanent want of reason, or a total temporary want of reason, but not a partial degree of insanity mixed with a partial degree of reason. Reason did not have to be complete,

'if there be thought and design; a faculty to distinguish the nature of actions; to discern the differences between moral good and evil, then upon the fact of the offence proved, the judgement of the law must take place ... My lords, in some sense, every crime proceeds from insanity. There were philosophers, in ancient times, who held this opinion ...

'My lords, the opinion is right in philosophy but dangerous in judicature. It may have a useful and a noble influence, to regulate the conduct of men; to control their important passions ... but not to extenuate crimes, nor to excuse those punishments, which the law adjudges to be their due.'

Whether it was the convincing argument of the Solicitor General, or Monro's less than unequivocal testimony, or Ferrers's overwhelming conceit and obnoxious character, the defence of 'occasional insanity' was unsuccessful, and the earl was convicted and executed.[14]

To summarize, the concept of madness which had legal significance in 1760 was quite restrictive: only defendants totally lacking in memory, totally mad, could confidently plead insanity, or 'senselessness'. To this was also added the conception of an inability to tell right from wrong. The implication of such a construction was clear. An acquittal was possible for the offender who – in the very narrowest sense – intended his act physically, perhaps 'purposefully', but at the same time was unable to appreciate the wrongfulness of his action. Just how to prove such a level of conscious functioning without a corresponding level of understanding was the substantial difficulty confronting defendants, and after 1760, medical witnesses in their efforts to substantiate a plea of insanity.

When John Monro entered the mid-eighteenth-century courtroom, he was not exactly breaking new ground as far as participating in a medical-legal dialogue. The use of medical evidence and sworn medical experts by judicial forums dates to at least the seventeenth century and very likely goes back a good deal further given the existence of opinions on impotence, premature births, and insanity in the codes of Theodosius and Justinian. Erwin Ackerknecht locates the first actual reference to medical testimony in 1511, when Phillip the Handsome spoke of his 'well beloved surgeons, sworn experts to the courts of Paris'.[15] In general, the sorts of crimes which attracted the attention of physicians in court included abortion, infanticide, and homicide, the last often involving an enquiry to determine which of several wounds had been mortal. According to Ackerknecht, the end of the eighteenth century witnessed the decisive stage in the growth of legal medicine with its search for the sort of scientific and technical detail manifested in, for example, the establishment of a systematized technique for autopsy, experimentation with post-mortem wounds, and close inspection of various degrees of subcutaneous haemorrhages.[16] Surgeons' memoirs were apparently a rich source of medico-legal knowledge with their careful descriptions of hanging and drowning, and identification of rigor mortis as one of the signs of death.[17] Parallel to the growth in knowledge of general medicine, legal medicine had progressed from an observational to an experimental stage, with the morgue playing an analogous role to the hospital in general medicine. Whether the late eighteenth, early nineteenth-century flurry of activity was the result of a 'push' from the courts in requesting more definitive medical opinion, or a 'pull' from those physicians mindful of the professional hazards of offering tentative opinions in what could be a fiercely adversarial setting, one sees in the late eighteenth-century creation of academic chairs of legal medicine, the recognition that physicians and lawyers had much to say to one another.

Beginning with Monro's appearance in the Ferrers case, forensic witnesses faced the difficulty of substantiating their opinions that substantive mental impairment existed in defendants who were not deteriorated intellectually and who consequently appeared in court in a somewhat pacific state. The classic raving madman could of course be identified without 'expert' guidance; it was the subtle twists and turns of moral insanity, of inhibitory insanity, and of irresistible will which required the special insight of a physician to 'bring the pathology to light'. While these varieties of insanity received generous treatment in medical tracts, one wonders to what extent medical testimony also incorporated these more esoteric terms and behavioural states. To appreciate the importance of social setting in the offering and the reception of such specialized medical knowledge, an actual examination of the late eighteenth-century criminal trials is required.

One's ability to grasp exactly what transpired at the Old Bailey between 1760 and 1815 is limited by the fact that no actual court transcripts exist. What is available is a rather peculiar set of tabloids known as the Old Bailey Sessions Papers (hereafter OBSP) which report the eight annual sittings of the court. These papers provide verbatim transcripts of some of what transpired at most of the trials. They were not meant to serve as legal writings – in fact, as John Langbein has pointed out, they resemble an earlier style of literature, the crime 'chapbooks' dating from Elizabethan times.[18] Although the OBSP provide a rare and valuable glimpse into legal procedure 300 years ago, they must be read with care. Written and sold on the street for lay readers, they often emphasize sensational testimony at the expense of more routine day-to-day procedure. Fortunately, trials in which insanity was a feature were an infrequent enough occurrence, and carried sufficiently bizarre accounts of the defendant's behaviour apparently to merit sustained attention in the papers. Even so, writing legal history from the OBSP must be done with a caution against what one cannot say. If an event is described in the papers, there is a strong possibility the event occurred in the manner described by just those words. But if something is missing from the papers, one cannot be sure it did not happen.[19] The narratives that do exist, however, allow for a reconstruction of the pace of the trial, the interactions between judge, witness, and jury members, and most of all, provide a vivid illustration of the overarching power of the judge to steer cases toward a 'proper' conclusion.

No reading of the OBSP, no matter which trial or which year one is investigating, can fail to reveal the extent of the judge's influence on the jury. Not only did the judge serve as examiner-in-chief for both the witness and the accused, he also possessed what appears to be unlimited power to comment on the events of the trial while the court was in session. These comments, often reported in detail in the papers, reveal that the bench hardly regarded juries as autonomous fact finders. Judicial 'direction' ranged from the broad hint – 'That the Witnesses which appeared to the Prisoner's character seemed to stand in need of some persons of reputation to support their own' – to the even more explicit instruction: 'then you will acquit him to be sure, gentlemen'.[20] Into this judicially dominated social setting entered the first medical witnesses in insanity trials, whose testimony we now turn to.

Between the years 1760 and 1815, 165 defendants at the Old Bailey raised some form of mental derangement as a possible exculpatory condition in their defence. The form this 'plea' took varied; some spoke of insanity, some of derangement, often the defendant would say simply, 'I was out of my senses.' The relative frequency of 'insanity trials' to all other trials ranged between 4 and 8 per 1,000 during the fifty-five years. When an allegation of insanity was raised at the Old Bailey, what was the offence likely to be? *Figure 2.1* gives these data.

Figure 2.1 Offence type as a percentage of total cases alleging insanity

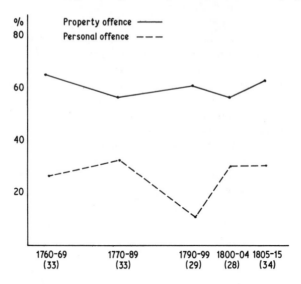

As revealed in the preceding array, stealing comprised the largest proportion of cases in any one time period in which an allegation of mental condition was raised. For the entire fifty-five-year sequence, fully 60 per cent of all defendants entering an insanity plea were on trial for some form of theft. This percentage should be seen in light of the usual case-load at the Old Bailey because stealing predominated here as well. In fact, the great majority of cases heard at London's central criminal court during the 1700s and 1800s was for some form of petty theft: shoplifting, stealing from pubs and inns, 'borrowing' household and workshop items by servants and apprentices.[21] As these offences figure most prominently in the yearly criminal case-load, they also serve as the most frequent crimes alleging mental derangement as well. One observation then to be made at the outset is that although the jurisprudence of insanity may have originated in homicide or treason cases, the Old Bailey became familiar with the insanity defence as a result not of charges of murder or violence, but through experience of rather routine, run-of-the-mill thefts; offences with which the court was only too familiar.[22] This may have had something to do with the medical and lay witnesses' difficulty in characterizing the defendant's mental condition as distinctly beyond the range of the ordinary (reasonable?) person.

But did witnesses – lay or medical – have difficulty persuading a jury of an offender's mental impairment? In other words, what were the chances of success in raising a defence of insanity? According to previous research, acquittal rates remained fairly stable both before and after 1800, the year of the Hadfield decision. This relatively constant rate (approximately 45 per cent) has been cited to argue that this celebrated case did not appear to have a demonstrable effect on the chances of convincing a jury of the defendant's insanity.[23] *Figure 2.2* shows, however, that after 1800 there is a noticeable shift in acquittal rates by offence.

Hadfield's importance to the jurisprudence of criminal insanity is that it introduced the concept of delusion to the courts. An act could be coolly and 'rationally' planned, yet still be the product of a madman, owing to his delusive construction of the circumstances surrounding the event. No longer need the accused be totally mad or totally devoid of memory; he could not intend his acts if he were incapable of appreciating the moral wrongfulness of his actions. The 1800 decision therefore had a potentially profound effect on the chances of raising a successful insanity plea. Yet the failure of Hadfield to play a significant role in subsequent prosecutions as manifested in the relatively constant total acquittal rate has led to a downgrading of Hadfield's contribution. However, when personal and property crimes are separated, it becomes apparent that the year 1800 does indeed witness a shift in acquittal rates: enhanced chances of success in personal crimes, somewhat lower risks of conviction for property offenders. Chances for acquittal in personal crimes increase for the next fifteen years and there is reason to suspect that they remained high for at least the next twenty years.[24] After Hadfield, then, defendants on trial for personal crimes were roughly twice as likely to convince a jury of a debilitating mental condition than were offenders prosecuted for property offences.

It is of course tempting to speculate on the reasons for the increase in acquittal rates after 1800. However, the twentieth-century student of the courts will recognize the hazards of such an undertaking. The difficulties encountered in trying to account for differential conviction rates in contem-

Figure 2.2 Acquittal rates in trials alleging insanity

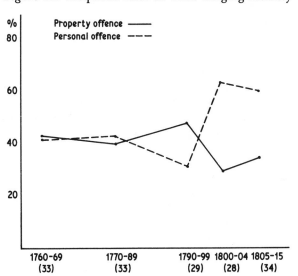

porary cases are formidable enough; hoping to explain the variation in court decisions 200 years ago with less-than-complete court data would be next to impossible. Still, it is worth asking how cases heard at the Old Bailey after 1800 differed from the pre-Hadfield trials, and what changes might have had a bearing on the jury's willingness to accept an insanity plea. For example, was there a change in the form of evidence? *Table 2.1* shows the frequency of medical witnesses appearing in felony trials at the Old Bailey.

Table 2.1 *Participation of medical witnesses in insanity trials (%)*

	(1760–99)	*(1800–14)*
property offences	7	11
	(61)	(38)
personal offences	13	27
	(23)	(22)

The array in *Table 2.1* reveals that the overwhelming majority of insanity pleas between 1760 and 1815 were made without the support of corroborating medical testimony. Most often, lay witnesses offered a description of the accused's conduct, and juries acquitted or convicted on the basis of this, and other 'non-expert' testimony. Only in personal offences after 1800 did the participation of medical witnesses reach a sizeable level.

When medical men did appear, the results are somewhat suggestive. Regardless of type of offence (personal or property) or time period investigated (1760–99 or 1800–15) trials in which medical testimony was offered always secured higher acquittal rates than those in which they were absent. Of course, one interprets this finding with caution. The proportion of cases in which medical witnesses appeared is so small (19 out of 143) and the number of possible factors accounting for an acquittal so numerous, that one must be careful not to attribute the rise in acquittals in personal offences to the mere appearance of a medical witness. Indeed, after 1800, one observes a slight increase in acquittal rates for personal crimes when no medical opinion was given whatsoever. Although it is clear that something happened in the early 1800s with regard to juries associating insanity much more with personal than property offences, it remains to be demonstrated how Hadfield actually contributed to this change. The concept of delusion, for example, so skilfully introduced and applied by Erskine in the Hadfield trial featured very seldom in subsequent insanity cases.[25] And, as the preceding discussion suggests, one cannot rely on the argument of medical witnesses overwhelming juries with their scientific expertise since their participation in trials was such an infrequent event.

Although the actual number of medical witnesses who testified in the period from 1760 to 1815 is quite small (31), one does notice an interesting shift in the professional background of the 'mad-doctor'. Where surgeons and apothecaries predominated as specialists to the courts in the latter half of the eighteenth century, physicians make up fully half of all medical witnesses after Hadfield.

It must be kept in mind that we are dealing with a quite small number of medical witnesses and that the precise professional affiliation was supplied by the witnesses themselves. Owing to the absence of regulation during these years regarding who could call himself 'physician' or 'surgeon' – especially when the practitioner was not from London – one must be cautious not to typify the apparent shift in professional background as definitive evidence that physicians had 'captured control' of the witness box away from other medical professionals. Even if the designated professional labels were completely trustworthy, it is still unclear what a shift in background would signify in terms of the 'respectability' of giving medical evidence because the status of 'mad-doctors' – whether physician, surgeon, or apothecary – is a matter of some debate.[26] What is revealed in these transcripts is that medical evidence was offered by men who were in positions of authority in the organizational world of prisons, hospitals, and in one case, academe. Included among those who testified were the apothecary and physician to St Luke's, the surgeon to Clerkenwell, Newgate, and the Royal Marines, and a Mr Hudson, identified as a 'medical professor'. If indeed the shift to 'physicians' is borne out by future research, it may suggest that the basis of professional opinion was moving away from descriptions of madness based on acquired experience with those afflicted, to a more theoretical abstraction of 'disease'. This level of testimony would lie more properly within the scope of the physician, who was distinguished from surgeons and apothecaries by a course of study requiring residence at a university. One might expect to find such a shift after 1823 with the inauguration of the first medical lectures on insanity, given by Alexander Morison. Although it has been reported that these lectures were not particularly well attended – between 1823 and 1845, his total audience numbered 150 – the number of medical men who testified in court was also quite small. The question worth asking is whether these medical specialists testifying in court were drawn from Morison's circle. As Scull writes, 'the availability of special education – regardless of its specific content or scientific validity – bolstered the medical profession's claims to expertise and esoteric knowledge'.[27]

When medical witnesses did appear in court, what was the lay juror likely to hear? An analysis of medical testimony up to 1815 is remarkable for its utter lack of technical terms, esoteric jargon, or physicalist imagery. Most often, the medical witness appears to have served a legitimating function. After several neighbours testified that the accused exhibited bizarre behaviour, the physician was sworn and simply stated that the defendant was indeed deranged. No 'diagnosis' as such was given beyond the usual statement, 'I have looked upon him as a man insane.' When an explicit rationale was given for the professional opinion, it most often rested on the defendant's inability to carry on a conversation: to have question and answer follow one another. Medical witnesses often discussed the defendant's random mumbling of ideas which were seldom connected in any apparently rational way. 'Incoherency' and 'flightiness' were the two most commonly heard characterizations of conversations of the insane.

The importance of conversation in diagnosing insanity featured prominently in a medical text published in 1816 by no less a medical authority than John Haslam, apothecary to Bethlem and himself a medical witness. 'All that we can know about the mind of an individual is from the communication of his ideas in terms or signs which are conventional between us. Disease is thus imparted by the ear or conduct which enables us to characterize the character of the mind.'[28] The ability to listen carefully and critically was in fact a point made by the author in support of medicine's unique qualification to discern madness. To the layman, the superficial conversation of the insane may appear to be rational – but 'the smallest rivulet flows into the great stream of derangement if the physician persists in drawing out the patient'.[29]

Other than 'inability to converse rationally' and 'a want of connected ideas', it appears that the medical witness had little else to offer. The physicalist arguments that were mentioned in court – 'taken in fit after a horse accident', 'being in a kind of stupor', 'fracture on the bone, which joined with liquor might produce derangement' – were also often made by neighbours and carried immediate intelligibility to the jury members. In fact, a perusal of the disease terms used in testimony reveals a vocabulary far removed from 'schizophrenic conversion hysteria'. Given the existence of many materialist explanations for insanity present in medical literature of the day, one wonders why there was such a scrupulous avoidance of a physicalist basis for the testimony.

One possible reason for the rather straightforward testimony may have been that at the time many of these cases were heard, an active and at times, quite vitriolic debate was taking place regarding some members of the medical profession's assertions that only doctors could effectively administer mental institutions. Insanity was argued to be a 'medical disease', cure depended on medical treatment, and anyone not trained in insanity (and this included apothecaries and surgeons) would operate, at best, inefficient institutions. The physicalist origin and basis for treatment became one of the key issues in a series of intensely bitter parliamentary debates between 1815 and 1817. 'Lesions of the brain', 'malformation of the skull', 'hereditary disposition to insanity' were all bandied about as aetiological factors of insanity causation despite the fact that dissections had failed to produce a standard malformation or lesion in the brains or skulls of lunatics.[30] Additionally, medical treatments were reported to be totally ineffective by other physicians who also administered asylums.[31] There was clearly no consensus on the precise medical nature of insanity – and while this is not always apparent in contemporary medical tracts which linked melancholia with abdominal viscera and mania with brain (not mind) disorder, physicians in the courtroom were extremely careful to phrase the basis for their expert opinions in clearly understandable terms that enjoyed wide usage.

Although the courtroom may have seemed to be an attractive forum to profess unique qualifications and 'scientific insight' into insanity, medical practitioners carefully avoided basing their testimony on materialist foundations of insanity which had yet to be reliably demonstrated.

Perhaps these early forensic witnesses were aware of the scepticism which could be the reaction to technical knowledge, especially when madness was hardly a novel or unique occurrence requiring a 'scientific' diagnosis. Technical terminology was of course not unheard-of in the courts; general medical witnesses often used esoteric terms to describe the relative lethality of wounds or lacerations, in giving testimony concerning the victim's appearance. Insanity, however, was not a wound, but a category of behaviour. Technical terms and scientific nosology could easily have generated scepticism on the part of a lay jury for whom madness was hardly the product of some unseen force other than, perhaps, the moon. For whatever reason, early medical witnesses in insanity cases chose to base their claims to expert authority on their extensive familiarity with the mad; familiarity, which among other things, enabled them to spot instances of shamming, or 'counterfeiting' madness, which the lay observer would not be likely to recognize.[32] Early medical witnesses therefore drew on their experience and their positions of authority in the caretaking of the mad to establish their credentials as the experts in the field.

In searching out the social and historical setting which witnessed the increase in acquittal rates after 1800, it now seems clear that at least one standard explanation is in doubt: that the increasing presence of medical experts in the courtroom and a corresponding display of esoteric knowledge impressing and mystifying a lay jury easily susceptible to the 'proofs' of science simply tipped the scales in favour of the defendant. The OBSP in fact reveal that acquittal rates in personal crimes increased even when medical witnesses did not appear, and even when they provided the court with specialized accounts of insanity, the testimony was hardly at a level likely to mystify anybody. Instead of concentrating exclusively on medical witnesses and medicine's claims, one would do well to remember the social setting in which the negotiation of madness was argued, for it is at once apparent that any change in the fortunes of the defence could only have taken place with a parallel change in judicial attitudes regarding insanity as an 'appropriate' defence in personal crimes, but less so for property offences. To look once more at the scope of comments offered by the bench serves as a reminder of the overarching influence wielded by the judges – influence which could undercut the impact of one (expert) witness's testimony; while at a different moment and for a different type of crime, support another's claim. In a 1796 murder case, the judge answered one witness's articulate description of the defendant's 'melancholy despair' with: 'Do you know that his wife had a little money of her own, independent of him?' In another trial the court queried: 'Was his insanity of a sort that you thought led him to pick pockets or steal spoons?' However, the bench was also capable of producing an acquittal by interrupting the flow of testimony to announce: 'such a clear case of lunacy, we may with perfect confidence rely upon it – that he was a lunatic at the time the act was committed'.

Judicial comments, which could either work on behalf of, or very much to the detriment of the defendant, were not the only way a judge could influence the reception of testimony. Another source of information about what the jury heard, and was encouraged to consider carefully, was the tone and thrust of the cross-examination. The investigation of medical witnesses is sometimes quite explicit in the OBSP, and other times must be inferred from the testimony narrative. An analysis of these cross-examinations reveals that the judge's choice to question closely the medical (or non-medical) witness may well have directly affected conviction risks; judicial challenges of testimony in personal crimes were accompanied by a substantial drop in the chances for an acquittal. The most frequent questions asked of medical witnesses included the following. After reciting the history of bizarre behaviour in order to substantiate their claim that the defendant was indeed insane, the bench would simply ask: 'Why didn't *you* commit him?' Medical witnesses who were able to supply graphic descriptions of mental derangement were finally asked if the raving defendant could 'tell good from evil' – a conclusion physicians were as reluctant to draw then as now. Perhaps the most telling query concerned not the content of the mental deviance or the inability to tell right from wrong, but an investigation into the time lapse between the physician's examination of the defendant, and the criminal offence. These are all 'logical' questions and certainly within the bounds of acceptable judicial enquiry, however the effect of asking them was very telling. Juries appear to have received medical (and non-medical) insanity testimony rather uncritically unless and until they were reminded that the penultimate question was not how sick, how strange, or how bizarre was the defendant's record of functioning but whether this 'supposed' mental condition sufficiently affected his ability to tell right from wrong, that is, impaired his ability to act intentionally.

The quintessential importance of intentionality was made abundantly clear in one of the few judicial instructions to the jury which the OBSP reports in detail: the trial of John Bellingham for the murder of Spencer Perceval. At the conclusion of the trial, Mr Justice Mansfield reminded the jury that, regarding insanity, 'the law is very clear: a man deprived of reasoning so as not to be able to distinguish between right and wrong can have no intention at all'. After listing various 'species' of insanity, the judge described an insane state, which 'fancied the existence of injury and sought an opportunity for gratifying revenge' (exactly the features of the Bellingham case). 'If such a person were capable, in other respects, of distinguishing right from wrong, there is no excuse for the atrocity which he might commit under the description of derangement'(!) Further, Lord Mansfield did not stop with 'the law' but instead proceeded to consider the medical testimony. 'What might have been the state of his mind some time ago is perfectly immaterial. The simple question is, whether at the time this act was committed, he possessed a sufficient degree of understanding to distinguish good from evil, right from wrong.' The judge then recounted the content of the witnesses' testimony emphasizing the rational aspects of Bellingham's conduct: he came to London by himself, was under no restraint, no medical man attended him, in short, 'perfectly regular in all his habits'. Finally, there was no proof to show his understanding was so deranged as not to know that murder was a crime. 'On the contrary, the testimony adduced in his defence has most distinctly proved [!] . . . that he was in every respect a full and competent judge of all his actions.' To no one's surprise, certainly not today's reader of the OBSP, Bellingham was convicted and executed forthwith.

The Bellingham case serves to remind contemporary historians of jurisprudence that any investigation of the effect of introducing medical witnesses and 'scientific' testimony into the insanity trial would be seriously shortsighted were it to rely on acquittal rates as a measure of medicine's capacity to 'prove' insanity. Even if the arrival of medical witnesses in court had been accompanied with a dramatic increase in the success of raising an insanity plea, one would still need to look further than 'professional dominance' to account for a change in the jury's willingness to follow medical opinions. Although the current literature on madness and the courts tends to highlight an 'incompatibility of competing discourses' (between medicine and law), it is important to remember that the ensuing dialogue was conducted in a highly structured social setting where the language of disease was decidedly subordinate to the legal concern with intent. When and if the jury was reminded of this, defendants faced much greater risks of conviction. Competing dialogues were certainly in evidence, but it was not a dialogue between equals.

Medical specialists in insanity trials found themselves in a forum characterized by an almost unbridled range of judicial control and influence. Those historians and social scientists who seek to chart the rise of medical hegemony in the 'mad business' and want to include a consideration of courtroom which after all provided a highly visible setting in which to argue medicine's professional claims, must take care to avoid the image of portraying doctors as usurping or imposing their will on an unsuspecting legal community. For what these papers suggest is that the greater use of medical testimony in insanity trials, and the growing credibility of medical claims to be the rightful caretakers of the mad, could only have been accomplished with the approval of a powerful judiciary who ultimately controlled what jury members heard and how they were to regard such testimony.

Notes

I am grateful to Professor Nigel Walker, Wolfson Professor of Criminology for graciously allowing access to his earlier work with the Old Bailey Sessions Papers which greatly facilitated my data collection. I benefited also from discussions with

Professor Hyman Gross of Corpus Christi College, and Dr John Forrester of King's College – all at Cambridge.

The research was conducted at the Institute of Criminology in Cambridge during the tenure of a Visiting Fellowship, 1982–83.

1 Lawrence Stone, *New York Review of Books* 9 (20), 16 December, 1982.
2 E.G. Michel Foucault, *Madness and Civilization* (New York: Mentor Books, 1967); William Ll. Parry-Jones, *The Trade in Lunacy* (London: Routledge and Kegan Paul, 1972); Andrew Scull, 'Mad-doctors and Magistrates: English Psychiatry's Struggle for Professional Autonomy in the Nineteenth Century', *Archives Européenes de Sociologie*, no. 27 (1975): 279–305.
3 Hyman Gross, *A Theory of Criminal Justice* (New York: Oxford University Press, 1979).
4 According to Gross: 'What in fact distinguishes the sane from the insane under the criminal law standards is the inability of the insane to appreciate the culpability, not the punishability, of their conduct. Because of their abnormality, the insane cannot at the time apprehend what justifies condemnation of their conduct'. (Gross, *A Theory of Criminal Justice*, p. 304).
5 Insane offenders were apparently subject for special disposition prior to the sixteenth century as well. Juries, however, were not empowered to acquit in these instances; their role was only to certify the facts of the case and refer dispositions to the king. Nigel Walker has located a number of thirteenth-century cases where this procedure can be inferred: *Crime and Insanity in England*: vol. 1 *The Historical Perspective* (Edinburgh: Edinburgh University Press, 1968), pp. 24, 25.
6 Walker, *Crime and Insanity*, p. 16.
7 Walker, *Crime and Insanity*, p. 26.
8 John Haslam, *A Letter to the Lord Chancellor on the Nature and Interpretation of Unsoundness of Mind* (London: 1823), p. 16.
9 George Dale Collinson, *A Treatise on the Law of Idiots, Lunatics, and Other Persons 'Non Compotes Mentis'* (London: 1812).
10 John Johnston, *Medical Jurisprudence on Madness* (Birmingham: J. Belcher, 1800).
11 Cf. Walker, *Crime and Insanity*, p. 56.
12 Walker, *Crime and Insanity*, p. 57.
13 Walker, *Crime and Insanity*, p. 59.
14 Walker, *Crime and Insanity*, p. 63.
15 Erwin Ackerknecht, 'Early History of Legal Medicine', in C.R. Burns (ed.), *Legacies in Law and Medicine* (1977), p. 250. In fact, the expert medical witness appears in legal documents much earlier. See *Select Cases in the Court of the King's Bench under Edward I*, ed. G.O. Sayles (Selden Society 55), pp. 126 ff.
16 Ackerknecht, 'Early History', p. 260.
17 J.A. Paris and J.S.M. Fonblanque, *Medical Jurisprudence* (London: W. Phillips 1823), vol. 1, p. xix.
18 John H. Langbein, 'The Criminal Trial before the Lawyers', *University of Chicago Law Review* 45 (2) (Winter 1978): 263–316.
19 Langbein, 'The Criminal Trial'.
20 Walker, *Crime and Insanity*, pp. 63–4.
21 Langbein, 'The Criminal Trial', p. 286.
22 Langbein, 'The Criminal Trial', p. 277.

23 Cf. Walker, *Crime and Insanity*, p. 74.

24 Analysis of acquittal rates for the years 1834–36 reveals that the success rate in personal crimes continued to rise to 70 per cent.

25 For the text of Erskine's argument, see Thomas Erskine, 'Speech for the defence in the Proceedings of the Trial of James Hadfield, 1800', in R. Hunter and I. MacAlpine (eds), *Three Hundred Years of Psychiatry 1535–1860* (London: Oxford University Press, 1963), pp. 567–72.

26 Roger Smith suggests that owing to their 'association with poor and criminal elements', most physicians avoided the 'mad business' (*Trial by Medicine*, Edinburgh: Edinburgh University Press, 1982). Andrew Scull on the other hand, argues that doctors who specialized in the growing field of mental derangement 'were not drawn from any one of these three classes (that is, physician, surgeon, or apothecary), nor did they differ in respectability or skill from the rest of physicians' (Cf. Scull, 'Mad-doctors and Magistrates' p. 255). For a detailed discussion of the relative status of these three strata within the medical profession see also George Clark, *A History of the Royal College of Physicians of London*, vol. 2 (Oxford: Clarendon Press, 1966), esp. chs 30 and 31. The doctors themselves are listed in the Appendix.

27 Cf. Scull, 'Mad-doctors and Magistrates', p. 271.

28 John Haslam, *Medical Jurisprudence as It Relates to Insanity According to the Laws of England* (London: C. Hunter, 1817), p. 78.

29 Haslam, *Medical Jurisprudence*, p. 18.

30 Cf. Johnston, *Medical Jurisprudence on Madness*.

31 A. Scull, 'From Madness to Mental Illness, Medical Men as Moral Entrepreneurs', *Archives Européenes de Sociologie*, no. 26 (1975): pp. 218–51.

32 Cf. Haslam, *Medical Jurisprudence*, p. 60.

Appendix

Table 2.A1 *Preliminary list of medical men offering testimony concerning mental condition of the accused, 1760–1815*

name	title mentioned at trial	year of trial and case number	comments
Ainsley, Dr	physician	1812: 537	Henry Ainsley, 1760–1834. MD Cambridge 1793. FRCP. Phys. to St. Thomas's, 1795. Resigned 1800 (Munk)
Barney, Mr	surgeon	1790: 360	
Chapman, Mr	surgeon	1760: 261	
Coleman, Thomas (Mr)	navy surgeon	1784: 493	warranted 1778 (MR'83)
Combes	doctor	1780: 415	
de Casto, Benjamin		1789: 494	
Diggan, Mr	surgeon	1780: 325	Diggins, apoth, in St. Albans Street (MR'83)
Gosner, John	apothecary (at Bethlem)	1784	John Gozna, apoth. Bethlem 1772–96 Collected statistical data on the insane which Haslam made use of
Haslam, John	apothecary	1813: 11	b.1764. apoth. Bethlem, 1795–1816. MD Aberdeen 1816. LRCP. Author of books on madness, medical jurisprudence, also criticism, comic pieces, etc. d.1844
Hodson, Mr	'medical professor'	1809: 605	Hodson, surgeon or apoth. at Preston (MR'83)
Hyatt	surgeon and apothecary	1812: 527	active in Ealing
Leo, Louis	doctor	1798: 470 / 1801: 446	physician active in the Sephardic community: 'Dr Leo of Houndsditch'
Leslie, Mr	surgeon and apothecary	1813	Leslie, —, post unknown, at Tocherford. Leslie, John, regimental surgeon, Coldstream Regiment, 3rd warrant 1779. Leslie, William, navy surgeon, warrant

Lowndes, Francis	'medical gentleman', physician	1805: 457	1781 author of two books on medical electricity (BL Cat.)
Meyers, Joseph Hart	physician	1789: 494	b. New York. MD Edinburgh 1779. Physician, Portuguese Hosp., General Disp., and Hosp. for German and Dutch Jews (dates unknown). d.1823. 'I live on John Street, America-Square'
Munro, Dr	surgeon	1780	Physician at Bethlem
O'Donnell, John	apothecary	1787: 599	
Ramsden, William	apothecary	1797: 512	active at Charing Cross
Reynolds, Thomas	apothecary	1784: 971	b. 1750. MD Leyden 1776. LRCP, FRCP, FRS. Physician Westminster Gen. Disp. 1780–81, St Luke's 1781–1800. Edited London Medical J. Private asylum owner (1781). Treated George III, d. 1813
Simmons, S.F.	physician	1787: 599	
Sims	doctor	1787	Probably James Sims (1741–1820) DNB
Sutherland, A.R.	physician	1813: 11	MD Edinburgh, 1805 LRCP. Physician St Luke's 1811–?6. d. 1861
Turner	doctor	1814: 360	
Waldron	surgeon	1814	
Walker, William	'medical man'	1798	'medical man at Newgate'
Willis	doctor	1800: 315	Willis, Francis 1718–1807. MD Oxford 1759. Son: Willis, John, also MD. Family owned private madhouse and were active in treatment of George III
Webb	surgeon	1812: 527	Surgeon, Clerkenwell Prison and House of Correction

CHAPTER THREE

Moral treatment at the Retreat, 1796–1846[1]

Anne Digby

'No term has of late years been more profusely and empirically employed, and none has been less understood, than "the moral treatment of insanity" ... If the English physician looks to the writing of his countrymen ... he finds little more than vague generalities. The most inflexible firmness must be combined with never-failing kindness and gentleness, and sympathy; the patient is to be taught habitual self-control, by habitual indulgence.'[2]

SO WROTE TWO eminent psychiatrists, J.C. Bucknill and D.H. Tuke, in 1858 when moral therapy had largely replaced the older regimes of physical coercion and medical depletion in English asylums. This gentle regimen had been pioneered in several institutions in the eighteenth century. However, the publication in 1813 of Samuel Tuke's *Description of the Retreat* (the first full-length description of any asylum) made the term moral treatment virtually synonymous in the public mind with the name of this small Quaker psychiatric hospital in York.[3] Daniel Hack Tuke (a member of the family which had done so much to initiate and develop this pioneering institution), served as a medical officer there. His irritation at the uninformed vagueness in much contemporary analysis and practice of moral treatment is understandable. What is perhaps more surprising is that this generalized description has continued to the present day. This paper aims to supply a more detailed analysis of moral treatment, as practised at the Retreat during the first fifty years of its existence. During this period the institution was under the control of lay therapists and was unconstrained by externally imposed legislation. This era ended in 1846 after the Lunatics Act of 1845 made it necessary for the Retreat to appoint its first medical superintendent and also led to the first visit of state-appointed lunacy commissioners to the Retreat.

The historical context of treatment

During the eighteenth century theoretical perceptions of insanity had changed and had begun to emphasize curability through the moderate management and re-education of the patient. To a limited, if problematic extent, the practical treatment of the mad had also altered: some Georgian patients benefited from a 'moral treatment' which was characterized by calmness and kindness and aimed to build up their self-esteem and self-restraint.[4] By the time that the Retreat opened its doors in 1796 moral treatment was not a novel phenomenon, so that rather than being a pioneer of such treatment, the York institution was a successful practitioner of received ideas.[5] However, the Quaker nature of the asylum imprinted these ideas distinctively. Created by local members of the Society of Friends after a Quaker patient died in obscure circumstances within the York Lunatic Asylum, the Retreat was designed solely for mentally-ill Friends.[6] Its pragmatic therapy emphasized the religious framework that sustained Friends when sane, and which it was hoped would prove to be even more effective in meeting the needs of insane members of the Society of Friends. The withdrawal from secular pressures evident in this Quaker environment was symbolized in its earliest name – 'a retired habitation' – and formalized in its eventual title – the Retreat.

Broadly defined, moral treatment as practised at the Retreat, and else-where, meant a concentration on the rational and emotional rather than the organic causes of insanity. It was not so much a specific technique as a range of non-medical treatments designed to involve the patient actively in his re-covery.[7] The spectrum of treatments therefore varied with the practitioner. At the Retreat, the central emphasis in moral treatment was given to trying to help the patient gain enough self-discipline to master his illness. To this end, it was thought important to create a comfortable environment which would facilitate this process of self-control by means of the patient's daily experience of civilized living conditions. The importance of spiritual values was stressed, and thus the Retreat's therapy gave explicit acknow-ledgement to what was often implicit elsewhere – the ethical component in moral treatment. Until 1820 patients at the Retreat were exclusively Quaker; even by 1846 only one-eighth of its first admissions had been non-Quakers. Thus, an ethical emphasis was a natural element in the lives of the majority of patients and a necessary precondition for recovery and resumption of normal life outside the asylum. The findings of associationism were accepted on the importance of the emotions in the well-being of the patient: the grounds at the Retreat were made as varied and interesting as possible to manipulate the patient's emotions and so to cheer the melancholics. The need to balance the emotions and distract the patient from painful thoughts and associations led to a central feature in the Retreat's moral therapy: the creation of varied employment and amusements.

The 'external' control of the patient, either through physical restraint or through medication, was practised on a lesser scale at the Retreat than had been usual in some earlier asylums, although neither means of treatment were eschewed entirely. But, as some commentators have suggested, the overt chains of the older tradition might be replaced by subtler methods of social control in reformed asylums such as the Retreat. Indeed, Michel Foucault has referred to the 'gigantic moral imprisonment' of patients by the

Tukes.[8] This has some validity in so far as the Retreat encouraged the self-control of its patients through what was effectively a system of rewards and punishments. Serious loss of self-control led to seclusion from the community (and ultimately, if the patient was violent, to physical restraint), while a reassertion of self-discipline led to readmission to the family. The social, or milieu, therapy by which individuals participated in domestic life at the Retreat necessitated active co-operation by the patient with the staff of the Retreat. Whether this amounted to 'moral imprisonment' in the *subjective* estimation of patients turns on the extent to which they shared in the moral values of those who ran the establishment. What evidence exists on this difficult issue suggests that in these early years there was sufficient identity of outlook between Quaker therapists and Quaker patients for this kind of social control not to have been perceived by most patients. Whether it was *in fact* operating is a question to which we return at the end of this paper. It might also be asked whether the related concept of the asylum manager acting as a moral guardian imposing conformist ideas on deviant patients was relevant to the Retreat in these early years.[9] It has a limited applicability, most obviously in the small numbers of cases of 'moral insanity', and also where social non-conformity in the form of alcoholism, chronic masturbation, opium addiction, or 'dissolute living' was labelled as insanity, and the lay therapist cast in the role of moral missionary.[10]

A fundamental problem in assessing the degree of control or repression arises from the nature of the historical evidence on the asylum, much of which emphasized the therapists' rather than patients' viewpoint. While patients' views on their treatment are available, both at the Retreat and elsewhere, such testimony remains highly problematical as far as interpretation is concerned.[11] We need to be aware of these difficulties in turning now to a more detailed analysis of the records of moral treatment.

A therapeutic environment

William Tuke and his fellow Quakers took as their objective to 'have studiously avoided that gloomy appearance, which frequently accompanies places appropriated for those who are afflicted with disorders of the mind.' The architect of the Retreat, John Bevans, commented at an early stage of planning that 'if the outside appears heavy and prison-like it has a considerable effect upon the imagination'.[12] This sensitivity to the feelings of patients and their friends and relatives, stemmed from a strongly-held view among these Friends that the insane retained their essential humanity, and that by placing them in civilized surroundings they would more readily recover the full use of their reason. It was therefore important not only to reduce physical coercion to a minimum but also to avoid any *appearance* of prison-like confinement.[13] Visits to some other institutions which housed the insane revealed the habitual assumptions which dictated their regime; the animality of the mad was seen as making them immune to discomfort, while their brutish nature was thought to require coercive cruelty.[14] In contrast, the York Quakers were clear that they were designing a home, rather than an institution, and that solid but unpretentious buildings, plain but well-designed furniture and fittings, were what was required in an environment for the mentally ill.

This 'retired habitation' was constructed on an unostentatious scale when compared with other asylums, for its pleasant brick and slate buildings were designed initially to accommodate only thirty patients. Its most distinctive features were the windows which had cast iron sashes concealed behind glazed wooden ones. In appearance they were unexceptional but in reality they combined the security, usually given by the unglazed barred gratings of the traditional asylum, with the comfort and amenity of a domestic, glazed window.[15] Since the numerous panes of glass in each window were only eight inches by six and a half inches the cost of replacing the glass – when a violent patient had shattered it – was only sixpence.[16] Indeed, the 'comfort combined with economy' which marked this aspect of the building was the pervading characteristic of the entire household economy of the Retreat, as the annual report of 1824 noted. The comfort, cleanliness, and good order of the house were frequently admired by visitors to the establishment,[17] and its polished wood floors and gleaming mahogany furniture must have given an impression of a well-run country house. However, in certain respects it was at first an austere, somewhat gloomy establishment with its high windows, lack of pictures or carpets, and its chilly, dark, and narrow corridors.

Initially the house was set in eleven acres of land, and by 1839 this had grown to some twenty-seven acres. The boundary walls round the perimeter, and those encircling the airing courts, were low and designed to avoid the impression of a prison. The grounds were carefully laid out into gardens, orchards, walks, and wooded areas.[18] Beyond the low walls patients could see the open countryside which surrounded the establishment. As Doerner suggests, this symbolized the Retreat's acceptance of a natural moral order.[19] But it is important to emphasize that this was a natural order which was divinely ordained. The significance that was attached to country walks in the Retreat's moral treatment was as much because of the spiritual as the physical benefits derived from them. Patients could regain their serenity through contact with beautiful, unspoilt surroundings.[20]

A controlled openness, which contrasted with much contemporary practice in English asylums, characterized the Retreat. Both the gates and the front door of the Retreat stood open to the world; a practice which was only discontinued when the cholera outbreak of 1832 made it dangerous for the patients.[21] There was frequent social contact between the small Quaker 'family' within the Retreat and the wider community of Friends in York and further afield. Convalescent patients from the Retreat attended meetings in York on Sunday mornings, while York Friends came up for tea on Sunday afternoons. Young women Friends often helped with mending the Retreat's household linen on a Thursday and the sewing circle of patients, staff, and visitors formed a cheerful forum for the exchange of news. When quarterly meetings took place in York, Friends from the region customarily took meals at the Retreat, and a long table was provided for the numerous visitors for dinner and tea. On a more formal basis Visitors to the Retreat were appointed from local Quaker families; on their regular inspections of the Retreat they would talk to the patients and inquire into their welfare.[22] When patients were in a later stage of convalescence they were allowed to take tea at one of the Quaker schools in York, or in the house of a local Friend. Occasionally, a patient whose recovery seemed complete would try out his fitness for the outside world by staying for a few weeks with one of these local families.[23] If one accepts the definition of recovery made by a later superintendent of the Retreat as 'the restoration of the patient to a previous condition of harmony with his surroundings',[24] then the Retreat's intercourse with the outside world provided a gradualist path by which its inmates might achieve this. The interpenetration of the asylum by the outside world meant that the patient's isolation was minimized and his social identity – usually that of a Quaker – was retained as much as possible.

Lay therapy

The crucial significance of Quaker values in constructing this asylum for the mentally ill was emphasized in the earliest records of the Retreat. The care of sick Friends by their fellows would 'render the minds of patients more easy in their lucid intervals, and consequently tend to facilitate and promote their recovery'.[25] A logical extension of this viewpoint was to give greater emphasis to the religious character and personal qualities of the Retreat's officers than to any specifically medical skills they might possess. The everyday care of the insane was seen as a divine art of healing, a fusion of medicine with religion, which for its success required qualities of integrity, humility and selflessness in its practitioners. 'The founders of the Retreat had a great object of humanity before them: their knowledge of the actual capabilities of the insane, or of their general condition in the country must have been imperfect.'[26]

George Jepson, who became superintendent of the Retreat in 1797, was considered especially fit for the post by the founder of the Retreat, William Tuke.[27] He emphasized first that Jepson was 'a steady religious Friend', and only after this did he mention that 'his knowledge of medicine would be of great use to the institution'.[28] This emphasis on character rather than medical skills was to be repeated in the appointment of the second superintendent, Thomas Allis, in 1823. Allis wrote an honest appraisal of his abilities in relation to the post and stated that he had 'no medical knowledge ... just common rate abilities, with general knowledge, powers of perception and habits of observation, attention and perseverance'.[29] Allis's successor was John Candler, superintendent from 1841 to 1846, whose previous work had been as a Quaker missionary where his moral qualities had presumably been well developed. Since the treatment at the Retreat was at first centred on moral not medical means, this stress on the personality of its chief officer was perhaps justified, for the key to moral treatment lay in the quality of personal relationships between staff and patients. This is what makes the term moral treatment so elusive, and also made the treatment so difficult to translate successfully from the Retreat to other institutions in the mid-nineteenth century.

Jepson was the creator of the Retreat's moral treatment. In a judicious assessment Samuel Tuke wrote that Jepson had discovered 'the almost infinite power of judicious kindness and sympathy on disordered minds; and consequently – the extensive applicability of moral agency in the management and curative treatment of insanity'.[30] George Jepson's genius was to see the mad individual not as an object outside the boundaries of human reason, as did so many of his contemporaries, but as a man or woman whose disordered mind could be steadied by calm kindness. His object was not to categorize and condemn the mentally ill to an existence outside a normal, domestic routine. Instead, he placed them in a social setting except when his insight into their special needs indicated that they needed temporary seclusion from it. His overriding objective was to restore the self-esteem of the patients through treating them with sympathy for their affliction, and respect for their individuality, and hence to build up their powers of self-control. In this he worked pragmatically, and over the years gained an unrivalled perception into 'how far the insane might be influenced through the medium of the understanding and the affections, and how far they might be beneficially admitted to the liberty, comfort, and general habits of the sane'.[31]

Soon after Allis had succeeded Jepson as superintendent of the Retreat its annual report spoke of the 'system of gentleness united with firmness'[32] having been continued and found to be as effective in new hands. A significant reason for this uninterrupted sequence lay in continuity of female nursing staff. The matron who headed the female establishment during the time of Thomas Allis was Harriet Ponsonby, who had been for several years the assistant to Catherine Jepson and like an adopted daughter to her. Catherine Jepson (née Allen) had been at the Retreat almost from its opening, first as female attendant, then housekeeper, and finally as wife to George Jepson.[33] But while there was some continuity in staffing and hence in knowledge of the external elements in moral treatment, the key to successful therapy lay in the exercise of individual personality. Allis – a kindly, sincere, forthright individual – did not possess Jepson's exceptional professional insight and sensitivity. Thus, some of the qualities which informed moral therapy were lost although its external appearance and systematic practice remained unaltered.

In its everyday practice this system depended crucially not on the Retreat's superior officers but on the attendants. It was their vigilant oversight which made it possible for the Retreat to do without much of that physical coercion found necessary in other asylums and madhouses. Attendants were responsible for the day-to-day care of the patients in their galleries, assisted them in washing, dressing, and feeding them where this was necessary, as well as seeing to the cleanliness and good order of bed chambers and day rooms. Indeed, the Retreat's insistent preoccupation with cleanliness and order reduced the amount of time available for the more therapeutic duties of its attendants: conversation with patients, organization of amusements, or participation in walks.[34] Also, the hours of work demanded compared unfavourably with those of attendants in other asylums.[35] In difficult cases Retreat attendants might be called on to sleep in the same room as a patient and effectively to provide care for twenty-four hours a day. Long hours, inducing fatigue and irritation, may have increased the likelihood of patient abuse, although what evidence we have on this difficult issue, suggests that it was infrequent. Dismissals of Retreat attendants for 'falling down on the job' were rare. In part, this reflected a good standard of performance and in part continuing difficulties in recruitment, and hence in replacing a less than perfect attendant with anyone better. Those managing the establishment found that it was impossible to recruit as attendants sufficient numbers of Quakers to look after increasing numbers of patients, and by the 1840s only a small minority of the attendants were Friends.[36] But the employment of those who were not Quakers, to look after the majority of patients who were, may have made it that much more difficult to create the kind of personal relationships on which successful moral treatment depended.

The Retreat's moral treatment imposed exacting standards on its un-trained attendants. The institution acknowledged that this was so by providing a more generous ratio of attendants to patients than was common. At the end of our period, the proportion was one to eight at the Retreat, which compared favourably with those in public institutions (one to eleven at the York Asylum, one to seventeen at Hanwell, or one to twenty-two at Wakefield), but unfavourably with the more expensive private establish-ments (one to two at Brislington House and almost one to one at Ticehurst).[37] It was recognized that the Retreat's objectives were compromised because of deficiencies in the nursing staff. If the attendants had had a sufficient amount of judgement, patience, and gentleness then George Jepson considered that physical restraint could have been reduced still further.[38] John Thurnam (the first resident medical officer), concurred and might on his morning round free a patient who had been placed in a strait-waistcoat by an attendant during the night.[39]

Self-control or external restraint

'The old system of treatment consulted, primarily, the ease of the attendant, the new one, the welfare and comfort of the patient.'[40] On a patient's arrival at the Retreat, Jepson insisted that any form of restraint should be removed, that he should be spoken to as if he were a rational being, and that he should be assumed to be capable of living in a community and partaking of its social life. In this way it was impressed on the patient from his first moments there that he was not a madman who had lost all claims to kindness and respect but one who would be helped to regain control over his malady by living in a protected community.

Quakers at the Retreat viewed the insane as possessing many attributes of the sane. This view of the mentally ill was to inform the later systematization of moral treatment: Samuel Tuke wrote in 1841 that 'the cultivation and extension of the remaining healthy feelings and associations forms one of the most important parts of moral management'.[41] Jepson and his successors felt that most of the patients were aware of the kindness shown to them, and could understand and appreciate the reasonable procedures of the Retreat.[42]

The case of William W. illustrates in an extreme form the progress which could be achieved by the substitution of moral treatment at the Retreat for the traditional regimen of restraint which had been suffered by an insane person before admission. William W. was a 39-year-old Whitby man, diagnosed as a maniac, who was admitted in July 1805. The notes made on his admission stated that he had

'been many years in a state of derangement, under the immediate care of his parents who had him shut up in a room fastened with chains, and mostly naked being unable to keep any clothes upon him. He has had frequent paroxysms of violence when he beat the walls and everything or person that happened to be in his way. A great degree of fatuity has taken place.'

With such an entrenched pattern of behaviour the mild therapy of the Retreat could produce only a slow improvement. However, four years later he was 'generally at liberty, regularly clothed, and much improved in his bodily appearance'. By 1813 he had 'pretty much got off the habit of beating the walls and scratching his forehead', and by 1815 was 'much improved in appearance; seems comfortable, and was useful in pumping, churning, mangling, etc.'.[43] A man whose previous behaviour had been that of a ferocious, caged beast, had gradually been assimilated back into the community, and had gained sufficient discipline and self-confidence to play a useful role there.

This social therapy presupposed a flexible system of classification and accommodation which could allow for a patient's withdrawal into seclusion or restraint, and then his reintegration into the community when recovery was under way. One of Jepson's gifts was both to see when seclusion would be advantageous, and also to be able to phase in very slowly the convalescent's re-entry into 'the family' at the Retreat. This is exemplified particularly well in the case of Samuel W. who entered the Retreat in 1803 and continued there until his death in 1824.[44] Suffering from intermittent mania he experienced several intervals of complete sanity each year divided by periods of extremely violent and anti-social behaviour. In his lucid phases he dined and talked with the rest of the family, walked in the garden, attended meetings in York on Sundays, went on visits to the York Quaker schools, the minster, local shops or on outings further afield with his relatives to places which included Castle Howard. He also took meals with Friends' families in York or stayed at their houses. This more prolonged hospitality could be cut short as when, during a stay at Henry Tuke's home, he suddenly became deranged and 'seemed to have lost the government of himself in a great degree'.

Jepson's growing experience with Samuel W. enabled him to detect the early warning symptoms of an impending paroxysm; the flurry of letter writing, the malicious comments, the volubility at meetings, and the sing-song tone of voice. When his behaviour, either verbally or physically, became sufficiently violent he was secluded in his room. If the violence escalated into tearing his blankets, breaking windows, or attacking his attendant he was physically restrained by a strait-waistcoat, or tied to the bed with straps at night. When coercion was necessary, overwhelming force was used to effect it so as to minimize the struggle with this patient. An instance of this was on 13 November, 1813 when, 'in the evening he had become quite outrageous and was by three men jacketed by force'. As soon as an aggressive phase became less severe the restraint was removed: 'This afternoon he appeared less violent and at his own request with promises of good behaviour had the waistcoat taken off.' Samuel W. did not always keep his promises but the staff in his (and other) cases accepted his word, thus emphasizing the trust on which moral treatment was based. By slow degrees as he became calmer and more rational he was allowed into company again: 'the 6th inst. he was a little calmer, smoked his pipe in the upper dining room in the evening very quietly. Yesterday and today at liberty and quiet.'

The Retreat, although breaking sharply with the traditional pattern of an unconsidered use of restraint, never abandoned the practice altogether, reserving its occasional use for violent patients whose aggression endangered others, or for suicidal patients whose destructive impulses threatened their own lives. Evidence on the use of restraint is incomplete but suggests that around 5 to 7 per cent of patients were restrained at any one time.[45] Restraint might be requested by the patients themselves: William W. requested that his arms should be restrained so that he should not beat them against the wall. Others had restraint imposed upon them: Mary S., a melancholic, 'snatched a knife from one of the servants and threatened to cut her throat, seeming quite frantic. Jacketed and held down.' Or James H., diagnosed as a maniac and melancholic, whose hands were confined to his sides with a belt and straps because he hit other patients and attempted to go about naked. As a result, the staff did 'not think ourselves justified in trusting him at present'.[46]

In general, the officers tried to keep restraint to a minimum and because this led to accidents or escapes this might attract censure from the Committee of Management.[47] In certain cases, however, the violence of the patient made strong coercive measures inevitable, as in the case of Wilson S.

(a maniac and melancholic), who was in the Retreat from 1814 to 1816. His attendant had to be changed to a bigger and stronger man and having thus obtained 'a complete ascendancy by superior strength he steps in between [W.S. and other patients] when necessary to prevent affrays'. Even so, W.S.'s murderous attacks on his attendant led to his being restrained by jacket or straps on more than one occasion. There were some patients who were scarcely amenable to moral treatment and who required almost constant restraint or seclusion. James H. was 'the terror of the place' for nearly the first quarter of the nineteenth century, requiring nearly constant restraint with wrist straps and the management of two attendants. And one religious melancholic lived in almost continuous seclusion from 1831 to 1841, refusing to leave his room or wear anything but a shirt. He was conscious of his condition, 'I am brutish and irrational and have lost all sense.'[48]

With the development of the non-restraint movement at Lincoln, Hanwell, and elsewhere in the late 1830s and early 1840s, the Retreat felt it necessary to review even their minimal use of restraint.[49] It is interesting to notice, for instance, that instead of using straps, a recognized form of restraint used to keep a patient in bed, the institution substituted the tying down of the four corners of the quilt; equally effective but presumably not regarded as restraint. By the end of our period, restraint was considered 'a serious deviation from the general practice of management at the Retreat'.[50] In the last quarter of 1845, when systematic weekly returns were begun under the Lunatics Act, no cases of restraint were minuted, but on average some 13 per cent of the patients were stated to be in seclusion at any time.[51] This practice of seclusion had been found in earlier years, on a small scale. No more than two patients were found secluded in the refractory rooms from 1828 to 1834, and frequently there were none in this situation. However, the informal and temporary use of seclusion by confining a patient to his bedroom for a short period seems to have been used quite frequently. It was employed for example, for Esther H. who in April 1806 'has gradually lost the control of herself so as to render it necessary now to keep her close in her room'.[52] Presumably, this use of solitary confinement was based on the sensationism of Locke's psychology: through a reduction of sound and light it aimed to subdue the excitement of patients.

> 'The Retreat, although its first principles of treatment at once abolished all cruel forms of restraint, and although it has undoubtedly been beneficially influenced by the experiment of entire non-restraint made at Hanwell and elsewhere, has not considered it wise to pledge itself to the non-restraint practice as a principle, conceiving that there may still be exceptional cases in which mild restraint is the best and kindest, as well as the most scientific mode of dealing with them.'[53]

The Friends associated with the Retreat felt that abolition of physical coercion did not necessarily preclude the torment or degradation of the lunatic.[54] While they acknowledged the stimulation given them by the non-restraint movement they preferred pragmatically to determine the individual needs of each case rather than to abrogate their judgement under the force of absolute principle.

Social therapy

'When returning reason indicates a restoration of mental powers, it may greatly tend to advance and establish this desirable event to be under the direction of persons who, whilst they are careful to promote cheerful and salutary amusements will, at the same time, be concerned at suitable seasons to cherish in them the strengthening and consolatory principles of religion and virtue.'[55]

This Retreat circular of 1794 indicated the concern which had been felt by its founders at the plight of Friends incarcerated in asylums and private madhouses where their disordered minds might be unduly influenced by the corrupt or vicious habits of those around them. To replace this by a Quaker environment in which patients might be assisted by appropriate religious sentiments, cheered by conversations with those of similar persuasion, and allowed when convalescent to attend meetings, seemed self-evidently desirable.

The moral and religious sentiments of the Friends who were treated there were not always obliterated by their mental affliction. Sarah G., a frequent patient there, was not untypical in that she conversed in such a manner as to show 'that religious affections are not or do not *appear to be* uncultivated and her ideas of what is called "consistency as a Friend" are decidedly high'.[56] For most of the inmates reading the Bible was their favourite occupation, and many carried it around in their pockets, so as to facilitate frequent reference to it. A number of patients were afflicted with religious delusions, and found conversation with visiting Quakers, or the Retreat's officers, a useful form of psychotherapy. About three-quarters of the patients attended the religious readings given by the superintendent, which were held on a Sunday afternoon. Not all of those present were Quakers, since in 1818 the decision had been made to admit non-Quakers to the Retreat if there was room for them, in order that their higher fees might subsidize some of the poorer Quaker patients. Their numbers grew until by the period from 1842 to 1846 they comprised some 12 per cent of the Retreat's patients. At this stage of the institution's history, however, their presence does not seem to have eroded the sense of Quaker community as it was to do later. For convalescents, whether Friends or belonging to other persuasions, there was freedom to go to meetings or other services in York on a Sunday morning. About one in six of the patients fell into this category.[57] This religious activity may be said to have been a very significant element in the moral treatment at the Retreat.

Another important element in moral treatment was the employment of the patients. Originally intended for the curable and convalescent, it was gradually extended to the chronic patients. Occupational therapy took a growing variety of forms. At first, the best-occupied inmates were the women – a feature common to most types of nineteenth-century institutions – since it was comparatively simple to employ them in household tasks, or in needlework, and knitting. Female patients, who made up slightly more than half of the total, might help in the kitchen or assist in cleaning the house or work in the laundry. Sewing was usually functional at first and involved mending domestic linen and clothes. Later, there was greater variety and besides knitting, worsted, or coarse work the more skilled did fancy work of different kinds.[58] It was the activity that was thought to be therapeutic rather than the end-product: one patient deluded herself that she was pregnant and knitted baby clothes; another gained happiness through knitting curious pincushions; while a third knitted garters which she unravelled as fast as they were created.[59]

The opportunities for male employment and recreation were always there, but it proved to be more difficult to interest the male patients in them. One of the Retreat's reports spoke of the institution's care to lead convalescents 'into some regular employment adapted to their taste or former habits'.[60] The problem of matching possible work to previous life habits was an enduring one; in the early days few wished to participate in the heavier domestic jobs such as pumping, mangling, churning, or chopping wood because these were regarded as menial tasks. When Thomas Allis had extended the range of occupations to garden or field employment there was resistance to involvement in manual labour. While suitable for pauper patients in public asylums the social status of the Retreat's patients made them view it as degrading. Perhaps because of this the Retreat had been slower than several other institutions in initiating the spade husbandry which had been found as early as 1818 in the West Riding Asylum at Wakefield. But the arrival of an energetic resident medical officer was to change this situation. The Retreat's report of 1839 spoke of the benefits obtained by male patients in digging out a two-acre field and planting it with potatoes and turnips under the supervision of an attendant employed for the purpose. Apart from this agricultural work there were attempts to occupy patients along the lines of their former posts; a surveyor's assistant made a survey of the estate, while a watch repairer and a carpenter were employed in their customary tasks.[61] By 1844 two carpenter's shops had been set up to provide a greater variety of occupational therapy for the men.[62]

'To relieve the languor of idleness, and prevent the indulgence of gloomy sensations'[63] through occupying the patient had been one of the prime objectives of the Retreat since its inception. Walking in the gardens and surrounding countryside, or the occasional excursion in a chaise (later a carriage), were designed to raise the spirits by avoiding the monotony of an institutional existence. Under Thomas Allis, there were arrangements for convalescents to stay for longer periods away from the Retreat at Scarborough. Between 1811 and 1822 it was possible for a few patients, who were those least in need of confinement, to be housed at the Appendage; a small house just outside the city walls where the transition to a more sociable and domestic pattern of existence could be effected more easily than at the Retreat.[64] As we have seen previously, there were also opportunities for convalescent patients to go shopping or attend meetings in York, or to take tea with Friends in the locality. At the Retreat itself there was a growing recognition that the enjoyment of a patient in an occupation was of greater importance than its intrinsic value. So a patient who liked boyish games might play marbles, while another played with a doll, and a third whistled on a comb and paper.[65] In contrast, an enterprising inmate appropriated a strip of garden, constructed a greenhouse, and bred rabbits and fowls for sale.[66] Many patients found solace in reading: usually this was the Bible, but a variety of other books was also enjoyed. Some inmates might play the violin or sing, while others wrote letters, or played games such as bagatelle. Pet therapy was practised: some patients looked after kittens and birds, while others found pleasure in the rabbits and poultry that were kept in the airing grounds. Outdoor amusements were also available, from helping in the hayfield, to archery, or cricket. At Christmas, the waits visited the Retreat, and on Plough Monday, the morris dancers. Indeed, the lunacy commissioners commented in 1847 that 'every means of amusement and occupation appear to be provided for the patients'.[67]

Yet although the Retreat was before its time in pioneering the rehabilitation of its patients through occupational therapy, its shortcomings were obvious. Inevitably, not every patient was capable of, or was attracted by, the occupations provided. The case books contain numerous sad little observations to the effect that patients (especially melancholics), were reluctant to start anything, or would not settle to it once they had begun. Gardening and agricultural labour were unsuitable for older patients or for those whose previous habits or occupations had made such a pursuit unappealing. Most of the occupations available for the women were indoor or sedentary ones. Samuel Tuke grew despondent at the monotony of the patients' lives at the Retreat, and at the transient impact of its employment and amusements. He wanted more occupations and ones which were self-evidently useful because he felt, with good cause, that this would have greater benefit for the patients. With less justification, perhaps, he also argued for occupations at the Retreat that would engage the mind in some rational object.[68]

Efforts to employ patients at York grew more intense as work therapy became recognized more generally as a desirable element in progressive asylum management. Dr Thurnam's efforts had apparently increased numbers engaged in useful pursuits to two-thirds by the 1840s, although the commissioners in lunacy's more realistic figure was somewhat lower – at just over half.[69] Yet in spite of this numerical advance, the case books began to give an impression that the purpose of increasingly ambitious programmes of occupational therapy was no longer self-evident. Rather than forming a vital part of the coherent way of life that had made up moral therapy at the

Retreat, employment seemed rather to be a venture that filled in the yawningly long hours of the asylum day. One reason for this devaluation was to be found in the declining importance of moral treatment itself, and the increasing value attached to medical treatments.

Medical and moral treatment

The first Physician to the Retreat, Dr Fowler, gave a full trial of the usual medical means employed in asylums but concluded that

> 'medical means were so imperfectly connected with the progress of recovery, that he could not avoid suspecting them to be rather concomitants than causes ... and led him to the painful conclusion ... that medicine, as yet, possesses very inadequate means to relieve the most grievous of human diseases.... The physician plainly perceived how much was to be done by moral, and how little by any known medical means.'[70]

This passage from Samuel Tuke's *Description of the Retreat* is followed by an analysis of how medical means were limited to: the warm and cold bath; a generous diet; plenty of air and exercise; some topical bleeding to arrest the paroxysms of maniacs; and medication for physical ailments. He contrasted this with the indiscriminate emetics and bleedings employed at Bethlem and elsewhere.[71] Although this analysis of the limited value of medication guided practitioners of moral treatment elsewhere,[72] the later case-books at the Retreat indicated that medical remedies were resorted to on an increasing scale.

Although medical treatments were not indiscriminate they were applied quite frequently. For example, although Tuke condemned opium as a means of facilitating sleep at night for maniacs, and stated that liberal diet and porter were preferred, the case books indicated that a variety of narcotics were being employed during the first half of the nineteenth century, including opium, laudanum, and morphia, as well as the milder hyoscyamus. Topical bleeding for maniacs – whether by cupping to the neck and shoulders or leeches to the temple – was used (as Tuke had acknowledged), but so also were counter-irritants of blisters, scarifications, and setons (which Fowler was said to have found to be ineffectual). These were employed to inflame the skin and induce suppuration and, so it was thought, to divert morbid action from the centre to the periphery of the body. Although the Retreat was said to have rejected violent evacuations and nauseous draughts the case books indicated that aperients and emetics of varying strengths were extensively employed to keep the bowels regular and the biliary functions in a healthy state. Laxatives ranged from rhubarb through castor oil, epsom salts, saline or calomel mixtures to the occasional use of mercurial blue pills (if the flow of bile was deficient). Emetics were prescribed less frequently but included salines and tartrate of antimony. To this must be added the increasing complexity of the medical means used to treat the physical ailments of the Retreat's patients. It is interesting that the medication employed at the Retreat, which in its first years, had been much less extensively employed than in the previous establishments in which some of its patients had lived, had by the end of the period become as intensively employed as was the custom elsewhere. Admittedly, the influence of the Retreat's moral treatment had helped in the decline of violent medical means employed in asylums generally. Yet it is clear that whereas the Retreat's medical treatments had in its earliest years been notably mild and infrequently administered, by the end of our period they were not noticeably distinctive either in quality or quantity from those employed elsewhere.[73]

However the milder treatments, which Tuke had emphasized in the *Description*, continued to be employed. The liberal diet of the Retreat, with its generous quantities of food of high quality, was particularly efficacious for patients who had been subjected before their arrival to a depletive regime. One patient 'was much reduced in flesh on admission and ate immoderately'. Another patient was described in 1843 as gaining four pounds in weight during her first week at the Retreat.[74] A nourishing diet, which was supplemented by alcohol, was thought to be especially suitable for melancholics instead of the traditional remedy of purging away the black bile which, it was alleged, had produced their depression. Melancholics who would not take the house diet at first were built up with beef tea, arrowroot, and glasses of wine or sherry. Later, they graduated to the Retreat's normal diet of: coffee or milk, toast or porridge at breakfast; meat or broth, vegetables, fruit or rice pudding at lunch; tea or coffee in the afternoon; and bread, cheese, and milk at supper.[75] In the earliest years, beer was served with the main meals but this was later removed because of the adoption of a more temperate regime in which alcohol was avoided except on medical prescription. While the finer regulation of the dietary needs of the patients received increased emphasis over the years, the use of hydrotherapy was not increased to the same extent. The near veneration of warm baths in the earliest case notes was not sustained although they continued to be used. To this was added the shower bath and the use of friction gloves by the end of our period. But the case-notes increasingly gave the impression that water treatments were just one, among many, medical treatments.

In the first years of the Retreat, the physician visited several times a week and prescribed medicines which the superintendent (acting as the apothecary), then made up and administered to the patients at his discretion.[76] Before his appointment as the first superintendent to the Retreat George Jepson had gained a considerable local reputation for his medical skills among the ordinary people, and this was recognized by Dr Fowler in devolving the day-to-day care of the patients upon him. The appointment of Thomas Allis as superintendent in 1823 (who acknowledged that he had no medical knowledge or skills), led to an increased influence of the medical men at the Retreat. Caleb Williams was appointed as visiting surgeon and made three visits a week, which were additional to an equivalent number made by the then visiting physician, Dr Belcombe.[77] Even this was later felt to be insufficient and in 1838 a resident surgeon, John Thurnam, was also appointed as resident medical officer 'to improve the medical and moral oversight of the patients'.[78] The annual report of 1842 stated that the Retreat had

> 'obtained through the zeal and efficiency of their present Medical Officer, the objects which they had chiefly in view in his appointment, viz: a more vigilant observation of the cases – a better record of the history and progress of the disease – and a more effective inspection of the patients and their attendants, in connexion with moral management.'

This internal reform, the appointment of a resident medical officer, presaged the end of the old regime at the Retreat and initiated the changes which were to be completed by the externally imposed reforms of the Lunatics Act of 1845. Although he was responsible for some initiatives in the moral treatment of patients, Thurnam's case notes revealed an acceleration of the trend towards medication. His appointment as the first medical superintendent of the Retreat was not only a recognition of what was legally necessary under the Lunatics Act of 1845, but an overt acknowledgement of an underlying situation in which the medical man had imperceptibly achieved ascendancy over the lay therapist. This predominance was not unique to the Retreat, but was part of a wider movement in which mad-doctors achieved control of the asylum in early nineteenth-century England. But the Retreat's capitulation had a certain irony since its approach to the mentally ill through moral treatment had earlier threatened the domination of medical men in this field.[79]

Moral and medical treatment

The paradoxical description of moral treatment with which this paper opened hinted at a creative tension within moral treatment. Did the Retreat during its first half century balance firmness with gentleness so that patients were treated humanely? Was moral therapy in fact the mild treatment that contemporaries believed it to be, or was Foucault correct in seeing it as fundamentally repressive?

The open character of the York institution which permitted visitors to test its practice against its publicity meant that much of its humane reputation was well founded. The permeability of the Retreat, which enabled patients to mix with visitors or to go out into the world outside the asylum walls, also reduced the amount of social control that the institution was able to exercise over them. Foucault's view of Retreat patients serving a penal term in thus an exaggerated one.

Yet the Retreat did have repressive elements: Samuel Tuke himself acknowledged the force of the 'principle of fear'.[80] Although mechanical restraint was used for only a very small minority of Retreat patients, its psychological resonance in a small institution, and hence its indirect power to control patients, was much greater than its actual use would have indicated. Similarly, the prevailing view of patients as being in a state of childhood dependence involved not only indulgence but also discipline. Although Foucault overemphasized the disciplinary function both of religious exercises and of employment at York he was surely right to suggest their controlling power.[81] But rather than following Foucault in emphasizing the single-mindedness of these activities it would be historically more accurate to distinguish several. Thus, while attendance at religious worship involved self-discipline, religion was also seen as the key which might unlock the door of insanity since the soul could rise above disease. Similarly, if, on the one hand, work for the patient might involve subordination to routine, the acceptance of discipline or the attainment of concentration, on the other hand, relearning these habits was also seen as an important way in which the convalescent patient prepared himself for re-entry into the world outside the asylum gates. Thus, in stressing its diversity of purpose we also underline the ambiguity of moral treatment. The fundamental values that informed the Retreat's moral therapy were those of the Society of Friends. Without an appreciation of the self-disciplined nature of Quaker life we may be in danger of interpreting the moralistic regime of a Quaker asylum as exclusively repressive, and further, of miscalculating the response of its typical Quaker patients to what they may have experienced only as a familiar lifestyle.[82]

The familiar could be imposed unsympathetically like a strait-jacket that stifled individuality in the interests of conformity or alternatively might provide a confidence-inducing background in which patients could forget their sense of failure and build up their own self-esteem. In its earliest years the Retreat was sufficiently small for individual idiosyncrasies to be accommodated in what was in many ways a surrogate home. One patient, who was diagnosed as suffering from 'monomania of pride', was allowed to wear a hat decorated with tinsel and peacock feathers, and was occasionally carried around shoulder high in his self-appointed role of Duke John. Another, who was worried about the iron frames in the windows, was comforted by the superintendent's assurance that they protected the household from burglars.[83] Thus, under Jepson and Allis there was a genuine attempt to govern 'rather by esteem than severity'. Yet this was an easier task for Jepson (1796–1823), who never had more than 72 patients in his care, than for Allis (1823–41) under whose direction numbers rose as high as 108.[84] One patient commented sadly that 'to one that has always been used to a small family, this is just like being in a show'.[85] This inmate clearly felt that she was an object to be managed rather than a subject to be treated. Already, seeds were planted at the Retreat that were to grow into a more repressive system of moral management in the second half of the nineteenth century. And a significant contributant to this subtle evolution from moral treatment to moral management was the enhanced importance given to medicine at the Retreat. Since recoveries were seen increasingly as the result of medical 'science' rather than moral therapy, so the latter became a series of techniques to be practised rather than the creative act of healing that it had been earlier.

How significant was this half-century of moral treatment at the Retreat? Historically, the publicity given to its early successes by the publication of Samuel Tuke's *Description of the Retreat* in 1813 had led to widespread imitation. But the therapy this York asylum had practised successfully in an establishment atypical in size, sectarian character, and social composition of its patients, did not necessarily transfer effectively to the very different pauper asylums which tried to adopt moral treatment. These institutions, as John Walton argues elsewhere in this volume, were reformatories first and refuges second. In contrast, in these first decades the Retreat was more a refuge than a reformatory, although a reforming element was to become increasingly evident in the mid-nineteenth century, when the more rigid procedures of moral management gradually replaced the individualized care that had characterized moral treatment. This pervasive development was the product of a number of convergent factors, including the need to replace mechanical or physical restraint of patients by a more systematic form of psychological control, and also the growing size of the asylum which resulted in a small egalitarian 'family' being succeeded by a more hierarchical, bureaucratically organized institution. Most crucial in this transition was the progressive dilution of the Retreat's Quaker character through the recruitment of growing numbers of affluent non-Quaker patients whose high fees were necessary to subsidize poorer Quaker inmates. This was conducive to a situation where therapy was more likely to produce mere outward conformity in non-Quaker patients, whereas the earlier successes of moral treatment appear to have sprung more from inducing self-control in Quaker patients who shared the values, assumptions and objectives of their therapists. In this context it is not without interest that the 'recovery' rates of the Retreat's patients (admittedly highly problematical in character[86]), were much higher in these early years than subsequently, when the Quaker nature of the Retreat had been attenuated. This poses the fascinating but unresolvable question of whether the distinctively religious character of the Retreat's moral treatment did not rely for its efficacy, at least in part, on an unseen kernel of spiritual healing.

Notes

The Retreat records are in the Borthwick Institute of Historical Research, York, referred to in the footnotes as BIHR.

1 The support of the ESRC in financing this reseach is gratefully acknowledged.
2 *A Manual of Psychological Medicine* (London: John Churchill, 1858), pp. 506–07.
3 A. Scull, *Museums of Madness* (London: Allen Lane, 1979), p. 102.

4 R. Porter, 'Was There a Moral Therapy in the Eighteenth Century?' *Lychnos* (1981–82): 12–26.
5 A. Digby, *Madness, Morality and Medicine: A Study of the York Retreat, 1796–1914* (New York: Cambridge University Press, forthcoming), ch. 1.
6 A. Digby, 'Changes in the Asylum: the Case of York, 1777–1815', *Economic History Review*, 2nd series, 36 (1983): 218–39.
7 E.T. Carlson and N. Dain, 'The Psychotherapy That was Moral Treatment', *American Journal of Psychiatry* 117 (1960): 519–24; E.A. Woods and E.T. Carlson, 'Psychiatry of Phillippe Pinel', *Bulletin of the History of Medicine* 25 (1961): 18–19.
8 M. Foucault, *Madness and Civilization: A History of Insanity in the Age of Reason* (London: Tavistock, 1971), p. 278.
9 V. Skultans, *Madness and Morals: Ideas on Insanity in the Nineteenth Century* (London: Routledge and Kegan Paul, 1975), p. 9; P. McCandless, 'Liberty and Lunacy: The Victorians and Wrongful Confinement', *Journal of Social History* 11 (1978): 376, 379.
10 See Digby, *Madness, Morality and Medicine*, ch. 5, for a lengthier analysis of this type of case.
11 Digby, *Madness, Morality and Medicine*, chs. 8, 9; M. Donnelly, *Managing the Mind: A Study of Medical Psychology in Early Nineteenth Century Britain* (London: Tavistock, 1983), pp. 91–2.
12 BIHR L/3/2, State of an Institution; H/1, John Bevans to William Tuke, 20 January, 1794.
13 R. Hunter and I. MacAlpine, 'Samuel Tuke's First Publication on the Treatment of Patients at the Retreat, 1811', *British Journal of Psychiatry* 111 (1965): 771.
14 D.H. Tuke, *Chapters in the History of the Insane in the British Isles*, 2 vols (London: Kegan Paul, 1882), vol. 1, pp. 14, 126.
15 BIHR A/1/1, Circular of 28 June 1792 in Directors' Minute Book, 1792–1841; H/1, Retreat Building: Letters and Receipts, 1793–6; S. Tuke, *Description of the Retreat*, facsimile edn (London: Dawsons, 1964), pp. 98–100.
16 S. Tuke, *Practical Hints on the Construction and Economy of Lunatic Asylums*, 2nd edn (Wakefield, 1819), p. 11.
17 BIHR D/3/1–2, Visitors Books (1798–1822, 1822–35).
18 BIHR H/1, Bills for plants etc.; BIHR, A/1/1, Circular of 25 September, 1794; Annual Report, 1839, p. 5; S. Tuke, *Review of the Early History of the Retreat* (York, 1846), p. 11.
19 K. Doerner, *Madmen and the Bourgeoisie* (Oxford: Blackwell, 1981), p. 66.
20 S. Tuke, *Description*, pp. 94–5.
21 BIHR, L/1, E. Pumphrey, 'Recollections of the Retreat of 50 years ago' (1896), pp. 75, 79, 90, 94–5; S. Tuke, *Practical Hints*, p. 13.
22 This is particularly evident in the women's visits; BIHR, D/2/1, Female (Committee) Visitors Book (1815–39).
23 For example, BIHR K/2/2–3, cases 25, 408, 420.
24 Bedford Pierce, 'Recovery from Mental Disorder', *Proceedings of the Royal Society of Medicine*, 15 (1922): 1.
25 BIHR A/1/1, Circular of 28 June, 1792.
26 Tuke, *Review*, p. 10.
27 The first appointments at the Retreat were of short duration: Timothy Maud, the first superintendent died in July, 1796; while the first 'matron', Jane King, resigned in April 1797.
28 BIHR H/2, W. Tuke to T. Maud, 13 February, 1797.

29 BIHR L/1, T. Allis to S. Tuke, September, 1822.
30 Introduction by S. Tuke to M. Jacobi, *On the Construction and Management of Hospitals for the Insane* (London: 1841), p. xix.
31 S. Tuke, *Review*, p. 16.
32 Annual Report, 1824.
33 Pumphrey, 'Recollections', p. 76; BIHR A/3/1, Committee Minute Book (1796–1825).
34 *Memoirs of S. Tuke*, 2 vols (London: 1860), vol. 1, p. 232.
35 J. Walton, 'The Treatment of Pauper Lunatics in Victorian England: the Case of the Lancaster Asylum, 1816–70', in A. Scull (ed.), *Madhouses, Mad-doctors, and Madmen* (London: Athlone Press, 1981), p. 180.
36 BIHR C/1, S. Tuke to T. Stordy, 22 November, 1826.
37 Introduction in Jacobi, *Construction and Management*, p. xxi; W.L. Parry-Jones, *The Trade in Lunacy* (London: Routledge and Kegan Paul, 1972), p. 186.
38 S. Tuke, *Review*, p. 24.
39 For example, BIHR K/2/5, case 639.
40 S. Tuke, *Review*, p. 33.
41 Introduction in Jacobi, *Construction and Management*, p. xxix; S. Tuke, *Review*, p. 22.
42 S. Tuke, *Review*, pp. 16, 19.
43 BIHR K/2/2, case 97.
44 BIHR K/2/2, case 85. (The case notes are reproduced in an appendix of Digby. *Madness, Morality and Medicine*).
45 BIHR, D/1/1, Committee Visitors Book (1815–67); S. Tuke, *Description*, pp. 165–66; *Review*, p. 26; *Sketch of the Origin, Progress and Present State of the Retreat* (York, 1828), p. 30.
46 BIHR K/2/1–2, cases 97, 78, 15.
47 Pumphrey, 'Recollections', pp. 85–6.
48 BIHR K/2/1, K/2/2, K/2/4, cases 171, 15, 260.
49 S. Tuke, *Review*, p. 27; Annual Report, 1839; cf. the essay by Andrew Scull in Volume I.
50 S. Tuke, *Review*, p. 29.
51 BIHR K/3/1, Medical Journal and Weekly Report (1845–50).
52 BIHR D/1/1, Committee Visitors Book (1815–67); K/2/1, case 101.
53 *Eighth Report of the Commissioners in Lunacy*, Parliamentary Papers, 1854, pp. xxix, 157.
54 S. Tuke, *Review*, p. 29.
55 BIHR A/1/1, Circular of 25 September, 1794.
56 BIHR K/2/3, case 178, Observation 31 October, 1838.
57 BIHR A/1/1, Directors' Minutes; S. Tuke, *Practical Hints*, p. 13.
58 S. Tuke, *Review*, p. 30; BIHR Case Books, K/2/2–6.
59 Cases 70, 183, 548.
60 Annual Report, 1839.
61 Cases 559, 671, 450.
62 Annual Report, 1844.
63 Annual Report, 1797.
64 This 'half-way house' was discontinued because of its high cost to the institution.
65 Cases 438, 465, 144.
66 Case 278.
67 BIHR G/1/1, Lunacy Commissioners Visitors Book, Entry 3, February, 1847.
68 Introduction in Jacobi, *Construction and Management*, p. xxviii; S. Tuke,

Memoirs, vol. 2, pp. 450–51.

69 BIHR D/1/1, 11 December, 1827, Committee Visitors Book (1815–67); Annual Report, 1839; BIHR G/1/1 Lunacy Commissioners Visitors Book.

70 S. Tuke, *Description*, pp. 111–12.

71 S. Tuke, *Description*, pp. 112–30.

72 Scull, *Museums of Madness*, pp. 188–89.

73 A comparison of the certificates filed on admission (which gave medical histories of the patients) with the histories of patients recorded in the Retreat's medical case books makes this very obvious (K/1/1–3 and K/2/2–6).

74 Cases 75, 666.

75 S. Tuke, *Description*, p. 124; letter written by case 637 in K/2/5 which described the diet approvingly.

76 S. Tuke, *Review*, p. 16.

77 S. Tuke, *Sketch of the Retreat*, pp. 56–7.

78 Annual Report, 1838.

79 Scull, *Museums of Madness*, p. 162.

80 S. Tuke, *Description*, p. 141.

81 Foucault, *Madness and Civilization*, pp. 243–48.

82 See ch. 4 of Digby, *Madness, Morality and Medicine* for a fuller discussion of the nature of the Retreat's management and of the character of the Retreat 'family'.

83 BIHR K/2/4, case 122; Pumphrey, 'Recollections', pp. 41, 43, 83–4.

84 Numbers at the Retreat were usually less than in the more recently established county and borough asylums: they had an average of 298 inmates by 1850.

85 BIHR K/2/4, case 544.

86 See Digby, *Madness, Morality and Medicine*, for a more detailed discussion of this point.

CHAPTER FOUR

Aspects of non-conformity: Quakers and the lunatic fringe[1]

Fiona Godlee

THE RETREAT AT York was above all a Quaker asylum, initially run by Quakers exclusively for Quaker patients. Though not the first people to conceive of or practise a moral treatment for insanity,[2] the Quakers' success with the method, and Samuel Tuke's published description of it,[3] gained it widespread acceptance and application. As a psychological means of producing behavioural conformity in the insane, (in Scull's words) it 'made redundant the harsh and barbaric methods previously connected inescapably with the concentration of large numbers of madmen together in an institutional environment.'[4] This paper seeks out the irony in the position of Quakers as keepers of the insane, and in the Tukes's contribution to the history of psychiatry. To do this it will first examine the aims of moral therapy as practised at the Retreat, and then develop a historical comparison between the Tukes and their early Quaker forebears.

Aims of moral therapy

In her paper, 'Moral Treatment at the Retreat, 1796–1846',[5] Anne Digby shows that, with all the changes in the management of patients which occurred over this period, a constant feature was the emphasis on kindness, respect, and the cultivation of self-control. The system was not only more humane than methods used previously and elsewhere for controlling the insane, it also proved more efficient at producing behavioural improvement; and it was more aesthetically acceptable, a vital consideration for the refined sensibilities of the new generation of reformers. On these two bonuses of the Tukes' moral therapy rests the irony so neatly revealed by Andrew Scull in his *Museums of Madness*. When similar techniques were adopted in the vast pauper asylums established under the legislation of the early nineteenth century, all humane and individualistic aspects disappeared, and emphasis was placed instead upon the latent strength of moral therapy as a socially acceptable mechanism for enforcing conformity. The techniques developed at the Retreat placed

> 'a far more effective and thorough-going means of control in the hands of the custodians [of the large, new asylums], while simultaneously, by removing the necessity for the asylums' crudest features, it made the reality of that imprisonment and control far more difficult to perceive.'[6]

This last point, only touched upon by Scull, is elaborated in a different context by Thomas Szasz.[7] He considers three famous examples of so-called 'progressive' and 'enlightened' reform: Guillotine's invention, Charcot's authentication of hysteria, and Pinel's liberation of the lunatics. Each act, he concludes, had deeper and darker implications than those superficially perceived. While the guillotine embodied humanitarian principles in providing a less painful means of execution, it also made the task of the executioner less unpleasant and the conscience of the judge less heavy. Charcot's recognition of hysteria as a real disease relieved hysterics of the trauma of unsympathetic treatment by sceptical doctors. But in making it easier to receive treatment he made it easier to treat, to disqualify, to control. Equally, Pinel's insistence that the insane be treated as human beings facilitated their confinement by removing concern for their physical well-being. All three developments, when viewed through Szasz's jaundiced lens, become acts not of reform but of mere cosmetic change by which the fundamental issues – execution, control, confinement – disappear from view.

The Tukes's reform may also be seen in this light. Moral therapy projected onto different circumstances was, says Scull, put to very different uses to those for which it was originally intended. In this he clearly designates the large pauper asylums as the first to stress the conditioning potential of moral therapy rather than its greater humanity. I intend to question this idea of Scull's, and the implication it carries that the Tukes were unaware of, or indifferent to, the power of moral therapy as a force for conformity.

The Tukes are often applauded for their empiricism in dealing with a subject as controversial as insanity. Unfettered by theoretical bias or professional loyalties, they simply made use of the techniques they deemed most effective. Commentators tend to see this as productive of a refreshingly uncomplicated approach to the treatment of the insane; and after reporting heated discussions on the nature of insanity and the correct therapy for it, they quote with apparent relief Samuel Tuke's common-sense justification for the use of moral therapy – namely, that it worked.[8]

Tuke would naturally have been keen to demonstrate to the world the effectiveness of moral therapy, knowing that this, perhaps more than its obvious benefits in humanitarian terms, would be a major criterion in the evaluation of its worth. Yet his concentration on the success of the method seems to run deeper than a simple desire for its public acceptance. At every decisive point in the development of the techniques employed at the Retreat considerations of efficacy, not humanity, appear to hold sway. This can be shown with reference to the major innovative features of moral therapy as initially practised at the Retreat. For example, the reliance on non-medical therapies for insanity[9] was not justified by Tuke in terms of the violence or interventionist nature of medical therapies, or even on the premise that the insane did not require therapy as such; but because none of the popular medical treatments were found to be of any use.[10] In their place Tuke advocated such things as warm and cold baths. Similarly, Tuke advised the use of the patients' 'desire for esteem' rather than the principle of fear, not so much for reasons of compassion as because the former was found to operate 'more powerfully'.[11]

Having considered the Tukes's empiricism as represented by Samuel Tuke, it is necessary to ask, at what was this empiricism aimed? What was it that constituted success for the keepers of the Retreat? Tuke writes, 'The persuasion which is extended to the patients is confined to those points which affect their liberty and comfort. No advantage has been found to arise from reasoning with them, on their particular hallucinations.'[12] This attitude is in keeping with the favoured phenomenological approach to insanity, but it is worth considering for whom the hoped-for 'advantage' was intended. Tuke provides the answer to this question. Of the patients' desire for esteem he writes,

'though it has obviously not been sufficiently powerful, to enable them to resist the strong irregular tendencies of their disease: yet when properly cultivated, it leads them to struggle to conceal and overcome their morbid propensities; and at least materially assists them in confining their deviations, within such bounds, as do not make them obnoxious to the family.'[13]

The techniques of moral therapy bring the patients to attempt to conceal their antisocial tendencies. Of more importance, it was Tuke's stated aim that such attempts at concealment and suppression should succeed; that the patient should conform for the good of the community. The power of moral therapy as a mechanism for enforcing conformity was not discovered for the first time in the large institutional asylums. It was already clearly acknowledged by Tuke in his *Description of the Retreat*.

Tuke celebrated the efficacy of the Retreat's regime in a regrettable though, for the purposes of this argument, ironically relevant context – the Quaker meeting house.

'A profound silence generally ensues [after a reading from the bible]; during which as well as at the time of the reading, it was very gratifying to observe [the patients'] orderly conduct, and the degree to which those who are disposed to action, restrain their different propensities.'[14]

The implication is clear. Outward appearance was deemed more important than the state of the inner being. This is the very antithesis of Quaker belief, a major focus of early Quaker protest having been empty religious observances associated with the established Church.

In an earlier section of his book, Tuke reports on the privilege, allowed to certain patients, of taking tea with the female superintendent. He writes, 'all who attend dress in their best clothes, and vie with each other in politeness and propriety'.[15] This confirms the impression of preoccupation with social niceties, and introduces another feature of patient management at the Retreat which is inconsistent with original Quaker testimony, this time concerning dress. Tuke tells us that 'all patients wear clothes and are generally induced to adopt orderly habits',[16] clearly an improvement on the indecent and filthy state of inmates in the majority of insane asylums. Yet throughout their history the Quakers have used clothes to achieve conspicuous non-conformity. Quaker dress, distinguished along with their peculiar form of speech as 'plain', achieved great notoriety and, as will be shown with regard to 'hat-honour', became an extremely effective means of social protest. George Fox, the founder of the Quaker movement, was widely recognized as 'the man in leather breeches'. Of relevance to the compulsory clothing of the insane, Quaker testimony at the height of their early enthusiasm included 'going naked for a sign'.[17] Later, as Quakers succeeded to wealth and social respect, clothing became a symbolic means of announcing their separateness from a world by which they were increasingly accepted.

The use of clothes to assert individuality or flout convention was of course not unique to the Quakers. Protesting groups of all types, especially the rising generation, have always employed peculiar modes of dress and language to these ends. The Retreat however provides an interesting paradox in the insistence that inmates conform in this matter by which Quakers traditionally celebrated their non-conformity and continued to uphold their identity.

My first conclusions then are these. The cardinal feature of moral therapy was undoubtedly its emphasis on kindness and humanity. But kindness was not the aim of moral therapy, only the intended nature of its administration. The aim of moral therapy was to achieve a degree of social conformity in the insane as a means of non-violent management and in order to reclaim them, if possible, for society. That this was recognized by those involved with the Retreat, and was not a distortion of motive later inflicted by more generalized use of the method, is suggested by the principles according to which Tuke evaluated different techniques. For this he referred not to a technique's humanity or ability to cure, but to its success in bringing patients to behave. Tuke's ambition for his patients seems to fall short of the deeper restoration of reason which the reputation of the Retreat and of the Quakers in general leads one to expect, and it is in several details strangely inconsistent with much of Quaker history and belief. In the light of these conclusions, I will now consider the Quakers' changing relationship with orthodox society, from early religious enthusiasm to nineteenth-century respectability. The Tukes and their colleagues developed techniques for encouraging conformity in the insane; while their Quaker forebears, as religious and social non-conformists, were persecuted and disqualified as madmen.

Historical contrast

The Quaker movement began in the north of England in the late 1640s with the wanderings of an apprentice leather worker, George Fox. The derisive name was inspired by the convulsive trembling exhibited by converts.[18] Nearly a century later it was described as 'one of the most pestilent sects that ever infected the Christian church'.[19] What was it about the early Quakers that made them so menacing?

THE QUAKER THREAT

In his account of the Levellers, Brailsford suggests that a prime function of religion is to maintain authority.[20] The great social changes that marked the late sixteenth and seventeenth centuries, caused by the cumulative effect of the Reformation and the English revolution, brought a call from the clergy for stricter discipline and orthodox religious observance.[21] In such uncertain times religious conformity was equated with piety and the rejection of orthodox religion with sin. H.S. Becker writes, 'society creates deviance by making rules whose infraction constitutes deviance'.[22] In Szasz's terms,[23] theology was the major rule-maker of seventeenth-century society, and religious rather than rational non-conformity was recognized as deviant. Like the insane a century later, seventeenth-century religious non-conformists repudiated the core values of orthodox society and so constituted a major threat to its stability.

With their challenge to institutionalized and dogmatic religion and their obstinate affirmation of social and sexual equality, the Quakers struck at the heart of English social structure. Matthews has summarized their beliefs:

'They taught the immediate presence of God in the heart of each believer. To know what was right one had only to listen with quiet attention to the words of that inner voice. It followed that outward forms of ecclesiastical organisation were worse than useless; they were dangerous, for they detracted from the reality of religion that spoke from within.'[24]

The Quakers therefore by-passed orthodox religious organization, dispensing with its rites of baptism, marriage, and burial, refusing to attend church or receive the sacraments, and withholding tithes, priests' fees, or any rates intended for the building and conservation of churches or other 'superstitious uses'.[25]

Their religious protest was augmented by specific social challenges aimed against established hierarchy. These were most notoriously manifested in their refusal to doff their hats to any person, and their insistence on addressing anyone they were talking to, whatever their social status, by the familiar term 'thou'. It is tempting to view these 'testimonies', both borrowed from the Anabaptists and probably fortified by aversion to the Ranter practice of being too 'complimental',[26] as meaningless breaches of good manners or tasteless eccentricities. On the contrary, they represented some of the boldest gestures in social life. The generalized use of the term 'thou', with its connotations of familiarity and even of contempt, constituted a threat of insubordination if not of actual revolt, while the refusal to pay 'hat honour' has been called 'a revolutionary act'.[27] Sewel wrote,

> 'though it was pretended that the putting off of the Hat was but a small Thing: which none ought to scruple: yet it was a wonderful Thing to see what great Disturbance this pretended small Matter caused among people of all sorts, so that even Men that would be look'd upon as those that practised Humility and Meekness soon shew'd what Spirit they were of when this worldly Honour was denied them.'[28]

The severity with which these affirmations of human equality were viewed[29] is evident from the heavy-handed legal reaction they provoked. James Naylor, on trial in 1652, was told by the Justice that 'if he would not put off his hat he would send him to prison; and also because he had said thou to him, for, said the Justice, my Commision runs Ye'.[30] Illustrations abound of the fear generated by what was seen as the 'inveterate malice of the Quakers'.[31] A petition sent to Richard Cromwell in 1659 complained that Yorkshire

> 'has been miserably perplexed and much dissettled by the unruly sect of people called Quakers, whose principles are to overturn, overturn, overturn Magistry, Ministry and Ordinances, all that which good men would keep up by their prayers and endeavours. These will not know, nor acknowledge any subjection they owe to any powers upon earth ... It is these men's common practice to meet by Hundreds in or near to our public places for worship, on purpose to disturb the Preacher and People assembled, causing and speaking all manner of evil against those Things that all sober minds deem good, to the great Terror of some and no small trouble of other Ministers, seeing they so frequently give out, that in a short Time they shall be the greater number.'[32]

A major cause for concern among those in authority was the Quakers' adherence to St Paul's injunction to 'swear not at all'. In an age of great social upheaval, political and judicial oaths took on peculiar importance.[33] At the Old Bailey in 1664, Judge Keeling warned that the Quakers 'have an interest to carry on against the government, and therefore they will not swear subjection to it; and their end is rebellion and blood'.[34]

In addition to the threat of social and political insubordination, there was the need for vigilance against blasphemy. Messianic pretenders, because not uncommon, were usually dismissed by the authorities as 'brainsick' or 'frantic'.[35] But in the case of James Naylor there were fears that his 'sin' would prove 'a national sin and consequently a national judgement'. His ride into Bristol, amidst palm-strewing followers on a rainy day in 1656, was deemed 'the height of horrid blasphemy' and set parliament in turmoil. A specially appointed committee debated for ten days what should be done in this 'special emergency', and confusion reigned on matters of theology and constitutional and legal procedure. Finally the death sentence was commuted to one in which, said the Speaker of the House, 'mercy is mingled with judgement'. Naylor was pilloried and whipped through the streets of London; his tongue was bored through and his forehead branded with the letter 'B'; he was made to re-enact his blasphemous ride into Bristol in parody, 'with his face backward', and imprisoned at parliament's pleasure.[36]

Such an aggressive response to this and other Quaker actions is easier to understand in the context of its religious and political setting. As well as the specific reaction to religious enthusiasts, it involved aversion to the more general concept of enthusiasm which was perceived as an increasingly ubiquitous and threatening phenomenon.

THE THREAT OF ENTHUSIASM

In his study of the French Prophets, Hillel Schwartz writes that the events of the seventeenth century 'argued persuasively for an inevitable relationship between overstrong religious feeling, enthusiasm and political fanaticism'[37]; and after the emotional chaos of the Civil War, the people of the Restoration had cause to distrust the emotions and the imaginative rhetoric that worked upon them.[38] George Williamson has explored the revolt against enthusiasm within Restoration literature.[39] Taking as his starting point Elizabethan dualism between Reason and the Passions, he follows the change in attitude towards the imagination from the beginning to the end of the seventeenth century; from its celebration as an idealizer of reality, to its rejection as a deceiver and 'the greatest enemy of Reason'.[40] Schwartz considers the scientific and medical objections to emotional extravagance.[41] Physical agitations were seen as harmful to the highly valued harmony between body and soul since any upset to the animal spirits could readily progress to mania, convulsions, and delirium. Medical, literary, and social commentators alike were anxious to defend both the individual and society from the unruly and the unpredictable, and above all from enthusiastic disregard of Reason, which held all things together.

'In matters of Faith and Religion', wrote Francis Bacon, 'we raise our Imagination above our Reason'.[42] Yet Schwartz confirms that, by the time of the Restoration, true inspiration and true religion were firmly believed to be in complete accord with and never to override Reason.[43] By the same token, if the Holy Spirit were indeed to enter a body, as the religious enthusiasts claimed that it did, it was sure to do so gently. Thus the forces which, according to one description, caused the Quakers to 'fall, foam at the mouth, roar and swell in their bellies',[44] must prove other than divine.

Of the alternatives put forward to explain the enthusiasts' strange behaviour, that of possession was favoured by the clergy, fighting as they were against the secularization of public outlook. Ex-enthusiasts, on the other hand, deflected embarrassment by asserting that they had been, as their former brothers continued to be, the victims of delusion.[45] Writers on the subject tended to agree with this assessment, at least in part. Henry More wrote in 1656, 'Enthusiasme is nothing else but a misconceit of being inspired.'[46] Yet, like Meric Casaubon, whose *Treatise concerning Enthusiasm*[47] appeared a year earlier in 1655, More believed that the delusion was itself the result of melancholy. Both writers referred to Robert Burton[48] who elaborated the concept of 'religious melancholy' in 1621. Inspired by fears for ecclesiastical and civil harmony,[49] he described it as an affliction of Papists and sectaries and warned that they spread it to the populace.

The idea that enthusiasm was a contagious disease – one which 'sews itself, and like the blood of a wart cut off, brings twenty for one'[50] – was both attractive and enduring; and it added a sense of urgency to the anti-enthusiasts' campaign. Here the connection between enthusiasm and mental disturbance, forged by Burton and increasingly accepted by others, proved a highly effective weapon. Roy Porter identified this addition to the anti-enthusiasts' armoury in his article, 'The Rage of Party'.[51] The labelling of enemies or deviants as mad, to disqualify them and invalidate their claims, is a common political device. It was used, for example, according to Szasz and others, against witches and heretics in the middle ages, and is fundamental to Foucault's 'great confinement'.[52] But whereas Foucault described its use in the context of a conspiracy against the remnants of eighteenth-century society who existed outside the normal control of the privileged elite, Porter believes that its victims were in fact the religious enthusiasts. He writes, 'Elite society was indeed closing ranks . . . to defame their enemies as insane. But pace Foucault, the prime target, the focus of the danger, was not the dregs but the godly.'[53]

ENTHUSIASM AS MADNESS

MacDonald states that, by the middle of the eighteenth century, the prevailing view among the educated elite was that people who claimed to have divine inspiration were mad.[54] Porter gives examples of the medical profession's support for this idea. Religious trances were equated with epileptic seizures, and diagnosable somatic seats suggested for the madness. Physicalistic explanations included lesions of the womb, dyspepsia, and an excess of bile. Dr Nicholas Robinson, writing in 1729, dismissed the visions and revelations of Fox and Naylor as 'nothing but the effect of mere madness [which] arose from the stronger impulses of a warm brain'.[55] Further retrospective denunciations of Fox as insane included a description of his journal as 'that Rhapsody of Madness',[56] and of Fox himself as 'of so dull and heavy parts' that 'he wanted wit to invent a name for his party, till the name Quakers was bestowed upon them by others from their monstrous Quaking and Distortions'.[57]

The extraordinary manifestations of conviction displayed by religious enthusiasts were perhaps reason enough – once such things were viewed in more secular terms – to elicit the charge of insanity. Epilepsy in particular seemed akin to their convulsions. More declared that each case of religious ecstasy was 'a degree and species of epilepsy'[58]; and Higginson, reporting on a Quaker meeting, wrote that listeners would 'fall suddenly down . . . as

though they were surprised with an epilepsy'.[59] Ronald Knox concluded
that 'the unbeliever hesitates whether to explain all this as hysteria or
diabolism'.[60] By choosing the former explanation and labelling threatening
religious expression as a medical rather than a divine phenomenon, sacred
witness was neatly transformed into meaningless gibberish and the threat to
the social order effectively removed. [61]

The accusations of insanity presented religious enthusiasts with a dilemma. Their claims that the convulsions they experienced were involuntary,
involving abandonment of the will to passionate and irresistible forces,
provided critics with all they needed to diagnose insanity. Yet, as Schwartz
points out, it was exactly this appearance of succumbing to an irrational and
overriding influence which guaranteed the purity of the divine communication. Faced with this problem, and a growing barrage of hostility, enthusiasts tended to adjust their perception of what occurred under inspiration to
include the survival of intellect and memory.[62]

The Quakers, for their part, began to stress the role of reason in their
worship. The Naylor episode, and others like it, forced them to consider the
wider effects of uncontrolled enthusiastic behaviour, and combined with the
unprecedented persecution of the Restoration period to divert the Quakers
from evangelism to self-preservation through organization and discipline. In
1664, Baxter acknowledged that 'pretended' ecstasies were no longer a part
of Quaker worship, and that now 'they only meet, and he that pretendeth to
be moved by the Spirit speaketh, and sometimes they say nothing but sit an
hour or more in silence and then depart'.[63] The Quakers are here represented on
the brink of quietism, experiencing the first effects of Weberian routinization.
Many historians have documented this change, from loosely structured
charismatic movement to classical religious sect.[64]

EIGHTEENTH-CENTURY QUAKERS

Quakers of later generations tended to adopt an apologetic stance when
speaking of the religious excesses of their spiritual forebears. John Gough,
for example, assured readers of an underlying rationality when he wrote of
the Quakers in 1790:

> 'Being themselves animated and deeply affected in spirit ... testifying
> against vice and wickedness might produce warmth of expression and
> action also, which to an uninvideous eye might appear convulsive: But
> their convulsions did not bereave them of understanding; they spake with
> the spirit and with the understanding also.[65]

Such apologies reflected a more generalized anxiety amongst Quakers of
the eighteenth and nineteenth centuries. Years of persecution and, more
especially, of 'marrying in', were believed by many Quakers to have led to
an increased incidence of insanity.[66] They were therefore sensitive on this
issue; and Samuel Tuke reported that a major objection to the establishment
of an asylum specifically for insane Friends was the aversion of some in the

Society 'to the concentration of the instances of this disease' amongst them.[67] In direct contrast, it was now generally believed that, as a group, Quakers were less afflicted by insanity than the population at large. Haslam, writing at the beginning of the nineteenth century, claimed that their judicious religious beliefs and personal habits made them 'almost exempt' from the ravages of madness[68]; an opinion which reflected the widely held belief that rigorous physical and spiritual discipline was a sure talisman against the loss of reason.

Indeed the Quakers' sober reputation, and the stress laid by them on the importance of self-discipline, made them a valued, even exemplary group in English society. They had emerged from 'the deadly age of Quietism'[69] depleted in number but greatly increased in wealth, respect and social status.[70] In his review of Tuke's *Description of the Retreat*, Sidney Smith described the Quakers as 'a very charitable and humane people', and declared that Tuke – 'a respectable tea dealer' – had written a book 'full of good sense and humanity, right feelings and rational views'. Above all, Smith had little doubt that the Retreat was 'the best managed asylum for the insane that has ever yet been established'.[71]

And so we have come full circle. Once the worst of madmen, the Quakers were now the best of mad-keepers and the most rational of men. In the combined effect of changes in the nature of Quakerism and the advent in society of new rules and new renegades lies the irony this paper has sought to demonstrate. It lies in the historical contrast created by the Quakers' gradual transformation from enthusiasts to institutionalized sectarians, from social revolutionaries to representatives of respectable society, from non-conformists to vehicles of conformity; and in particular, from their position on the lunatic fringe to their decisive role in the development of orthodox psychiatry.

Notes

1 The help and advice of Dr Roy Porter, Dr W.F. Bynum and the Quaker scholar, Barbara Godlee, are gratefully acknowledged.
2 See Roy Porter, 'Was There a Moral Therapy in 18th Century Psychiatry?', *Lychnos*, 1980–81: 12–26.
3 Samuel Tuke, *Description of the Retreat* (York: W. Alexander, 1813; reprint, ed. by R. Hunter and I. MacAlpine, London: Dawson's, 1964).
4 A. Scull, *Museums of Madness* (London: Allen Lane, 1979), p. 120.
5 Anne Digby, 'Moral Treatment at the Retreat, 1796–1846', in this volume.
6 Scull, *Museums of Madness*, p. 121.
7 Thomas S. Szasz, *The Myth of Mental Illness* (London: Paladin, 1972), pp. 42–3.
8 Tuke, *Description of The Retreat*, p. 132.
9 This was of course never total, and medical therapies came increasingly into use. See Anne Digby, *Madness, Morality and Medicine: A Study of the York Retreat, 1796–1914*, (New York and Cambridge: Cambridge University Press, in press).
10 Tuke, *Description of the Retreat*, p. 112.

11 Tuke, *Description of the Retreat*, p. 157.
12 Tuke, *Description of the Retreat*, p. 151.
13 Tuke, *Description of the Retreat*, p. 157.
14 Tuke, *Description of the Retreat*, p. 161.
15 Tuke, *Description of the Retreat*, p. 158.
16 Tuke, *Description of the Retreat*, p. 178.
17 See Richard Bauman, *Let Your Words Be Few* (Cambridge: Cambridge University Press, 1983), ch. 6, pp. 84–94, for an analysis of this Quaker testimony.
18 George Fox claimed that the name came from his own demands that his persecutors tremble at the name of the Lord. See William C. Braithwaite, *The Beginnings of Quakerism*, 2nd edn (Cambridge: Cambridge University Press, 1955), p. 57. See also Bauman, *Let Your Words Be Few*, pp. 79–80 for the conversion process.
19 Joseph Trapp D.D., *The Nature, Folly, Sin and Danger of being Righteous Overmuch*, 3rd edn (London, 1739), p. 61.
20 H.N. Brailsford, *The Levellers and the English Revolution* (London: Cresset Press, 1961), p. 44.
21 Michael MacDonald, *Psychological Medicine* 7 (1977): 565–82.
22 H.S. Becker, *Outsiders* (New York Free Press of Glencoe, 1966), quoted by Thomas S. Szasz, *The Manufacture of Madness*, (London: Routledge and Kegan Paul, 1971), pp. 279–80.
23 Thomas S. Szasz, *The Age of Madness* (London: Routledge and Kegan Paul, 1975).
24 Ronald Matthews *English Messiahs* (London: Methuen, 1936), p. 6.
25 Willen Sewel, *The History of the Rise and Progress of the Christian People called Quakers* (London: The Assigns of J. Sowle, 1722), p. 19.
26 Christopher Hill, *The World Turned Upside Down* (Harmondsworth: Penguin, 1972), p. 191.
27 Brailsford, *The Levellers*, p. 45.
28 Sewel, *History of the Rise*, p. 19.
29 The violent hostility aroused by them is explained by Bauman, *Let Your Words Be Few*, pp. 43–62, in terms of their encroachment into everyday life, as compared to specialized religious challenges.
30 J. Besse, *A Collection of the Sufferings of the People called Quakers*, 2 vols (London: 1753), vol. 2, p. 3.
31 Trapp, *The Nature of being Righteous*, p. 64.
32 Besse, *Collection of The Sufferings*, p. 98.
33 See Bauman, *Let Your Words Be Few*, ch. 7, pp. 95–119.
34 Quoted by John Gough, *A History of the People called Quakers from their Rise to the present time* (Dublin: 1790), vol. 11, p. 123.
35 Keith Thomas, *Religion and the Decline of Magic* (London: Weidenfeld and Nicolson, 1971), p. 158.
36 Matthews, *English Messiahs*, pp. 23–36.
37 Hillel Schwartz, *Knaves, Fools, Madmen, and that Subtile Effluvium: A study of the opposition to the French Prophets in England, 1706–1710* (Gainesville, Fla.: University of Florida, 1978), p. 78.
38 Bauman, *Let Your Words Be Few*, pp. 63–83, discusses the role of rhetoric in conversion and convulsions.
39 George Williamson, 'The Restoration Revolt Against Enthusiasm', *Seventeenth Century Contexts* (London: Faber and Faber, 1960), pp. 202–39.

40 Henry More, *Enthusiasmus Triumphatus* (London: 1656), p. 50.
41 Schwartz, *Knaves, Fools, Madmen*, pp. 31–41.
42 Quoted by Williamson, 'The Restoration Revolt', p. 204.
43 Schwartz, *Knaves, Fools, Madmen*, p. 40.
44 Braithwaite, *Beginnings of Quakerism*, p. 108.
45 See George Keith, *The Magick of Quakerism* (London: 1707). Claims of having been bewitched and deluded by magic were often laid before the law courts; A.M. Gunmere, *The Quaker* (Philadelphia, Pa.: 1901), pp. 194–95.
46 More, *Enthusiasmus Triumphatus*, p. 2.
47 Meric Casaubon, *Treatise concerning Enthusiasm* (London: 1655).
48 Robert Burton, *Anatomy of Melancholy* (London: 1621).
49 Michael MacDonald, *Mystical Bedlam*, (Cambridge and New York: Cambridge University Press, 1981), pp. 223–24.
50 Sophronius, *Censura Temporum* 1 (June, 1708) p. 168, quoted by Schwartz, *Knaves, Fools, Madmen*, p. 54.
51 Roy Porter, 'The Rage of Party: A Glorious Revolution in English Psychiatry?', *Medical History* 27 (1983): 35–50.
52 Szasz, *Myth of Mental Illness*, pp. 188–206; Michel Foucault, *Madness and Civilisation* (London: Tavistock, 1967); also *Discipline and Punish: the birth of the Prison*, (New York: Pantheon Books, 1977).
53 Porter, 'The Rage of Party', pp. 39–40.
54 MacDonald, *Mystical Bedlam*, p. 170.
55 Dr Nicholas Robinson, *A System of the Spleen* (London: 1729), quoted by Porter, 'The Rage of Party', p. 40.
56 Trapp, 'The Nature of being Righteous', p. 59.
57 Theophilus Evans, *The History of Modern Enthusiasm*, 2nd edn (London: 1757), p. 38. Rachel Knight's retrospective psychoanalysis of Fox in *The Founder of Quakerism* (London: Swarthmore Press, 1922), finds him merely abnormally sensitive.
58 More, *Enthusiasmus Triumphatus*, p. 95.
59 Francis Higginson, *A Brief Relation of the Irreligion of the Northern Quakers* (London: 1653), quoted by Bauman, *Let Your Words Be Few*, p. 80.
60 Ronald Knox, *Enthusiasm* (Oxford: Clarendon Press, 1950), p. 4.
61 For a consideration of the modern analogue of this response to new religious sects see Herbert Richardson (ed.), *New Religions and Mental Health: Understanding the Issues* (New York: Edwin Meller, 1980).
62 Schwartz, *Knaves, Fools, Madmen*, pp. 39, 72.
63 Richard Baxter, *Narrative of his Life* (1696), p. 77, quoted by Knox, *Enthusiasm*, p. 150.
64 Braithwaite, *Beginnings of Quakerism*; Arnold Lloyd, *Quaker Social History, 1669–1738* (London: Longmans, Green, 1950); Bauman, *Let Your Words Be Few*, pp. 137–53; Richard Vann, *The Social Development of English Quakerism, 1655–1755*, (Cambridge, Mass.: Harvard University Press, 1969).
65 Gough, *History of The Quakers*, vol. 1, pp. 96–7.
66 M.H. Bacon, *The Quiet Rebels* (New York: Basic Books, 1969), p. 139; Elizabeth Isichei, *Victorian Quakers* (Oxford: Oxford University Press, 1970), p. 168.
67 Tuke, *Description of the Retreat*, p. 25.
68 John Haslam, *Observations on Madness and Melancholy*, 2nd edn (London: 1809).
69 D.E. Trueblood, *The People Called Quakers* (New York: Harper and Row, 1966), p. 95.

70 For a breakdown of nineteenth-century Friends by class see Isichei, *Victorian Quakers* pp. 288–89.
71 *Edinburgh Review* (April, 1814): 189–98.

CHAPTER FIVE

Locked up or put to bed: psychiatry and the treatment of the mentally ill in Sweden, 1800–1920

Roger Qvarsell

WHEN STUDYING THE history of psychiatry and the hospital treatment of the mentally ill during the nineteenth century, several matters ought to be considered. First, the establishment of psychiatry as a science was a long and complicated process. It involved the coming of the new discipline to the universities and medical schools, the formulation of a classification scheme for mental diseases, the publishing of textbooks, and, during the second half of the century, the acceptance of a common theoretical framework for the new discipline which connected it with the medical sciences.

Second, the idea that it was possible to cure the insane with medical and educational methods, an idea with roots in the philosophy of the Enlightenment, was established as a base for the mental hospital system during the nineteenth century. We can perhaps say in this context that for the first time a secularized ideology of treatment influenced the organization of the asylums. Earlier types of treatment had been of a more accidental nature.

Third, it is very important to stress that the changes in the treatment of the mentally ill were related to changes in the social conditions of the insane, as society moved from an agrarian to an industrial economy. I will illustrate these matters by surveying the history of psychiatry and the treatment of the mentally ill in Sweden from the beginning of the nineteenth to the beginning of the twentieth century.

This will not be a history of scientific discoveries, new theories or original ideas. Sweden was at that time a cultural satellite to the European continent, especially Germany and France. A history of psychiatry in Sweden is therefore a history of the spreading of ideas from other countries and of the transformation of these ideas in the special social and cultural context in Sweden. For centuries Sweden has been a rather centralized society, with a strong state apparatus trying to control both economic and social processes. During the nineteenth century, the power and cultural influence of civil servants and the intellectual middle class, such as teachers, doctors, and clergymen, increased. This group often shared a political ideology where the most important goal was to secure order and harmony in society.[1]

At the beginning of the nineteenth century, the situation of the insane in the asylums was terrible. They dwelt in small, dirty, and dark buildings, with almost no medical assistance and with nothing to occupy their minds. In a report of an inspection tour of some of the asylums, Wilhelm Ronander (1794–1847) wrote that the care of the insane was everywhere neglected. Inmates were often naked, locked up, and sometimes even chained. According to Ronander, some of them were not insane at all and should have been released, while some of the genuinely insane were in such miserable physical condition that they looked like the preparations pathologists put in glass showcases.[2]

During the first two decades of the century, very little was known in Sweden about the intense discussions among psychiatrists in England, France and Germany. Eric Gadelius (1778–1827) seems to have been alone among his countrymen in having read of the works of such eminent contemporaries as Philippe Pinel and Johann Christian Reil. Gadelius was professor at the medical school in Stockholm, Karolinska Institutet, where surgeons were trained, and in his lectures he gave a brief introduction particularly to the psychiatry of Pinel. In a number of articles he discussed some modern therapeutical instruments, among them Joseph Mason Cox's revolving chair. Gadelius did not himself have any practical experience of the treatment of the mentally ill, but he must have influenced the first generation of Swedish psychiatrists.[3]

As a result of visits abroad, a little was known about the attempts made at some foreign asylums to practise the 'moral treatment' methods that were recommended in the psychiatric debate. 'Moral treatment' was first used by psychiatrists in England during the second half of the eighteenth century, but came to Sweden especially via German authors and practitioners. It is important to note that almost all the psychiatric writers of the time, irrespective of their theoretical framework, emphasized the importance of re-education, diet, a daily routine, and occupation as well as more special medical treatments.

The 1820s were a decade of great reform in the Swedish mental hospital system, as in several other countries. In 1823, the Swedish Riksdag, or Parliament, decided that a large number of small asylums ought to be closed and a limited number of central hospitals established for the insane. Each of these hospitals was to be of a size that made it possible to have a physician working there full-time, in order to give the insane the curative medical treatment to make discharge possible.

The first and most important of these mental hospitals during the following three decades was that in the little town of Vadstena on the eastern shore of the Vettersea. But before I discuss this hospital further, I shall make some remarks on the historical background to the changed policy towards the insane in the 1820s. Why did the government give instructions for the mental hospitals in accordance with the psychiatric theories of the time when in fact no one in the country had any experience of the new psychiatric methods?[4]

First, it is to be stressed that most of the debaters thought that with the new psychiatric methods it would be possible to cure at least some of the insane, after which they should be able to support themselves. Both the conservatives and the radicals, who were inspired by early liberalism, wanted to lessen the costs of supporting the poor and therefore eagerly adopted the optimistic view of curability. One of the historical roots of this optimism was the Enlightenment view of the nature of man, wherein the way of life and education are thought to mould human character. This means that the political decision to change mental hospital policy in a way had the same ideological roots as 'moral treatment' in psychiatry.

Second, the changing policy towards the insane was caused by changing social conditions of the poor. During the nineteenth century, Swedish society exchanged an agrarian for an industrial economic structure. Industrialization was most intense during the second half of the century, but some of the social problems often connected with industrialization were already to be seen at the beginning of the nineteenth century, partly because of the rapid growth of the population. In the agrarian society, social control of different types of deviances had been managed by the local ecclesiastical authorities and the heads of households. Even the primary moral and religious education was in the hands of local authorities. But as geographical mobility increased as a result of the difficulty of finding agricultural work, this system of social control was no longer adequate. It is possible to see the building of great institutions for the insane as a way of establishing another and a more centralized system for social and moral control, as David Rothman has emphasized for America.[5] In this sense mental hospital policy must be seen in the same light as the legislation of the 1840s concerning compulsory primary school education and prison reform.

Third, the policy towards the insane was influenced by the philanthropic and humanitarian ideals of the time but, as may be seen from the intense discussions among historians of psychiatry, it is difficult to evaluate the real historical importance of these ideas.[6]

Humanitarian ideals were widespread among the members of the intellectual middle class, and several of the men who dominated asylum reform were influenced by evangelism or utilitarianism. The first Swedish psychiatrist for instance, was brought up in a family where most of the members were active in the Moravian evangelical movement. The important thing here is that the view of the nature of man in the evangelical movements was to some extent similar to that of 'moral treatment' psychiatry. The insane were not seen as condemned creatures, like Nebuchadnezzar, but as unhappy men or neglected children, who could be changed for the better with Christian love and fatherly education. The idea of the malleability of man was very important at the beginning of the nineteenth century.[7] Despite the difficulties of describing the historical effects of the humanitarian ideals, it is quite clear that they influenced the ideology of asylum reform in the 1820s.

Let us now turn to the mental hospital in Vadstena, where the first attempts were made in Sweden to use psychiatric treatment in a systematic way.[8] In 1826, a central hospital was established, a doctor was employed, and the buildings of a former nunnery were altered to provide premises. According to government instructions, the hospital and the doctor were to treat and cure the insane so that they should be able to leave the institution. But this goal partly contradicted the aims of local authorities who sent patients to the asylum in order to avoid supporting them and were therefore not interested in having them back again. Here the conflict between two points of view concerning the goal of a mental hospital is illustrated. According to the local authorities, the asylum should support those who could not support themselves; from the doctors' and the officials' points of view, the hospital should treat and cure the insane and then let them go back home.

One of the main focuses of 'moral treatment' psychiatry was the influence on mental health of the patient's 'lifestyle'. Consequently, the internal organization of the hospital was a matter of some moment. At the hospital in Vadstena, great importance was attached to the organization of the daily life of the patients, in accordance with the directives issued by the central authorities. An attempt was made to separate different types of patients. Those who were considered curable were installed in one building, while incurables were housed elsewhere. A special first class ward was established, as was a convalescent ward so that fortunate patients could avoid contact with their less fortunate fellows.

The activities of the institution, which may be followed in the records, give the impression of a large institution designed for care and treatment undergoing rapid change. The board of directors began increasingly to see their job as a profession rather than simply a Christian duty. The number of employees increased and their jobs became more specialized. The family ideal of the period influenced activities, and the regulations for employees testify to a general attitude that senior officials, the manager and the doctor, should perform their duties with a mixture of authority and benevolence, as should the ideal father. Nurses, orderlies, and work organizers were assigned the same role *vis-à-vis* patients as would have been expected of a governess and maids *vis-à-vis* the children of a bourgeois family of the period.

Most remarkable was perhaps the role assigned to the doctor. He was the institution's most distinguished official, alone responsible for the treatment of the patients. The influence of the doctor may also be observed in changing terminology. During the 1820s and 1830s, the terms used to refer to both patients and staff were changed so as to bring them more in line with the medical field in general.

In 1826 the surgeon Georg Engström (1795–1855), educated at the medical school in Stockholm, was employed at the hospital in Vadstena. He was to be the first doctor in Sweden who can properly be called a psychiatrist. Engström never worked out any consistent psychiatric theory, neither did he invent any new therapeutic methods. He was more like a cautious official than an investigator. He was eclectic, trying to put the ideas of others into practice. He was well read in psychiatric literature and acquired a library in which the different schools, especially of German psychiatry, were represented. As an official, he wrote journals and medical records and sent official reports to Stockholm every third month. These make it possible to study the psychiatric ideas and the therapeutic methods of an unknown practitioner in the field of psychiatry during the 1820s, 1830s and 1840s.

Engström's view of disease and his system of classification had much in common with those of Reil. He distinguished four main types of mental illness. The first was *idiocy* (Amentia) which was distinguished by a lack of energy. The second type of illness was *mania*, which was the direct opposite of idiocy and was distinguished by the presence of an excess of energy together with an irresistible urge to behave maniacally. The third type of illness was labelled by Engström *insanity* (Wahnsinn). The patient was distinguished by an apparent spiritual imbalance. The imagination had taken the upper hand over reason, the capacity to reason logically had broken down and the relationship between the spiritual elements was disturbed. The fourth and final type of mental illness in Engström's system was *paranoia* (Fixer Wahnsinn), which often manifested itself as a feeling of being threatened, but which was always characterized by the patient's suffering from a fixation so strong that it monopolized his entire consciousness.

The implication has already been drawn that Engström's view of mental illness may be interpreted as an energy theory of the human psyche. Mental illness arose whenever there existed a surplus, a shortage, or an imbalance in psychological energy. Engström thus aligned himself with that school of psychiatry that had been influenced by the Platonic tradition and which had received the acclaim of many theorists during the Romantic period.

Engström's notations of the causes of illness reveal his conviction that almost all the circumstances of a person's life are able to provoke mental illness. Inherited predispositions, physical maladies, head injuries, menstrual disturbances, masturbation, repressed footsweat, neglected childhood, poverty and drunkenness, all could provoke mental illness. The prime cause of mental illness was, however, strong emotions and passions such as agitation, anxiety, arrogance, love, or jealousy.

Both physical and mental circumstances could thus provoke mental illness, but the most interesting aspect of this catalogue of causes becomes apparent if we make an experiment: how should a person live if he wishes to run the least risk of succumbing to mental disease, according to what we know about Engström's ideas about the causes of illness? This ideal healthy person ought to inherit good health, have received a good upbringing, be relatively well-off, abstain from excessive drinking, and live a tranquil existence requiring the exercise of no strong emotion or intense passion. This coincides, of course, with the ideal of living that increasingly characterized the urban middle class to which Engström himself belonged. Engström's view of mental illness may therefore be seen as constituting a reverse picture of all the norms that suffused the bourgeois family. In this way, his view of mental illness takes on a normative or moralistic character, a concept of disease that was very common in the literature about health and prolongation of life.

The most important type of treatment at the hospital concerned the organization of a daily routine. Engström felt that work, order, cleanliness, fresh air, and suitable company were decisive to recovery. He therefore took great pains to organize opportunities for work, walks, and social life. Any patient who was up to it was found work in the park, in the garden, in the kitchen, or spinning and weaving for domestic needs. Some patients worked outside the hospital for citizens of the town, returning to the hospital in the evenings. Engström cultivated a dream in which the hospital would become self-sufficient as regards food and other necessities. His idea was that hospital life should as closely as possible resemble life outside the institution, and thus patients from higher social strata, who were not used to physical labour, were treated in a different way. These patients were to occupy themselves by reading selected geographical and historical works, with conversation in small groups, and by playing music.

Of course, compulsion and punishment were not unknown in the hospital, even if such phenomena were not as common as one might gather from the literature on the history of psychiatry. The most common form of compulsion was the isolation of a difficult patient in a cell, but strapping to a chair also occurred.

Various forms of showers and baths were commonly used in treatment, almost forming part of the daily routine. Engström was especially keen to redistribute areas of heat and cold among parts of the body with the use of water. Medical authorities such as Brown and Reil considered this to be beneficial. A particularly common form of this treatment was immersion in a warm bath with a simultaneous cold shower playing on the head. At the beginning of the 1830s, Engström acquired both a revolving chair and an electric appliance, his reasoning being that no hospital could be considered complete without them. Neither of these apparatuses became therapeutic fixtures, however. The revolving chair is mentioned only ten times in the medical records and the electric appliance was used only once in a while. It would seem that the optimism surrounding the concept of curability drove Engström to apply methods of treatment that were very quickly abandoned and which to a great extent had become obsolete even as they were being installed.

A large number of patients were treated with skin irritants or with drawing compounds. Setons and moxa were used to produce septic sores; mustard compresses, antimony salves, and cantharides were used to produce blisters; flailing with nettles or enclosure in a sack full of ants were methods used to provoke skin irritation. Irritants were generally assumed to increase vitality. The use of drawing compounds derived from the view of man in which the balance of elements was stressed in the Hippocratic fashion, or in which the various parts of the body were seen to exist in counterpoint to each other, as Reil had taught.

The majority of patients also received some form of medication, but it is difficult to be sure whether Engström felt that this treatment had any psychiatric significance or if the medication was prescribed for purely physical ailments. The most common medications were those with a laxative effect: quint (Tinctura colocynthidis), celandine (Extractum chelidonnii), or asian rhubarb (Radix rhei). Emetics like antimony salts (Tartarus anti-monialis), tartar emetic, and emetic root (Ipecacuanha) were used. Medical science at this time directed much attention towards the digestion process, and the hospital used Radix gentianae, aloes, and chalk mixture (Musilago cretacae) in order to fortify the stomach.

Among tranquillizing agents, henbane (Hyoscyami) was used; and as stimulants, Peruvian bark (Cinchonae), vanilla (Vanillae), rhubarb wine (Vinum rhei amarum), and oleo gum resin (Asa foetida). Also camphor drops (Liquor nervinus Bangui), tincture of the legendary amber (Tinctura succini aromatica), saffron (Crocus), and opium were used as stimulants.

Some of the preparations found in the pharmacopoeia of the day were thought to have a direct and beneficial effect on mental illness, and these were to be found at Vadstena hospital. Belladonna was considered to affect mental illness, and vanilla was thought to be able to cure hysteria, hypochondria, and melancholy. Gratiola was recommended against mania and the black Christmas flower (Helleborus niger) was used in the treatment of mental illness, as it had been since antiquity.

The treatment that the patients at Vadstena received thus comprised a wide variety of elements, but it would seem that Engström nevertheless felt that social upbringing, as well as work and regular habits of living, were of the greatest importance for the cure of his patients.

The organization of the hospital at Vadstena was founded on therapeutic optimism, but it is not possible to say that it was successful. Very few patients were discharged, and most stayed for their whole lives at the asylum. As a consequence, psychiatric thought in the 1840s and 1850s showed a much more pessimistic attitude towards the possibility of curing the insane than was the case in the 1820s. The debate around the middle of the century concentrated more on philanthropic ideals, and the economic motives for hospital treatment fell to the background.

This development, from an optimism concerning the possibility of reducing the number of the mentally ill towards a more pessimistic attitude and an emphasis on philanthropic motives, was typical of changing attitudes towards social problems in Sweden during this period. In what we call the time of Karl Johan, the king who reigned to 1844, social problems were often thought to be very easy to solve. This belief was inspired by the social thought of the philosophers of the Enlightenment and by economic doctrines in the liberal tradition. But as the social problems increased and the paternalistic ideology became more important in the middle of the century, the basis for this optimism was reduced and philanthropic attitudes towards social problems became more important.

When Carl Ulric Sonden (1802–75), head of Danviken outside Stockholm, the second most important mental hospital in Sweden, and Magnus Huss (1807–90), Director of the Board of Health, argued the necessity of building a new hospital in the capital, their chief concern was for the living conditions of long-stay patients. They thought the old hospital crowded and damp, the grounds too small, but they did not, as their forerunners might have done, suggest that improved conditions would produce cures.[9]

But in spite of this diminished therapeutic optimism in the middle of the century, it was stressed in the first law dealing with the mental hospital system, which was passed in 1858, that the goal of hospital treatment was to cure the insane and send them out into society again.

This law was the first of several occurrences around 1860 that were to establish psychiatry as a medical discipline and the ideology of treatment as an official goal for mental hospital organization. In 1859, the mental hospital doctor Gustav Kjellberg (1827–93) started to give clinical lectures to the students of medicine at the University of Uppsala, and from 1861 it was compulsory for future doctors to take a two-month course in psychiatry. During these years, the universities and the medical school in Stockholm appointed professors in psychiatry, and in 1863 Kjellberg published the first book in Swedish that can be called a textbook of psychiatry.[10]

Kjellberg also worked out the classification scheme for mental diseases used in the annual statistical reports the hospitals published from 1861. These reports also gave a large amount of personal data on the patients: sex, age, the duration of the disease and suchlike, in accordance with the statistical scientific ideals of the time.

In the 1860s, the debate among psychiatrists about the real nature of mental disease was over, at least for some decades. Almost all medical scientists and medical authorities were at this time convinced that mental diseases were of the same nature as somatic disorders. In accordance with authorities like Wilhelm Griesinger and others, mental diseases were seen as disorders or damage of the nervous system.

In the 1860s, psychiatry had taken a large step towards the establishment of a scientific paradigm and a professional role for psychiatrists. Achievements included a general theoretical framework, a common terminology, teaching positions at the universities, and the official recognition of the psychiatrists' positions at mental hospitals. But by the turn of the century, both the scientific character of psychiatry and the professional status of the psychiatrists were once more to be questioned.

During the last decades of the century, medicine secured its position as a science. The debates about homoeopathy, magnetism, and the medical philosophy of romanticism were over, and the bacteriologists thought that they had found the key to the mystery of disease. The reputation of hospital care improved when standards of cleanliness became higher, and as nurses became better educated doctors were liberated from many of the dirty parts of their work.

Medicine became a natural science at a time when the cultural importance of scientific ideals was very great. In late nineteenth-century literature, the doctor often played an important role. Strindberg and Ibsen, to mention just two Scandinavian examples, were fascinated by the men who, with a chilly attitude, reigned over life and death, but nevertheless often showed a tenderness towards human beings. This position of medicine influenced psychiatry both in theory and practice.

The belief in the connection between mental disease and the nervous system stimulated pathologists to study the brain. A Swedish example of this is a dissertation of Carl Hammarberg (1865–93) in which he argued that idiocy always had its roots in a lack of efficient cells in the cortex, an opinion he based on a large number of post-mortem examinations.

Inspired by anthropology, some psychiatrists became interested in phrenology again and started in the 1880s to measure the crania of all the patients at the large mental hospital in Stockholm. Others, perhaps inspired by social Darwinism, tried to find out whether mental deviance was an effect of a special hereditary personality.

But even more important was the fact that the organization of the mental hospitals at the turn of the century took the hospitals for somatic diseases as models. A pavilion system was preferred and the rooms for the sick were built with big windows to let light and fresh air in. The most distinctive similarity with the treatment of the somatically diseased was that almost all patients were put to bed. 'The mentally sick patient is even somatically ill and therefore ought to be treated like any other sick man', the doctor and medical official Gustaf Bolling (1839–1901) declared in 1896 in a lecture at the Swedish Society of Physicians; and in a textbook for future nurses published in the 1920s, one hospital doctor wrote that 'the mental diseases are somatic diseases as much as typhoid fever, tuberculosis, cancer and fractures'.[11] The Professor of Psychiatry at Uppsala, Frey Svensson, authorized this treatment and said that to put the mentally ill in bed was the most important treatment because it kept the patients warm and it stimulated the circulation of the blood in the brain.

Another important principle in the treatment of psychiatric patients in the years around 1900 was the continuous supervision of the sick. The nurses never left the patients' rooms and everything that happened was reported to the doctor and written down in special diaries. The third important principle was always to try to calm the patients down. The patients were put in lukewarm baths for hours, they were packed in wet sheets and they were given different sedatives, like chloral, barbitone, sulphonal, and morphine.

If we compare the treatment of the insane in the 1830s with that at the turn of the century, the most distinguishing feature is that the ideal of activity, work, and idleness had been replaced by quietness, tranquillity, and confinement in bed.

The influences on psychiatry of pathology and neurology and other medical disciplines were very important, but several circumstances complicated the situation in psychiatry at the turn of the century.

Around 1890, an intense discussion of the use and abuse of hypnotism started. The most important and well-known of the Swedish psychiatrists who used hypnosis was Otto Wetterstrand (1845–1907), who also published books and articles on the subject. But most of the psychiatrists and medical officials, among them Fredrik Björnström and Magnus Huss, warned against the use of hypnosis because of the power the doctor had over the hypnotized patient.

In 1896, the influential psychiatrist Bror Gadelius (1862–1938) introduced Freud's and Breuer's theory of hysteria in a Swedish medical context, but he thought it was too narrow to be useful. Gadelius was also one of the main opponents of psychoanalysis in the more intense discussions on the subject at the Swedish Society of Physicians around 1910. The psychiatric practitioners Paul Bjerre (1876–1964) and Emmanuel af Gejerstam (1867–1928) argued in articles and lectures for a psychiatry that was inspired by Freud, although they were not orthodox followers. But almost all official psychiatrists followed Gadelius in his attempts to show that psychoanalysis was not a scientific theory.

The introduction of hypnosis and psychoanalysis complicated the position for psychiatry and made it more difficult to establish a psychiatric paradigm. Another problem for psychiatrists at the turn of the century was the existence of several debates in which the scientific character of psychiatry was questioned. The background to this was a number of cases the newspapers had written about, in which psychiatrists had declared some patients incapable of fulfilling their citizens' duties and responsibilities under pressure from relatives who wanted to get control over the patients' economic transactions. Therefore some physicians, especially the temperamental anatomist of the brain, Salomon Henschen (1847–1930), declared that they did not recognize psychiatry as a special branch of the medical profession. The Professor of Psychiatry at Uppsala, Frey Svensson (1866–1927), responded and declared that psychiatry certainly was a science with both theories and therapeutic techniques, which put it on the same level as other disciplines. The psychiatrists' attempts to obtain recognition for their professional status were, as we can see, not entirely successful.

But even more important for psychiatry at the beginning of this century in Sweden was the expansion of its sphere of activity. Many new mental hospitals were built, the number of patients increased rapidly, and more and more patients from the middle and upper classes entered the institutions. This expansion of the hospital system will perhaps confirm the theory of Andrew Scull of a connection between the changed social situation in an industrialized and urbanized society and the requirements of public care for the insane.[12]

Psychiatry even expanded in another direction. Deviant behaviour of different kinds was labelled as illness and incorporated into the domain of the psychiatrist. Most important was the fact that many criminals were treated as if they were insane. The first Professor of Forensic Psychiatry, Olof Kinberg (1873–1960), who was deeply influenced by Cesare Lombroso, attempted to get all criminals exempted from punishment and sent to mental hospitals. During the first three decades of the twentieth century, a lot of young criminals were treated as if they were insane.

In this survey of the history of psychiatry in Sweden I have tried to show how psychiatry and the organized treatment of the mentally ill arose during the nineteenth century, and that if we want to understand its historical roots we must study nineteenth-century society.

The asylum reform of the 1820s had its roots in changing social conditions for the insane and the organization of the mental hospital system was very much influenced by the social and moral ideals of the expanding intellectual middle class. It is also important to stress that hospital treatment of the insane started several decades before psychiatry was established as a science in the medical schools in Sweden in the 1860s. Consequently, it is not possible to see the treatment of the insane as an applied science in the narrow meaning of that concept.

In the last decades of the nineteenth century psychiatry was on the threshold of formulating a scientific paradigm that could be endorsed by most psychiatrists, but at the turn of the century the nature of the discipline was more and more questioned. The development of nineteenth-century Swedish psychiatry was, generally speaking, shaped by two factors: the establishment of medicine as a science and the emergence of institutions for the insane.

Notes

1 This essay is based on R. Qvarsell, *Ordning och behandling. Psykiatri och sinnessjukvård i Sverige under 1800-talets första hälft [Order and Treatment. Psychiatry and the Care and Treatment of the Mentally Ill in Sweden during the First Half of the 19th Century]* (Umeå Universitetet, 1982) and 'Från förvaring till behandling i medicinsk regi' ['From Custody to Medical Treatment'] *Kritisk psykologi* (1981): 1.
2 Letter from Ronander to the Board of Health 1824. The Swedish National Archive. ÄK 693.
3 G. Hardin, 'Psykiatriundervisningen i Sverige före 1860' ['The Teaching of Psychiatry in Sweden before 1860'] *Lychnos* (1973/74): 193–216.
4 A more extensive analysis in Qvarsell, *Ordning och behandling*, ch. 2.
5 D. Rothman, *The Discovery of the Asylum* (Boston Mass.: Little, Brown, 1971).
6 A. Scull, 'Humanitarianism or Control?', *Rice University Studies* 67 (1981): 21–41.
7 M. Mandelbaum, *History, Man and Reason* (Baltimore: Johns Hopkins Press, 1974), p. 144.
8 The presentation of the hospital at Vadstena and the psychiatric thoughts of Georg Engström is based on the medical records of the hospital (Qvarsell, *Ordning och behandling*), chs 5–11.

9 C.U. Sondén, *Daniks hospital* [*The Mental Hospital at Danviken*] (Stockholm: Qvarsell 1853); 'M. Huss, *Kan eller bör hufvudstaden längre undvara en väl ordnad kuranstalt för sinnessjuka*' ['*Can or ought the capital city any longer do without a well-arranged hospital for treatment of the mentally ill*'] (Stockholm: Qvarsell, 1853).

10 G. Kjellberg, 'Om sinnessjukdomarnas stadier' ['About the stadiums of insanity'], *Uppsala universitets årsskrift* (1863): 9 ff.

11 G. Bolling, 'Om användandet of sängvilan för behandling of sinnessjuke' ['About the Use of Rest in Bed as a Treatment of the Insane'], *Hygiea* (1896): 2; M. Söderström, *Undervisning i sjukvård för sinnessjukvårdens personal* [*Teaching Medical Attendance for the Staff at Mental Institutions*] Stockholm: (1929), vol. 1, p. 651.

12 A. Scull, *Museums of Madness* (Ann Arbor, Mich: University of Michigan Microfilm, 1974), p. 637.

CHAPTER SIX

A slavish bowing down: the Lunacy Commission and the psychiatric profession 1845–60

N. Hervey

MUCH HAS BEEN written about the growth of central administration in nineteenth-century England, and study of the Lunacy Commission provides further comparative material, while highlighting several new issues. Before examining these, however, it is important to provide some introduction to the history of asylum inspection and the forces at work prior to the 1845 Lunacy Acts which eventually established a full time board, responsible for the nationwide visitation of asylums.

Early inspection of the insane 1774–1845

The earliest proposal for the licensing and inspection of asylums was in 1754, when the College of Physicians were asked to undertake the supervision of private madhouses.[1] They rejected the idea as too troublesome, although it also probably ran counter to the vested interest some physicians had in these institutions. Not until 1763 was a House of Commons Select Committee appointed to investigate claims of cruelty and illegal confinement in madhouses. Leave was given to bring in a bill, which finally reached the statute books in 1774, as the Madhouse Act.[2] This established the licensing and inspection of madhouses in London and within a seven-mile radius thereof, by five commissioners, annually appointed by the College of Physicians.[3] In the provinces a group of visiting magistrates appointed by quarter sessions in each county were to fulfil the same task, accompanied by a doctor.

The main aim of this legislation was to prevent illegal reception of the sane, and for this reason it concerned itself little with the mechanics of inspection, or indeed with the real plight of madhouse inmates. It failed to provide the new inspectorate with sufficient executive powers, and hampered them by placing limitations on the performance of several tasks. The commissioners were unable to refuse a licence whatever the state of an asylum, and visitations were only to take place between 8 am and 5 pm. Furthermore, the new system of certification, whereby a patient could be admitted only on an order signed by a doctor, did not apply to pauper patients, who were left unprotected. Until the enactment of legislation in 1828, the commissioners and provincial magistrates were often forced to accept conditions inferior to those found in the best houses, owing to the obdurate refusal of proprietors to implement changes. The greatest weakness of this Act, however, was that it established an inspectorate composed of men who already had close personal and professional links with asylum proprietors.[4] Allied to this, the continual rotation in the appointment of commissioners meant that no corpus of administrative expertise was established in the metropolis, and little continuity was possible.

Further moves were initiated between 1814 and 1819 to improve the inspection provided by the College of Physicians, but these did not stem from within. A group of interested philanthropists, evangelicals, asylum governors, and magistrates led by Sir George Rose,[5] began to campaign for more efficient controls over the management of asylums, following revelations of the maltreatment of patients at Bethlem and York in 1814. In 1815, a Select Committee to consider the better regulation of madhouses was established, which exposed the lax attitude adopted by the College commissioners to their duties since 1774. The Quaker businessman, Edward Wakefield, suggested that medical persons were the most unfit of any class of persons to be inspectors, and cited as evidence of their perfidy the fact that most public asylum superintendents kept private madhouses elsewhere which diverted them from their public duties.[6] Dr John Weir, the Inspector of Naval Hospitals, testified that the only solution was a permanent board of three members,[7] under the Home Secretary, who would be salaried and empowered to visit, report on, and control every institution for the insane throughout England.

The idea of a new inspectorate independent of the College of Physicians appealed to some asylum owners with a surgical background, who resented superiority affected by the College.[8] Other proprietors such as G.M. Burrows, who had close links with the College, were anxious to prevent the Home Secretary usurping its authority. He was not uncritical of the College, decrying the continual turnover of commissioners, but feared that if in control, the Home Secretary would appoint unqualified lay commissioners, thus passing control of the subject out of medical hands.[9] Despite the drafting of bills in 1814, 1816, 1817, and 1819, however, no legislation was enacted. Lord Chancellor Eldon opposed any interference in the privacy enjoyed by Chancery patients and objected to clauses in these bills which envisaged an extension of state control over private enterprise in this field.

The issue of further state interference then receded until 1827, when Garrett Dillon, surgeon to St Pancras Parish, who had been gathering evidence of abuses at the Hoxton madhouses, approached Lord Robert Seymour asking him to move for another Select Committee.[10] Seymour, a

Middlesex magistrate and active governor of Bethlem, had remained interested in this subject since his involvement with the 1815 Select Committee, but was reluctant to act, believing that too many parties were still opposed to government interference. Dillon however persuaded him and Robert Gordon, a fellow magistrate, to become involved. As Seymour was a sick man, Gordon assumed control. He became the driving force behind the Select Committee and its resultant legislation.[11] Two related issues emerged strongly from this enquiry. One was the struggle for paramountcy between physicians and surgeons where inspection of asylums was concerned. The other was a generalized resistance amongst doctors to outside interference in regulation of this subject.

The Select Committee clearly illustrated how defective the College commissioners' visitation had been. Their secretary, John Bright, acknowledged that they had never framed any regulations for madhouses and the testimony of different commissioners as to the purpose of their superintendence was confused. William Macmichael [12] stated that their visits were to monitor the management of asylums rather than adjudicate precise points of insanity in individual cases, whereas Thomas Turner[13] claimed he was not looking to the treatments offered, 'but only whether people were mad or not'. The Select Committee were keen to remedy this state of things.

Of its twenty-nine members, seven were leading evangelicals and these men formed a core who were in favour of promoting the role of magistrates as visitors.[14] Some proprietors supported this. Edward Long Fox, owner of Brislington House stated that he would be sorry to be entrusted with 'so much of that power as necessarily is given to me ... without the supervision of those persons in whom the country ought to confide'.[15] In its report, the Select Committee specifically recommended that the Home Secretary take charge of visitation, appointing at least five magistrates amongst those to inspect metropolitan asylums. The evangelicals influenced the whole spirit of this Select Committee, and the questionnaire circulated to asylums reflected their dominant preoccupations: the desirability of personal control, the prejudicial effects of indolence, and the benefits of religious consolation. They went much further, however, in seeking to establish basic standards of asylum management which could be universalized by a central authority. For them, the paternalistic management of patients advocated within the pastoral model of the York Retreat[16] was preferable to the establishment of a medical model of treatment. In his evidence, Sir Anthony Carlisle, suggested that doctors' treatments should be made public, as their professional mystique had led to a great want of knowledge amongst practitioners.

This did not, however, reflect the thinking of most physicians. In 1828, two bills were referred to the Lords, who set up their own Select Committee. The madhouse doctors and College commissioners who gave evidence before this all expressed opposition to outside interference in professional practice. They were opposed to the concept of keeping registers which would be open to inspection and disagreed with night visitations as disruptive for patients. Most were antagonistic to daily medical attendance on patients, and to a man the College commissioners opposed the introduction of surgeons to visitational duties.

It became evident that a large measure of collusion had existed between the commissioners and those they supervised, since 1774. John Latham, a former commissioner and President of the College of Physicians expressed himself in favour of coercion, quoting from the Bible on the use of chains, while William Heberden favoured the use of cribs and straw for dirty patients. His reasons for continuing the College's role as commissioners were quite laughable. He wrote, 'There is this reason for wishing to continue it, that it is a little slur upon persons, after having had such a thing for a time, to have it taken away from them.' More damaging for the future of the commission however were Thomas Turner's attitudes. He remained a commissioner until 1856, and was firmly in the mould of a gentleman physician. Not for him the robust, prying qualities demanded of an inspector. He opposed any enquiry into medical treatments and, contrary to the beliefs of the evangelical reformers, was opposed to divine service in asylums, stating that it was a profanation of such a holy ceremony.[17]

Inevitably, in face of the traditional role of the College and the need for some expertise, a compromise was reached in which lay members were introduced alongside medical members in the new board. The Madhouse Act of 1828 established a Metropolitan Lunacy Commission consisting of five doctors and up to fifteen lay commissioners. The professional commissioners alone were to be paid and the powers afforded this body were considerably greater than those of its predecessors. It could revoke or refuse to renew a licence after due notice to the Home Secretary. The commissioners were to visit licensed asylums quarterly and might discharge those improperly detained. The certification system was tightened up, as were the requirements concerning returns of patients and records of their treatment. A resident medical officer was now required in establishments with over 100 patients and the Lords inserted a clause that divine service should be performed in licensed houses on a Sunday. Most important of all, the Act instituted several penalty clauses which required the prosecution of certain offences.[18]

Both the College and madhouse owners campaigned hard against the bill, on the grounds that it infringed on professional practice, and disturbed the private contract made between doctors and their patients, or patients' families.[19] S.W. Nicoll, the Recorder of York, opposed the new board on the grounds that it would be administratively top heavy and ineffective.[20] In the event both fears proved to be without substance. The new Metropolitan Lunacy Commission started inauspiciously, however, as the Home Secretary Peel, was quite unprepared for the rapid appointment of commissioners required by the Act.[21] He inadvertently approached Gordon to head it, before realizing that Granville Somerset was the senior parliamentarian of the two interested in this subject.[22] Peel was, however, keen to select the best physicians and referred their appointment to Sir Henry Halford, President of the College, ensuring that its interest was by no means disregarded.[23] As

for the lay commissioners, Gordon suggested several fellow county magistrates, and the rest were chosen from parliamentarians who had sat on the
Select Committee.[24]

The only precedents for such a body were the unwieldy boards established in the eighteenth century which had been designed to remove sole
executive decision making from powerful individuals and render their
departments accountable to Parliament.[25] Attachment of this commission to
the Home Office clearly had a similar object in mind, a view which is
strengthened by evidence that between 1828 and 1845 there was always a
member of the commission who was also attached, in some capacity, to the
Treasury, providing the government with financial leverage over its
workings.[26]

Initially there was great interest in this board, and its immediate impact
was considerable. Two private asylums had their licenses revoked, and other
asylums subsequently made wide-ranging alterations to their management.
Before long, however, rather than proving top heavy, the commission ran
into difficulties owing to the reluctance of some lay commissioners to
participate at all. In 1833 Shaftesbury reported to Lord Brougham, the Lord
Chancellor, that 'many whose names are on the list, are either unwilling or
unable to take any share in the business'.[27] It was mostly the parliamentarians who were unable to assist the commission in its work,[28] and
Shaftesbury therefore increasingly recommended magistrates as lay members, although several important parliamentarians were subsequently
appointed.[29]

Brougham had in fact already contributed to a significant change in the
commission's structure the previous year. He disliked the preponderance of
Tory MPs on the commission, a view shared by several doctors. John
Haslam believed the commission's first report reflected only the influence of
its parliamentary members,[30] while Halford in a memorandum prepared for
Brougham referred to the unwieldy contrivance of attaching Middlesex
magistrates to the commission, when physicians alone should have
sufficed.[31] Brougham's 1832 Act for the Care and Treatment of Insane
Persons effected a compromise by reducing the lay commissioners and
increasing the professionals. He had written to Halford in 1831, 'the Bill we
have got quite altered – My plan has been nearly taken up to have the Board
professional chiefly. I wanted the college to appoint the medical portion –
but the whole has been given to the Great Seal.' He now pledged that while
he remained in office medical appointments would be referred to Halford,
thus giving the College of Physicians a prominent voice, but also undermining the establishment of a truly independent inspectorate.[32] More important, the Act drafted two barristers onto the commission, and Brougham's
nominees, Mylne and Procter, were to play a vital role in future developments. Without them, Shaftesbury stated in 1845, the doctors would have
been nearly powerless and the whole Board would have stagnated.[33]

Other clauses in the Act lowered the numbers rendering commission
meetings quorate and abolished the requirement that lay commissioners

must accompany doctors on visitations. Now a barrister could fulfil this role. As Brougham intended, these changes increased the influence of professional commissioners, and it is important to acknowledge that the change from a large commission in 1828 to a streamlined one in 1845, went through intermediate phases. As O. MacDonagh has suggested, the process of government growth was a gradual one, built on the experience of field executives who pointed up deficiencies in the system.[34]

From 1832 to 1845, an uneasy alliance existed between the lay and professional commissioners. A significant measure of disagreement existed concerning the importance of religious consolation, the use of work as therapy, and other tenets of the moral treatment canon, which the evangelicals were keen to embrace. Shaftesbury even undermined the emphasis his medical commissioners placed on the paramountcy of medical superintendents in public asylums, by secretly supporting the appointment of a lay governor to overall charge of Hanwell Asylum in 1841.[35] These tensions were played down by their Secretary, Edward Dubois,[36] whose letters illustrate the problems of communication between lay and professional commissioners who did not meet regularly as a board. Contrary to previous accounts, however, they did establish some successful strategies for improving the condition of London madhouses, but were always aware of the deficiencies in provincial asylums.

In 1842, Granville Somerset obtained legislation which added two barristers and two doctors to the board. Their powers of inspection were extended to provincial asylums and the professionals' emoluments for extra-metropolitan visitations increased. In 1844 they produced a report on the condition of asylums in England and Wales which amply illustrated the terrible state of provincial madhouses, and the following year a full-time commission was established. The 1845 lunacy bills were the work of the legal commissioners, not Lord Shaftesbury or the medical ones, and Dubois claimed they were 'concocted in the dark', by R.W.S. Lutwidge and the other lawyers who hoped to feather their own nest.[37] In fact, Procter (a lawyer) mapped out most of the clauses, which were based on the experience of his fellow commissioners,[38] and it is clear that the professional commissioners already held a strong position on the board. The choice of personnel for the new commission was clearly going to be of vital importance.

Shaftesbury and the commission's personnel

The Lunacy Commission, established in 1845, consisted of six full-time professionals (three medical and three legal). Their duties included visitation of private asylums, county asylums, workhouses, and hospitals throughout the country,[39] although local magistrates retained the main responsibility for provincial asylums. The board were empowered to visit and make a return of all single patients kept for profit, and were afforded some powers to alter the regime of private asylums. Also, in conjunction with the Home Secretary, they were to supervise construction and management of the new county asylums. For the first time, a central body was authorized to monitor practice and establish standards relating to medical certification, asylum management, and the care of patients on a nationwide basis. It was essential to select an inspectorate of the highest calibre.

Shaftesbury recognized this and noted,

> 'the success of the Commission will depend humanly speaking on the character of its officers. We must have the best men in every sense of the word; men who can speak with authority to the skilful and experienced persons with whom they will always be in contact and sometimes collision.'[40]

In fact, Shaftesbury perpetuated the weakness of former inspectorates by selecting commissioners whose long acquaintance with private practice and traditional forms of care undermined the board's standing as an independent and impartial authority. Before turning to these men, though, it is important to provide some account of Shaftesbury's views in order to understand how he made his choice and what he expected from the commission.

In parliament Shaftesbury usually rehearsed a well-worn theme of the prodigious advances which had occurred since he first assumed office in 1828, depicting former barbarities such as the use of manacles, straw, and hosing down for dirty patients.[41] The horrific scenes he witnessed as a young man had indelibly stamped his memory and to some extent explain the undemanding yardstick he subsequently employed for the board's progress. Shaftesbury was noted for his interest in scientific innovations, and was not slow to grasp the significance of moral treatment and non-restraint. However, he retained a lay view of them and never acknowledged the scientific basis medical practitioners claimed for them. Tuke and Conolly had both eschewed medicine to a large extent in promoting treatments which rested on regimen,[42] and Shaftesbury shared their perspective. He was less convinced by the medical profession's claim to expertise in this field than in others such as public health, and throughout his career piqued psychiatric practitioners with references to the incompetence of medical men. He stated on several occasions that a layman could give as good an opinion on the existence of insanity as a doctor.[43]

These views had serious implications for the commission, which constantly proved reactionary when confronted with new treatments.[44] Shaftesbury often gave the lead to his colleagues, making crude generalizations about mental illness. In 1859 he informed the Select Committee on Lunatics that the main cause of insanity was intemperance, claiming that it was instrumental in 50 per cent of cases, and that because temperance societies had reduced the level of alcohol consumption, the numbers of insane were diminishing. In fact they were increasing rapidly. His evidence contained similar generalizations concerning the greater prevalance of insanity in Roman Catholic countries, and amongst High Church rather than Low Church adherents.[45] These remarks were a congeries of imperfect observations, preconceived prejudices and direct falsehoods, but carried weight because of Shaftesbury's importance. There was indeed a self-deceptive dishonesty about the way he passed off personal opinions as the received knowledge of the commission.

Shaftesbury never lost this loose and popular perspective of lunacy, ascribing it at other times to commercial speculation and railway travel, and yet he could lay aside his moral and political prejudices when considering individual cases, where the boundaries of mental illness came under closer scrutiny. A highly sensitive man, he saw himself as a victim of the perpetual agitation in Victorian society. He clearly suffered from disparities created by the conflicting demands of his aristocratic background and the kind of work he undertook, by the gap between his moral beliefs and the existing state of society, and by the struggle between the cancer of personal ambition and the self-denial enjoined by his evangelical convictions. Several contemporaries noted a hint of instability in his make-up,[46] and he himself dwelt on the possibility of becoming mentally ill. Often overworked and ill, Shaftesbury impressed fellow commissioners with his irritable, morose, and introspective nature[47] and often contemplated giving up public office.[48]

Shaftesbury retained a special feeling for the Lunacy Commission, however, which he believed was a pioneering body. He claimed it was unique because the inspectorate were also an integral part of the executive, being free to interpret board policy with almost invariable endorsement for their actions.[49] It was a matter of some pride to him that decision-making was a democratic process, although he underestimated the inhibiting nature of his presence on other commissioners. As the board's parliamentary spokesman, Shaftesbury's apolitical nature was important in negotiating with successive governments, but alongside this must be placed the damaging effects of his social and religious beliefs.

Like most of his colleagues, he had long acquaintance with asylum owners, and in some respects was not unsympathetic to them. The scion of a noble family, Shaftesbury employed a double standard. Privately he considered the upper classes had a right to absolute privacy, and yet publicly he inveighed against the licensed houses and lodgings in which they were kept. With this perspective he could not initiate his threatened closure of private asylums, as these classes would then have had no provision but single lodgings.[50] Shaftesbury did attempt to found subscription hospitals for the wealthier classes, but his appeals failed to kindle support.[51] His true beliefs are highlighted by the fact that when his son Maurice became mentally disturbed with epilepsy, he arranged private lodgings in Lausanne, Switzerland, for him, rather than asylum care.[52] These lodgings are interesting in view of his lifelong opposition to placing patients abroad, where they had no protection, by way of visitation.

As for Shaftesbury's religious convictions, these were most influential, because he often appointed commissioners who shared his views. Gordon, Vernon Smith, Lutwidge, Nairne and Campbell constituted an important group, whose moral beliefs were reflected in many of the board's policies.[53]

They constantly stressed the need to separate the sexes and maintain appropriate social conduct and standards in asylums. As Foucault noted, quiet and tranquil behaviour was praised at York Retreat, where patients were encouraged to emulate Quaker standards.[54] In later nineteenth-century asylums, the call for tranquillity was a reflection of Shaftesbury's sabbatarianism. The literature in asylum libraries, the emphasis on work and neat dress, were all an extension of this bias, and eventually led to a collapse of therapeutic initiatives. In fact Shaftesbury's recruitment of personnel explains many of the difficulties subsequently experienced in the board's relations with the psychiatric profession.

Between 1828 and 1845 a philosophy of practice had evolved, and Shaftesbury felt obliged to reappoint former commissioners. In August 1845 he recorded,

> 'Dr Southey has resigned, and I have implored the Chancellor to appoint Dr Prichard in his place ... Prichard has a reputation and is by far the most superior of the remaining former Commissioners and as being one of these we cannot pass him over. But he wants capacity as a Visitor of asylums.'[55]

Here Shaftesbury faced the dilemma that in selecting men who could exert influence over asylum superintendents, namely those noted for their private practice, and in fact the type of practitioners later shunned as commissioners, he was also appointing a group essentially empathic to the private sector. There are many examples of this empathy. Prichard and Hume continued to attend parties given by leading alienists such as Morison and Sutherland,[56] Lutwidge was a long-standing acquaintance of F.B. Winslow who was often dealt with leniently by the commission[57] and Procter mentions his sympathy for Forster's friend Charles Elliott of Munster House who was hauled up before the board for some infringement of the laws.[58] These sympathies did not altogether prevent the board from acting, but it is evident that they instituted more stringent controls over licensed asylums and single patients only after the appointment of two ex-county asylum superintendents as commissioners in the 1850s.[59] The original 1845 appointees had all been brought up on a pabulum of fees and connections and were heavily indebted to patronage.[60]

The result of this recruitment policy, was the appointment of men who provided a prop to many of Shaftesbury's prejudices, men who subsequently found it difficult to depart from the collective influence of the board. While Shaftesbury spoke of the harmony existing within the department, the result of gradually adding members to a long-standing nucleus, several commissioners felt unable to express their opposition to the board's policies openly. Gaskell campaigned in the *Journal of Mental Science* for the voluntary admission of patients, while Lutwidge and Wilkes voiced their differences of opinion, when appointed to a commission investigating the condition of Irish asylums.[61] Both Procter and Forster also used public journals to air their views.[62] In 1863 Forster asked the *Examiner* to highlight Colonel Jebb's unhealthy influence at the Home Office, which had secured the exclusion of someone he favoured for the new Broadmoor Asylum Commission. This too at a time when the board was collaborating with Jebb on plans for Broadmoor.[63]

These individual attempts at dissent, were complemented by the formation of interest groups within the commission, which attempted to act in concert. From 1855 onwards, Procter, Forster, Gaskell, and Wilkes formed a clique which dined together, covered one another's duties and attempted to bypass Lutwidge for whom they shared a mutual dislike.[64] The latter more naturally gravitated towards the churchmen on the commission. In many respects, however, the greatest threat to the board's workings was posed by the lay commissioners. The role of these men has been undervalued, although Shaftesbury considered them of indispensable importance. He claimed that they provided the board with the status needed to influence county magistrates who were responsible for the local administration and inspection of asylums.[65] His view of them was not shared wholeheartedly by the professional commissioners. Procter thought Gordon a zealot of the worst kind, remarking of him: 'He did not come to the last Board. Thank God for all things. He should never be here without Lord Shaftesbury to control him.'[66] Nevertheless, lay commissioners played an important role in visitation, special enquiries, and formulation of policy. They were also employed as go-betweens to various government offices, often with verbal instructions alone. It was this style of government, which Shaftesbury endorsed, that Chadwick had objected to at the Poor Law Board, because it bypassed other members of the board and had no clear accountability attached.[67] In August 1846 Shaftesbury was furious with Lord Seymour, who had been briefed by his professional colleagues but failed to appear in parliament to defend the commission, in the Haydock Lodge scandal.[68] More culpable still was Colonel Clifford, another lay commissioner. In 1863 Procter wrote to Forster concerning a clause inserted at the last minute into the new lunacy bill:

> 'It will doubtless have the effect of converting workhouses into asylums, unless we are very firm in restricting it. Now I am going to tell you a secret. The new clause, I believe, was suggested ... by Clifford ... not a word of this, I will explain.'[69]

Clifford was also a magistrate in Hereford and Monmouth, where local justices were anxious to avoid expense on asylum care. In this instance he was supporting a move to allow workhouses to draw patients from a wide catchment area for their lunatic wards, in opposition to everything the commission stood for. Evidently the two hats he wore were incompatible, and he was not serving the board's best interests.

Generally speaking, however, the commission presented a united front in public, although it was often at the expense of innovative policy-making.

The early formulation of policy

Given the men selected for the new commission, it was not surprising that it was the Home Office which initially took the lead in promoting minimal standards of asylum care, to be uniformly applied nationwide. The medical commissioners wanted to leave the management of asylums and keeping of records to the discretion of individual superintendents. In May 1846 the board informed the Home Secretary, Sir James Graham, that having considered the regime at various asylums it was scarcely practicable to frame any general rules. However, under pressure from the Home Office, which had been appointed to superintend the county asylum building programme, the board consulted Mr Perry, a prison inspector, concerning administrative systems they might adopt. The medical commissioners were opposed to the rigid categories Perry recommended for recording information in medical casebooks, but their views were overridden, and detailed registers implemented.[70] Some practitioners saw the failure of Hume, Turner, and Prichard to perpetuate the old regulations and methods of care as a sign of weakness and assumed that the General Asylum Rules promulgated in 1846 were the handiwork of the legal commissioners. Wakley remarked in the *Lancet* that Hume and Turner were 'hardly fitted to uphold their profession against the three active lawyers who act as the legal Commissioners',[71] and others suggested that they were not sufficiently acquainted with the new moral treatment and non-restraint systems, being wedded to the old concept that a quantity of physick would do.[72]

Certainly, apart from Prichard's reputation as an alienist, the medical commissioners could not be termed experts in this field. In order to get round this, the board centred its attention on the physical condition of asylums and libertarian issues surrounding the freedom of patients. When the scandal at Haydock Lodge erupted in 1846, Grey stoutly defended the commission in parliament, suggesting that it should not be seen as a cure-all. He was keen that the board should establish its status as a repository of expertise and argued that it needed longer to raise standards throughout the country. He willingly empowered the board to employ architects, public health inspectors, and engineers, which gradually increased its standing as a body with specialized knowledge in the field of asylum construction and management. The authority of individual commissioners remained limited at this time however. They completed their circuits of visitations and presented reports to the board, who took decisions as a group. Initially, many people continued to approach the Home Office as the ultimate authority in matters relating to lunacy but, increasingly, as they were referred to the commission its position became established.[73]

In view of the fact that none of its medical commissioners had experience as asylum superintendents, one would have expected considerable resistance to the new commission from practitioners managing asylums in both the public and private sectors of psychiatry, who had their own systems of care to defend. This was especially true of the public asylums from which the board had drawn its model of practice, and we must now turn to an examination of their response to the commission.

The Lunacy Commission and public asylums

In the late 1850s, James Huxley,[74] the superintendent of Kent County Asylum, was one of a number of doctors who began to voice serious misgivings about the relationship developing between the commission and practitioners working in county asylums. In a series of articles, he delineated the gradual intrusion of a central authority which had resolved as early as 1846 that with a few exceptions, 'where peculiar systems have worked and some deviation may be permitted, in all asylums hereafter to be erected ... a substantial adherence to the Printed General Rules should be enforced'.[75] Huxley saw the board's desire for uniformity as the thin end of the wedge, claiming that 'a slavish bowing down' was what they wanted as the 'best preparation of the soil, for their crop of encroachments'. In particular he noted a want of proper independence in the tone taken by some superintendents towards the commission.[76] To some contemporaries this resulted from the exclusive position the Board had created for superintendents in public asylums. The *Medical Circular* suggested that whenever a particular duty was confided exclusively to one group who were protected from external control, there was a tendency to passive sloth, maintenance of the status quo, and resistance to innovation.[77] Andrew Scull has argued a similar thesis, remarking that the board essentially collaborated with the medical profession in establishing a hegemony for doctors in public asylums. He stressed the commission's basic acceptance of the asylum solution for growing numbers of insane paupers, and traced their subsequent theoretical legerdemain in accepting a degeneration from curative ideals to custodial reality.[78] David Mellett has also suggested that public sector doctors were more attuned to the principle of state control than private practitioners, provided medical prerogatives were recognized.[79] What these commentators have failed to highlight was the instrumental role Shaftesbury's commission played in turning county asylums into cocoons of dullness, and the considerable resistance many superintendents attempted to put up to central control.

With the imposition of specific guidelines, it was inevitable that local magistrates responsible for managing public asylums, many of whom were very experienced, would begin to question the board's knowledge base. In 1847, the governors of Lincoln Hospital roundly criticized Turner and Mylne for interference in their therapeutic regime. These commissioners impugned the monthly rotation of three medical officers which produced a confused treatment programme. They also objected to the lack of classification, the absence of a steward, indiscriminate admission of visitors, and the poor quality of keepers. Finally, in opposition, as the commission saw it, to the spirit of non-restraint founded at Lincoln, the lack of a seclusion room was noted. The governors interpreted these criticisms as a 'hasty pledge' to erase local differences and an attempt to prevent the development of new forms of treatment. In particular, they questioned the board's espousal of seclusion rooms, preferring that patients should associated with each other. The governors implied that the board had deduced this and several other practices from the economy of prisons and condemned its use of words such as 'keeper' and 'cell' which implied the care of felons. Lincoln's plea was that they had developed their regime through years of trial and error and it was suited to local conditions.[80] It is evident that the board feared Lincoln's ability to set up an alternative model to their own, especially as subscription hospitals did not have to submit their rules to the Home Secretary for approval at this time.[81] Indeed, several of the policies they criticized for the sake of establishing uniformity and therapeutic control were later adopted by the board itself.[82]

Many public asylums had developed their own practices, and the above scenario was enacted at other institutions, although not always so publicly. The commission made ruthless use of their annual reports to shame institutions into change, and when finally granted access to Bethlem in 1851, observed only the barest decencies in their assault on the hospital.[83] Shaftesbury was anxious not to afford any special status to charity hospitals, and was annoyed by Bethlem's exclusion from the 1845 Lunacy Acts. The commissioners entered Bethlem with a preconceived notion of what to expect, and made extensive use of leading questions in their enquiry to elicit faults they intended to find. They undoubtedly failed to treat testimony favourable to their case with the same care applied to other evidence, and during their investigation broke all the rules of evidence. Nevertheless, doctors at the hospital found it difficult to defend themselves on any other grounds than that the board's enquiry was unfairly conducted. The evidence was clear. There were no specialist wards for sick patients, virtually no medical records existed, the attendants were insufficiently supervised, and very little was done to provide work or entertainment for patients who spent most of their time in damp, dark, straw-filled cells. The rapidity with which the commission forced change on the hospital, and the collapse of their medical officers when questioned about their professional practice, were a further warning to doctors that they no longer had sole possession of the field.[84]

It was this that concerned Huxley most, as the boundaries between administrative authority and medical autonomy were still fluid at this time. Until the mid-1850s a symbiotic relationship existed between practitioners and the commission, in which the former felt free to advise, criticize, and correct the board. Since then, Huxley believed, asylum superintendents had abdicated their role as arbiters of correct medical practice by their servile approach to the commission. To some extent this was understandable as many feared an outspoken attitude would cost them their posts.[85] Unfortunately, the consequence of conceding that the commission could force statistics and information, gathered nationwide, into a giant alembic, and produce universally applicable policies, was that they relinquished their position as experts in the field. In 1859, Lutwidge claimed that the board did not dictate medical practice, but in the absence of a consensus amongst doctors it was in fact quite willing to do so. Three years earlier, considerable controversy had erupted over the use of shower baths following a death at Surrey Asylum. The board having researched existing practice laid down strict guidelines for their future employment.[86] Huxley was among those who refused to return questionnaires about this treatment on the grounds that it was a medical matter, but with each issue that arose, more practitioners gave way to the board.

Even superintendents like Bucknill, who ostensibly supported the commission, differed from them on many treatment issues.[87] Bucknill believed the medical commissioners failed to represent the interests of scientific medicine, and welcomed the appointment of Gaskell, an ex-county asylum superintendent, in 1848. He still felt however that the latter's opinions suffered deterioration by being averaged with those of less qualified medical commissioners. Huxley interpreted this appointment, and that of Wilkes in 1855, as the cue for further dictation from the board. In order to trace the way in which the board developed its relations with county asylums, it is proposed to chart their contact with one in particular, Kent Asylum.

Established in 1833, Kent had an involved local magistracy, drawn from the local conservative landowning gentry who resented the encroachment of central authority. Initially the magistrates welcomed the new board but soon changed their attitude. In 1847 they refused to provide details of the attendants hired and sacked, and resisted attempts to alter their statistical recording in line with other asylums.[88] More significantly they provided Huxley with support on medical issues, endorsing his criticisms of the board in Kent's Asylum Reports.[89] In 1856 he attacked the night-watching scheme for dirty patients which stemmed from Gaskell's experience. He ridiculed the lack of thought behind the commission's blanket injunctions, juxtaposing their recommendations of long exhausting walks to procure sleep for patients with the idea of waking them four times a night to keep them clean.[90] Huxley also disliked the vigorous new form of visitation. Gone were the gentlemanly exchanges with Turner and Hume. Gaskell and Wilkes were to be found rummaging through cupboards, tasting food, and ransacking beds, and their thoroughness rubbed off on colleagues who felt obliged to adopt higher standards.

Unfortunately the Board's assumption of superior expertise made them increasingly intolerant of opposition. Huxley felt they were wedded to petty restrictions which deadened all therapeutic initiative. It seemed they wanted patients to eat, work, and sleep in a dull round of perpetual drill. He cited their refusal to allow patients to sit or lie on the floor as a tacit return to coercion, because attempts to move them on inevitably ended in struggles. Above all, he related Kent's problem to enforced enlargement of the asylum under pressure from the Board.[91]

Certainly its growth led to an increasing turnover of staff and a less caring regime. The average working life of attendants dropped from three years in the 1840s, to only one year in the late 1850s. Those employed at Kent were mostly farming people or ex-forces personnel, who had few skills and certainly not the ability to manipulate patients' environments as part of their moral treatment. Between 1876 and 1878 the words most frequently used to describe them were 'brutish', 'dirty', 'ugly', and 'rude', and a fifth of those who left at this time were sacked, for cruelty, neglect of patients, or drinking while on duty.[92] Unlike nurses in the 1840s, they were not trained on the job, and many more left because of restrictive rules at the asylum. It is clear from the servants' book that size and strength were the important criteria in staff selection, and the average age on employment was only twenty-four. Under the board's new regime, treatment consisted mainly of labouring in the fields which attendants had to participate in against their wishes. Medical casebooks reflect the minimal care afforded each patient and the much-lauded therapeutic value of the diet seems to have been exaggerated, as many staff left owing to its poor quality.[93] The extent to which Kent had changed under the commission's influence is reflected through the public's eyes. In 1851, at the time of the West Malling scandal concerning use of restraint in a local madhouse, several locals wrote to the board praising the county asylum,[94] but by the 1860s relatives' letters of complaint began to multiply. One nurse gave as her reason for leaving in 1879 that: 'The Maidstone people regard all nurses from this asylum as bad characters and insult them in the streets ... too many of our nurses by their conduct in the open roads well justify the treatment they receive and bring disgrace on the Institution.'[95]

Given the existence of the Association of Medical Officers of Asylums and Hospitals for the Insane,[96] why did this process of degeneration take place? One explanation is that superintendents, themselves products increasingly of the county asylum system, reflected it in their lack of initiative. Numerous patients discharged on trial were needlessly recalled to the asylum, because the requisite confirmation of their recovery was not forthcoming from the relieving officer. This lack of creative thinking had not been present before the 1850s. There was, in fact, considerable local resourcefulness from magistrates. Using family connections, justices had set up their own communication between asylums, spreading ideas and information.[97] The Asylum Officers Association had fulfilled a similar role before 1845, and, although less organized than the commission, had acted more in a spirit of free exchange.[98] But once the traditional composition of the magistracy lessened in the 1860s and 1870s, its commitment to fighting the board waned. Without their support, superintendents were unable to oppose the remorseless progress of the commission.

The board's relations with public asylums provide a classic illustration of divide and rule. The initial medical commissioners were not sufficiently forceful to insist on a wider range of discretion for superintendents, and the latter failed to unite against the outside dictation of practice. Hopes that Gaskell and Wilkes could change this pattern were ill-founded, as they had already shown themselves to be imitators of Conolly, who already provided the board's model. In fact, their appointment ended all hopes of a commission committed to investigation of the pathology of mental illness. Could the private sector provide any sterner opposition?

The Lunacy Commission and private care of lunatics

Parry-Jones has stated that private asylum owners and practitioners were never able to achieve a corporate identity, failing to integrate or identify with county asylum superintendents within the Asylum Officers Association.[99] I believe this is wrong on both counts. There was, in fact, an extensive and cohesive network between licensed houses and private practitioners in lunacy, which stretched throughout the country and provided considerable opposition to the board, both on its own and through the Association. Before turning to this however, it is necessary to examine the board's attitude to the private sector.

D.J. Mellett has suggested that the formulation of lunacy legislation was generally in government hands, implying that the commission was a passive recipient of Home Office initiatives.[100] In fact, they were instrumental in drafting all legislation enacted after 1845, systematically storing information on loopholes in the law.[101] Increasingly they sought authority to dictate the management of private asylums, but it was only after the appointment of Wilkes that the board made significant inroads into private practice. Initially, however, commissioners were ambivalent about the stance they should adopt. Despite Shaftesbury's antipathy towards them, private asylums continued to flourish. Parry-Jones suggested the most obvious reason for this, that they filled gaps in the provision of county asylums. Even when the latter were built, and madhouses forced to give up their pauper patients, proprietors could obtain new patients from the chronic population in workhouses, or increase their private patients.

An equally cogent explanation is that the board failed to work out a consistent ideology towards them and, in reacting to situations as they arose, found it impossible to maintain a credible consistency. In 1846, they licensed Camberwell House, last of the huge London pauper licensed houses. This would seem to be a torsion of everything Shaftesbury stood for. The commission's minutes, however, suggest that they had provisionally approved this new establishment while Shaftesbury was away, as he subsequently informed a deputation campaigning against it that the board 'would not feel justified in refusing a licence after the heavy outlay of expense made under reasonable expectation of its being granted'.[102] It was not until 1851 that the commission systematically attempted to reduce the number of paupers in licensed asylums, and even then they merely substituted private patients for paupers, thereby perpetuating these institutions. In time, stipulations were made about the sex of patients and categories of dangerousness that might be accepted, and, as the board showed no sign of phasing out these institutions, accusations were made that they were creating a monopoly for a few owners they favoured.[103]

Like many bureaucracies attempting to impose controls over private enterprise, the Lunacy Commission fell into the trap of making it explicit that there were certain organizations they looked more kindly on than others. In years to come, asylum owners complained that they never singled out houses for praise, but this was a direct result of their experience.[104] Those houses the board had commended invariably used this in their advertising, and subsequently rested on their laurels. Despite its ambivalence about these asylums, the board did initiate some improvements almost immediately. They were inaccurately criticized by Conolly in 1849 when he claimed that the previous occupation and education of licence applicants were immaterial to the board.[105] In fact, Shaftesbury proposed a series of conditions for licence applicants that were enforced as early as 1846. His scheme epitomizes the commission's dilemma. In establishing conditions to ensure only applicants with the requisite capital and experience were chosen, he was in effect promoting the continuance and growth of these institutions, in contradistinction to his public utterances.[106]

It was the imposition of controls over the appointment of madhouse medical officers, the levels of staffing and financial dealings of owners, rather than the much-vaunted visitation that eventually began to effect change. All these, however, were implemented only because of the board's control over the granting of licences.[107] David Roberts is among those who have referred to the moral authority, 'auctoritas', commissioners used to influence those they supervised,[108] but in practice the Lunacy Commission increasingly held the threat of licence revocation over proprietors to effect change. They were reluctant to use this ultimate weapon as it would mean ruin for the owner, and showed a persistent leniency towards offenders that went beyond a mere acknowledgement that repeated recourse to revocation would have been impractical.[109] In March, 1851, seven months after categorically resolving not to, they renewed Mrs Pierce's licence. Nevertheless they did impose myriad new conditions on owners, under threat, which gradually altered the therapeutic climate of asylums. In 1856, for instance, they agreed to license Grove End Villa only if Mrs Kerr gave assurances 'of her disposition to give effect therein to the recommendation so repeatedly made and entirely disregarded for an alteration of the system of non-association pursued there'.[110] Their more stringent approach to private asylums however only emerged after 1855. Before that, the open sympathy of some commissioners for asylum owners was quite clear, and several continued to feel the same way. In 1859, W.G. Campbell suggested they should not degrade proprietors by showing such extreme suspicion of their motives. The previous year an inquisition at Acomb House, York, on Mrs Turner commented adversely on the conduct of Mr Metcalf, the proprietor, for offensive language and improper behaviour. Procter however commented that he was sorry for the man 'who has had to deal with a woman of a decided character

... in many ways'.[111] Ultimately, it was this sympathy, that led to open opposition from the private sector.

The network existing between licensed houses and private practitioners in lunacy found physical form only in Sir Alexander Morison's Society for the Protection of the Insane.[112] This organization provided a forum for doctors who espoused a certain amount of restraint and heavily endorsed single lodgings, many of which were illegal. These men regularly exchanged patients, in the sort of trade deprecated at the time, and included amongst their number many leading metropolitan madhouse owners.[113] Many proprietors also met up in other societies, including the Asylum Officers Association.[114] Most of the major London alienists, and others less well known, had consulting rooms in the area between Mayfair and Regents Park, and regularly made joint consultations, sharing the work around.

There were several satellite organizations on the fringes of this network, none of which came under the board's control. Chapman and Potters provided servants and nurses for asylums, and Messrs Lara and Lane, founded in 1828, advertised themselves as 'Medical Agents and Lunatic Asylum Registrars'.[115] In 1851 they announced the opening of a registration office, with a view to establishing a medium of communication and negotiation between proprietors and friends of the insane. They proposed collating a list of good asylums and competent attendants which would be open to the public. In doing this, they deliberately usurped the board's role, stating that because of their inquisitional manner in trying to establish a register of attendants they had 'forfeited the confidence of those parties they had invited to cooperate with them'. They also expressed surprise that the proprietors hadn't formed their own association before and suggested that they should unite: 'Union is strength. The Central Office of Registration now proposed may form a *point d'appui* . . . a nucleus around which such an association might be organised.'[116]

Some proprietors preferred, however, to raise a spirit of resistance through the more official medium of the Asylum Officers Association. Although outnumbered within this organization, they exerted considerable influence on its proceedings. In 1856 the board issued a circular asking for details of the amounts received by proprietors for patients' accommodation to ascertain if they were correctly provided for from their estates. A group of proprietors set up a committee in response, to monitor implementation of the laws, and obtained a judgement from the Solicitor General to the effect that this request for information was illegal.[117] This decision did not stop the commission pressuring owners for these details, and they continued to threaten them with the loss of their licence if it was felt they were milking their patients financially, without providing proper care. Unfortunately, this weapon was not open to them when they approached doctors concerning the system of private lodgings.

Under the new Act in 1845, Ashley, Mylne, and Turner formed a private committee to deal with patients cared for in lodgings.[118] In response to a circular they found only twenty-one patients still legally registered under certificates, and further circulars asking for returns met with a stony silence.[119] Clearly they needed to establish how widespread this form of care was, in order to initiate regulations governing it, but from the outset they failed to impose themselves on the situation. In 1845, the board informed Samuel Newington of Goudhurst, Kent, that he did not require an official casebook to record his single patient, an act which immediately placed single patients on a different footing from all others, except workhouse lunatics, where the same problems of identification and registration subsequently arose.[120] This was despite the fact that the Act specifically mentioned a medical visitation book. In referring to the visitation of these patients, Shaftesbury implied that it was troublesome and done of the board's 'own free will'. Certainly the Act did not lay a specific duty on the commissioners, and they did have many other responsibilities, but this is symptomatic of their approach. The penalty of this reluctance to structure a systematic registration and visitation was open defiance from practitioners.

The career of Alexander Morison[121] provides a good example of how single lodgings, although connected to the network of private asylums, remained beyond the commission's reach. Morison never owned an asylum, but his practice revolved around them. In the 1830s he referred patients to Elm Grove and Southall Park, was visiting physician at these houses, and also Earls Court House and London House.[122] He was able to place recovered patients out into lodgings from these asylums, and also move them back if they relapsed. Like many doctors however he failed to notify the commission of these transfers. Private lodgings were the ideal form of care for wealthy families, as they avoided the stigma of asylum admission, allowed a greater degree of family contact and, above all, were secret. Unfortunately they were also used as a form of social control. Scull has described how paupers who crossed the boundaries of normalcy were incarcerated, and P. McCandless demonstrated a similar process in private asylums.[123] Single lodgings were used in the same way. Morison attended patients in lodgings who were victims of the mesmeric craze, wanted to contract undesirable marriages, or had joined fringe religious groups, and in several cases was given a specific brief by parents to straighten out their wayward children.[124] As his patients were rarely registered, they had no safeguards to their liberty at all, and with the increasing difficulty of confining these borderline cases in asylums, due to better certification procedures, it is tempting to speculate that the number of patients in single lodgings rose.

Most doctors saw the board's interest in these patients as an unwarrantable intrusion. E.J. Seymour, the former Metropolitan Lunacy Commissioner was among those who favoured lodgings with the right protections, but did not envisage these safeguards emanating from a government board. He believed lodgings were effectual only when the family were involved and helped care for the patient. This combined with regular medical attendance was the best way to obtain a cure.[125] He and Dr Winslow cared for Sir Robert Peel's brother in this way, without any notification to the

Board.[126] The latter's failure to enquire more closely into this system owed much to Ashley's reluctance to antagonize the moneyed classes, even though he knew that many lunatics spent weeks and months alone in the company of an attendant who provided little intellectual stimulation. In most lodgings, the new methods of moral treatment and non-restraint were ignored, and some patients kept under an excessive amount of restraint, owing to their violence.[127] If calm, a few were afforded greater latitude, with one of Morison's patients being allowed out to attend a temperance meeting on her own, where she was entrusted with a reclaimed drunkard. However, apart from dining with the family or occasional rides in a carriage, most patients received little in the way of moral treatment; rather, they were liberally supplied from the pharmacopoeia and bled.[128]

The commission, although conscious of the system's deficiencies, proved unable to gather reliable statistics of the numbers involved. Morison refused to give accurate information concerning his activities when questioned,[129] and it was not until 1860 that the board acknowledged a widespread evasion of the law, stating that it had been sanctioned, 'if not suggested, by medical men in attendance upon insane patients who, from their position, could hardly be ignorant of its requirements'.[130] What the board failed to admit was that their initial reluctance to intervene had led to a growth in this form of care, most of which they were ignorant.

Like many practitioners, Morison endorsed from ten to twenty lodgings at a time, supplying many more with patients.[131] Several housed more than one patient, which was illegal, and they were generally run by a widow or couple, with an attendant to care for the patient. Attendants were recruited from various sources, many approaching Morison having left other asylums. Most asylums had a 'call' list, and keepers on this could be sent out to lodgings at any time. Winslow, Sutherland, and Burrows were amongst the proprietors who used this, and it was not until the late 1850s that the board realized what was happening and attempted to prohibit 'call' lists. This was a precarious existence, as Burrows pointed out. Keepers who discharged themselves from the permanent service of an asylum, taking a single patient on full-time, risked the possibility of his recovery or death. In this situation they were effectively blacklisted by other proprietors who had been kept informed of the initial breach of contract with their former asylum.[132] Some attendants, however, rose to the challenge.

Frederick Horne is a good example of this type. He was placed out from Bethlem's 'call' list by Morison, but then went freelance using his relationship with Morison to secure a succession of patients.[133] This became a two-way process however as Horne obtained patients elsewhere and recommended Morison as the medical attendant to the relatives. In 1849 Morison recommended that Horne should get 31s. 6d. a week, and by 1850 he was charging two guineas a week to care for patients and four if it was at his cottage in Camberwell.[134] In 1859 Shaftesbury claimed that doctors were paying attendants a yearly stipend, supporting them when unemployed, but taking from two-thirds to three-quarters of their fees when they found work.[135] This was untrue in Horne's case, although other less able attendants were undoubtedly used in this way.

It is difficult to estimate the number of single lodgings, but there were certainly well over the 115 recorded by the board in 1860. By that time, 6,000 pauper patients were registered as being in lodgings, most of whom lived in terrible conditions, and it is probable that from 1,500–2,000 private patients were kept in them as well.[136] Further evidence of their presence was the existence of a Keepers' Association at Lisson Grove in north London. Founded in 1840 to service the lodgings system, it was still flourishing in 1860, and seems to have attracted attendants blacklisted elsewhere.[137] Morison was most offended when two of their keepers demanded two bottles of wine each a week while caring for one of his patients. It is a measure of the board's failure to penetrate the private sector that they did not uncover this organization until nineteen years after its foundation, despite its unsavoury activities.[138] This failure was due in part to the medical profession, which systematically concealed its interest in private patients, but the board was also to blame for not acting decisively. Firms such as Lara and Lane were left to foment trouble, and it was only with the appointment of Gaskell and Wilkes that a more pragmatic approach was taken, in which powers were sought through parliament and individual asylums questioned more closely about their connection with lodgings. The board remained ambivalent though, concerning the private sector, and this, combined with the opposition of practitioners, led to a healthier dialogue than existed with the public sector. Ultimately, the proprietors' opposition to initial attempts at casting their houses in the mould of county asylums, combined with the limitations placed on their size, meant that they had more to offer in terms of a therapeutic environment, than the latter which lost their way and became vast repositories for chronic patients.

Conclusion

Examination of the board's evolution demonstrates that it had few Lamarckian qualities. Unable to adapt to change, the commissioners preferred to impose a model on psychiatry, one heavily influenced by Shaftesbury's evangelical outlook and developments at Hanwell. Selection of the board's personnel was crucial, and contributed much to its failings. In *Representative Government*, J.S. Mill espoused a degree of paternalistic rule only as a staging post on the way to a system employing more enlightened civil servants, who would express their opinions without fear of losing office.[139] Unfortunately, Shaftesbury's dominant position as chairman and the traditional perspectives inherited from previous inspectorates hampered individual commissioners, and prevented later appointees from challenging the collective orthodoxy. In 1859 Shaftesbury resisted enlargement of the board on the grounds that he could foresee a time 'when it would be almost impossible to carry on the business of the Commission, as it would be so much in the nature of a debating society'.[140] Probably he was right to defend the commissioners' unique position, an inspectors and members of the executive, because in time they increasingly took control of the board's affairs. Whilst he remained active, however, much constructive dialogue was stifled by his desire to follow a 'middle road' in all things.

In this essay, I beg the question whether political theorists such as Bentham had any influence on the practical workings of the board,[141] although it is clear that Lutwidge was a Chadwickian who applied the devastating test of utility to every aspect of their work.[142] Rather, it is important to acknowledge that the commission evolved gradually, promoting internal change in its structure and methodology, initiating legislation and extending central control into the provinces, from a knowledge base founded on its field executives' experience. To understand why it developed into such an unimaginative organization, one must distinguish between explanations derived from its constitutional position and those based around its personnel. Clearly there were numerous constraints imposed by the Treasury and Home Office, but it was the limitation of its staff which compounded these.

Its most able professionals were lawyers, whose interest lay in administrative systems and legislative change. In these spheres the board rapidly became the acknowledged authority. As a leader in the field of scientific medicine however it left a lot to be desired. The early medical commissioners had no experience of managing large asylums, and would have been content to allow superintendents to develop their own regimes. It was the Home Office which insisted on uniformity, and the county superintendents were largely at fault in their failure to prepare a sound case defending individual practices. Nevertheless, the medical commissioners were also culpable in contributing to an atmosphere which discouraged research into the pathology of mental disease and promoted a lay perspective of lunacy. In the private sector, their leniency to proprietors delayed the imposition of effective controls until after the appointment of Gaskell and Wilkes.

By the 1870s, the board had developed a *modus operandi* that not only encouraged an unhealthy adherence to the Moloch of administrative perfectibility, but also carried in its train the seeds of a 'long sleep' for what had been an emerging professional group, the county asylum superintendents. As Huxley had foreseen, the commission's desire for authority had led to an intolerance of opposition which effectively curtailed growth. Only further research will reveal the full extent to which central authority came to dominate the practice of psychiatry.

Notes

1 R. Hunter and I. MacAlpine, *Three Hundred Years of Psychiatry 1535–1860* (London: Oxford University Press, 1963), pp. 451–56.
2 Madhouses became known as licensed houses or private asylums in the

nineteenth century. The terms are interchangeable and have been used in this way throughout, although the former came to be used mostly in a pejorative sense.

3 These men will be referred to as the College commissioners hereafter.

4 The Diaries of E.T. Monro, 1806–1833 (in private hands, Sevenoaks, Kent). These illustrate that many physicians who acted as commissioners, had patients at Monro's asylum, Brooke House. Among these were Halford, Powell, Tierney, Baillie, Heberden, Maton, Bree, and Hue to name but a few. Also Thomas Turner the future full-time commissioner, who dined often with Monro.

5 Sir George Henry Rose (1771–1855), diplomatist. MP Southampton 1794–1813, Christchurch, Hampshire, 1818–44; Metropolitan Lunacy Commissioner 1828–31; Member of Commons' Select Committees concerning Lunacy, 1807, 1815, and 1827.

6 PP 1814–15, IV, pp. 15–18.

7 PP 1814–15, IV, pp. 27–30. Weir's suggestion was for one active citizen, one man of the law and one physician.

8 *Times*, 20 June, 1814. XYZ attacked the College accusing its members of aggrandizement in promoting Rose's bills, which sought to widen its powers.

9 G.M. Burrows, *Cursory Remarks on a Bill Now in the House of Peers for the Regulating of Madhouses* (London: T. and G. Underwood, 1817), pp. 19–22.

10 University College London, Brougham MSS, 44208, Letter, Dillon to Lord Brougham 14 December, 1832. See also PP 1826–27, VI, pp. 57–60. Dillon was very critical of the College commissioners, and suggested public asylums managed by magistrates were the answer.

11 House of Commons Journals, vol. 36, 1828, pp. 85, 411. Gordon was the only member of the select committee who helped prepare both bills.

12 William Macmichael (1784–1839) MD 1816, 1822–31 Physician to the Middlesex Hospital; was on close terms with a number of madhouse owners, and from 1833–37 was a Lord Chancellor's Visitor to Chancery patients.

13 For details of all the Metropolitan Lunacy Commissioners see Appendix A. Turner (1776–1865) has been confused with the surgeon Thomas Turner (1793–1873) who pioneered medical schools in Manchester, a mistake the former would not have found amusing. See D.J. Mellett, 'Bureaucracy and Mental Illness: The Commissioners in Lunacy 1845–90', *Medical History* (July 1981): biog. app.

14 Lord Ashley, Spencer Perceval, Robert Gordon, Williams Wynn, Calthorpe, and Rose all became Metropolitan Lunacy Commissioners. Villiers did not.

15 PP HL CCXXXVII, p. 1. Minutes of evidence taken before the Select Committee of the House of Lords to whom were referred the bill entitled An Act to Regulate the Care and Treatment of Insane Persons, p. 19.

16 For further discussion, see, A. Digby, 'Moral Treatment at the York Retreat' in this volume.

17 PP HL CCXXXVII, pp. 99, 65, 102–03.

18 9 Geo IV c. 41, ss. 2, 17, 20, 37, 29, 30, 32, 35, 38, and 44.

19 Monro Diaries, 1828. Monro consulted regularly with Drs A.J. Sutherland, G.M. Burrows, E.L. Fox, G.G. Bompas, and J. Willis, all prominent madhouse owners. He called on Lord Malmesbury with Dr Willis, and himself approached the Lord Chancellor, Robert Gordon, the Bishop of Llandaff and the Home Secretary. Entries dated 17 March, 25 March, 3 April, 12 April, 29 April, 14 May, 16 May, and 17 May.

20 S.W. Nicoll, *An Enquiry into the Present State of Visitation in Asylums for the*

Reception of the Insane and into the modes by which such visitation may be improved (London: 1828), p. 89.

21　British Museum Addit mss, Peel Papers, 40397 ff. 210–12, letter from Peel to G. Somerset, 2 August, 1828; see also Leicester County Record Office, Halford mss DG 24/872, Peel to Halford, 2 August, 1828.

22　Peel Papers, 40397 f. 206, letter from Peel to Gordon, 1 August, 1828; ff. 210–12, Peel to G. Somerset, 2 August, 1828. Peel, having informed Somerset of his inadvertent offer to Gordon, before receiving a reply from the latter, asked whether Somerset would accept the chairmanship if Gordon declined. He also had the nerve to ask if Somerset would serve under Gordon.

23　Halford mss, DG24/872 Letters from Peel to Halford, 2 August, 1828; Halford to Peel, 3 August, 1828 and 5 August, 1828. Peel asked for Halford's opinion on several doctors who had approached him for commissioners' posts, including A. Halliday, J.A. Gordon, and W. Lambe. Halford however recommended staunch College men; Turner, Bright, and Southey who were chosen, Macmichael and Hewett whom he later recommended to Brougham as Lord Chancellor's visitors of lunatics and four others.

24　The fellow magistrates suggested by Gordon, B. Bouverie, G.F. Hampson, and J. Clitherow, all had evangelical leanings.

25　For discussion of these see H.W. Parris, *Constitutional Bureaucracy: The Development of British Central Administration since the Eighteenth Century* (London: Allen and Unwin, 1969), pp. 84–90; also Sir N. Chester, *The English Administrative System 1780–1870* (Oxford, 1981), pp. 300–42.

26　1828–30, G. Somerset, Jr Ld of Treasury; 1830–32, F.T. Baring, Ld of Treasury; 1830–34, R. Vernon Smith, Jr Ld of Treasury; 1835–39, E.A. Seymour, 12th D. of Somerset, Ld of Treasury; 1839–41, R. Gordon, Sec. to Treasury; and 1841–45 J.M. Gaskell, Ld of Treasury.

27　Brougham, mss, 44556, letter from Ashley to Brougham, 20 February 1833; 43992, Ashley to Brougham, 20 May 1833.

28　Buckinghamshire County Record Office, Freemantle mss, D/FR/130/8, Secretary of the Lunatics Office to Sir T.F. Freemantle asking if he wished to continue in office as a Metropolitan Lunacy Commissioner, 29 August, 1832. In reply Freemantle stated that he hadn't fulfilled his duties because of pressure of parliamentary business.

29　The most important of these were Sir R. Inglis, commissioner 1833–35, Sir G. Grey 1833–34, and E.A. Seymour 1836–51.

30　John Haslam, *A Letter to the Metropolitan Commissioners in Lunacy containing some strictures on the Act of Parliament and observations on their Report* (London: 1830), pp. 3, 9.

31　Halford, mss, DG24/835/1 Report on and suggested regulations for the keeping of lunatics, n.d.

32　Halford mss, DG24/866/20, letter from Ld Brougham to Halford, 10 April, 1831.

33　Brougham mss, 33670 Letter from Shaftesbury to Brougham, 18 July, 1845. It is clear that the new legal commissioners rapidly applied pressure to become salaried, persuading Shaftesbury and Brougham to support this, but not G. Somerset. For this see Brougham mss, 43992, Shaftesbury to Mylne, 1 August, 1833 and Somerset to Shaftesbury, 10 August 1833. Also 44155, Mylne to Le Marchant, 2 November, 1832. Mylne wanted Le Marchant to inform Brougham that it might be out of his power, unless paid, 'long to continue an efficient member, without interfering with my other professional engagements'.

34 O MacDonagh, *A Pattern of Government Growth, 1800–60* (London: MacGibbon and Kee, 1961).

35 National Register of Archives, Diaries of the 7th Earl of Shaftesbury, SHA/PD/3, 15 November, 1844. The complete unfitness of William Godwin for this post badly dented Shaftesbury's confidence in his own judgement.

36 Edward Dubois (1774–1850). Barrister, wit, and man of letters. Contributor to the *Morning Chronicle and Observer*. Editor of several magazines. Secretary to the Metropolitan Lunacy Commission 1833–45. A Brougham appointee who kept the latter informed of the board's activities.

37 Brougham mss, 572 Letter Dubois to Brougham, n.d.; see also 585 Dubois to Brougham, n.d. Dubois remarked, 'in one thing [his principles] Lord Ashley has been duped. He understands and says that the Commissioners, Medical and Legal, shall devote their whole time to lunacy.... Now, I hear from those well informed on the subject that the Doctors mean to retain other offices and the Lawyers such practice as they may have.'

38 Brougham mss, 17962, Procter to Brougham, 22 July, 1845.

39 This included 21 county asylums, 11 hospitals, 96 provincial madhouses, 48 metropolitan madhouses, *c.* 750 workhouses, and 20 gaols. They were also empowered to visit Bethlem, and the military and naval hospitals with permission from the Home Secretary or Lord Chancellor. Thus totalling 949 institutions in all.

40 Shaftesbury Diaries, SHA/PD/4, 9 August, 1845.

41 Hansard 3rd. S, vol. 76, pp. 1257–264; also PP 1859, 1st Sess. III, pp. 64–5 and PP 1877, XIII, pp. 520–35.

42 S. Tuke, *Description of the Retreat, an Institution Near York for Insane Persons of the Society of Friends* (York: W. Alexander, 1813; reprint by Dawsons, London, 1964); J. Conolly, *The Construction and Government of Lunatic Asylums and Hospitals for the Insane* (London: John Churchill, 1847); and the essays of Andrew Scull and Anne Digby in these volumes.

43 Hansard 3rd. S, vol. 61, p. 806; PP 1859, 1st Sess. III, p. 23; and Journal House of Lords, 24 March, 1862.

44 H. Newington, 'Some Incidents in the History and Practice of Ticehurst Asylum' *Journal of Mental Science* 47 (1901): 70–1.

45 PP 1859, 1st Sess. III, pp. 7–10.

46 *The Journal of the Honorable H.E. Fox 1818–1830*, ed. The Earl of Ilchester (London: Thorton Butterworth, 1923), p. 131. Henry Edward Fox (1802–59), 4th Baron Holland, MP 1826–27, was an Oxford contemporary of Shaftesbury's. In 1820 he wrote, 'Ashley's character seems to me quite unintelligible and can only be accounted for by a dash of madness.' See also Mabel Countess of Airlie, *Lady Palmerston and Her Times*, 2 vols (London: Hodder and Stoughton, 1922), pp. 146–48. Florence Nightingale remarked that 'had he not devoted himself to reforming lunatic asylums, he would have been in one himself' (C. Woodham Smith, *Florence Nightingale 1820–1910* (London: Constable, 1950), p. 589).

47 Victoria and Albert Museum, Forster mss, 48/E/32, letter from Procter to Forster, 1865.

48 Shaftesbury Diaries, SHA/PD/5, 24 April, 1852, 13 July, 1852.

49 PP 1860, XXII, pp. 22–4.

50 Single patients: In law, it was illegal after 1828 to care for a single patient, unless they came under a Chancery Committee or it was not undertaken for profit, until an order and two medical certificates were obtained. These patients were cared

for in lodgings generally.

51 PP 1859, 1st Sess. III, pp. 59–60. In 1845 Shaftesbury raised only £1,200 after an appeal, and had to return the money to subscribers two years later.

52 Shaftesbury Diaries, SHA/PD/5, 13 July, 1849, 5 September, 1851. Before Select Committees Shaftesbury always gave evidence that he was opposed to the lodgings system.

53 Shaftesbury Diaries, SHA/PD/6, 1 June, 1852. Shaftesbury would occasionally take communion with Lutwidge. See also, Victoria and Albert Museum, Forster mss, 48/E/32, Procter to Forster, 26 October, 1858. Procter mentions doing a visit with Gaskell on a Sunday, contrary to the board's custom.

54 Michel Foucault, *Madness and Civilisation: A History of Insanity in the Age of Reason* (London: Tavistock, 1967), ch. 9; see also F. Godlee, 'Aspects of non-conformity', in this volume.

55 Shaftesbury Diaries, SHA/PD/4, 9 August, 1845.

56 Royal College of Physicians Edinburgh, Diaries of Sir Alexander Morison, 6 May, 1846.

57 *Journal of Mental Science* 3 (19), (October, 1856). Vote of Congratulation to R.W.S. Lutwidge.

58 Forster mss, 48/E/32, Procter to Forster, 21 July, 1863. Procter also spoke of his friendly relations with the Drs Mayo (Procter to Forster, 20 October, 1863).

59 The visitation books at all asylums illustrate how enquiries became more searching after 1856. The appointment of Lutwidge as a visitor also contributed to this.

60 In addition to those mentioned already Lutwidge owed his appointment to Shaftesbury whom he knew from the National Society for Promoting Religious Education and the Statistical Society. Hancock Hall to Lord Lyndhurst, and Campbell to Sir Robert Peel.

61 Samuel Gaskell, 'On the Want of Better Provision for the Labouring and Middle Classes when Attacked or Threatened with Insanity', *Journal of Mental Science* 6 (1860): 321–27.

62 John Charles Bucknill, 'Article Concerning the Eighth Report of the Irish Inspectors of Lunatic Asylums, 1857', *Journal of Mental Science* 4 (24) (1857). They advocated flue systems of ventilation and less hard labour for patients, in opposition to current board policies.

63 British Museum Add mss, Layard Papers, 34624 f. 523, letter from Procter to MacVey Napier, 13 July, 1844; Brougham mss, 24545, 10 January, 1863.

64 Forster mss, 48/E/32, Procter to Forster, 17 August, 1856.

65 PP 1859, 1st Sess. III, p. 2.

66 Forster mss, 48/F/65, Procter to Forster, 4 November, 1859.

67 R.A. Lewis, *Edwin Chadwick and the Public Health Movement, 1832–54* (London: Longmans, Green, 1952), pp. 7–26.

68 Shaftesbury Diaries, SHA/PD/4, 28 August, 1846. Haydock Lodge was a grossly overcrowded private asylum in Lancashire. Paupers were underfed and ill treated there, which resulted in a high mortality rate. Also its owners were implicated because they used their position as poor law officials to direct paupers there.

69 Forster mss, 48/E/32, Procter to Forster, 27 July, 1863.

70 Public Record Office (PRO), HO 45/OS/1452, letters from the Lunacy Commission to the Home Office, 19 May, 1846, 13 June, 1846, 24 June, 1846, and 5 September, 1846. See also HO 44/70 Home Office to Lunacy Commission, 3 November, 1845.

71 *The Lancet*, 13 January, 1849. Wakley suggested their weakness would lead to the profession losing its hold over insanity.

72 *The Medical Times*, no. 415 (September, 1847), pp. 573–74.

73 Home Office correspondence in HO 34 and HO 43 classes illustrates that both Graham and Grey (a former Metropolitan Lunacy Commissioner) made great efforts to impress magistrates and others that the board should be the final authority on most matters relating to lunacy.

74 James Huxley (1821–1907) MRCS 1843, LSA 1843, MD St Andrews 1844, Resident Medical Officer and Superintendent Kent County Lunatic Asylum 1846–1863. Brother of T.H. Huxley.

75 PROM H50/1, 3 September, 1846. This is the class containing the Lunacy Commission's minute books; see also HO 45/OS/1452, Lunacy Commission to the Home Office, 5 September, 1846.

76 Kent County Asylum Annual Report 1861–62, p. 33.

77 *Medical Circular* 4, no. 94: 279–80.

78 A. Scull, *Museums of Madness: The Social Organisation of Insanity in Nineteenth Century England* (London: Allen Lane, 1979), pp. 194–210, 226–33.

79 D.J. Mellett, *The Prerogative of Asylumdom* (New York: Garland Press, 1983).

80 PP 1847–48, XXXII, Appendix H.

81 The Lunacy Commissioners remedied this by inserting a clause in the Regulation of the Care and Treatment of Lunatics Act, 16 and 17 Vict., c. 96, s. 30 stipulating that charity and subscription hospitals must have their rules approved by the Home Secretary, which effectively meant, by them.

82 Most notably a register of all violent incidents.

83 The commission had had an earlier request for a special visit turned down by the Lord Chancellor in 1847, and had shelved further applications in 1848 and 1851 feeling they had insufficient evidence to justify them. It is perhaps not insignificant, that Shaftesbury's father, the 6th Earl, a governor of Bethlem and lifelong opponent of his son's activities, had died that summer. The commissioners' letter announcing their initial visitation, arrived the day after they did.

84 Bethlem Hospital, *The Report of the Commissioners in Lunacy to the Secretary of State, Together with a copy of the Evidence on which such report is stated to be founded* (London: Spottiswoode and Shaw, 1852), and the essay by Patricia Allderidge in this volume.

85 Scull, *Museums of Madness*, ch. 5 for the case of John Millar, sacked by the Buckinghamshire magistrates from their county asylum. He subsequently became the medical officer at Hoxton Madhouse.

86 For detailed discussion see, Charles Snape, *Wandsworth Asylum – A Letter to the Committee of Visitors of the Surrey County Lunatic Asylum* (London: 1856); Surrey County Asylum Fifteenth Annual Report, 1857.

87 For example Bucknill felt the board overemphasized the use of work (*J. Ment. Sci.* 1 (6) (July, 1854). He resented their praise of Samuel Hill's use of 'hard labour' at the North and East Ridings Asylum, suggesting that in future magistrates would be asking for superintendents with a recommendation from Mr Pusey's Agricultural College at Cirencester.

88 Kent County Record Office (KCRO), Q/GCL8 House Committee Minute Book Kent County Asylum, September, 1843–December, 1849. Entry for 15 May, 1847.

89 Lunacy Comissioners Seventeenth Annual Report 1863, PP, XX, pp. 74–78. In 1863, the magistrates claimed that they did not sanction these reports, although as

the commission pointed out, this was a meaningless statement, as they had been publishing them alongside their own for twenty years.

90 *J. Ment. Sci.* 4 (23) (October, 1857).

91 Kent Asylum Annual Report 1861–62, p. 29.

92 Of the sacked staff at Kent, seven were dismissed for leaving their patients unattended all night whilst out drinking, four for prostitution in Maidstone, three for playing cards in a corner of the suicide ward whilst a patient cut his throat, and several for sleeping whilst on night duty. Others were sacked for sending inexperienced staff out with large numbers of patients on their own, during the cold weather. KCRO, MH/Md2/As6.

93 The above statistics are based on Kent Asylum Servants Books. KCRO, MH/Md2/As6, 7, AS22.

94 PRO, MH51/44A. The Commission's case notes on the West Malling investigation.

95 KCRO, MH/Md2/As7, 24 September, 1879.

96 Hereafter referred to as the Asylum Officers Association.

97 Examination of family papers in Kent and Surrey shows the magistracy taking great interest before the 1860s. Several Surrey magistrates were also Bethlem or Hanwell governors, as were one or two Kent visitors. Five Surrey magistrates joined Sir A. Morison's Society for the Improvement of the Condition of the Insane, and at least two attended his lectures on insanity. Their correspondence confirms links with justices in other countries, for instance, the Hanwell bench writing about their method of non-restraint. See KCRO, Marsham mss, U1515, OQ, L1, Serjeant Adams to Lord Marsham, 7 December, 1839.

98 Royal College of Psychiatry, minute book of the Medico-Psychological Association, June 1841–October, 1892. See 1st meeting, 4 November, 1841, and subsequent meetings to 1856. In 1851, the Association's secretaries suggested that their scheme to distribute asylum reports abroad had been rendered unnecessary, by 'a more direct interchange that takes places between the British and American establishments'.

99 W.Ll. Parry-Jones, *The Trade in Lunacy: A Study of Private Madhouses in England in the Eighteenth and Nineteenth Century*, (London: Routledge and Kegan Paul, 1972), pp. 89–90.

100 Mellett, *Prerogative of Asylumdom*, ch. 4.

101 PRO, HO 45/OS/2222, Lunacy Commissioners to HO, 3 July, 1848. They suggest that legislation should be postponed concerning wandering lunatics, because there are other changes they want 'which the experience of the Commission in its working has suggested, and of which memoranda for that purpose have been carefully made'.

102 PRO, MH50/1, pp. 148–49, 23 January, 1846.

103 W.J. Corbet, 'Ought Private Lunatic Asylums to Be Abolished?', *Westminster Review* 142 (September, 1894): 378–80.

104 L. Weatherly, *A Plea for the Insane: The Case for Reform in the Care and Treatment of Mental Diseases* (London: Grant Richards, 1918), pp. 60–2.

105 Parry-Jones, *Trade in Lunacy*, pp. 88–9.

106 PRO, MH50/1, 8 October, 1846.

107 PRO, MH50/11, 7 November, 1860. Having finally managed to establish that the proprietors of Hoxton were the Lord Mayor John Carter, and Recorder of the City, Russell Gurney, the board renewed the licence for only four months, with a further renewal conditional on a full written statement detailing the exact duties

of every officer employed in the house, and to what extent they were under the control of the proprietors.

108 D. Roberts, *The Victorian Origins of the British Welfare State* (New Haven, Conn.: Yale University Press, 1960), ch. 4.

109 PP 1859, 1st Sess. III, pp. 34–5.

110 PRO, MH50/8, 27 August, 1856; see also MH50/9, 21 April, 1858. The board made renewal of Halliford House's licence conditional on discontinuation in the use of their 'seclusion' room; MH50/9, 23 March, 1858, Dr Finch of Fisherton House, Wilts, threatened through the magistrates, owing to his continued use of a 'ducking bath', water gruel as punishment for patients, and his infrequent ward rounds.

111 PP 1859, Sess. 2 VII, p. 47; Forster mss, 48/F/65, letter from Procter to Forster, 29 August, 1857.

112 Co-founded by Shaftesbury's father, this society contained six Bethlem governors and three Surrey Asylum visitors. Other wealthy patrons such as the Duke of Norfolk and the Earl of Arundel had relatives or friends who had been treated by Morison.

113 J. Purdie and E.L. Bryan (Hoxton), G.M. Burrows and J. Bush (Clapham Retreat), J.G. Millingen (York House), W.B. Costello (Wyke House), W. Wood and F. Philp (Kensington House), E.T. Monro (Brook House), A.J. Sutherland (Blacklands House), H.W. Diamond (Twickenham House), G.W. Daniell and Lady Ellis (Southall Park). There were also some provincial owners, including C. Summers (Great Forsters), G. Hitch (Sandywell Park), and J.B. Daniel (Bailbrook House). These men met regularly at Morison's house and elsewhere.

114 Other societies regularly used, were the Ethnological, the London Medical, the Royal Medical and Chirurgical, the Provincial Medical and Surgical Association, the Society for the Relief of Widows and Orphans of Medical Men, and the Royal Medical Benevolent College of which Shaftesbury was the chairman.

115 These agents were only four doors down from the Metropolitan Lunacy Commissioners' office in Adelphi Street, and round the corner from E.T. Monro's house.

116 *Medical Times* vol. 2 (May, 1851): 537–38.

117 *Medical Circular and General Medical Advertiser* vol. 9 (January, 1856): 8–9.

118 8 and 9 Vict., c. 100, s. 89. The fact that only three commissioners were empowered to be on this committee proved very inconvenient. In 1853 the board got this extended to all their members. See 16 and 17 Vict. c. 96, s. 27

119 PRO, MH 51/236 Circular Letters Book No. 1, 1845–63. Circulars Nos. 3 and 5.

120 PRO, MH50/41 the Minute Book of the Private Committee, September, 1845–No. 1846, 25 September, 1845.

121 Sir Alexander Morison (1779–1863), visiting physician of Surrey Madhouses 1809–62, visiting physician Bethlem 1835–52 and Surrey County Asylum 1841–56. Remembered for his book on physiognomy and the fact that he initiated lectures for nurses. Also visiting physician at Hanwell, 1829–48.

122 Royal College of Physicians, Edinburgh, The Morison Diaries, 19 December, 1833, and diary for 1840. Elm Grove was owned by Mrs Wood, the sister-in-law of his colleague at Hanwell, Sir W. Ellis; Southall Park by Ellis himself, and then his widow.

123 Scull, *Museums of Madness*, pp. 201–04; P. McCandless, 'Liberty and Lunacy: The Victorians and Wrongful Confinement', in A. Scull (ed.), *Madhouses, Mad-doctors and Madmen: The Social History of Psychiatry in the Victorian Era*

(London: Athlone Press, 1981); and the essay by John Walton in this volume.

124 Morison Diaries, 10 April, 1850, 4 September, 1844. In 1844, a Captain Greathorpe approached Morison about his daughter who wanted to marry a common soldier. He recommended Dr Belhomme in Paris who had an 'Institution for the children of parents who had difficulty in managing them'.

125 E.J. Seymour, *Thoughts on the Nature and Treatment of Several Severe Diseases of the Human Body* (London: Longman, Green, 1847), vol. 1, p. 216; Seymour (1796–1866) was a commissioner from 1830–38. He was also well known to Robert Nairne, a colleague at St George's Hospital and in private practice. He was appointed to the Metropolitan Lunacy Commission in 1857 amidst an outcry from the county asylum superintendents.

126 Peel, mss, 40609, ff. 149, 151, 208, 215, 221, 258, 259, 268, 277, 279, and 314. Correspondence relating to William Yates Peel (1789–1858).

127 The Reverend Howard whom Morison placed with an ex-Hanwell magistrate, Mr Trimmer, was under restraint almost continuously for eight years until moved to Ticehurst Asylum. In 1842 Morison recorded another patient as 'still requiring restraint, although nearly reduced to a skeleton and his back excoriated with sores', Morison Diaries, 11 November, 1842.

128 Many of Morison's private patients also had their heads shaven.

129 PRO, MH50/5, 10 July, 1851.

130 Lunacy Commissioners Fourteenth Annual Report, 1860, p. 68.

131 PP 1859, 1st Sess. III, p. 42. Shaftesbury claimed in 1859 that some great physicians controlled up to forty houses in this way. Morison supervised lodgings in Maidstone, Sevenoaks, Tonbridge, Gravesend, Canterbury, Plaistow, and Farley, and many in London. He would also obtain patients for doctors, clergymen, and others to care for at home, most of whom were not registered.

132 George Man Burrows, *Cursory Remarks on a Bill Now in the House of Peers for the Regulation of Madhouses* (London: Underwood, 1817), p. 83.

133 Lunacy Commissioners Seventh Annual Report, PP. 1852–53, XLIX, pp. 30–2. The commission prosecuted another Bethlem attendant set up in this way by Morison.

134 Morison Diaries, 27 October, 1849 and 8 December, 1850. See also *The Medical Directory*, part 2, 1848, p. 28 in the advertisement section; Horne even made two attempts to obtain a licence for several patients, MH50/11, 31 October, 1860 and 13 December, 1860.

135 *The Lancet* 1, 2nd ser. (23 January, 1847): 82. In fact Wakley had highlighted this system some years earlier. Wakley who had a nephew under Morison's care in Elm Grove, was always a stern opponent of the worst practices in the private sector, although supporting it generally.

136 This figure is a very rough estimate. Chancery Bonds (PRO/J/103/1–3) illustrate that 50 per cent of Chancery patients were in lodgings, that is 300. There were 117 officially registered lodgings. Almost all 186 licensed houses in the country had four or five former patients in lodgings, *c.* 840 patients. Many other practitioners, clergymen and others were also looking after patients as is evidenced by advertising in *The Times* and other newspapers.

137 In the advertisements section of the *Medical Directory*, 1847, p. 25, the Association begged leave 'to return their sincere thanks to the gentlemen of the medical profession and the public for their liberal patronage'. See also *Medical Directory*, 1857, p. 23, advertisements section.

138 PP 1859, 1st Sess. III, pp. 189–90.

139 J.S. Mill, *Considerations on Representative Government* (London: Longmans, Green, 1861), pp. 334–35.
140 PP 1860, XXII, pp. 22–33.
141 For discussion of this issue see, S.E. Finer, 'The Transmission of Benthamite Ideas 1820–50', in G. Sutherland (ed.), *Studies in the Growth of Nineteenth Century Government* (London: Routledge and Kegan Paul, 1972); cf., *inter alia*, O. MacDonagh, 'The Nineteenth Century Revolution in Government: A Reappraisal', *Historical Journal* 1 (1958): 52; H. Parris, 'The Nineteenth Century Revolution in Government: Reappraisal Reappraised', *Historical Journal* 3 (1960).
142 Other members of the board were well aware of Benthamite traditions. Shaftesbury through Chadwick; Forster from his vast collection of pamphlets on them; Vernon-Smith, Seymour, and Lutwidge via the Statistical Society. In many respects, Procter believed that Lutwidge with his numerous ideas created extra drudgery for the board, although it is also true that he elevated the position of secretary almost to that of a seventh full-time commissioner making visitations, interviewing at the board, representing them in court and helping devise legislation. In this sense he was in the mould of Chadwick, Kay Shuttleworth, and Horner, rather than the mere clerk pictured by David Roberts, *Victorian Origins of the Welfare State*, p. 239.

Appendix A

Lunacy Commissioners' and secretaries' length of service.
Medical commissioners: John Robert Hume (1845–57), Henry Herbert Southey (1845), Thomas Turner (1845–56), James Cowles Prichard (1845–48), Samuel Gaskell (1848–66), James Wilkes (1856–78), Robert Nairne (1857–83).
Legal commissioners: John Hancock Hall (1845), William George Campbell (1845–78), Bryan Waller Procter (1845–61), James William Mylne (1845–55), Robert Wilfred Skeffington Lutwidge (1855–73), John Forster (1861–72).
Secretaries: Lutwidge (1845–55), Forster (1855–61).
Lay commissioners: Lord Shaftesbury (chairman) (1845–85), Edward Adolphus Seymour, 12th Duke of Somerset (1845–52), Robert Gordon (1845–64), Robert Vernon Smith, Baron Lyveden (1845–72), Francis Barlow (1845–79), Colonel Henry Morgan Clifford (1853–84).

BIOGRAPHIES

MEDICAL
John Robert Hume (1781–1857). MD St Andrews 1816, LRCP 1819, FRCP 1836. Physician to Wellington during the Peninsular War and on return to England. Inspector General of Hospitals 1818–21. Private practice in London. Metropolitan Lunacy Commissioner 1828–45.
Thomas Turner (1776–1865). Educated Charterhouse and Göttingen. MB Cantab 1799, MD 1804, MRCP 1804, FRCP 1805, Treasurer RCP 1822–45. Physician St Thomas's Hosp. 1802–16. Physician Extraordinary to Queen Adelaide 1830–49. Metropolitan Lunacy Commissioner 1828–44.
Henry Herbert Southey (1783–1865). Younger brother of Robert Southey. MD

Edin. 1806, FRCP 1823, FRS 1825. Practices in Durham and London. Physician Middlesex Hospital 1815–27. Physician to George IV and Queen Adelaide. Metropolitan Lunacy Commissioner 1828–45.

James Cowles Prichard (1786–1848). MD Edinburgh 1808, Physician St Peter's Hospital, Bristol 1811–21 and to the Bristol Infirmary 1814–45. Private practice in Bristol. Famous ethnologist and President of the Ethnological Society. FRS 1827. From a Quaker background, Prichard was a committed Christian. Member of the Association of Medical Officers of Asylums and Hospitals for the Insane 1841–45. Metropolitan Lunacy Commissioner 1841–45. Author, *A Treatise on Diseases of the Nervous System*, 1822; *A Treatise on Insanity and Other Disorders Affecting the Mind*, 1835; *On the different Forms of Insanity in Relation to Jurisprudence*, 1842.

Samuel Gaskell (1807–96). Born Warrington. Educated locally owing to reduced family circumstances. Despite discouragement because of eye weakness, completed medical education at Manchester and Edinburgh after initial apprenticeship to a Liverpool bookseller. Resident MO Stockport Cholera Hosp. 1832–34, RMO Manchester Royal Infirmary and Lunatic Asylum 1834–40, medical superintendent Lancaster Moor Asylum 1840–48, where he abolished restraint. Retired in 1865 after a street accident. Pioneer in work with the mentally handicapped.

James Wilkes (1811–94). LSA 1834, MRCS 1835, FRCS 1854. Studied General Hospital Birmingham and Kings College London. RMO Staffs County Lunatic Asylum 1841–56. Member of Commission of Inquiry into State of Lunatic Asylums in Ireland. Honorary Lunacy Commissioner 1878–94.

Robert Nairne (1804–87). Educated Edinburgh and Trinity College, Cambridge MB 1832, MD 1837, FRCP 1838. Physician St George's Hospital 1839–57, an institution with evangelical sympathies. Appointed by Lord Chancellor Cranworth, a governor of the hospital (as were Robert Gordon and Sir George Grey, the Home Secretary). Moderate private practice as well. Treasurer of the Royal Medical and Chirurgical Society. Member of the deputation of private asylum owners and private practitioners to the Home Secretary in 1853, concerning the lunacy bills.

LEGAL

John Hancock Hall (1797–1845). Eldest son of Revd John Hancock Hall LLB, Risley Hall, Derbyshire. Admitted MT 1817, Barrister 1825. Metropolitan Lunacy Commissioner 1842–45.

William George Campbell (1810–81). Barrister MT 1836, Special Pleader 1838–43, Northern Circuit 1843–45. A protégé of the Duke of Argyll, who tried to obtain a post as assistant solicitor to the Excise for him in 1845. A convinced churchman. Honorary Lunacy Commissioner 1878–81.

Bryan Waller Procter (1797–1874). Born Leeds. Educated Finchley and Harrow. Articled to a solicitor in Calne, Wiltshire. Barrister G.I. 1831. Mostly practised in conveyancing. Began contributions to the *Literary Gazette* in 1815. Minor poet, pseudonym Barry Cornwall. Friend of Leigh Hunt, Lamb, Hazlitt, Landor, Carlyle, Swinburne, Coleridge, Macaulay, Dickens, and Browning. Metropolitan Lunacy Commissioner 1832–45, Honorary Lunacy Commissioner 1861–74. Author, *Dramatic Scenes and Other Poems*, 1819; *Poetical Works*, 1822; *English Songs*, 1832; *Memoir of Lamb*, 1866.

James William Mylne (1800–55). Educated Glasgow Grammar, Glasgow University and Balliol, Oxford. Barrister L.I. 1827. Metropolitan Lunacy Commissioner 1832–45. Co-author, with Benjamin Keen, of *Reports of Cases in the High Court of Chancery 1832–35*, 3 vols, 1834–37; and, with R.D. Craig, *Report of Cases in The*

High Court of Chancery, 1835–48, 5 vols, 1837–48.

Robert Wilfred Skeffington Lutwidge (1802–73). From an established county family in Cumberland. Educated St John's Cambridge. Barrister L.I. 1827. Auditor of the National Society for Promoting Religious Education 1828–43. Member of the Statistical Society from its foundation in 1834. Pioneer photographer and favourite uncle of Lewis Carroll. Lutwidge and Carroll shared their interest with Dr Diamond of Surrey County Asylum. Metropolitan Lunacy Commissioner 1842–45. Member of Commission of Enquiry into the State of Lunatic Asylums in Ireland 1856. Killed by a patient while visiting Fisherton House, Salisbury, Wiltshire.

John Forster (1812–76). Son of a Newcastle butcher and cattle dealer. Educated Newcastle Grammar School, University College, London. Barrister I.T. Drama critic *True Sun* 1832. Editor *Foreign Quarterly Review* 1842–43; *Daily News* 1846; *Examiner* 1847–55. Prolific writer, moved in Dickens's circle. A good friend of Lord Shaftesbury. Author *Lives of the Statesmen of the Commonwealth*, 5 vols, 1836–39; *Life and Adventures of Oliver Goldsmith*, 1848; *Life of Charles Dickens*, 1872. Winslow recalled him as 'severe and blunt' but 'sympathetic'.

LAY COMMISSIONERS

Anthony Ashley Cooper, 7th Earl of Shaftesbury (1801–85). Educated Harrow and Christ Church, Oxford, BA 1823, MA 1832, DCL 1841. Styled Lord Ashley 1811–51. MP Woodstock 1826–30, Dorchester 1830–31, Dorset 1831–46. Commissioner of the Board of Control 1828–30. Lord of the Admiralty 1834–35. Metropolitan Lunacy Commissioner 1828–45. Ecclesiastical Commissioner 1841–47. MP Bath 1847–51. Chairman of the Ragged School Union 1843–82. Lord Lieutenant. Dorset 1856–85. Commissioner on the Board of Health 1848–54.

Edward Adolphus Seymour, 12th Duke of Somerset (1804–85). Educated Eton and Christ Church, Oxford. Styled Lord Seymour until his father's death in 1856. MP Okehampton 1830–31, Totnes 1834–55. Lord of the Treasury 1835–39. Secretary to the Board of Control 1839–41. First Commissioner of Woods and Forests (and *ex officio* President of the Board of Health, where he clashed with Shaftesbury) 1849–52. Metropolitan Lunacy Commissioner 1836–45. Lord Lieutenant. Devon. Author, *Christian Theology and Modern Scepticism*, 1872; *Monarchy and Democracy*, 1880.

Robert Gordon (1786–1864) Born Kirkcudbrightshire, Educated Christ Church, Oxford, BA 1808. MP Wareham 1812–18, Cricklade 1818–37, Windsor 1837–41. A committed Whig, known as the Dorsetshire Joseph Hume. Commissioner of the Board of Control 1832–33, secretary 1833–34 and 1835–39. Secretary to the Treasury 1839–41. Metropolitan Lunacy Commissioner 1828–45. Governor of St Luke's Hospital for the Insane and St George's Hospital.

Robert Vernon Smith, Baron Lyveden (1800–73). Educated Eton and Christ Church, Oxford, BA 1822. Student at I.T., but never called to the Bar. MP Tralee 1829–31, Northampton 1831–59. Jr. Treasury Minister 1830–34, Joint Secretary to the Board of Control 1835–39, Under-Secretary of State for War and Colonies 1839–41. President of the Board of Control 1855–58. Deputy Lieutenant Northampton. Metropolitan Lunacy Commissioner 1828–45.

Francis Barlow (1799–1887). Educated Trinity Hall, Cambridge, BA 1821, MA 1824. Barrister M.T. 1825, L.I. 1837. Also a Master in Lunacy under the Lord Chancellor. Appointed to liaise between the two offices. Honorary Lunacy Commissioner 1879–87.

Henry Morgan Clifford (1806–84). Educated Eton and Christ Church, Oxford. Chairman of the Hereford Quarter Sessions 1845. MP Hereford 1847–65. Colonel of the Monmouth Militia.

CHAPTER SEVEN

Casting out and bringing back in Victorian England: pauper lunatics, 1840–70

J.K. Walton

THE MIDDLE DECADES of the nineteenth century in England saw a great expansion of the county and borough asylum system for pauper lunatics. This had begun with the piecemeal, gradual and patchy adoption of an Act of 1808 empowering county justices to build and maintain asylums out of the county rates, and was extended by the Lunatic Asylums Act of 1845, which nominally made adequate specialized provision compulsory for this controversial sector of the deviant and disadvantaged. The rise of the county asylum was part of a more general trend towards the isolation of the dangerous, deviant, and socially incompetent in total institutions. This was also the age of the workhouse, the reformed prison, and the reformatory, all of which, not excepting the workhouse under the less-eligibility regime, sought not merely to contain, repress, and quarantine undesirables, but also professed to aim at their rehabilitation, their resocialization into an acceptable, responsible, disciplined mode of existence.[1] But why this concentration on expensive institutional solutions to problems which were not essentially new, especially at a time when ratepayer and taxpayer resistance to increased public expenditure was deep-rooted, vituperative, and often crippling? This question is especially problematical when we look specifically at pauper lunatic asylums, which were conspicuously expensive institutions, especially when compared with the workhouses and more informal means of confinement and control which constituted the main alternatives, though not, it seems, when compared with the private asylums which were beginning to specialize in pauper lunatics.[2]

Any explanation must take account of several elements. It must embrace the contemporary perception of growing problems of social disorder and cultural conflict, not necessarily in an urban or industrial setting, which encouraged expenditure on institutional solutions with pretensions to re-education as well as repression. Alongside this 'social control' perspective, it must also take on board a humanitarian concern for the protection, against visible abuses, of people who were coming to be seen as curable sufferers whose condition was not their fault. These perspectives were merged and blurred by the convergence of medical and moral definitions of mental disorder, as the range of behaviour definable as 'insane' was extended by the adoption of such nebulous concepts as 'moral insanity', propagated by the empire-building architects of the new profession of psychiatry. Indeed, the rise of the psychiatric profession is itself an important explanatory variable, as its proponents pushed along the tides of humanitarian concern and the imperatives of custodial control, and as their elastic definitions of insanity helped to create an appearance of alarming growth in the incidence of mental disorder, impelling local and national government towards urgent action. The new psychiatrists made asylum-building seem all the more attractive by their promise of large numbers of cures, if only they were given adequate levels of investment in the right sort of premises. The economically derelict could, it seemed, be turned back into orderly and productive citizens under a wholesome and humane regime of 'moral treatment' in a properly appointed, therapeutic asylum.[3]

The medicalization of lunacy also helped to remove barriers to funding by making it easier for local authorities to accept the suspension of the principle of less-eligibility for paupers whose indigence was seen to arise from a distressing form of illness which was no fault of their own. But such perceptions were very far from being universal in this period. Boards of guardians often complained about the luxurious conditions in which their pauper lunatics were maintained, at extra cost to the ratepayers. But in this respect county asylums usually had a great advantage over workhouses. Their funding was organized not through bodies elected by local ratepayers, like the boards of guardians and local boards of health whose purse-strings were tightly controlled by parsimonious farmers, shopkeepers, and tradesmen, but through justices of the peace who were nominated by central government (subject to the consensual approval of the leading county gentry) and were therefore less vulnerable to pressure from those who paid for their policies.[4] Justices, indeed, were usually drawn from a wealthy and well-educated class whose members were particularly receptive to reputable-looking medical opinion and advice, although they were not averse to treading on asylum superintendents' toes in autocratic supervision of established asylums. Asylum expenditure, along with police and prisons, was one of the main sources of complaint brought forward by objectors to the traditional system of county government at mid-century.[5] So asylums were cushioned by their funding system against the ratepayers' reactions which consistently held back public health and other improvements in early and mid-Victorian towns, for example.[6] A further important aspect of the medical model of insanity was that a widening range of problematic behaviour and circumstances could be blamed on the medical problems of individuals rather than the deficiencies of society at large: a mode of explanation which was conveniently compatible with *laissez-faire* principles, and posed no challenge to the existing economic order.[7] The efforts made by asylum superintendents in the 1840s to correlate environmental conditions with insanity might have disturbed this cosy state of affairs, but these were soon abandoned as impracticable.[8] Despite their comparative advantages, even the county asylums needed all the help they could get from central government in pursuit of what their national inspectorate, the Lunacy Commissioners as established under the 1845 Act, regarded as minimum standards of staffing and amenities.[9]

Despite the importance of the medical interpretation of insanity, and the associated efforts of humanitarian reformers for whom religious considerations often bulked large, the scales were tipped in favour of the asylum builders by the fact that insanity was visibly a threat to life and property: a problem of law and order. Without this dimension the insane poor would probably have been left, like the sick poor generally, to the workhouse infirmary and the occasional charitable foundation. Indeed, many lunatics were kept in the workhouse, in spite of legislation to the contrary, simply because it was cheaper than the asylum. The widespread opposition among Poor Law guardians after 1845 to paying expensive asylum maintenance charges for lunatics who were deemed harmless is indicative of the importance of the custodial aspect of asylum provision in conciliating public opinion, or at least ratepayer opinion. The rise of the 'non-restraint' system in pauper asylums in the 1840s and early 1850s may seem to contradict this emphasis on the custodial, but we should remember that attendants and nurses at Lancaster Asylum, and no doubt elsewhere, faced severe financial penalties if patients escaped from their custody.[10] Moral treatment, and even 'non-restraint', had to be backed by sanctions and strict vigilance if it was to survive.

The county asylum was, then, part of an increasingly wide-ranging, if ramshackle, unco-ordinated and often ineffective network of formal and informal institutions for the restraint and modification of behaviour which appeared to threaten property, propriety, religion, order, and the constitution. Its acceptability to taxpayers, ratepayers and county elites was greatly assisted by its associations with public order and the security of life and property. It was less controversial than other initiatives for public order and 'social control', such as police reform, education, church-building, the temperance movement, and the campaigns for 'rational recreations' and against cruel sports, because it did not become identified with existing fault-lines of conflict in the wider society, and because it did not offend substantial established vested interests. Controversies over 'wrongful confinement' or criminal responsibility were sometimes embarrassing, especially when psychiatrists contradicted each other or made outrageous statements during court hearings, but the parade of scientific detachment, objectivity, and humanitarianism deployed by the advocates of the reformed asylum system was generally disarming.[11] The asylum advocates' claim to offer cures in generous measure, especially if patients were admitted early, was a further useful weapon, even though it was soon falsified, or at least undermined, by the asylum superintendents' own statistics.

The 'social control' dimension is clearly very important to our understanding of the rise of the pauper asylum system. As F.M.L. Thompson and others have reminded us, there is more to 'social control' than mere coercion, a point which has always been central to those historians who have taken the Marxist route to this polymorphous concept by way of Gramsci and bourgeois hegemony. 'Social control', in the sense in which most historians now use the phrase, is about the attempted recasting of values and attitudes in an approved framework imposed or provided from above.[12] This certainly went on within the asylum walls, where the role of 'moral treatment' was to resocialize the patient into behaviour patterns acceptable to those in authority, while making his or her presence tolerable to family and neighbours. These concerns overlapped but were not necessarily congruent. But how far did the asylum become acceptable to the working-class community at large? Did it succeed in legitimizing itself as a humane and therapeutic institution, or was it viewed, like the workhouse, as an instrument of repression, a place to be shunned and hated?[13] An answer to this question would help us to evaluate the asylum's success at influencing values and expectations in the wider society.

Andrew Scull believes that the asylum did become an acceptable place for working-class families to send relatives whose anti-social behaviour was very difficult to cope with in the confined space of the working-class home, under circumstances where there were many claims on the financial, physical, and emotional resources of their relatives and neighbours. He emphasizes the pressure to maximize income associated with the increasing penetration of the market economy, and he suggests that the separation of home and workplace also made it increasingly difficult to organize the domestic care of the insane. He argues that the continuing growth in demand for asylum places, and the concomitant rise in the recorded insanity rate in nineteenth-century England, were fuelled to a significant extent by the increasing willingness of families to consign aged, incompetent, or otherwise burdensome relatives to asylums, as the successful propaganda of the reformers reduced or removed the stigma attached to such an apparent abandonment of the obligations of kinship.[14] I am sceptical about aspects of this interpretation. It is easy to exaggerate the extent of the separation of home and workplace in the mid-nineteenth century, and the family seems to have been remarkably resilient in the face of economic change and migration, except perhaps in parts of the largest cities.[15] Moreover, the aged, at least, did not bulk large in asylum admissions, and the median age of arrivals in the asylum at Lancaster, Wakefield, and no doubt elsewhere, remained in the high thirties during the 1850s and 1860s.[16] More important, this discussion leads us into an issue of central importance to the role of the pauper asylum in early and mid-Victorian society. Scull does not really address the question of how working-class people came to be defined or labelled as insane, and as fit candidates for asylum admission.[17] Who performed this exercise in casting out? Was it, in the first instance, the patient's hard-pressed relatives and neighbours? Or did the initiative come from those in authority, selecting people who visibly posed problems of regulation, order, and control and consigning them to the safe custody and re-educative influences of the asylum? Was the casting out of pauper lunatics a desperate grass-roots response to practical problems on a novel scale by working-class families themselves, or was it an exercise in social engineering by magistrates, Poor Law officials and medical men? These questions cannot, of course, be answered straightforwardly in terms of such a simple dichotomy: examples can be found in support of either contention, and both sets of influences no doubt interacted in many cases. It may well prove impossible, from the unsatisfactory evidence available in registers and case-notes, to assemble a convincing quantified profile of the social and administrative background to asylum admissions. But the issue merits further exploration.

Before we take this further, we must remember that the asylum was not the only way of casting out those whom Scull calls 'inconvenient people'. It was only the most specialized, expensive, and complicated of a range of options, though its importance was steadily being extended during the middle decades of the nineteenth century. Working-class families and neighbourhoods often did their own casting out in informal ways, and the significant number of asylum admissions who were picked up as vagrants must often have been on the road as a result of some such process, though an element of choice must also often have entered the equation. Working-class families – and people higher up the social scale – also sometimes preferred to cast out their mad relatives domestically, consigning them to outhouses, cellars, or locked rooms where they were hidden from neighbours and authorities alike, often in squalid and humiliating conditions. The Lunacy Commissioners were well aware of this practice, and after new legislation in 1862 strengthened their powers, they inaugurated a series of prosecutions for the cruel treatment of lunatics kept singly in private premises.[18] But the cases that came to court were the tip of a substantial iceberg. The domestic confinement of lunatics was particularly likely to arise where families had a breadwinner in regular work and a reasonable standard of living – 'the self-supporting classes', those 'in the middle ranks of life, or who are poor, but not paupers', as the commissioners put it in 1864.[19] In such cases the relatives were expected by the Poor Law authorities to pay all or part of the asylum costs themselves, and many preferred their own cheap, informal solutions, with all the abuses this might entail. In other cases, no doubt, families and neighbours might conspire to supervise and protect people whose problems were mild enough not to pose a threat, but sharply defined enough to lead those in authority to regard them as insane if they came to their attention. Many people who might have been labelled as lunatics must have been kept out of institutions in such ways, and because of this they remain largely hidden from history.[20]

Many other potential lunatics, and a substantial proportion of those who were actually certified insane, were retained in the hands of the Poor Law authorities without reaching the asylum. The Lunacy Commissioners report cases of relieving officers refusing to offer more than a small measure of outdoor relief to families attempting to cope with violently irrational or severely subnormal members.[21] More common was the practice whereby a relieving officer would dispatch an apparent lunatic to the workhouse in the first instance, and pass him or her on to the asylum only if the workhouse authorities specifically requested it. Such attempts to maintain the insane at a cheaper level of purely custodial care were made illegal by legislation in 1853 and 1862, but the commissioners were constantly coming across examples of this kind of administrative abuse.[22] Only the violent and intractable, those who were disruptive of workhouse routine and difficult to handle, were likely to be passed on to the asylum, unless external pressure was brought to bear.

Of the 44,695 lunatics known to the authorities in 1864, just under half were in county and borough asylums. Most of the rest were in workhouses, but 5,523 were with relatives, and 1,018 were 'boarded out or in lodgings'.[23] So the asylum was only part of the story, and we must broaden the focus to bear in mind the large number of lunatics who never experienced the controversial benefits of asylum treatment. But the question we posed earlier remains important, and it is best documented in asylum sources, though nowhere, as far as I know, in a really satisfactory way. Who stuck the label 'pauper lunatic' on an individual? To what extent did the initiative come from those in authority, from workhouse masters, police, justices of the peace, medical practitioners, employers? To what extent did it come from the lunatics' own families, in response to behaviour that was so intolerable that it overrode the usual antipathy to the Poor Law system in general and the workhouse, through which most lunatics passed, in particular?[24]

The short answer is that we do not know. We can identify a range of influences and possibilities, but we cannot yet quantify a pattern. The basic administrative procedure is clear enough. A deposition had to be sworn before two JPs to the effect that the individual in question was 'a Lunatic or Insane person'. Usually, no doubt, this was initiated by the overseers of the parish or township, who then had to bring the candidate along for examination by the JPs, after which, if satisfied that he or she was mad and chargeable to the parish in question, the JPs caused a 'medical person' to conduct a further examination. If all were agreed, a certificate of lunacy was duly signed, and the new patient was supposed to be conveyed to the asylum.[25] But we cannot reconstruct the circumstances leading up to the involvement of the officials in any regular or systematic way. We do not usually know what social processes lay behind the initiation of the administrative procedures. Sometimes the route to the asylum is traceable back to the workhouse, the prison or the magistrates' court, and often, as D.J. Mellett suggests, 'the first link in the chain of decision making remained the relieving officer', who could decide to 'transmit an insane pauper to the workhouse', from which the asylum might be the next step; but even this is only part of the story.[26] We can take matters a little further by looking at some evidence from Lancaster Asylum.

Some asylum admissions clearly did originate with people in authority, anxious to dispose of the difficult and dissolute. Workhouses, especially, sent their quota of the hard-to-manage, many of whom might not have been regarded as insane on initial admission; although the Lunacy Commissioners were complaining in 1866 and 1867 that excited or uncontrollable work-house lunatics were being disciplined by spells in prison instead of being referred to the care of the asylum.[27] The courts also brought the attention of JPs to bear on habitual drunkards and petty offenders, and one route to the asylum was that taken by a Wigan man in 1871, when the chief constable remarked that he had been in prison forty-six times for disorderly conduct in the street, and 'this morning when in the dock he made faces at the bench'. He was duly dispatched to Lancaster Asylum.[28] Vagrants, too, were often passed on to asylums through the courts, and of course there was the numerically small but controversial and difficult category of criminal lunatics as such, 'homicidal maniacs' and the like. But it is difficult to show, despite the vagrants and the occasional prostitute, and a disproportionate representation of unskilled labourers and domestic servants among asylum admissions, that the asylum population was dominated by a subculture of the disorderly poor, chosen for the threat they posed to property, decorum, and the social order.[29] There might be an element of deliberate coercion or repression of perceived anti-social attitudes, but it was one influence among many.

Any such repression did not extend to the systematic persecution of political or religious deviants, although political or religious delusions, and delusions about property, are frequently noted by asylum officials. We cannot recreate the context or nature of these utterances, however, and it is highly likely that they were usually, if not always, the garbled and distorted products of more generally disordered minds. Admissions deemed to be politically related form a very thin trickle from the early 1820s through to the 1870s. In 1821 Henry Whittaker 'appears to have been deranged by the constant, petty vexations together with great violence attempted, and partly effected on his person by several radicals who were his fellow workmen in a manufactory', so here our causal mechanisms are inverted; but in the early 1840s we find odd cases ascribed to '*politics*' and to excitement occasioned by attending a meeting of the Anti-Corn Law League, and in 1843 we have the interesting case of a former grocer whose religious persuasion was described as 'freethinker' and his habit of life as 'eccentric', while his insanity was said to have shown itself by 'peculiarity of conduct and eccentricity of manner'.[30] This is a classic example of the problems of interpreting sources of this kind. Read one way, this is a straightforward account of symptoms, if couched in value-laden and decidedly unclinical language. Read another way, it looks like the persecution of a man whose attitudes and beliefs were unacceptable to neighbours and authorities. The 'correct' reading, if such a thing exists, can almost certainly never be recovered. But more striking still is the case of Emma Blackburn, a 19-year-old rover in a cotton mill, who was admitted to the asylum in 1871 after five months' confinement in

Haslingden workhouse. The cause of her insanity was said to be 'political excitement', and the comments on her case after a month in the asylum are particularly interesting:

> A fine healthy looking young woman, well nourished and of robust frame. Since admission has continued to shout and cry at intervals. Her countenance and eyes are much suffused. She does not occupy herself in any way and is occasionally quarrelsome. Frequently will not respond to questions put to her. Takes her food well but is restless at night.

All this seems entirely consistent with a horrified response to wrongful confinement; and the patient steadily declined thereafter, losing weight, being dosed with morphia, chloral, bromide, and chloroform, and being given a punitive shower bath after cursing and swearing at the attendants in 1875. Two years later she died of peritonitis.[31] This looks a very suspicious case, and one wonders whether other patients with similar 'symptoms' continued to languish in workhouses without coming to the attention of the asylum authorities. Indeed, in 1870 the commissioners found two women in Blackburn workhouse, confined as lunatics without proper certification and paid for by relatives. In one case a husband paid 10s per week to keep his wife on pauper fare; and 'the second case was that of a girl who had been dissipated and disobedient to her parents, who sent her to the workhouse as a lunatic, and paid for her maintenance. In this case, also, there seemed no proof of her being of unsound mind'.[32] The commissioners found all this very objectionable; and although these three examples were isolated cases, and additional evidence might show them in a different light if it were available, the implications are disquieting. The concept of 'moral insanity' could provide particularly potent ammunition against an indiscreet, passionate, or assertive woman in the heyday of the double standard.[33]

To return to the point about the relationship between political dissent and asylum admissions, it should be stressed that even Lancaster Asylum, large and close to centres of unrest as it was, generated no more than a handful of suspicious-looking cases in the sample years I have studied, and Michael Shepherd's Birmingham investigations seem to have yielded no examples at all.[34] After all, why bother to use the complicated and controversial machinery of certification for insanity when, as the events of 1839–42 made abundantly clear, straightforward physical and legal coercion could do the job of repression admirably without compromising the appearance of ruling-class legitimacy?[35] In any case, the roots of most asylum committals clearly lay in domestic troubles, as families at the end of their tether sought succour even though it meant the Poor Law and the asylum. The typical case was very far removed from Emma Blackburn or James Malone, for whom the admissions register entry read, 'Cause of insanity: *politics*'.[36] It was nearer to the experience of Eliza Hartley's family, who told the relieving officer that she was 'constantly rambling about the house and removing furniture, and bringing it downstairs as if the family were going to remove. Constantly blowing kisses to everyone she meets.'[37] A more severe level of stress is epitomized by a case from Staffordshire in which 'the Lunatic was constantly attacking his mother, as well as his brothers and sisters'. The mother, too, was eventually certified insane.[38] The invocation of the asylum brought relief from impossible circumstances to many families, and at this stage and under these conditions its availability and use became an unalloyed benefit, not least to those patients who were rescued from squalid confinement in locked rooms and filthy workhouse wards. The Lunacy Commissioners may have been professional empire-builders who sometimes indulged in special pleading, but in this respect at least their opinions carry conviction. Scull, too, is probably right about the growing acceptability of the asylum for desperate working-class families, but the evidence is more problematic than he allows, and the causal mechanisms he suggests are sometimes simplistic and out of line with empirical evidence and recent historiography.

The analysis of case-registers may provide some clues as to the kinds of behaviour families found intolerable and those in authority frowned upon: categories which remain analytically impossible to separate in studying the vast majority of asylum admissions. A small experimental sample from the medical registers of Lancaster Asylum for 1842–43, which provide the asylum authorities' perceptions of patients' 'habits of life', the 'exciting cause' of their insanity, and their 'particular propensities and hallucinations', offers interesting food for thought.[39] This source is at two (or more) removes from the start of the process of defining an individual as insane. The asylum officials' comments on new admissions give us what they chose to retain from the evidence sent in from the localities, which in turn must have been variable in reliability, outlook, and depth of knowledge. The officials' selection of material for inclusion in the registers was itself coloured by their own preconceptions and by their initial impressions of the patient. But a sample of 400 admissions, evenly divided between the sexes and between the years 1842 and 1843, produced the results shown in *Table 7.1*.

It would be dangerous to read too much into these figures, but this approach may point a way forward towards a wider understanding of the stresses and modes of behaviour which contemporaries saw as having a causal relationship with insanity, or which helped families and authority figures to decide to cast people out into custodial (and, it was hoped, curative) care. Drink and violence (especially intra-familial violence, usually of husbands towards wives, or involving a wife's rejection of her husband), bulk largest in the table, along with the threat of suicide, which was at once crime, sin, and evidence of derangement in contemporary eyes. Drink and sexual misdemeanour (included in category 3 of *Table 7.1*) are more in evidence among men than women, perhaps surprisingly in the light of contemporary attitudes; and among women the patriarchal family and the behavioural expectations which surrounded it were probably more important than the figures suggest. Physical debility was noted in only a small minority of cases, even in the economically depressed year of 1842, although the stresses of unemployment and the poverty cycle are regularly mentioned in the registers as contributory factors, and must have reduced families' ability to cope with, and to survive without, psychologically ailing members. Many female patients were discharged from Lancaster Asylum 'not improved', at the request of husbands who were presumably desperate for whatever help and comfort they could get; and this is itself an eloquent commentary on the problems faced by the families of pauper lunatics.[40]

The most misleading aspect of *Table 7.1*, and of the source on which it is based, is probably the lack of weight given to passive depression and withdrawal, which tends to attract a diagnosis of 'melancholia' in the register, and little other comment. When this neglected form of quiescent desperation is added to the violence, delusions, and bizarre behaviour that lie behind the categories analysed in the table, it becomes apparent that the asylum was not resorted to lightly by families and Poor Law authorities. It was the final resource when all else had failed, in the vast majority of cases; and most of those who were admitted and remained within its walls were not so much 'inconvenient people', in Scull's terminology, as impossible people in the eyes of families, neighbours, and authorities. Attitudes may have changed in late Victorian times, but in the middle decades of the nineteenth century the county asylum provided relief for desperate families rather than an easy option for the uncaring or irresponsible.[41]

I have examined the problems involved in trying to understand the process of 'casting out' pauper lunatics at some length. There is less to say about 'bringing back' in this context, largely because there was so little of it. The percentage of patients discharged 'cured' at Lancaster Asylum, calculated on the average number resident during the year in question, fell from 23.5 in 1837 to 13.4 in 1841, and after a short recovery it bottomed out again successively at 7.1 in 1847, 4.9 in 1852 and 4.6 in 1860 before making a

Table 7.1　*Aspects of behaviour of patients admitted to Lancaster Asylum, 1842–43, as recorded in the medical registers*

characteristics of admissions	men	women	all
	%	%	%
1　violence or threat of violence	22.5	17.0	19.75
2　suicidal	12.5	14.5	13.5
3　'intemperance', 'irregularity', 'dissipation', etc.	24.0	12.0	18.0
4　religious delusions	6.0	5.0	5.5
5　problems involving family and sexual relationships	2.5	11.5	7.0
6　physical feebleness	2.5	5.5	4.0

Note: These are minimum figures: many entries provide little or no information, especially when patients were picked up as vagrants. On the other hand, several individuals appear in the table under more than one heading.

modest recovery for the rest of the decade.[42] After 1850 the figure never again reached 10 per cent, and the death rate was almost always higher than the cures. Lancaster was not exceptional. In 1867, according to the superintendents, the county and borough asylums and registered hospitals of England and Wales held 2,491 patients who were 'probably curable', and 22,257 who were 'probably incurable'.[43] The asylum superintendents had given up hope for about 90 per cent of their patients; and the ratio in the workhouses must have been much worse. An expensive system had promised cures, and failed to deliver; and if Lancaster is at all representative, most of the successes were alcoholics who had dried out, exhausted half-starved over-worked women who recovered after a few weeks of limited exertion and reasonable diet, and cases of post-natal depression.

This was a disastrous failure for the moral treatment system, which had begun with confident claims about the prospect of socializing the deviant, dissolute, and depressed into sober, hard-working citizens. The failure was partly due to limited resources, unsuitable patients, and the rapid growth in asylum size; but the psychiatrists' claims were extravagant from the beginning, and when the capable, sympathetic staff and favourable staff/patient ratios they needed were not forthcoming, the embryo psychiatrists had nothing to put in their place until the empirical study of the brain brought new claims to understanding and cure in the later nineteenth century. Attempts to reclaim patients as useful members of society through steady work in appropriate jobs increased the efficiency of the asylum as a unit of production, but it was easier to get inmates to contribute to the smooth running of the asylum than to decant them into the outside world. A patient like Mary Ann Cooke might graduate over time from being withdrawn and incontinent to potato-peeling, and ultimately to scrubbing and flock-picking in the gallery, but this kind of success was contingent on an adaptation to asylum routine that amounted to institutionalization.[44] Most of the patients who were discharged 'cured' were out within a few months, and it became a rare event for someone to be 'cured' after five years or more in the asylum.[45] Long-term chronics increasingly predominated.

Not only did the asylum regime encourage regular and disciplined habits at the cost of growing dependence on its machinery of support and coercion; it was also very difficult, in practical terms, for inmates to be reintegrated into the outside world, even if supportive families awaited them. Jobs were likely to be hard to come by, accommodation might be hard to find, and pauper lunatics ceased to be entitled to relief on leaving the asylum. As these problems of adjustment became apparent, widespread attempts were made to mitigate them during the 1860s. In 1862 Gloucester Asylum began to allow selected patients leave of absence to visit family or friends for the day or even, occasionally, a few days, and the scheme was warmly endorsed by the Lunacy Commissioners.[46] Despite this enthusiasm, other asylums seem to have been slow and very cautious in following up the idea; but this judgement is based on the annual reports of the commissioners, and it may be that schemes were started unobtrusively elsewhere, and were not picked up by the commissioners after their early enthusiasm had passed. At Lancaster, the visiting justices' minutes record in 1864 that Joseph Walmsley was being given several weeks' leave of absence, with an allowance from the asylum of 5s per week; and in December he was discharged. In 1865 a female patient was similarly treated; and two years later another basic practical problem was solved for George Blake, who was loaned £1 to pay the fare of himself and two sons home to Whitehaven on his discharge. By this time the allowance paid to convalescent patients had gone up to 8s. 2d.[47] It is hard to say whether the handful of patients mentioned in these minutes were the only beneficiaries of these policies, or whether they were being applied more generally, but usually without comment. But the necessity for such assistance, and the slow and gradual way in which it began to be offered, illustrate the way in which the administrative inertia of the asylum system developed a built-in bias against cures and discharges, especially when patients' families and friends were less than eager to have them back. Poor Law penny-pinching and concern for custodial control combined to make a gentle assimilation into the outside world almost impossible: patients had to be released suddenly and without resources, into a harsh and unfriendly world. No wonder many of them reappeared, an aspect of the asylum system which, like so many others, needs further research.

The definition and treatment of pauper lunatics raises difficult issues, conceptually and in terms of the interpretation of the abundant but ultimately frustrating evidence. It is worth taking a few concluding sentences to clarify my own position. I would argue that the pauper asylum system justified its rapid expansion and high funding levels by a potent mixture of coercive and humanitarian attributes, among which the claims of moral treatment to provide plentiful cures through exposure to a regime of industrious discipline and virtue bulked large. It was at this point that the asylum system approximated most closely to a master plan for winning the assent of deviants to the social system by encouraging the internalization of appropriate value systems; and it was at this crucial dimension of 'social control' that the asylum failed most abjectly, except in terms of integrating patients into their own separate and peculiar worlds, from which escape thereafter became all the more difficult. In terms of the wider society, it was much easier to be 'cast out' as a pauper lunatic than to be reclaimed, although the actual mechanism of 'casting out', with its important implications for the workings of early and mid-Victorian society, remains tantalizingly difficult to unravel. In policy terms, asylums were intended, on balance, to be reformatories first, refuges second, and motives of public safety and 'social control' predominated over humanitarian aims; but in practice, and with all the faults of these problematical institutions, it was the humanitarian goals that were, in a limited but significant way, more effectively met.[48]

Notes

This paper was presented to the Victorian Studies conference on "Casting out and bringing back in Victorian England" at the University of Leicester, September 1982. My thanks go to Robert Colls for devising such a stimulating theme, and to the participants for their critical comments and suggestions.

1 A. Scull, *Museums of Madness* (London: Allen Lane, 1979); M.A. Crowther, *The Workhouse System 1834–1929* (London: Batsford, 1981); M. Ignatieff, *A Just Measure of Pain* (London: Macmillan, 1978).

2 Parliamentary Papers (PP) 1844, XL, p. 191.

3 Scull, *Museums of Madness*, ch. 3; D.J. Mellett, *The Prerogative of Asylumdom* (New York and London: Garland, 1982), pp. 9–10 and ch. 4.

4 But for an alternative perspective see D.J. Mellett, 'Society, the State and Mental Illness 1790–1890' (Ph.D. thesis, University of Cambridge, 1978), p. 48.

5 D. Gregory, 'Rates and Representation: Lancashire County in the Nineteenth Century', *Northern History* 12 (1976): 158–71; PP 1850, XIII, Select Committee on County Rates, minutes of evidence; C.H.E. Zangerl, 'The Social Composition of the County Magistracy in England and Wales 1831–87', *Journal of British Studies* 11 (1971): 113–25.

6 See especially E.P. Hennock, *Fit and Proper Persons* (London: Edward Arnold, 1973).

7 D. Ingleby, 'Mental Health and Social Order', in S. Cohen and A.T. Scull (eds), *Social Control and the State* (Oxford: Martin Robertson, 1983), p. 163, remarks that, 'The great value of medical knowledge as a basis for maintaining social order is that it can be used to regulate morality without seeming to do anything of the sort': an important related point.

8 M.A. Shepherd, 'Lunacy and Labour', *Bulletin of the Society for the Study of Labour History* 34 (1977): p. 64.

9 Scull, *Museums of Madness*, ch. 3; and the essay by Nicholas Hervey in this volume.

10 Lancashire Record Office (LRO) QAM.5/42 Rule 12.

11 P. McCandless, 'Liberty and Lunacy: The Victorians and Wrongful Confinement', *Journal of Social History* 11 (1977–78): 366–86; Roger Smith, *Trial by Medicine* (Edinburgh: Edinburgh University Press, 1981); Scull, *Museums of Madness*, ch. 4.

12 F.M.L. Thompson, 'Social Control in Victorian Britain', *Economic History Review* 34 (1981): 189–208; A.P. Donajgrodzki (ed.), *Social Control in Nineteenth-Century Britain* (London: Croom Helm, 1977), esp. pp. 9–26; Cohen and Scull, *Social Control*, pp. 1–49, 106–17.

13 But for a gloss on this comment see Crowther, *Workhouse System*, ch. 9; for a private asylum, cf. Anne Digby, 'Moral Treatment at the Retreat, 1796–1846,' in this volume.

14 Scull, *Museums of Madness*, ch. 7; and for a different emphasis Mellett, 'Mental Illness', p. 34.

15 M. Anderson, *Family Structure in Nineteenth-Century Lancashire* (Cambridge: Cambridge University Press, 1971), and especially 'Smelser Revisited', *Social History* 1 (1976), pp. 317–34.

16 J. Walton, 'The Treatment of Pauper Lunatics in Victorian England: The Case of Lancaster Asylum, 1816–70', in A. Scull (ed.), *Madhouses, Mad-doctors and Madmen: The Social History of Psychiatry in the Victorian Era* (Philadelphia, Pa.:

University of Pennsylvania Press, and London: Athlone Press, 1981), pp. 188–89; and information on Wakefield from Richard Russell, University of Sheffield.

17 For some comments on this theme see M. Ignatieff, 'Total Institutions and Working Classes: A Review Essay', *History Workshop Journal* 15 (1983): 169–72; and compare Mellett, 'Mental Illness', p. 21.

18 PP 1864, XXIII, Eighteenth Report of the Commissioners in Lunacy, p. 79. There are sometimes echoes here of the idea of the madman as beast, which no doubt survived tenaciously in popular consciousness alongside other stereotypes of the mad: compare M. Foucault, *Madness and Civilization* (London: Tavistock, 1971), ch. 3; Mellett, *Prerogative of Asylumdom*, ch. 5.

19 PP 1864, XXIII, Eighteenth Report p. 89; S.M. Gaskell, 'On the Want of Better Provision for the Labouring and Middle Classes When Attacked or Threatened with Lunacy', *Journal of Mental Science* 6 (1860): 321–27.

20 J.K. Walton, 'Lunacy in the Industrial Revolution: A Study of Asylum Admissions in Lancashire, 1848–50', *Journal of Social History* 13 (1979–80): 13–18.

21 PP 1864, XXIII, Eighteenth Report, p. 80; 1865 XXI, Nineteenth Report, pp. 47–8.

22 PP 1864, XXIII, Eighteenth Report, p. 79; 1865 XXI, Nineteenth Report, p. 43.

23 PP 1864 XXIII, Eighteenth Report, p. 108.

24 For some comments on this theme see Mellett, *Prerogative of Asylumdom*, pp. 8–9.

25 LRO QAM.1/36 Committal Warrants.

26 Mellett, *Prerogative of Asylumdom*, p. 136.

27 PP 1866, XXXII, Twentieth Report, pp. 20–1; 1867 XVIII, Twenty-first Report, p. 232.

28 LRO HRL.2/5 Case of David Green.

29 Walton, 'Pauper Lunatics', p. 189.

30 LRO QAM.1/30/19 Admission No. 3942, July, 1843.

31 LRO HRL.3/4 Case of Emma Blackburn.

32 PP 1871, XXV, Twenty-fifth Report, p. 77.

33 See E. Showalter, 'Victorian Women and Insanity', in Scull, *Madhouses*, pp. 313–36.

34 Shepherd, 'Lunacy and Labour', p. 65.

35 See especially C. Godfrey, 'The Chartist Prisoners 1839–41', *International Review of Social History* 24 (1979): 189–236.

36 LRO QAM.1/30/15. Italics in original. For another interesting case, in 1843, see QAM.1/30/19 Admission No. 4027: a block maker from Lancaster, religion 'socialist', intellect 'superior', exciting cause of insanity 'disappointment', 'insanity showed itself by painful emotions, false perceptions, &c.'. This is a further case with disquieting possibilities, but perhaps it is all too easy for another Lancaster socialist to build up a misleading empathy with this inmate, in the aftermath of the 1983 General Election.

37 LRO HRL.3/4 Case of Eliza Hartley.

38 PP 1865, XXI, Nineteenth Report, p. 44.

39 This sample consists of two blocks of consecutive admissions, each of 100 men and 100 women, taken from LRO QAM.1/30/19, beginning at Admission No. 3643 in 1842 and No. 3918 in 1843.

40 See also Mellett, *Prerogative of Asylumdom*, pp. 76–80.

41 Compare A. Scull, 'A Convenient Place to Get Rid of Inconvenient People: The

Victorian Lunatic Asylum', in A.D. King (ed.), *Buildings and Society* (London: Routledge and Kegan Paul, 1980), pp. 37–60.

42 LRO QAM.5/19 table IV, facing p. 22.

43 PP 1867, XVIII, Twenty-first Report, p. 268.

44 LRO HRL.1/10 Case of Mary Ann Cooke.

45 Walton, 'Pauper Lunatics', p. 186.·

46 PP 1863, XX, Seventeenth Report, p. 465.

47 LRO QAM.1/38 from 1 November, 1864.

48 Scull's recent conclusions in this general area seem apposite and sensible: A. Scull, 'Humanitarianism or Control? Some Observations on the Historiography of Anglo-American Psychiatry', in Cohen and Scull, *Social Control*, pp. 118–40.

CHAPTER EIGHT

Social factors in the admission, discharge, and continuing stay of patients at Ticehurst Asylum, 1845–1917

Charlotte MacKenzie

BARRISTER H.B. WAS admitted to Ticehurst Asylum on 8 April, 1880. He had indecently assaulted two daughters of the medical man with whom he was lodged. His condition was described as 'more or less congenital', and he was said to have 'chiefly sinned in over-drinking and in unnatural lust for boys and small girls'. He disliked being confined, and when another patient commented to him during a game of billiards that: ' "We are two b—y lunatics" . . . Mr B. replied, "I don't mind being reminded of the fact, but it is hard lines to be shut up." ' He was discharged two years later, accompanied by an attendant. Before his discharge, when the proprietor of Ticehurst, Hayes Newington (1847–1917), 'asked why [Mr B.] would limit his choice of a mate to the ages outside 17 and 60', he replied cavalierly enough, 'that other people married within these ages and he always liked to be different to other people for the sake of originality.'[1]

As Hayes Newington wrote in a paper presented to a meeting of the Medico-Psychological Association on 9 November, 1886 'mere insanity' was not by itself a reason for admitting a patient, or for preventing their discharge.[2] In a recent article on 'Victorian Asylum Practice' Laurence Ray has suggested that emphasis by historians on the growth of institutionalization, and mid-Victorian concern over the accumulation of chronic cases in asylums, has obscured the high discharge rate and rapid turnover of patients in Victorian asylums.[3] In this paper, I hope to show that an analysis of admissions to Ticehurst Asylum between 1845 and 1915 suggests Ray's hypothesis may be equally true of patients in the private sector.

Opened in 1792 by Ticehurst's village surgeon and apothecary, Samuel Newington (1739–1811), Ticehurst Asylum was managed by the Newington family through four generations until 1917. Situated in the Weald of Sussex near the Kent border, Ticehurst was well-placed to take patients from all over the home counties and London. Initially offering a range of charges and accommodation which included some pauper patients, from the outset higher-class patients were sought after and catered for. Early admissions included three patients referred by the Willis family who had attended King George III during his first illness (1788–89), and by the late 1820s paupers were no longer admitted, although no county asylum was opened in Sussex until 1859.[4]

Samuel Newington's son Charles (1781–1852), who was also qualified as a surgeon, extended and improved the facilities offered at Ticehurst, laying out and 'ornamenting' the grounds in 1816, and building a chapel for the asylum in 1831. In addition to the accommodation offered in the main building, Charles Newington received some patients into his own house, the Highlands.[5] By 1845, the main building accommodated up to fifty-nine patients, and the Highlands five, at an average cost in the main building of 3 guineas per week.[6] This rates Ticehurst as expensive compared with the range of 15s. to 2 guineas cited as typical by Parry-Jones (1972).[7] An analysis of the former occupations of patients resident on 31 July, 1845, as given on their admission papers, shows the vast majority (all twenty-seven women patients, and twenty-one men) to have been 'independent'. The others pursued middle-class careers: there were four clergymen, three merchants and manufacturers, three clerks, two army captains, one physician, one surgeon, and one student barrister.[8]

August 1845 provides a convenient point at which to take up the history of admissions and discharge at Ticehurst, since the passage of the 1845 Asylums Act (8 & 9 Vict. c. 100) made it statutory to keep admission and discharge books. In addition, it made the keeping of medical case-notes compulsory, and these provide details not only of the patient's condition prior to discharge, but of the history of the case prior to admission. Together with other biographical sources, and letters from patients and their relatives and friends which were sometimes kept with the case-notes, it becomes possible to build up a picture of the kind of behaviour likely to lead to confinement or discharge, as well as a more complete overview of the patients' psychiatric 'careers'.

Under the auspices of Charles Newington's two eldest sons, Charles Edmund Hayes Newington (1813–63) and Samuel Newington (1814–82), both of whom were qualified physicians, Ticehurst continued to prosper. Admissions rose steeply between 1845 and 1885 (see *Table 8.1*). Following Charles Edmund's death, his widow and children moved to Blackheath, and their former home the Vineyards was opened to female patients.[9] From the late 1860s, patients of both sexes began to spend some time by the sea at St Leonards, in two houses rented by the Newingtons. In 1872, seven new rooms for male patients were provided above a new entertainments hall. Another house for female patients, Quarry Villa, was opened in 1874.[10] By 31 July, 1875, the number of patients resident had risen to seventy-nine, a level around which it remained until 1917 (see *Table 8.2*).

When the patient population is taken in profile at any one time, the prognosis most patients and their relatives or friends could look forward to appears bleak. The median length of stay for patients resident in Ticehurst at

Table 8.1   *Admissions to Ticehurst, 1845–1915*

	men	*women*	*all admissions*
1845–55	26(6)	24	56
1855–65	40(3)	39(6)	88
1865–75	84(9)	56(15)	164
1875–85	74(12)	75(27)	188
1885–95	48(11)	41(7)	107
1895–1905	46(10)	50(9)	115
1905–15	56(8)	45(6)	115
total	374(59)	330(70)	833

Note: Figures for House and Highlands. Numbers in brackets indicate readmissions. Years run 1 August–31 July. The House and Highlands were separately licensed until 1852, after which both houses, and all later additions (the Vineyards, Quarry Villa, etc.), were licensed together.
Sources: Register of Admissions, 1845–81 and 1881–90; *Register of Patients,* 1890–1907; *Civil Register,* 1907–19.

Table 8.2   *Resident in Ticehurst, 1845–1915*

	men	*women*	*both*
1845	36	28	64
1855	36	22	58
1865	31	26	57
1875	44	35	79
1885	42	36	78
1895	39	37	76
1905	43	35	78
1915	41	38	79

Note: Figures for House and Highlands. Numbers counted 31 July for each year. The House and Highlands were separately licensed until 1852, after which both houses, and all later additions (the Vineyards, Quarry Villa, etc.), were licensed together.
Sources: Register of Admissions, 1845–81 and 1881–90; *Register of Patients,* 1890–1907: *Civil Register,* 1907–19; *Register of Removal, Discharges and Deaths,* 1845–90 and 1890–1908: *Register of Discharges and Transfers,* 1907–30; *Register of Deaths,* 1907–30.

any one time fluctuated around twenty-five years (see *Table 8.3*). Between 60 and 80 per cent of those resident could expect to die in Ticehurst, and only between 2 and 11 per cent could expect to be discharged recovered (see *Figure 8.1*). Statistics like these have led Andrew Scull to conclude that: 'the rich could buy greater attention and more eminent psychiatrists for their

Figure 8.1 Outcome of stay – profiles, 1845–1915
Outcome of stay for those resident in Ticehurst on 31 July of every
tenth year, represented as successively cumulated percentage. (Sources: see
Table 8.2.)

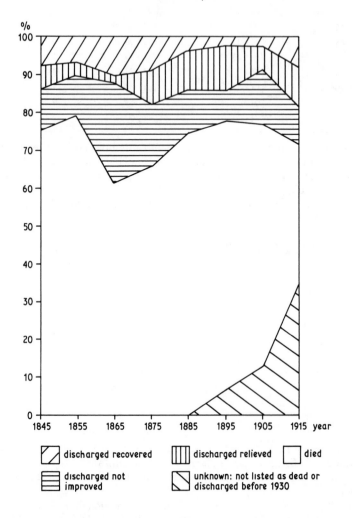

crazy relatives, but not more cures; so that for all the lavish expenditure of
funds, private asylums remained in Bucknill's words "institutions for private
imprisonment".'[11]

Looking instead at the outcome for patients grouped by date of admission, this picture is inverted. As at Brookwood and Lancaster (the two
asylums described by Ray), the median length of stay for patients admitted
between 1845 and 1915 was around one year (see *Table 8.4*).[12] Between 60
and 80 per cent of those admitted could expect to be discharged, although

Table 8.3   *Length of stay: profiles, 1845–1915*

	men	*women*	*both*
1845	29.6	24.2	27.8
1855	29.1	32.5	30.0
1865	28.3	14.2	23.75
1875	28.75	15.0	22.0
1885	30.8	23.1	26.5
1895	33.3	23.3	27.7
1905	27.0	27.0	27.0
1915	20.0	30.0	20.75

Note: Median length of stay *in years* for those resident in Ticehurst on 31 July of every tenth year.
Sources: See *Table 8.2*.

Table 8.4   *Length of stay: admissions, 1845–1915*

	men	*women*	*both*
1845–55	23.1	18.0	21.75
1855–65	22.0	12.0	13.6
1865–75	14.8	11.7	12.8
1875–85	8.25	5.9	6.9
1885–95	10.9	15.75	12.0
1895–1905	18.0	16.5	16.6
1905–15	16.2	11.5	13.6

Note: Median length of stay *in months* for all patients admitted to Ticehurst including readmissions. Years run 1 August–31 July.
Sources: See *Table 8.2*.

only between 16 and 39 per cent were actually 'recovered' (see *Figure 8.2*). Whilst this rate of recovery modifies Andrew Scull's assessment of the rate of 'cure' as 'abysmally low', more importantly the discharge of almost half of all admissions when they were not improved or recovered undermines the image of private Victorian asylums (like public ones) as dumping grounds for social misfits.[13] Only 26 per cent of those patients discharged as 'relieved' or 'not improved' between 1845 and 1915 remained under certificates and were immediately transferred to another asylum or to single medical care.[14]

This suggests that the attitude of the public to institutional solutions, and to the claims of the medical profession to new expertise in treating the insane, was pragmatic and sometimes incredulous. The picture which

Figure 8.2 Outcome of stay – admissions, 1845–1915
Outcome of stay for all admissions to Ticehurst between 1 August, 1845 and
31 July, 1915 (including readmissions) grouped in decades and represented
as successively cumulated percentages. (Sources: *see Table 8.1*.)

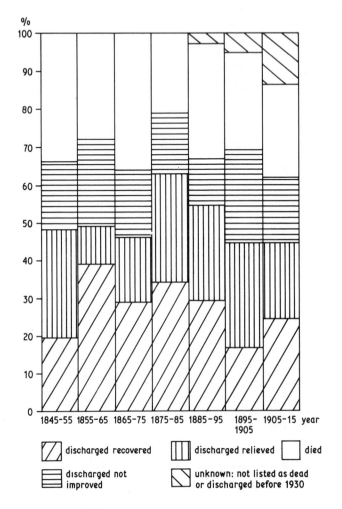

emerges from the Ticehurst records suggests that for upper and middle-class
Victorians the asylum was only one of a possible range of strategies to be
adopted when someone became disturbed, including travel abroad, single
confinement (not necessarily with a doctor), and treatment at home with a
nurse or attendant. In this paper, I hope to tease out some of the currents of
feeling and interest that informed individual decisions. Two case-histories
briefly illustrate some of the options available:

Washington Travers had already been a patient at Ticehurst once (from

September, 1854 to January, 1856) when he was placed in single confinement with a Revd Cawithen in Devon. After running away to his brother's in London, he went to where the Prince of Wales was bathing, laughed at him and called him names, and was returned to Ticehurst in July, 1858. He wandered off more than once from Ticehurst, and was allowed out several times on trial, spending the Christmases of 1858 and 1859 on the Isle of Man with a friend, and part of the summer of 1859 in Scotland with his cousin. In April, 1860, he left for Australia with an attendant, and travelled for about eight months, coming back via Shanghai and Japan. Shortly after his return he was discharged from his certificates, and returned to Australia, where he planned to stay five years.[15]

C.V. de V.B. (1870–1934) was described by the Hon. E. Lyttleton as solitary, eccentric, and difficult to influence when he was a pupil at Eton. After leaving school his physical health broke down, and he spent the winter of 1892–93 in New Zealand and Australia. In 1893, despite the opinion of a 'brain specialist' that he was mentally unfit because he believed his father and step-mother wanted to kill him, he was gazetted into the army. By 1896 he was badly in debt, and his father agreed to bail him out only on condition that he went to India as an aide-de-camp to Lord Elgin. He returned a year later with fever and dysentery, and publicly embarrassed his family by attempting to sue his father for the loss of his hair. Despite his increasingly eccentric behaviour – he became totally inactive, eating four or five helpings at each meal, and sleeping fourteen hours a night – it was only when he inherited his father's estate and title as a duke that his family decided to have him certified. He became a single patient with a Dr Douglas, before being admitted to Ticehurst in January, 1899, where he remained until his death in 1934.[16]

There is ample evidence from Victorian letters, diaries, and autobiographies that upper and middle-class families regarded the asylum as a place of last resort. Despite the impact of moral treatment and non-restraint on the ethos of asylums, the public image of (even private) asylums remained poor. After a visit to Lancaster prison in July, 1843, Catherine Winkworth (1827–78) noted in her journal that 'no sight can be more painful unless it be a lunatic asylum'. Her subsequent imaginative description of what asylums were like was edited out of the published journals by her sister Susanna (1820–84).[17] Such powerful fantasies must have made it difficult for Catherine to come to terms with her eldest brother Henry's confinement at Ticehurst two years later.[18]

Even personal inspection could not always allay families' fears about institutions. When Isabella Thackeray, the novelist's wife, became suicidal after the birth of their third child in 1842, William contacted Bryan Procter (1787–1874), one of the Lunacy Commissioners, for advice about asylums. Later William wrote to his mother: 'Procter ... took me to his favourite place which makes me quite sick to think of even now. He shook his head about other places.' They eventually made private arrangements with a Mrs Bakewell in Camberwell.[19]

High institutional standards of cleanliness and good order could go some way to alleviating relatives' anxiety at confining a patient, and the Lunacy Commissioners frequently commented on the 'perfect order' at Ticehurst.[20] However, concern for the patients' wellbeing in the 1840s and 1850s was also affected by a deeper lack of confidence in the curative capabilities of the medical profession.[21] This mistrust fostered a pragmatism in approaching treatment which could embrace homoeopathy and hydropathy as readily as psychological medicine.

As Terry Parssinen has pointed out, 'the medical heresies of the 1840s – mesmerism, homoeopathy and hydropathy – were patronized by an affluent, urban clientele.'[22] These were precisely the kind of people who might otherwise have sent patients to Ticehurst. Despite mesmerism's particular claim to the successful treatment of nervous disorders, I have found no evidence of patients being treated mesmerically before admission to Ticehurst, although one patient admitted in January, 1837 had his certificates signed by John Elliotson (1791–1868). This was, however, before Elliotson began his famous mesmeric experiments.[23]

In cases where the patient's symptoms did not lead to ostracism, the therapeutic scepticism which attracted patients to unorthodox medicine could lead to a total rejection of treatment. To give an example, Samuel Greg (1804–76), a reformist mill-owner whose sister-in-law was a patient at Ticehurst,[24] suffered a nervous breakdown in 1846, when the introduction of new stretching machinery to his mill at Bollington in Cheshire led to a walk-out by staff. He suffered from debilitating depression, did not go out for nine years, and was never able to resume management of the mill. Attributing his ill-health to the phreno-mesmerist experiments he had undertaken in the 1820s with his brother William Rathbone Greg (1809–81), he believed his nervous system had been irreversibly depleted of energy. Initially trying hydropathic treatment at Malvern and on the continent, he 'suffered many things from many physicians, but with little help or satisfaction, and came at length to feel that he must sit down under his burden and live with it as best he could to the end'.[25]

Such resignation could require tolerance and fortitude from family and friends. In cases where the patient became suicidal or violent, it was simply impracticable. The unitarian minister George Kenrick (1792–1874) had been in Samuel Newington's choice of word 'subjected' to hydropathic and homoeopathic treatment at home before being admitted to Ticehurst in March, 1860. His volatile temper and attempt one night to conceal a razor in his bed (with what were believed to be suicidal intentions) persuaded his wife Sarah to agree to his certification.[26]

The advantage which hydropathic treatment had over certification was that it could be clearly addressed to treating any physical disorder believed to be affecting the patient's state of mind, thereby avoiding the stigma of mental disease. In practice, many asylums included hydrotherapy in their range of treatments, although at Ticehurst more emphasis was placed on regimen through diet, exercise, and purging than on baths.[27] In his evidence to the select committee on the operation of the lunacy law in 1877, James Crichton Browne (1840–1938) alleged that many insane patients were illegally confined in hydropathic establishments to avoid the stigma of certification.[28]

The shame experienced by families when one of their members became mentally disturbed could be very intense. Susanna Winkworth's biography of her sister Catherine describes the close and affectionate relationships enjoyed in their evangelical family. Yet while the biography was privately printed for circulation within the family only and makes reference to physical illnesses and treatment experienced by various family members, the eldest brother Henry (who was confined at Ticehurst) is never mentioned by name. References which circumstantial evidence would suggest are to him in Catherine's diaries are represented by asterisks, and he is described in the footnotes simply as 'a close connection'.[29]

Such shame and embarrassment may have been particularly acute when families placed a high premium on intellectual achievement. In a letter to Eliza Fox in February, 1853, Elizabeth Gaskell remarked bitingly of Susanna Winkworth that she had been 'wiser than ever since the *Times* said she was no average woman'.[30] Yet this personal vanity may have been underpinned by the extent to which Susanna relied on her intellectual reputation (as translator of the life of Niebuhr) to maintain her social position.

The decline of the Winkworth family's silk-manufacturing business created financial problems. In 1859, Susanna's younger brother Stephen took over her housekeeping expenses so that she could afford to pay her doctor's bills.[31] Although the Ticehurst accounts do not record how much was paid for Henry Winkworth (partly because some of his time was spent at the higher-class Highlands), even if he had been paying the average rate at the time of 3 guineas per week, his annual bill would have come to more than his father eventually felt able to bequeath for his upkeep, £100 per annum.[32] Of course, having a son who was chronically dependent in this way must have contributed to the family's financial problems.

In a wider perspective, claims to intellectual strength were part of the liberal middle-class appeal for a larger role in government. William Rathbone Greg criticized the aristocratic inheritance of privilege in an article in *Fraser's Magazine* in 1868:

> 'Not only does civilisation as it exists among us enable rank and wealth, however diseased, enfeebled or unintelligent to become the continuators of the species in preference to larger brain ... but that very rank and wealth, thus inherited without effort and in absolute security, tends to produce *enervated and unintelligent* offspring. To be born in the purple is not the right introduction to healthy living.'[33] (italics in the original)

Mental disorder could pose a particular threat to those who felt their social position was already marginal.[34]

For W.R. Greg, a unitarian and author of the widely discussed *Creed of Christendom* (1851), the fact that his wife's delusions centred on religion

created social embarrassment. After a year's stay at Ticehurst, Lucy Greg
was still not free of the 'delusion' that she was a Roman Catholic. Whilst
staying with the Gregs in 1859, Susanna Winkworth confided to Catherine
that: 'Mrs Greg is such a sweet creature ... but evidently very weak and
can't bear much talking ... it was awkward in our talks that I don't know,
and can't make out, whether she is Protestant or Catholic.' Mrs Greg finally
openly went over to Rome in 1867.[35]

This is not to suggest that her case was one of 'wrongful confinement'
based on a lack of religious toleration. Her first period in an asylum, at Dr
Fox's in 1842, pre-dated her conversion. Any connection between her
religious beliefs and her confinement was more oblique. Each of Lucy
Greg's breakdowns followed childbirth or miscarriage. The Newingtons
dated her interest in Catholicism from the time of her third breakdown:

> 'when just beginning to feel aware that her feelings towards her husband
> were unnatural & groundless and casting about for some justification of
> them she accidentally saw some books which turned her mind towards
> the Roman Catholic views of the single state being the holiest.'

She became violent, and was separated from her family for the next five
years.[36]

In 1854 she was placed in a cottage near her family, and nursed by William
Greg's sisters, 'occasionally enjoying the intercourse and society of her
domestic circle'. The suggestion that she was well enough to return to her
family full-time precipitated the worsening of her condition which preceded
her admission to Ticehurst in 1857. The Newingtons weaned her off the
opiates with which she had been sedated whilst in single confinement, her
condition improved, and she was discharged recovered in 1858.[37]

That the Newingtons were proud of Mrs Greg's recovery after twenty
years of intermittent mental disturbance may be surmised from the fact that
they visited the Gregs in London after her return home.[38] Mrs Greg was
keen that her sister, also mentally disturbed, should become a patient at
Ticehurst.[39] Yet it seems likely that in addition to the treatment she received
at Ticehurst, the fact that she was past child-bearing age contributed to Mrs
Greg's willingness to return home, and that her former violence and the
beginnings of her interest in Roman Catholicism had a common source in a
fear of further pregnancies, which had previously precipitated her breakdowns. The case of Mrs Greg illustrates how complex personal needs could
be met through the assumption of a sick role,[40] and how once that role was
adopted other aspects of behaviour which the family found embarrassing
could be attributed to the patient's ill-health.

The decision to confine a relative or friend, even when it was believed that
this was in the individual's best interests, could lead to strong feelings of
guilt. Walter Marshall (b.1837), one of a Leeds flax-spinning family, had
been depressed for many years before he became a patient at Ticehurst in
May, 1876. Immediately prior to admission he had become very excited,
campaigning for the Liberals during the elections. He spent money backing

business deals his family believed to be bad investments. His wife Annie, other family, and friends were concerned by his change of character.[41]

Although Walter believed he had been wrongfully confined, the Newingtons were pessimistic in their prognosis. Walter had, in Hayes Newington's choice of word, 'confessed' that he had been treated for syphilis eighteen years previously. They began treating him with iodide of potassium, then commonly used in the treatment of syphilis. Sir William Gull (1816–90), physician to the Prince of Wales, saw Walter while at Ticehurst to visit another patient, and concurred with the Newingtons' opinion.[42]

Walter Marshall's cousin, the psychical researcher Frederic Myers (1843–1901), wrote to his friend Henry Sidgwick (1838–1900):[43] 'Gull has seen W. & expresses a very unfavourable opinion. (N)ewington tells me he thinks he will never leave Ticehurst. W. is now angry and complaining of plots etc. wh. much distresses A..'[44] The situation was compounded by the fact that for several years Myers had been in love with Annie, and although they had decided not to allow their relationship to become a sexual one, they were close friends. F.C. Gauld has dismissed the suggestion of a genuine conspiracy between Myers and Annie as unfounded, and indeed they reacted to news of the seriousness of Walter's illness by deciding it would be better if they stopped seeing each other.[45]

In August, Myers left for Norway, while Annie remained in the Lake District with her five children. On 19 August, the Marshalls held a family conference at Keswick to discuss Walter's illness, and Annie asked to be relieved of the responsibility of taking decisions concerning his welfare. Frederic's mother was concerned about Annie's state of mind:

'She grew silent towards me, after having been *quite* frank and loving – & I could not with all my entreaties get her to speak of what was in her mind, after she had once said that she saw she had been quite wrong in everything – in this last step for W. (the certif.) & altogether about religion – in rejecting Xianity – I hoped she wd. pass thro' this crisis.'

Annie committed suicide a few days later by drowning herself in Ullswater.[46]

It seems likely that Annie's decision to have Walter certified was precipitous. Her fears for his sanity may have been coloured by her experience of having had two sisters who died insane, and her knowledge that one of Walter's brothers was incapable of managing his own affairs.[47] Exhaustion from living with his intense activity and volubility, as well as his sleeplessness (he woke regularly at 5 am) may have contributed to her decision.[48] Her subsequent suicide testifies to how fragile her own state of mind was. Despite the doctors' prognosis, after Annie's death Walter was transferred to single care with a Dr Hall in Brighton, released a month later, and was well enough the following year to give evidence to the select committee on the operation of the lunacy laws.[49]

Because this case is so well-documented from the patient's point of view, it is a salient one through which to explore the difference between patients'

and doctors' perceptions of the patient's troubles. Marshall did not deny
needing treatment, but he argued that hitherto he had always been treated as
a 'nervous' patient, not as insane, and he objected to the loss of liberty
entailed in certification. Throughout his evidence to the select committee, he
insisted he and Annie had been on good terms, and that once she realized it
had been a mistake to have him certified, she had done all she could to assist
in his release.[50]

The role of the Newingtons seems less ingenuous. When Walter arrived at
Ticehurst, the case-notes suggest that his attendants had to search for signs
of mental disturbance. They commented that: 'His memory seems to be fair,
he is quite coherent, and though he has not expressed any definite delusions,
yet there seems to be working about him some idea of greatness.' He was
'never idle', and within two days of admission had 'already painted several
fairly executed pictures of the grounds etc.'. On the other hand: 'He wants
to get up at very early hours, wants to do several things, not absurd but
inconvenient.'[51]

Marshall recalled in his evidence to the select committee that he had first
seen 'Dr Newington' a few days after admission:

> 'I told [Dr Newington] all my case, and he talked very kindly. Of course,
> I told him all; I treated him with perfect confidence. He said, "Well, your
> former life shows that you require some medical treatment; suppose you
> stay here for six weeks; I understand your case. By that time you will get
> out perfectly well; and there will be no scandal or anything." That was
> reasonable, and I consented to that.'[52]

Unfortunately, Marshall does not specify which 'Dr Newington' he saw,
although the admission notes on his case were completed by Samuel
Newington's nephew and successor, Hayes Newington.[53]

Fresh from his training under David Skae (1808–73) and Thomas
Clouston (1840–1915) at Morningside Asylum in Edinburgh, Hayes
Newington had a particular interest in cases of syphilitic insanity, and had
written his first paper on one in 1873.[54] Syphilitic cases were amongst the
most common at Morningside,[55] and this would have both given Hayes
Newington clinical experience of their symptomatology, and perhaps led
him to anticipate its presence. Although syphilis and general paralysis were
thought of as independent diseases, Thomas Clouston listed syphilis as one
of the predisposing causes of general paralysis.[56]

Both Hayes Newington and William Gull interpreted Walter Marshall's
tremulous facial muscles and exalted state of mind as symptoms of the first
stage of general paralysis. In the case-notes, even Walter's paintings were
viewed in a different light: 'His room ... is decorated with very many of his
own paintings and drawings, mostly of a gaudy, sensational and jerky
character. Some present the typical G.P. appearance – lots of colour grouped
into purposeless masses.'[57] When two doctors sent by Walter Marshall's
brother declared themselves of the opinion that he was well enough to be

released on trial, 'Dr Newington' cautioned that they had seen Walter at his best. In any case, both doctors concurred with the diagnosis of general paralysis.[58] The commissioners decided that rather than being released on trial, Walter should be transferred to single care.[59]

Regrettably, I have been unable to trace what happened to Walter Marshall after he gave evidence to the select committee, but up until that time he had been living at home, apparently well. Speaking to the Medico-Psychological Association in 1900, Hayes Newington candidly admitted:

> 'We have had some mistakes in diagnosis. One case had all the usual symptoms [of general paralysis] well marked, left us relieved, has been cured elsewhere, and under various forms of control since, but after eleven years we believe he is as lively as ever.'[60]

The time-lag of eleven years is too short for this case-history to refer to Walter Marshall, but Hayes Newington's admission substantiates the likelihood that they may also have been mistaken in their diagnosis of Walter Marshall's case.

Despairing of being released, Walter Marshall became convinced he was being kept prisoner because of his radical political beliefs. Whilst this in itself was noted as a symptom, his political opinions were also seen as symptomatic. He is described, for instance, as 'talking in a very extravagant manner and saying that he should like to clear [everyone in the city] out altogether'.[61]

Arguments of 'social control' are less easily applied to private asylums than public ones, where there was a class difference between the people confining and those confined. For the middle and upper classes, apart from criminal cases which went through the police and courts, it was rather a question of self-regulation. It was families and friends, rather than doctors, who made the initial diagnosis of 'insanity' by referring someone for treatment.[62]

Most patients at Ticehurst were referred by their family (see *Table 8.5*). As in other areas of legal responsibility in Victorian England, men more commonly referred patients of both sexes than women: 70.7 per cent of married female patients were referred by their husbands, while only 52.1 per cent of married men were referred by their wives. When women did refer patients, it was sometimes made clear that they derived the authority to do so from their husbands. Thus in 1876 a woman called Amelia Pretyman referred her sister-in-law Emily Pretyman 'on behalf of her husband Revd J.R. Pretyman, clerk in holy orders, Bournemouth'.[63]

A letters book for 1857–73 shows that the most common reason for refusing patients was that the terms they were offering were too low.[64] In a letter to the *Journal of Mental Science* in April 1885, Hayes Newington argued that receiving doctors at an asylum could do little other than accept the opinion of the certifying doctors as to the insanity of the patient being admitted:

Table 8.5   *Person(s) referring patients to Ticehurst, 1845–1905*

	men	women	both
	%	%	%
spouse	20.0	23.5	21.7
brother(s)	19.8[a]	16.0[a]	18.0[b]
father	14.9	12.3	13.7
sister(s)	3.5	10.3[c]	6.8[c]
other male relation(s)	8.1	4.0	6.1
son(s)	4.9	6.6[d]	5.7[d]
mother	4.6	6.3	5.4
brother(s)-in-law	4.9	4.3	4.6
other man[e]	6.0	1.2	3.6
other female relation(s)	2.7	4.0	3.3
man with same surname – relationship not known	3.2	2.6	2.9
person with same surname – sex not known[f]	1.4	2.6	2.0
other[g]	2.2	1.7	2.0
unknown	2.2	1.7	2.0
other woman[h]	0.5	2.6	1.5
woman with same surname – relationship not known	1.1	0.3	0.7

a Including one referred by both a brother and a brother-in-law
b Including two referred by both a brother and a brother-in-law.
c Including one referred by both a sister and a male cousin.
d Including one referred by both a son and a daughter.
e E.g. friend, solicitor, guardian.
f E.g. cousin, with only initials and surname given.
g Lunatic by inquisition, or referred by the Court of Chancery, or committee.
h E.g. lady's companion, mother superior.
Note: Figures for 1 August 1845 to 31 July 1905. Details of the relationship between the patient and the person(s) who referred them are not generally given in the *Civil Register*, 1907–19.
Sources: Register of Admissions, 1845–81 and 1881–90: *Register of Patients*, 1890–1907.

'Are we, with but little knowledge of the facts, to take the responsibility of reversing, possibly to the public harm, two opinions founded on facts? ... All we can do is to watch the case, and if necessary get rid of it at once'.[65]

Once a case was known to them, the asylum doctors were in a position to be discriminating about admission. Thus in March 1879, Hayes Newington visited a former patient, Georgiana Carter, in Tunbridge Wells, and advised her father against readmission, instead prescribing chloral hydrate and mustard baths to be given at home.[66]

As asylum doctors, the Newingtons had to balance the social needs of their clients (primarily patients' families) against the requirements of the law. Once a patient was admitted, the continuing trust and confidence of the family depended on the ability of the Newingtons to negotiate the difficult feelings aroused by the patient's mental distress, and the decision to resort to certification. Describing mental disturbance in terms of individual organic pathology alleviated families' feelings of responsibility. As Nancy Tomes has argued:

'Hospitalization justified the removal of a disruptive individual while at the same time promising medical treatment and a possible cure. Hospital treatment thus addressed the powerful sense of guilt and helplessness expressed by so many families when dealing with an insane relative.[67]

The 'supposed causes' of insanity listed in the admission notes rarely point to family relationships as a source of stress. Rather, they attribute mental disturbance to accidents ('blow on the head', 'a fall'), physical ill-health ('influenza', 'fever'), natural processes ('childbirth', 'her age'), or the environment ('tropical climate', 'long residence in India'). Or it is attributed to the individual's role in society ('excitement from business', 'overwork in ministry'), an adverse change of circumstances ('loss of property', 'business failure'), or the individual's lack of moderation or self-control ('intemperance', 'irregular living', 'self-abuse'). Where mental disturbance is seen as resulting from the family, the stress referred to is generally beyond the family's control ('bereavement', 'sudden illness of adopted daughter'). The only other emotional circumstance seen as commonly affecting mental stability is rejection in love ('disappointed affections', 'disappointment in love').[68] Perhaps this is not surprising, since the 'supposed causes' might originate from the family, and were copied into the admission books from the certificates. The one patient whose breakdown was attributed to an 'unhappy marriage' was referred by her mother rather than by her husband.[69]

The potential for abuse in a system which left so much power in the hands of the family and doctors, either or both of whom might stand to gain personally or financially from a sane person's confinement was one of the most reiterated arguments of the lunacy reform movement. Ticehurst Asylum had been directly implicated in this campaign since its inception. John Perceval (1803–76), the secretary of the Alleged Lunatic's Friends Society (founded in 1845), which pressed for the 1858–59 parliamentary inquiry into the lunacy laws, had been confined at Ticehurst from February to December, 1832. In 1838 he published an account of his experiences, in which he alleged he had been sane during the time of his confinement at Ticehurst.[70]

Apart from the case of Walter Marshall, the 1877 enquiry considered the case of two other patients who had been confined at Ticehurst, and Samuel Newington was called to give evidence. Interestingly, he relied not so much on ideas of professional expertise to defend his opinion of one of the patients' insanity, as on long-standing personal knowledge of the individual: '[Mr Preston] was an old college friend of mine, so that I knew him very well indeed.' In the other case he blamed delays in the patient's release on the family: 'When I found that [Mr Thomas] was sufficiently well, I proposed to his family that he should be released, and they were dreadfully frightened because they thought that he would go home and commit all sorts of depredation about the property.'[71] Thus fear of the insane, and the stigma of certification, affected a patient's reception back into the wider society.

Another former patient at Ticehurst, Herman Charles Merivale (1839–1906), pinpointed this fear as the most difficult obstacle lunacy reformers had to overcome: 'Cowards at the best, all of us, we are all of us afraid of the very name of "madness" more than anything else; and in that fear lies the security of the present system against any attack that may be made upon it.' Yet equally, the stigma of certification could undermine the patient's own self-esteem: 'The feelings of fear and shame – for it has in one's own despite a sort of shame about it – that the experience left behind, died slow and hard.'[72] Merivale's own feelings of shame were sufficiently acute for him to publish *My Experiences in a Lunatic Asylum by a Sane Patient* (1879) anonymously, despite the blustering title.

Herman Charles Merivale was the son of Herman Merivale (1806–74) permanent under-secretary of state for the colonies and India. Trained as a barrister, he travelled on the western and Norfolk circuits with Matthew Arnold, served on the Boundary Commission, and heard cases for the Privy Council on Indian Appeals. His real ambition, however, was to be a playwright and novelist.[73] After his first period of confinement at Manor House in Chiswick, he wrote a one-act farce under the pseudonym Felix Dale, called *He's a Lunatic* (1868), in which the wrong person is taken to an asylum by mistake.[74] In *My Experiences in a Lunatic Asylum* Merivale denies having been suicidal before his admission to Ticehurst, which he calls 'Pecksniff Hall'. Like Walter Marshall, he did not deny having been in need of treatment at the time of his admission, but believed certification to have been unnecessary. He attributed his mental depression to natural grief at his father's death, and physical weakness caused by a disturbed liver, reduced diet, the enervating effects of an unsuccessful water-cure at Carlsbad, and excessive medicinal use of chloral hydrate.[75]

Merivale's story was taken up by a former secretary of the Lunacy Law Reform Association (founded in 1873), Louisa Lowe, in her diatribe against private asylums, *The Bastilles of England* (1883), although it is unclear whether or not she identified 'Pecksniff Hall' as Ticehurst. She also discussed in detail the cases of Thomas Preston and another former patient at Ticehurst, Sir Samuel Fludyer (1799–1876).[76] The motivation for both these patients being confined was seen as financial. She quoted a letter sent from Ticehurst by Thomas Preston on 25 August, 1873:

'Madame – I see by the *Standard* you are taking an interest in us so-called lunatics; perhaps you know someone who can help me. The Court of Chancery has appointed my younger brother my sole committee; he is hostile to me, our interests are opposed, and he will not allow me to use my own money to apply to the Court.'[77]

Sir Samuel Fludyer's father left a will in which if Samuel died without an heir, his money was to be transferred to other male relations on the father's side rather than his daughters. Louisa Lowe accused the sisters of having Samuel certified after an argument, and writing a will in their own favour.[78] Her information was inaccurate in so far as she claimed no lunacy commission had ever been held on the case: in fact, one had been held in 1858, and found him insane.[79] She was right, however, to suspect the Newingtons of having a high financial interest in Sir Samuel's confinement – at a charge of 12 guineas a week, he was the highest-paying patient at Ticehurst in the 1840s.[80]

Lowe's case was considerably weakened by the fact that the cases she chose to consider from Ticehurst died some years before her book was published (Sir Samuel in 1876 and Mr Preston in 1877). The 1877 enquiry had concluded Preston was properly confined, particularly in view of his propensity to attack women.[81] In the light of this, even the statement of a former attendant from Ticehurst, Robert Minchin, that Preston had been sane and that 'he also knows of other persons at Ticehurst perfectly quiet and harmless' would have carried little weight.[82]

The reputation of Ticehurst survived attacks from the lunacy reform movement. Even those who believed themselves victims of the lunacy laws, and were critical of the Newingtons' moral integrity, had good to say of Ticehurst's institutional standards. John Perceval believed that

'had he been placed at first under Mr C. Newington, he should within three or six months have recovered his understanding; but he doubts if he should have recovered his liberty any sooner; for that gentleman exercises a somewhat suspicious scrupulousness, and an officious tenderness respecting the too sudden return of his patients to society.'[83]

Walter Marshall, who spent a few days at Munster House in Fulham before arriving at Ticehurst said: '[At Ticehurst] I was very kindly treated, and it was a very pleasant change. I had much more liberty; I was able to walk about the country with an attendant, in place of being walked round the garden.'[84]

Ticehurst House was never advertised, like Shillingthorpe House in Lincolnshire, as being 'conducted in the style of a country gentleman's residence',[85] yet that is the ethos conveyed by Herman Charles Merivale. It is worth quoting at some length:

'During those months I had the advantage of living in a castellated mansion, in one of the prettiest parts of England, ... With carriages to take me out for drives, closed upon wet days, open on fine; with cricket and bowls and archery for the summer, and a pack of harriers to follow across country in the winter ... with five refections a day whereof to partake ... with a private chapel for morning prayers or Sunday service ... with little evening parties for whist or music amongst "ourselves", and a casual conjuror or entertainer from town to distract us sometimes for an evening'.[86]

Each residential unit at Ticehurst was relatively small. Allowing for patients who were out on trial, as well as those at St Leonards (about fifteen at any one time), by the mid-1870s even the main building can only have accommodated about thirty patients, and these were strictly segregated by sex. In March 1877 the visitors commented on fourteen male patients dining together in the main building, and seven or eight female patients dining together in the Vineyards.[87]

Under the proprietorship of Hayes Newington, new accommodation continued to be added to the asylum. In 1882, his personal home, Prospect House, was added to the licence, and in 1888 his co-proprietor cousin Alexander's[88] house, the Woodlands, was added on, and Quarry Villa was extended. A special house, Westcliffe, was built to accommodate patients from Ticehurst in St Leonards in 1889. In 1893, the house Hayes Newington had built for himself, the Gables, was adapted to accommodate one upper-class patient.[89] This expansion of space was not matched by an increase in admissions or patient numbers (see *Tables 8.1* and *8.2*). In 1900, Hayes Newington commented 'each patient requires more space as years go on'.[90] Fees rose accordingly. An Egyptian prince, Saaf ed Din, who became a patient in 1899, paid £2,020 per annum in the early 1900s for his single accommodation.[91]

Attendants at Ticehurst were expected to treat patients with the respect normally accorded by servants to members of a superior class. One attendant was dismissed 'for not saluting the ladies as provided in our regulations'.[92] In 1881, the commissioners commented that 'the fact that this is a private asylum, is, as far as possible, veiled by the comfort and elegancies of the house and furniture'.[93] The case-notes on a female patient called Lucy Bing Tinne record that she: 'Does not appear to recognize the ladies about her are insane, looks upon this building as an hotel.'[94]

This genteel ambience was maintained at a cost. Just as behaviour which was unacceptable socially often led relatives to confine patients, it was also one reason why patients were refused admission, or relatives were asked to remove them. The letters book for 1857–73 for example records that one patient was refused admission because he was 'definitely suicidal'.[95] Between 1845 and 1915 there were only three successful suicide attempts at Ticehurst.[96]

The commissioners frequently comment on the low incidence of seclusion and restraint at Ticehurst. They attributed this lack of violence to the high staff:patient ratio, which permitted the undivided personal attention recommended by the proponents of non-restraint to be a reality in a way in which it could not be in many asylums.[97] A reading of the case-books suggests another explanation. Patients who were violent and difficult to control were frequently transferred. In April, 1860, Revd Louis Davidson de Visme was described as 'very fond of striking when in close quarters'. This was tolerated for some years, until early in 1867 when he broke a poker over Samuel Newington's shoulder and was transferred.[98] (Pokers at Ticehurst had been made of wood ever since Charles Newington was hit over the head with one by a patient.)[99] When Mary Berryman threw her attendant downstairs in August 1884, she was sedated with potassium bromide. However, a year later an entry in the case-notes reads: 'Has smashed her piano, sofa, chairs, and is now breaking down the wall. Goes out once a day walking, but requires a man to accompany her, as she is murderous in her actions.' Two months later she was transferred.[100]

Other patients were transferred because their behaviour was felt to be unacceptable. Letitia Walker annoyed other patients by opening doors and windows when they wanted them shut. She would wander into their private rooms and insult them; she jeered at Ellen Farrer's dress when they were walking to church together. Five months after her admission her relatives were asked to remove her.[101] A year later, in 1858, Charles Mawley was described as 'much disliked by the other patients'. He used to mix cigar ash and grease together to make 'hair-dye', and kept rotting food in drawers so that he could demonstrate to visitors how bad the food was. Finally, he persuaded another patient to leave the grounds with him, and his relatives were asked to remove him.[102]

Through adopting such a strict attitude, the Newingtons were successful in creating an exceptionally tranquil environment for their patients, and one where relatives could feel happy about leaving them. In other respects, the asylum protected the family from the patient's behaviour: for example letters were censored, and sometimes not sent. One woman patient who posted a letter whilst out for a walk was afterwards confined to the grounds of the asylum.[103]

Praise for Ticehurst was so consistent in the commissioners' reports that Lord Shaftesbury commented to the select committee in 1877 that: 'To abolish such a house as Ticehurst, for instance, would be a positive loss to science and humanity.'[104] In attacking Ticehurst, lunacy reformers like Louisa Lowe struck at the core of the system to which they were opposed. If even the best private asylums could be shown to abuse civil liberties, then only total abolition could meet the reformers' demands. The publication in *Nineteenth Century* of an article by J.C. Bucknill (1817–97), a prominent mad-doctor, which favoured abolition led Hayes Newington to write a letter to the *Journal of Mental Science* defending private asylums.[105]

In this letter, Hayes Newington discussed the question of financial interest and the admission of sane patients, arguing that all doctors received fees for their services and, as quoted above (note 65), that asylum doctors were dependent on doctors in the community for reliable diagnosis. His comments on the low rate of cure in private asylums suggest that in 1885 the reputation of private asylums was still poor:

> 'Many of the upper classes can and do retain the services of independent specialists and get well without leaving home, or are sent away to medical men's houses. We, therefore, can say that ... what we ... get are not infrequently the residue of unsuccessful treatment elsewhere ... in the case of the wealthy it is well known that an asylum is generally the last thing thought of.'[106]

The following year, a bill proposing to end the issue of new licences for private asylums came before parliament. The possibility of total abolition was raised. Some patients at Ticehurst were anxious about what closure would mean for them. In June 1886, the commissioners visiting Ticehurst observed that: 'The bill before parliament for amendment of the Lunacy Laws was on the lips of many, and one lady especially inveighed against the abolition of private asylums, in which she has herself (here & elsewhere) passed many years of her life.'[107]

Hayes Newington was sceptical whether the lunacy reform movement spoke for the majority of patients. At a meeting of the Medico-Psychological Association in July, 1886 when abolition was discussed he argued that:

> 'it was quite a question whether that prejudice [against private asylums] was mainly on the part of those people most concerned, viz., the patients. There was, of course, much prejudice on the part of the patients' friends, but, taking patients themselves, the acute maniac did not care where he was, the melancholiac would be miserable anywhere, and it was principally the "moral insanity" cases which made the most noise from the patient's point of view, and they were just the people in asylums whose opinions should be considered the least.'[108]

Bluff as this was, it expressed a range of possible reactions to confinement which could not be given scope within the lunacy reform movement. The commissioners consistently reported most patients to be satisfied with their treatment at Ticehurst: 'not one complained of the treatment he receives here', 'several of them spoke in the highest terms of the kindness shown them', 'more than one patient expressed their satisfaction at the treatment they received, and acknowledged how much they were indebted to it'.[109] It is important to set these voices against those of Walter Marshall and Herman Merivale, both of whom, in addition to their personal experience of confinement, had a political investment as active liberals in the campaign for lunacy reform.

The bill was thrown out at its second reading on 11 June, 1886. The issues raised by the campaign, however, continued to be aired. One of the accusations levelled at private asylums was that they were slower than public asylums to discharge patients. In January, 1887, Hayes Newington published an article in the *Journal of Mental Science* asking 'What Are the Tests of Fitness for Discharge from Asylums?'.[110]

In this paper, Hayes Newington dealt particularly with suicidal patients, and the difficulty of assessing when it was safe to let them home. He pointed to the limits of the asylum doctor's powers, citing the case of a woman whose home circumstances he believed endangered her mental wellbeing. She was married to a man who drank heavily, and whom Hayes Newington described as 'little better than a besotted fool'. He went on: 'Her husband came to see her, and on at least one occasion abused our hospitality by taking more than was good for him. After a time he insisted on removing her. Had I had any means of conveniently resisting this, I certainly should have done so.'[111]

It is possible to identify this case from the case-books as that of a woman called Louisa Sicklemore. In fact, contrary to Hayes Newington's expectations she was able to remain out of treatment for sixteen years, and only became deeply melancholic and needed readmission following her husband's death.[112] This case provides an interesting example of a situation in which possible family causes were perceived, but the Newingtons felt unable to be frank to the family or the patient about their perceptions, although able to discuss them with professional colleagues.

Two years later in his presidential address to the Medico-Psychological Association, Hayes Newington again confronted the problem of getting families to refer patients promptly for treatment. Speaking on 'Hospital Treatment for Recent and Curable Cases of Insanity', he argued that the establishment of a separate hospital for acute cases within the asylum, and the introduction of voluntary treatment would go some way to mitigate the stigma of certification.[113] At Ticehurst, voluntary boarding of former patients had been considered even before the 1862 Act made it statutorily regulated (25 & 26 Vict., c. 111). In 1856 the commissioners considered the case of a Miss Thorpe, and suggested that 'as she has no home & expresses a wish to remain here it becomes a question whether she should not be discharged as a patient & reside here as a boarder'. In fact, the Newingtons opposed this idea, and she went instead to relatives in London.[114]

Once the practice had been regulated, some patients did stay on as boarders. For example, in February, 1873 a Mr Sullivan felt he did not have the 'nerve' to leave Ticehurst, and he became a boarder. He left Ticehurst fifteen months later, only to be returned after three months in a state of acute mania.[115]

The 1890 Lunacy Act finally established the principle of voluntary treatment (53 Vict., c. 5). During the first twenty-five years of its operation at Ticehurst however it was more frequently taken up by former patients than by new admissions (see *Table 8.6*). Patients who were suicidal or violent still legally required certification.

According to G.H. Savage (1842–1921), a prominent consultant in mental disorders who referred many patients to Ticehurst,[116] the stigma of certification was still strong. In an article in the *Journal of Mental Science* in 1901 he

Table 8.6   *Admissions to Ticehurst: voluntary boarders, 1890–1914*

	men	women	all admissions
From certificates in Ticehurst	8	5	13
former inmates admitted from home	1 (1)	2 (3)	7
new patients	6 (1)	7	14
total	15 (2)	14 (3)	34

Note: Patients admitted for treatment as voluntary boarders between 1 January, 1890 and 31 December, 1914. Numbers in brackets indicate second admissions.
Sources: Register of Voluntary Boarders, 1890–1930; *Register of Admissions,* 1881–90; *Register of Patients,* 1890–1907; *Civil Register,* 1907–19.

argued that many families still sent patients on extended trips abroad rather than face certification. Savage advised against this because the increased stress of travelling could lead to a worsening of the patient's condition – melancholics needed rest rather than distraction, and hysterics might pass into a state of acute mania because of excitement.[117]

Late-Victorian and Edwardian diaries and autobiographies, like mid-Victorian ones, document the extent to which asylums were still considered places of last resort. Virginia Woolf, or Virginia Stephen as she then was, broke down after both her mother's death in 1895, and her father's death in 1904. On the first occasion she was treated at home, and on the second stayed at Violet Dickenson's house, where she was attended by a private nurse. It was only on her third breakdown in 1910, when her sister Vanessa was unable to nurse her at home because she was pregnant, that Virginia became a voluntary boarder at Burley in Twickenham, a private asylum recommended by George Savage.[118]

When Edith Ellis, Havelock Ellis's wife, broke down in 1915, nursing at home was impossible because they did not have adequate accommodation to offer a private nurse. Edith's mental depression was complicated by diabetes, and she became a patient at a convent nursing home in Hayle. After a suicide attempt, closer attendance than they could give her was considered necessary. Havelock Ellis records in his autobiography:

'It was considered by the doctors, and I agreed, that admission to a hospital for the insane as a voluntary patient, would be the best method ... But the suicidal attempt proved an insuperable difficulty. They would not accept her as a voluntary boarder. The question of her certification as a lunatic was raised ... [but] the thought of carrying her off by some ruse, when she was still so alive to everything round her, and leaving her a prisoner in an asylum was more than I could bear.'[119]

In the end a trained mental nurse was sent from London, and temporarily cared for Edith in the convent nursing home, until a place was found for her in a convalescent nursing home for mental and nervous cases in south London.

In this paper, I have tried to give a dynamic account of the tensions between asylum doctors and their clientele, to modify the image created by the accumulation of chronic cases of an unremittingly low rate of discharge and cure. The 1890 Lunacy Act (53 Vict., c. 5), which forbade the issue of new licences, or expansion of existing ones, led to a falling off of admissions at Ticehurst, as elsewhere (see *Table 8.1*). Yet despite the falling percentage of private patients who were accommodated in licensed houses, numbers at Ticehurst remained at the same level between 1885 and 1915 (see *Table 8.2*).[120]

The increasing professionalization of medicine, and state recognition of the medical profession's claims to expertise in treating the insane, tightened the hold of the medical profession on the treatment of insanity.[121] The development of anaesthesia, antisepsis, and further bacteriological discoveries of the 1870s and 1880s made the medical profession's role in physical health increasingly plausible.[122] These discoveries led the public to hope for similar advances in psychological medicine, which were not forthcoming. Anticipating the introduction of new lunacy legislation, the *Times* reported in 1889 that 'our knowledge of the essential nature of insanity, of the causes which foster and produce it, of the means by which no doubt it could be cured, is scarcely greater now than it was a hundred years ago.'[123] Families still then referred patients as a last resort, expecting little. In the absence of recovery, they continued to remove patients, to try alternative treatments or simply to keep them at home.

The Ticehurst case-notes show how often individual patients' disturbances were part of a wider pattern of family problems. Removing a patient eased family tensions, and it was this social need which asylums like Ticehurst successfully fulfilled. The rate of discharge of patients who were not recovered or relieved suggests that often temporary removal was sufficient. Ray is right to argue that there was a more fluid interchange between the asylum and the outside world than is suggested by the emphasis on the accumulation of chronic cases.

Doctors like Hayes Newington worked to enhance this fluidity, to remove the stigma of certification and normalize hospital treatment for emotional disturbance. They also sought to extend the increasingly scientific image of medicine to the psychological arena.[124] As we have seen, their real diagnostic and prognostic skills were rudimentary, but their skill in creating a therapeutic ambience, and their tact in handling the feelings of their clients, won the confidence of patients' families.[125] Further research is needed to round out our picture of what happened to those who did not opt for the ayslum, or who left it unrelieved.

Notes

1 *Case Book* 26, pp. 112, 114, 116, 159.

2 H.F. Hayes Newington, 'What Are the Tests of Fitness for Discharge from Asylums?', *Journal of Mental Science* 32 (1887): 491.

3 Laurence J. Ray, 'Models of Madness in Victorian Asylum Practice', *Archives Européenes de Sociologie* 22 (1981): 229–64.

4 *Bill Book*, 1792–1802 and 1802–11. Accounts for Revd Chambers, 1797–1834; Revd Lofty, 1799–1800; and Mr Darnay, 1808–16. *Bill Book*, 1826–32.

5 H.F. Hayes Newington and A.S.L. Newington, 'Some Incidents in the History and Practice of Ticehurst Asylum', *Journal of Mental Science*, 47 (1901): 63; Visitors' Reports, 19 April, 1831, E. Sussex County Record Office, QAL/1/3/E10.

6 *Visitors Book*, 1833–45, entries for visits made in 1845. Fees calculated from *Bill Book*, 1840–46.

7 W.Ll. Parry-Jones, *The Trade in Lunacy* (London: Routledge and Kegan Paul, 1972), pp. 101, 125.

8 *Register of Admissions*, 1845–81.

9 *Visitors Book*, 1846–69, entry for 29 April, 1863.

10 *Visitors Book*, 1869–87, entries for 26 April, 1870, 27 October, 1871, 17 June, 1872, 23 March, 1874.

11 A. Scull, *Museums of Madness* (London: Allen Lane, 1979), p. 208.

12 Ray, 'Models of Madness', p. 233.

13 Scull, *Museums of Madness*, p. 208; for a similar argument applied to the public sector, see John Walton's article in this volume.

14 Eighty-seven out of 334 patients discharged 'relieved' or 'not improved' between 1 August, 1845 and 31 July, 1915. *Register of Removal, Discharge and Deaths*, 1845–90 and 1890–1908; *Register of Discharges and Transfers*, 1907–30.

15 *Case Book* 5, pp. 9–11, 44, 71, 80–1.

16 *Case Book* 39, pp. 132–35, 139.

17 Susanna Winkworth, *Letters and Memorials of Catherine Winkworth*, 2 vols (London: Clifton, 1883 and 1886) vol. 1, p. 67. Both Catherine and Susanna were German translators: for an account of their lives see the *Dictionary of National Biography*.

18 *Register of Admissions*, 1845–81, patient no. 53.

19 Gordon N. Ray, *The Letters and Private Papers of William Makepeace Thackeray*, 4 vols (London: Oxford University Press, 1945), vol. 2, p. 81.

20 *Visitors Book*, 1846–69 and 1869–87, entries for 17 June, 1947 and 26 April, 1870.

21 R.H. Shryock, *The Development of Modern Medicine* (Madison: University of Wisconsin Press, 1979), pp. 248–72.

22 Terry M. Parssinen, 'Professional Deviants and the History of Medicine: Medical Mesmerists in Victorian Britain', in Roy Wallis (ed.), *On the Margins of Science: The Social Construction of Rejected Knowledge* (Keele: Keele University Press, 1979), p. 109.

23 *Register of Admissions*, 1845–81, patient no. 35 – admission Daniel Bull of Clapton Sq., London. On Elliotson, see Terry M. Parssinen, 'Professional Deviants', p. 106.

24 *Register of Admissions*, 1845–81, patient no. 117 – Lucy Anne Greg (1811–73)

was married to Samuel Greg's younger brother, William Rathbone Greg the essayist.

25 Samuel Greg, *A Layman's Legacy* (London: Macmillan, 1877), pp. 17, 21–3, 33.

26 *Case Book* 9, p. 47; 5, pp. 146–49.

27 *Case Books, passim*; see also H.F. Hayes Newington and A.S.L. Newington, 'Some Incidents', pp. 69–72 for a description of treatment at Ticehurst.

28 *Report from the Select Committee on Lunacy Law*, PP. (1877), XIII, p. 75.

29 Susanna Winkworth, *Letters and Memorials*, vol. 1, dedication and p. 78.

30 J.A.V. Chapple and Arthur Pollard, *The Letters of Mrs Gaskell* (Manchester: Manchester University Press, 1966), p. 225.

31 Susanna Winkworth, *Letters and Memorials*, vol. 2, p. 267.

32 Henry Winkworth (d. 15 May, 1869), 1st codicil to his will, 23 May, 1861.

33 W.R. Greg, 'On the Failure of Natural Selection in the Case of Man', *Fraser's Magazine* 78, (1868): 361.

34 See the article by F. Godlee in this volume.

35 Susanna Winkworth, *Letters and Memorials*, vol. 2, pp. 265, 459.

36 *Case Book* 4, p. 114.

37 *Case Book* 4, pp. 71–2, 74, 75. *Register of Removal, Discharges and Deaths*, 1845–90, entry for 27 May, 1858.

38 *Case Book* 4, p. 114.

39 *Case Book*, 1857–73, letters received in 1858.

40 For a discussion of this in relation to hysteria, see Carroll Smith-Rosenberg, 'The Hysterical Woman. Sex Roles and Role Conflict in Nineteenth-Century America', in R.J. Brugger (ed.), *Our Selves/Our Past. Psychological Approaches to American History* (Baltimore, Md.: Johns Hopkins University Press, 1981), pp. 205–43.

41 *Case Book* 22, pp. 93–5.

42 *Case Book* 22, pp. 97–8. On nineteenth-century therapeutics for syphilis, see C.C. Dennie, *A History of Syphilis* (Springfield, Illinois: Charles C. Thompson, 1962), pp. 104–05.

43 See the article on 'Victorian Psychical Research' by P.J. Williams in The Companion Volume 1.

44 F.C. Gauld, *The Founders of Psychical Research* (London: Routledge and Kegan Paul, 1968), p. 121. Gauld quotes this letter as reading, 'Trewington tells me . . .', but this is almost certainly a misreading of the original manuscript.

45 Gauld, *Founders of Psychical Research*, footnote pp. 122–23.

46 Gauld, *Founders of Psychical Research*, p. 122.

47 Gauld, *Founders of Psychical Research*, p. 117.

48 *Case Book* 22, pp. 96, 104.

49 *Register of Removal, Discharges and Deaths*, 1845–90, entry for 3 September, 1876; *Report on Lunacy Law*, p. 423.

50 *Report on Lunacy Law*, pp. 422, 423, 424.

51 *Case Book* 22, pp. 96, 97.

52 *Report on Lunacy Law*, p. 421.

53 *Case Book* 22, pp. 96–9, 102–4, 154.

54 H.F. Hayes Newington, 'Notes of a Case of Insanity Dependent on Syphilis', *Journal of Mental Science* 19 (1874): 555–60.

55 Margaret Sorbie Thompson, 'The Mad, the Bad, and the Sad: Psychiatric Care at the Royal Edinburgh Asylum (Morningside), 1813–94' (unpublished PhD

thesis, Boston University, 1984), p. 208.

56 Thomas Clouston, *Clinical Lectures in Mental Diseases* (London: J. & A. Churchill 1886), p. 260.

57 *Case Book* 22, pp. 98, 102, 104.

58 *Report on Lunacy Law*, p. 422.

59 *Patients Book*, 1846–1904, 21 August, 1876.

60 Hayes Newington and A.S.L. Newington, 'Some Incidents', p. 68.

61 *Case Book* 22, p. 103.

62 For a discussion of this in a twentieth-century context, see David Mechanic, 'Some Factors in Identifying and Defining Mental Illness' *Mental Hygiene* 46 (1962): 66–74.

63 *Register of Admissions*, 1845–81, patient no. 377.

64 *Case Book*, 1857–73, *passim*.

65 H.F. Hayes Newington, 'The Abolition of Private Asylums', *Journal of Mental Science* 31 (1885): 142–43.

66 *Case Book* 26, p. 7.

67 Nancy Jane Tomes, 'The Persuasive Institution: Thomas Story Kirkbride and the Art of Asylum-Keeping, 1841–83' (unpublished PhD thesis, University of Pennsylvania, 1978), p. 13. A revised version of this thesis has now been published as *A Generous Confidence: Thomas Story Kirkbridge and the Art of Asylum-Keeping, 1840–1883* (Cambridge and New York: Cambridge University Press, 1984).

68 *Register of Admissions*, 1845–81 and 1881–90: *Register of Patients*, 1890–1907; *Civil Register*, 1907–19.

69 *Register of Admissions*, 1881–90, patient no. 5561 – admission of Nora von Bunsen, 3 November, 1886, referred by her mother Kittie Hill.

70 For an account of the lunacy reform movement, see Peter McCandless, 'Insanity and Society: A Study of the English Lunacy Reform Movement, 1815–70' (unpublished PhD thesis, University of Wisconsin, 1974). John Perceval, *A Narrative of the Treatment Experienced by a Gentleman, during a State of Mental Derangement*, 2 vols (London: Effingham Wilson, 1838 and 1840).

71 *Report on Lunacy Law*, pp. 365, 366. William Thomas Preston was a patient at Ticehurst from 26 March, 1870 to 10 December, 1873, when he was transferred to Barnswood Asylum in Gloucester. He was at Brasenose College, Oxford (1832–36), while Samuel Newington was at Worcester College (1834–42). John William Thomas, a clerk in holy orders, was a patient at Ticehurst from 25 January, 1873 to 11 February, 1874, when he was discharged recovered. (*Register of Admissions*, 1845–81, patients nos 275 and 309; *Alumni Oxon.*)

72 Herman Charles Merivale, *My Experiences in a Lunatic Asylum, by a Sane Patient* (London: Chatto and Windus, 1879), pp. 13–14, 71–2.

73 J.A. Blaikie, 'Herman Charles Merivale', in Alfred H. Miles (ed.), *The Poets and the Poetry of the Century*, 10 vols. (London: Hutchinson, 1891), vol. 6, p. 371.

74 Felix Dale, *He's a Lunatic* (London: Thomas Hailes Lacy, 1868).

75 Merivale, *My Experiences*, pp. 28–32.

76 Louisa Lowe, *The Bastilles of England; or, the Lunacy Laws at Work* (London: Crookende, 1883), pp. 20–32. She also discusses the evidence given by Samuel Newington on Revd Thomas's case.

77 Lowe, *Bastilles of England*, p. 23.

78 Lowe, *Bastilles of England*, pp. 20–2.

79 *Case Book* 3, p. 50.

80 *Bill Book*, 1840–46, pp. 18, 68.
81 *Report on Lunacy Law*, p. 440.
82 Lowe, *Bastilles of England*, pp. 24–5.
83 Third person in the original. Perceval, *Treatment Experienced*, p. xiv.
84 *Report on Lunacy Law* p. 421.
85 Quoted in Parry-Jones, *The Trade in Lunacy*. p. 106.
86 Merivale, *Experiences in a Lunatic Asylum*, pp. 7–8.
87 *Visitors Book*, 1869–87, 26 March, 1877.
88 Alexander S.L. Newington (1846–1914) was in general practice before returning to Ticehurst on the death of his father, Samuel Newington. He played a less prominent role professionally than his cousin Hayes Newington.
89 *Visitors Book*, 1869–87, 14 April, 1882; 1887–1904, 22 May, 1888, 17 November, 1888.
90 Hayes Newington and A.S.L. Newington, 'Some Incidents', p. 65.
91 *Patients Bill Book*, 1901–08, account Prince Ahmed Saaf ed Din.
92 *Attendants Book*, letter dated 7 January, 1909.
93 *Visitors Book*, 1869–87, 10 June, 1881.
94 *Case Book*, 32, pp. 5–6.
95 *Case Book*, 1857–73, application 21 September, 1872.
96 *Register of Removal, Discharges and Deaths*, 1845–90 and 1890–1908; *Register of Deaths*, 1907–30.
97 *Visitors Book*, 1869–87, e.g. 15 December, 1862, 17 November, 1882.
98 *Case Book* 9, pp. 16, 74.
99 M.A. Lower, *The Worthies of Sussex* (Lewes: Geo. P. Bacon, 1865), p. 255.
100 *Case Book* 28, pp. 233, 234.
101 *Case Book* 4, pp. 32, 37.
102 *Case Book* 4, pp. 59, 60, 124, 154.
103 *Case Book* 32, p. 246.
104 *Report on Lunacy Law*, p. 546.
105 Hayes Newington, 'The Abolition of Private Asylums', pp. 138–47.
106 Hayes Newington, 'The Abolition of Private Asylums', p. 143.
107 *Visitors Book*, 1869–87, 1 June, 1886.
108 *Journal of Mental Science* 32 (1886): 301.
109 *Visitors Book*, 1869–87, 20 September, 1859, 30 January, 1875, 25 June, 1879.
110 Hayes Newington, 'What Are the Tests of Fitness', pp. 491–500.
111 Hayes Newington, 'What Are the Tests of Fitness', pp. 491–500.
112 *Register of Patients*, 1890–1907, patient no. 650.
113 H.F. Hayes Newington, 'Presidential Address', *Journal of Mental Science* 35 (1889): 293–315.
114 *Patients Book*, 1846–1904, 16 October, 1856.
115 *Patients Book*, 1846–1904, 6 February, 1873, 24 March, 1873, 22 June, 1874, 21 September, 1874.
116 Savage certified twenty-five admissions to Ticehurst between 1885 and 1915, or about one in thirteen of all admissions during this period. (*Register of Admissions*, 1881–90; *Register of Patients*, 1890–1907; *Civil Register*, 1907–19.)
117 G.H. Savage, 'Travel in Mental Disorders', *Journal of Mental Science* 37 (1901), pp. 236–42.
118 Quentin Bell, *Virginia Woolf, a Biography* 2 vols (London: Hogarth Press, 1972), vol 2, p. 228. For an account of Virginia Woolf's breakdowns and medical treatment see Stephen Trombley, *'All That Summer She Was Mad': Virginia*

Woolf and her Doctors (London: Junction Books, 1981).

119 Havelock Ellis, *My Life* (London: William Heinemann, 1940), p. 487.

120 See Parry-Jones, *Trade in Lunacy*, p. 55 for a table of declining numbers in private licensed houses.

121 See Scull *Museums of Madness* for a description of the growth of asylums in relation to the professionalization of medicine.

122 Richard D. French, *Antivivisection and Medical Science in Victorian Society* (Princeton, NJ: Princeton University Press, 1975), p. 150.

123 Quoted in Hayes Newington, 'Presidential Address', p. 300.

124 Hayes Newington, 'Presidential Address', pp. 303, 307, 313; Hayes Newington argued for the presence of neurologists and doctors of general medicine with an 'extended knowledge of physiology and its most recent advances' in the asylum.

125 Nancy Tomes's discussion of this ('The Persuasive Institution') in relation to Thomas Kirkbride and the Pennsylvania Hospital is particularly helpful.

CHAPTER NINE

Aspects of the history of psychiatry in Italy in the second half of the nineteenth century

Annamaria Tagliavini

AS AN AREA of study, the history of psychiatry in Italy is of recent origin but has attracted considerable interest. It has ceased to be simply a study of past medical practice, written by medical practitioners for their colleagues, but has gained the attention of social historians and historians of science, as well as of radical psychiatrists wishing to examine critically the origin of their discipline.[1] These developments have led to a widening of perspectives, and historical work has now gone beyond the effective impasse of biographies of illustrious psychiatrists of the past on the one hand, and 'internal histories' carried out from a medical rather than a historical point of view on the other.[2]

There has thus been a rapid growth in research aiming to outline the various aspects of the relationship between psychiatry and the social marginalization of the mad in the poor classes, a relationship that developed side by side with the construction of the modern state, which in Italy took place in the second half of the nineteenth century. Key influences on much of this research have been the work of Foucault, which began to be translated into Italian in the mid-1960s, and the ideas of Klaus Doerner on the dialectic between social integration and the repression of the marginal. In the early 1970s, the strong political drive for the release of mental patients led occasionally to a simplified reading of the history of lunatic asylums. Some of this research in Italy has in fact the air of being a hunt for the 'villain', presupposing that a violent, conscious repression of the lower classes took place, being manifested in the 'great confinement' in asylums between 1870 and 1890: such work, however, fails to consider the internal contradictions of the new bourgeois state and its ideological apparatus. In other cases there has been a straightforward equation between psychiatry and positivist views of science such as evolutionary theory, with the latter being seen as a mere ideological cover for the rising industrial bourgeoisie. Such an equation fails to examine the theoretical basis of nineteenth-century psychiatry and the real political, cultural, and scientific formation of its exponents.

Historical accounts of the asylums in the various states of pre-unified Italy have attracted considerable interest,[3] and much research has been and is being carried out in the archives of major psychiatric institutions to investigate the huge heritage of original documents. This research has enabled us to reconstruct the various psychiatric traditions and relevant legislation of the pre-unification period, for example local histories which constitute a fundamental chapter for the history of psychiatry at a national level. The nineteenth century may in fact fairly be considered the 'golden age' of alienism in Italy[4]: while institutions designed to cater for the mad had already been established in the 1700s, it was in the nineteenth century that an institutional network developed on a vast nationwide scale. It was then too that psychiatrists declared their independence as a separate profession, distinct from medicine, and that a body of knowledge on mental illness was well established, with a precise programme and an autonomous sphere of influence.

The fortunes of Italian psychiatry during this period, at both national and international levels, were undoubtedly linked to the encounter of psychiatry with the spread of positivism: an encounter of which Cesare Lombroso, with his criminal anthropology, provides the most famous instance. While studies on Lombroso initially tended to see him as the number one villain of his day,[5] he is now being afforded more precise and less heavily ideological consideration, and his work and ideas are being examined within the scientific context of his age.[6] Thus historical and legal studies have lately begun to investigate the relationship between psychiatry and the *scienze carcerarie* – criminology, penology – in which Lombroso's work constituted a focal point. Key issues in this growing body of research are penal responsibility in mental illness, criminality or so-called deviance, and the effective social control exercised by asylums, prisons, and 'criminal asylums'.[7]

In what follows I shall outline, perforce somewhat summarily, the principal characteristics of Italian psychiatry in the second half of the nineteenth century. I shall do so by describing the psychiatrists' research interests, their role within the institutions, and the theoretical premises on which their activity seems to have been based. This will involve some considerations of the relationship between psychiatry and positivist culture in the period. It will also allow me to present to English-speaking scholars the most important results of the recent historical research in the field.

The main primary sources to which I will refer concern particularly the activities of the Società Italiana di Freniatria, the first professional association of Italian psychiatrists, at whose periodic congresses theoretical and institutional issues were debated with great interest.

1 Psychiatrists and asylums before the political unification of Italy: a brief historical sketch

It is difficult to refer to an 'Italian psychiatry' as a national enterprise, a *unique* body of knowledge, a definite and homogeneous profession, before the political and administrative unification of the country, which started in 1860[8] At the moment of unification there existed a wide variety of different cultural, political, and scientific traditions, different kinds of institutions for the care of the insane and different laws that had to be amalgamated into the new unified state.

At the beginning of the eighteenth century the care of madness had been isolated as an autonomous problem from those of poverty and endemic diseases.[9] In 1710, for example, in the Ospedale S. Orsola in Bologna, inside the Pontifical State, a special ward for mad people was created.[10] In Tuscany the process of modernization began early in the second half of the eighteenth century, and in 1774 the grand duke Pietro Leopoldo introduced the first law to regulate the confinement of the insane under the control of the state, a fundamental principle that would be inherited by the first national law, passed as late as 1904.[11] In 1788 the Ospedale di Bonifacio was headed by Vincenzo Chiarugi (1759–1820), one of the protagonists of the important reform movement in European psychiatry, like Pinel in France and Tuke in Great Britain.[12] In Turin Vittorio Amedeo II of Savoy in 1728 founded the 'Ospedale dei Pazzerelli'; run by the religious congregation of Santo Sudario.[13] In Lombardy-Veneto Maria Teresa of Austria ordered that the building 'Pia casa della Senavra' should be dedicated to the care of the insane and in 1781 it became the first lunatic asylum in Milan[14]; in Venice at the end of the century the hospital of San Servolo, governed by the 'congregation Fatebenefratelli' was opened.[15]

According to recent studies there are two fundamental moments of transformation, the first in the second half of the eighteenth century; the second, at the beginning of the nineteenth associated with the spread of Pinel's reform from France to Italy, where in several states lunatic asylums were founded. Psychiatry came to be considered a 'theoretical-practical paradigm'[16]; a more modern form of social control than the previous form of segregation of the marginalized.

In 1813, in Aversa under the enlightened government of Gioacchino Murat, brother-in-law of Napoleon, the first true lunatic asylum was opened. It was run by Giovanni Maria Linguiti (1773–1825) and combined care with segregation, hospital with prison: a model institution that became widely accepted in the nineteenth century throughout Italy.[17] Under Murat a law was introduced to regulate the 'Opere Pie' and to bring under the state's jurisdiction questions relating to the confinement of the insane.

The medicalization of madness and the state's regulation of the mad, together with a general humanization of the conditions of life of lunatics were the main characteristics of psychiatric reform as operated by Pinel in

France. The influence of French culture and experience on Italian psychiatry was very important throughout the nineteenth century, not only on the structure of asylums but also on theory; Pinel and Esquirol had great influence, as has been clearly demonstrated by recent studies.[18]

By the mid-nineteenth century the blueprint of psychiatric institutions had been effectively drawn; every Italian state had its lunatic asylums and physicians to supervise them. But it is only in the second half of the century, with the emergence of the new Italian state that a 'national consciousness' of psychiatry as an autonomous discipline with a distinct professional identity was born. During this slow process of political and administrative unification of the state there was also an attempt at moral and cultural unification: the realization of the programme of the 'Risorgimento'.[19] Psychiatrists tried to participate in this programme by actively attempting to achieve for the new profession the role of 'civil servant' of the state, the agents of the government in the building and management of a national network of lunatic asylums[20]: they were to exercise the exclusive control of madness.

According to statistics of the period,[21] in 1866 there were 27 public asylums and 5 private (4 in Milan and 1 in Turin) ones and 4 wards for mad people in general hospitals. A study in 1918 counted 59 public asylums and 30 private, plus 3 criminal asylums.[22] Unfortunately, no historical work has been done on the private psychiatric sector in Italy. By means of a law passed in 1865 the new state had given the Amministrazioni Provinciali – county administrations – the responsibility of funding the public asylums.[23] It is difficult to evaluate the character of the psychiatric profession before national unification and to trace the steps by which one became a psychiatrist or an 'alienist'. Certainly the profession emerged from the general field of medicine, and medical training was a necessary background. Before unification, psychiatry had been taught only at the Scuola Superiore di Medicina in Florence (since 1844) and at the University of Turin since 1850. In the 1860s the teaching of psychiatry was instituted in the universities of Bologna and Naples (1863), in Pavia (1864), in Genoa (1866), and Padua (1867). The psychiatric 'career', as a standard specialization was not well established until the end of the century, but in order to become the supervisor of a lunatic asylum practical experience within such an institution was usually preferred, even if it did not constitute a formal requirement. In fact, general practitioners were also eligible for such posts.[24]

A professional association for psychiatrists

In parallel with the expansion of the institutional network was the growing demand for a national professional organization of psychiatrists. In 1862 the first group met during the tenth congress of Italian scientists in Siena. It was composed of Serafino Biffi (1822–99) and Andrea Verga (1811–95), both from Milan, Giuseppe Girolami (1809–78), Carlo Livi (1823–77), and Francesco Bonucci (1826–69). The first specialist journal was first published in 1852 in Milan, the *Appendice psichiatrica*, or 'psychiatric appendix', of the *Gazzetta medica Italiana-Lombardia*, edited by Verga, supervisor of the lunatic asylum of Senavra from 1848 to 1852, and subsequently director of the Ospedale Maggiore of Milan.[25] From its inception the periodical campaigned for a new psychiatry at a national level and for a reform of psychiatry and asylums in general. In 1864 its title was changed to *Archivio Italiano peule malattie nervose e più particolarmente per le alienazioni mentali*, and until 1891 it remained the major organ of Italian psychiatry, promoting and sustaining the professional association. In 1891 it was amalgamated with the *Rivista sperimentale di freniatria e di medicina legale in relazione con l'antropologia e le scienze giuridiche e sociali*,[26] founded in Reggio Emilia (1875) by Carlo Livi, supervisor of the asylum of San Lazzaro and his colleagues Augusto Tamburini (1848–1919) and Enrico Morselli (1852–1929). Milan and Reggio Emilia must be considered, according to recent studies,[27] two very important centres of Italian psychiatry in the second half of the nineteenth century.

The lack of an autonomous professional body that could recognize specific psychiatric qualifications and represent the interests of the new profession was deeply felt. Thus in 1873, during the eleventh congress of Italian scientists in Rome, the Società Italiana di Freniatria was formed, rapidly becoming a major forum for the discussion of theoretical and institutional problems.[28] Andrea Verga was elected president and Serafino Biffi secretary. Verga's presidency lasted until 1891, when Biffi replaced the 'old father' of Italian psychiatry, flanked by Augusto Tamburini, who himself became the third president in 1896.

The association's statutes – a true programme of the new profession – envisaged a membership composed of those physicians who shared a commitment to positivist experimental method in anatomical and physiological research, along with a conception of mental illness as a strictly organic phenomenon. This must be considered a declaration of principle, and a programme of research with the aim of giving scientific credibility to the new profession, and to unify around positivism, as a creed of science, the different conceptual traditions of mental illness current before the unification of the country.

The sense in which these Italian psychiatrists were positivists should be understood by analogy to the 'scientific naturalism' claimed by Victorian psychiatrists in Britain, rather than as a direct legacy of Comte.[29] In the new national psychiatry, in fact, arguments as to possible psychogenic interpretations of mental disturbances, common up to and through the 1860s, had to cease.

Psychiatric physicians were to be considered the only true experts. The second point of the statutes established that lawyers, philosophers, and natural scientists could occupy secondary positions in the association, on condition that they had a sincere interest on behalf of 'miserable lunatics'.[30] Institutional matters were a central issue. Until the turn of the century, alienists saw themselves as serving the new state. They directed the construction of asylums, and most important of all, championed legislation that was finally approved in 1904, after many years of parliamentary struggles.[31] The new national law on public and private asylums established the concept of the danger to society of madness and its juridical and psychiatric control. With the new law the role of supervisor of the asylum became much more powerful; he had, in fact, complete authority over the sanitary organization of the institution and also great power over its economic and administrative management.

This role was reluctantly recognized by the state; in achieving their ambition of serving the new state psychiatrists had to fight against the state's slow and insensitive bureaucratic machinery, economically and politically backward-looking; moreover, they faced the difficulty of liberating themselves from the older and very powerful category of general medicine.

The new specialists considered it their task to put an end to the great curses of the nation: poverty, illiteracy, alcoholism, and endemic illnesses. The psychiatrists' commitment to 'scientific' solutions to these problems, through vast programmes of social hygiene and sanitary and moral education of the population, reflects a quite well-established Italian tradition which links scientific and above all medical practice with progressive political thinking and activism. This tradition involved a concept of science as the fundamental instrument of civil progress and emancipation, an idea coming from the Enlightenment, which became a heritage of the Italian 'Risorgimento', with its ideology of constructing a new state.[32]

This engagement also involved a wider battle by alienists against superstition of all kinds; in particular, the belief that madness was the work of the devil, an idea then still widely current in rural areas. Also by discrediting rural priests and exorcists, psychiatrists were able to make the care of the mad their sole prerogative.[33] An interesting example is given by a well-studied case of 'epidemic hysteria' in a small rural area in Friuli.[34] As late as 1878 psychiatrists were obliged to use the army to convince the population to use the asylum and medicine rather than exorcists. Such rationalistic conviction found support amongst many Italian scientists and also in the secular spirit of the new state: many scientists believed religion to be incompatible with modern scientific principles.

With regard to madness, alienists commonly felt that rites, penitence, and the fear of sin and punishment further excited the already disturbed mind of their patients;[35] the case of the asylum of Venice run by priests until the end of the century was considered an exception.

Several psychiatrists were active in politics; some of them – Andrea Verga and Leonardo Bianchi, for example – were senators of the kingdom of Italy; others such as Lombroso were sympathizers with the socialist reform movement. But generally, at the turn of the century the progressive attitude of the 'Risorgimento' seems to have become less evident in psychiatry; in that period there was an intensification of social struggles and disorder toward which psychiatrists on the whole took up a conservative position; social deviancy and anarchy were defined as forms of mental illness.[36]

At the first meeting of the Società Italiana di Freniatria (1873) the group of founders undertook to hold a national congress every three years in one of the towns where the major asylums were located. They thereby aimed to attract public attention to the new science, and to encourage membership of the association.

The society had 12 founding members; the first congress was held in Imola in 1874, with approximately 100 participants.[37] Numbers grew throughout the rest of the century; in 1894 there were 122 members and in 1907 approximately 300. The first split in the society occurred in 1907 with the birth of the Society of Neurology and the second in 1909 with the first conference of the Associazione fra i Medici dei Manicomi Pubblici – Society of Public Asylum Physicians. The aim of this society was a more active defence of their specific professional interests, especially those of psychiatrists working in public asylums rather than in the prestigious academic positions to which the most famous psychiatrists turned at the beginning of the twentieth century.

The fiercest debates throughout the last thirty years of the nineteenth century revolved around the asylum, which emerged quite clearly as the focus of psychiatric activity and as the key therapeutic instrument of the period. Physical and pharmacological therapies were considered merely additional measures that could be usefully employed only in conjunction with the principal one, namely the asylum. The central idea of institutional therapy was to place the patient in a deliberately artificial environment, healthy and organized according to sound scientific principles. The structure of the building, its furnishing, the hierarchical relationship between doctor and patient, the timetable and discipline all had assumed therapeutic value. Hydrotherapy, clinotherapy, physical restraint, the use of sedatives in cases of frenzy, and of tonics in moments of weakness could be of additional aid only within the determining context of this therapeutic microcosm.

With the dominant conception of mental illness as a disease of the brain or the nervous system – an idea that underlines the medical matrix of psychiatry, psychiatrists were first of all physicians – therapy in the asylum was based on a re-education of the patient in which hygienic and moral principles were dominant; clean air, personal hygiene, and correct diet reinforced the virtues of work, discipline, and isolation. The influence of Pinel was crucial to this therapeutic tradition of 'moral treatment' in Italy. There was a sort of split, or contradiction, between a medical diagnosis and a moral therapy. Madness was on the one hand considered to be an organic disease of the brain and the nervous system – a lesion, inflammation, atrophy, or malfunction in the structure, a disorganization, a weakness – and on the other hand was held to be curable by the moral means of the asylum, to which the medical was subordinated. Clearly the use of the medical model of madness helped support the validity and the scientificity of the psychiatric profession in the asylum, where moral therapy went together with social control and confinement. The hypothesis which argued the need to reorder moral conduct and instinctive behaviour had its roots in the eighteenth-century tradition, which was linked to a psychogenetic conception of mental illness: in the nineteenth century this was replaced by organicist theory, although at the level of treatment the eighteenth-century moral therapy was reinforced by the practice within the asylum.

In a paper given at the sixth congress of the Società di Freniatria, one psychiatrist claimed that

> 'the order and discipline that the madman finds in the asylum, the new impressions that are made on him, the assistance and care he receives, the advice, exhortations and occasional opportune reproof bestowed upon him by the doctor, the sight of the other patients, the isolation, the distractions, all combine to form a truly suggestive environment. This environment favourably influences the symptoms and progress of psychopathy. It produces in the estranged subject the feeling of dependence on a benevolent and intelligent will, creates in him an awareness of his own illness and restores his psychic personality.'[38]

The environment of the asylum of the period (albeit artificial) reproduced, on a smaller scale, the reality outside. In the 'model asylum' of San Lazzaro, for example, social classes were rigidly divided, with peasants in the fields and artisans in their workshops, while the landlords sat in their villas reading good books and engaging in social pastimes.[39] The asylum – as envisaged by alienists – had to be a faithful representation of the outside world, only without those disturbances that might impede the recovery of reason. But this therapeutic and philanthropic conception of the asylum as a means of, on the one hand, curing the interned madmen, and on the other protecting society from deviants, was not without its ambiguities. Psychiatrists were clearly aware that in most cases they were merely locking up their patients, thereby defending society from 'pathogenic germs' and the danger of madness. In many cases, of course, this programme could not be applied for practical reasons: for instance the increasing number of recoveries, the inadequacy of the existing institutions and the lack of financial support for building new asylums.

It has been calculated that from 1874 to 1913 the population in asylums increased enormously, from about 12,000 in 1874, to a peak of 40,000 in 1907.[40] This was the age of 'the great confinement' in Italy. There were certainly many social and economic reasons for this – all those changes in society for which the lower classes of the population had paid so high a price; after all alcoholism and 'pellagra' (a form of madness due to inadequate diet especially in rural areas) were frequent in asylums in that period.[41] The widening of the category of madness confirmed the need for experts: it was a psychiatric exercise in self-validation. Those problems, it was argued, could be answered scientifically, acceptably, usefully.

Therapeutic techniques of British origin (such as 'open door' and 'no restraint') obtained little following in Italy. They were considered to be impractical given their high cost, and moreover considered to lack any real symbolic value. After all, the madman had been set free of his chains more than a hundred years before. The interest of the Italian psychiatric scientific community in these English techniques is shown in the occasional discussions occurring at their meetings. In 1890 Augusto Tamburini, director of the asylum of San Lazzaro in Reggio Emilia, presented a paper on his experience of 'no restraint' with a positive judgement[42]; on the other hand, in 1901 Ruggero Tambroni, director of the asylum of Ferrara, gave a paper firmly opposing any kind of 'no restraint'. At the subsequent congress in 1904, Ernesto Belmondo suggested that physical restraint should be substituted by appropriate drugs; this position of acceptance in theory, but of ambiguity in practice was the one most widely accepted.

Medical knowledge on insanity

A major concern during the period was the theoretical and scientific foundations of psychiatry. Born out of the field of medicine, the main way in which the new science attempted to qualify its separate status was through research in the pathology of the brain and of the nervous system. The object of psychiatric study, madness, was considered a disease of the organ of thought, the brain:[43] 'so called mental disease, those called "frenopatie" or "frenosi" can be studied only as diseases of the cerebral organ, or of the whole nervous system,' wrote Livi[44]; he believed that the problem was to discover 'why and how, man by means of the brain thinks and becomes mad'. In the same article Livi affirmed that for investigating madness the 'experimental' method, of Bacon and Galileo, proceeding by means of observation and experiment, was the only one.

Madness was held to be caused by exogenous or endogenous alterations to which abnormal behaviour such as delirium and hallucinations could be directly traced. Thus in the research literature of the period we find predominantly anatomical and physiological studies on the nervous system that attempt to relate psychiatry to neurology. The need to establish precise links between morphological changes in lesions with functional alterations of the nervous system gave rise to intense research activity in the field of pathological anatomy, which took place in laboratories attached to psychiatric hospitals. This research was designed to elucidate precise cerebral locations for the various psychic functions, thereby providing an empirical basis for the theoretical model. These studies were principally concerned with the sensory and motor functions and their relationship to the cortex.

In 1896 the *Rivista di patologia nervosa e mentale* was born. It was edited under the auspices of the psychiatric clinic of Florence and the 'schools' of Genoa and Reggio Emilia; the editor was Eugenio Tanzi, the co-editors were Augusto Tamburini and Enrico Morselli, all of whom were important psychiatrists and were amongst the collaborators of the *Rivista sperimentale di freniatria*. This new periodical proposed to complement the old one; it did not represent a complete break. Nevertheless, it gathered together that original nucleus of ideas that in time would constitute the new field of neurology. Only ten years later it had become an autonomous discipline. The preface to the first number declared that the journal would take on the role of an Italian *centralblatt*, concerned mainly with studies and international reviews of the anatomy, physiology, and pathology of the nervous system.[45] Similarly, in inaugurating the first congress of the Società di Neurologia ten years later, Leonardo Bianchi could still maintain that this new body represented not so much a split with psychiatry as the creation of a parallel specialism, a natural development for a discipline whose dimensions had increased and whose functions had become more complex.[46]

We can, in fact, find numerous testimonies to the close links between the two disciplines. One of the most significant is provided by a paper by Enrico Morselli, in which he maintained that psychiatrists are both neurologists and alienists, and that the inseparable tie binding psychiatry to neurology is based on the equally close relationship between organ and function, brain and thought, man's nervous system and his higher faculties.[47] Morselli stated that the two specializations of psychiatry and neurology are like two intersecting circles, sharing a common sector. He viewed psychiatry as concerned with groups of constitutional anomalies of the psyche, so-called simple or typical 'vasanie', which cannot as yet be traced to a clear basis in pathological anatomy. Neurology was concerned with a larger number of illnesses, whose locations are in the nervous centres and which produce disturbances of the motor and sensory functions. Notwithstanding this distinction, Morselli remained convinced that the functional and the organic were directly related, that the physical and psychological nature of man formed a unity, and he therefore saw the two disciplines as operating in parallel. Thus, at the turn of the century, the vast increase in the numbers of neuropathological studies does not seem to have significantly modified the state of knowledge concerning the principal types of psychopathies. It was at this point that some psychiatrists began to argue the importance of a return to clinical work, in the sense of renewed attention to the symptoms, development, and remedies for various types of illness. Eugenio Lugaro, author of an important book on mental illness in the 1900s, was convinced that the advances made in knowledge of the nervous system had shed relatively little light on the physio-pathological mechanisms of the psychopathies, and in particular on the precise locations of disease. But notwithstanding the fact that such attitudes were being increasingly aired at psychiatric conventions, experimental neurological research continued to expand.[48] Let us consider briefly, as an example, one form of mental pathology – hysteria – the interpretation of which could not easily be fitted into the model of 'cerebral lesion', but whose cause and roots Italian psychiatrists continued, despite the doubts, to place in relation to the nervous system.[49] Hysteria occupied a relatively important place in Italian psychiatric literature in the last two decades of the nineteenth century and the first of the twentieth. Of course the most important studies were conducted in France by Charcot, Bernheim, and Pierre Janet and in Austria by Breuer and Freud.[50] In Italy it merited only a chapter in the main treatises and manuals and was the occasional topic of discussion in the pages of specialized journals, but was not the subject of specific monographs.[51] The problems of defining this disease turned on its double nature as an organic illness, with a precise, albeit varied, physical symptomatology, which nevertheless did not seem to correspond to specific cerebral lesions. Not all the patient's mental faculties seemed to be affected; rather, a functioning reason was accompanied by an incapacity of will (failure in the control of the 'instincts' and of consciousness itself). Hysteria seemed more closely related to moral madness than to any other pathological form. Above all, hysteria was understood as

> 'a morbid manner of feeling and responding to physical and moral stimuli, an excessive impressionability, a shaky equilibrium of the nervous element ... a dynamic alteration of the nervous apparatus encapsulated by the term irritability and which can concern one or other side of the cerebral-spinal axis.'[52]

As to the causes and mechanisms of hysteria various hypotheses were suggested; the possibility of an 'hydraulic disturbance' able to modify the chemical-molecular condition of the cerebral elements; or else a disturbance in the functioning of the 'electrical apparatus' which, according to the Jacksonian model, 'circulated, condensed and finally released its force in order to reproduce more'.[53]

Augusto Tamburini, in his experimental studies (1881) of hypnotic phenomena in certain hysterics, found a permanent state of excitability of the nervous system due to 'modifications in the molecular nature of the nervous system'.[54] In these patients the slightest emotion was capable of producing 'that violent discharge of nervous tension which characterised the hysteric attack'. The hypothesis of a hierarchial organization of the nervous system subdivided into superior and inferior centres operating through nervous energy was rehearsed again at the beginning of the twentieth century in Leonardo Bianchi's *Trattato di psichiatria* (1904). Although Bianchi quoted Janet and Freud, his own definition of hysteria is that of a psychological illness of psychic personality, whose cause nevertheless had to be sought in the absence of appropriate normal structure and solid relations between the various 'cerebral provinces'. The exaggerated excitability of the hysteric was caused by malfunctioning of the inhibitory mechanism of the superior central centres, themselves 'overloaded with high tension'. The superior centres, 'the true deposit of historical experience' which, according to 'the law of adaptation and conservation of personality,' stabilized behaviour, would be obstructed in the hysteric by the 'lower I' – *io inferiore*. It seems then that even at the beginning of the twentieth century, and despite early familiarity with the work of Janet and Freud, the attempt to establish a neurological or, better, neuro-dynamic basis continued unabated; it remained an important theoretical background to Italian psychiatric research. It would also perhaps be one of the reasons why the dissemination of psychoanalysis in Italy was relatively slow and late compared with other countries, as the few studies on this question have suggested.[55].

One important consequence of the 'clinical' proposal of Italian psychiatry was its effect on the debate concerning the introduction of a nationally standardized classification of mental illness, the search for which had lasted throughout the first three decades of the Società di Freniatria's existence. A first discussion of the problem of a national classification of mental diseases took place at the first congress of the society in 1874. On that occasion Andrea Verga proposed a classification that tried to unify the French model of Pinel and Esquirol, together with the new tradition of organic aetiology of mental pathology whose key figures were Morel and Griesinger.[56] In another paper at the same conference Clodomiro Bonfigli, director of the asylum at Ferrara, proposed two different kinds of classification, one for scientific purposes based on the 'morbid processes', the other for practical ends.[57] The congress decided officially to adopt the classification of Verga, which was considered more useful in subdividing the insane on the wards into 'curable' and 'incurable'. In 1901 at the eleventh congress Sante De Santis called for a new project in which the clinical ideas of Emil Kraepelin and of the German clinical school could be incorporated.[58]

Before it could unify the practices of classification previously in use in the various asylums of the individual states, however, the new science had to agree on a terminology to suit its requirements. In consequence, it would appear, discussion of the merits of possible classificatory models was pushed into second place with respect to the more pressing terminological issue. Had this discussion developed, it would clearly have revealed the underlying differences and disagreements within this apparently compact professional body.

In recent historical studies the main criticism levelled at the psychiatry of this period has concerned its organicist stance and its consequent failure to understand the whole process of mental illness. As we have seen in the example of hysteria at the end of the century, organicism became a wider concept and the restricted idea of the cerebral lesion was integrated with various conceptions of malfunction and disorganization of the entire nervous system. The conviction that every manifestation of madness had an organic basis, and the search for its physical location undoubtedly led to an unproductive interpretation of many kinds of mental diseases, for instance, the actual neuroses. However it should be remembered that it was precisely during this period that major discoveries were made in Europe concerning the structure and functions of the nervous system and that psychiatry and neurology made a major contribution to these discoveries. In Italy, for example, the important work of Camillo Golgi (1844–1926)[59] and Luigi Luciani (1840–1918)[60] threw light on very important aspects of the physiology and the pathology of the nervous system.

Psychiatry and positivism: the spread of evolutionary theories and the model of degeneration

An issue still debated in recent historical studies is the extent to which the growth of psychiatry in Italy was related to the spread of positivism.[61] There are clearly intellectual debts, a reciprocal influence on topics and language between the new science and the 'religion of science'. From the evidence for this interchange we may cite the interest of psychiatrists in sociology and anthropology, as well as experimental psychology. These disciplines developed in Italy in the positivistic climate of the last third of the nineteenth century.

Many of the doctors who were active members of the Società di Freniatria were involved in what we might call general cultural activity of a positivistic tone. Psychiatrists were among the founders of the *Rivista di filosofia scientifica*, effectively the official organ of Italian positivism from 1881 to 1891. Enrico Morselli, Cesare Lombroso, Eugenio Tanzi, Gabriele Buccola, all members of the Società di Freniatria, made important contributions to the journal, a sign of their additional commitment as men of science to theoretical and philosophical reflection. Important studies have shown the significant contribution of the *Rivista di filosofia scientifica* to the introduction of evolutionism in Italy.[62] They have also shown how within this Italian *milieu* of positivism the various human sciences – criminology, anthropology, sociology – were characterized by evolutionism.[63]

The impact of evolutionism in Italy in the age of positivism is still an object of research. Many such studies have alerted us to the fact that the issue is not just the spread of Darwin's work, but also a wider context in which Spencer's theory of cosmic evolution (from the inorganic to the mental), Moleschott's theory of the circulation of life, the work of Haeckel, the Lamarckian tradition in the natural sciences, and moreover the whole range of ideas on evolution before Darwin flourished together.[64] I will now consider briefly the use that psychiatry made of the concepts and language of evolutionism. Psychiatrists sympathetic to Lombrosian anthropology and human sciences in general defined their allegiance to an 'aetiological' current that runs alongside the neurological one in a shared organicist stream.[65] While neurological psychiatrists were studying the brain and the nervous system as the key to the cause of madness, aetiological psychiatrists were interested in discovering in the body of the mad patient the signs of a morbid past. They invoked evolutionary theory not only to describe but also to account for mental pathologies. The mechanism whereby characteristics are inherited was seen as the cause and enabling condition for most types of madness. But the psychiatrist's application of Darwin's theory of natural selection to man and the relationships of human beings to the natural and social environment seems to have been often hasty and superficial. In the case of psychiatry we must refer to an earlier tradition of evolutionary and hereditary ideas. The rise of the idea of hereditary madness preceded Darwinian evolutionism. It is an idea with a long history in the medical field and found an important systematization in the work of Benedict-Augustin Morel.[66] It is with his *Traité des dégénérescences, intellectuelles et morales de l'espèce humaine* (1857) and with his *Traité des maladies mentales* (1860), that, as has recently been noted,[67] 'The idea of time officially enters into psychiatry.' Morel's hypothesis outlined a temporal idea of the process of the hereditary development of mental illness in the individual and in the species. For Morel, madness, like certain other kinds of illness, develops in the individual as a progressive degradation towards a final state of degeneration.

Madness had predominantly moral characteristics but it was manifested in certain recognizable bodily signs. In Italy Morel's work was associated with evolutionary thought and his theory was pushed much further in this direction. The idea of degeneration, as well as the theory of atavism, found an important interpreter in Cesare Lombroso.[68]

The theory of atavism – according to which delinquency and madness could be seen as different forms of throwback to a past, more primitive form of behaviour – appeared for the first time in the first edition of *L'Uomo delinquente studiato in rapporto alla antropologia, alla medicina legale e alle discipline carcerarie* (1876). With the second edition in 1878 it became more widely known. As has been noted, Lombroso's work owed much to previous traditions of comparative anatomy, phrenology, and anthropology (especially that of Paul Broca) but his point of view located these ideas in a more general evolutionary perspective and in a cultural context characterized by the spread of Darwin's work. The degeneration hypothesis was most widely accepted in Lombroso's principles of criminal anthropology, in particular his stereotype of the 'criminal personality'; psychiatrists following his ideas set about the search for typical madmen. Psychiatric research of the period therefore pursued both the spatial organization of the brain and a temporal dimension represented by the past animal behaviour of man.[69] The idea of degeneration, the theory of atavism, heredity, together with the 'struggle for existence' and 'the survival of the fittest' were used at one time or another to account for madness.

> 'Atavism, degeneration, illness [declared the paper 'Degeneration and Primitiveness' at the eleventh congress of the Società di Freniatria in 1889[70]] do not exclude but penetrate and complete one another; they are the levelling instruments of biological energy; they constitute together the moving wheels of human life; they are always in action for the biological equilibrium of society and if through them degeneration occurs so too does regeneration.'

In Giuseppe Sergi's *Le Degenerazioni umane*[71] the carriers of the germs of madness are described as the vanquished in the battle for survival – the weak. The strong who had come through unharmed are the normal. Sergi conceived of various types of degeneration: on the one hand there were those with social consequences 'from the vagabond who produces nothing to the murderer, from the beggar who lives off others to the fraudulent bankrupt,' and on the other there were individual forms whose main characteristics were lack of balance or symmetry in the cerebral organs. The most frequently mentioned illness of this kind was epilepsy, considered by Lombroso to be a paradigmatic case of degeneracy. If we add to all this the fact that the roots of much 'deviant' behaviour were held to reside in atavistic or primitivistic regression, the extent of the influence of evolutionism, in general, on psychiatry in Italy becomes apparent. There was a clear propensity at the time to interpret psycho-pathological forms in hereditary, degenerative terms. To judge from the debates in the psychiatric congresses this propensity reached its peak in the 1880s. Toward the end of the century the idea of degeneracy and hereditary madness lessened in influence, as was clearly explained by Enrico Morselli. In 1905, in his preface to Raffaele Brugia's, *I Problemi della degenerazione* (1906), Morselli outlined a short history of the idea of degeneration in Italian psychiatry. According to him there had been three periods, the first involving a severe and restricted application of Morel's idea, exclusively to certain forms of intoxication; the second, an 'excessive extension' in which degeneration became a sort of all-encompassing form of explanation for every type of mental pathology; the third, almost heralded by this book of Brugia's, involved a critical, cautious re-examination of the use of the concept.

In the same preface Morselli discussed the scepticism he had felt since 1891 when in the sixteenth lecture of his course on general anthropology at the University of Genoa he had distinguished anthropological degeneration from its more strictly pathological equivalent. Even in his *Manuale di semejotica delle malattie mentali* (1898) he had insisted on the need to separate anthropological degeneration (the world of Lombroso's criminals) from the field of mental pathology where degeneration had its limits as a diagnostic term; but on his own admission he had remained for the most part unheard by the majority of his colleagues still involved in degeneration and atavism.

'All we alienists, following in the footsteps of Lombroso, of Krafft-Ebing and of Magnan (glorious footsteps but already superseded) for a certain period made the mistake of believing too much in the theory of degeneration; so much so that, in the end, we placed this internal factor – operating obscurely and indefinitely on the organism and on the functional activity of the new being – as its basis. Thus degeneration became almost the exclusive category in our classification and definition of illnesses and mental anomalies.'[72]

It has been suggested recently that inside this 'aetiological' interpretation of mental diseases – to which evolutionism gave support – as a throwback to the past, of the primitive man who 'sleeps' inside the civilized man and wakes up in madness, one could possibly recognize a primitive idea of unconscious activity.[73] Certainly we need much more research in this field to understand why this evolutionary conception of man and of his mental functions existed inside the 'organicist paradigm' and why this idea – the possibility of unconscious past activity – did not break the paradigm itself.

The relationship between psychiatry and evolutionism in general has been roughly pointed out; this is not the only link between psychiatry and positivist scientific culture. We should exercise care in evaluating the effect on psychiatry of certain key themes in positivist culture. First, it was not positivism as a philosophical system that was principally involved; this was mainly a backdrop that was never directly faced. The use of the term 'positivism' in Italy can be compared to the use that British psychiatrists made of 'scientific naturalism' in the Victorian age.[74] It can be considered a common tendency of psychiatry in the second half of the nineteenth century, across different cultural contexts, to use ideologies and philosophies which affirmed the predomination of scientific knowledge and of scientific experimental method in every field of reality; this affirmed a more important role for scientists in society, in this case, of psychiatrists in their institutions, and in society. Positivism became for Italian psychiatry a 'spontaneous epistemology', to use an expression of Georges Gusdorf, developing relatively late, merging within an old experimental tradition in medicine. The link with the latter was in any case more often declared than practised in the psychiatry of the time, dominated as it was by generalizations lacking substantial experimental evidence. What was taken from positivism, and developed and exalted by psychiatry, was the validity and certainty of scientific knowledge and its practical value in solving social problems, a conception of science which came to outlive positivism itself. Overall, rather than simply an instrumental or ideological use of positivism by the new discipline, we appear to be faced with a complex interaction whose extent and consequences have yet to be clarified.

Conclusions

All in all, nineteenth-century Italian psychiatry seems to have been concerned with solving practical problems rather than with discussion of major theoretical issues. But its clear concern with the organization of the asylum should not lead us to underestimate its emergence as a science. If, as some have attempted to do, we deny the psychiatry of the period scientific status and dignity, reducing it to asylum technology, we will fail to grasp the role it played in the spread of new attitudes toward madness where ideology and common sense often blend in an equivocal medical language. The consolidation of the conceptual apparatus of Italian psychiatry took place within the context of a neurological emphasis which aimed at using medical criteria to establish 'proofs' with ever-growing levels of certainty as to the origins and physical correlates of madness in its various forms. It was a faith in organic accounts of mental illness, a faith which was undaunted even while seeking more 'sociological' explanations in evolutionary theory.

Notes

I am very grateful to Bill Bynum and Roy Porter for their helpful comments on my work. I would like to acknowledge the Italian CNR for the support of my research with a NATO fellowship and the generous hospitality of the Wellcome Institute for the History of Medicine.

1 The numerous interdisciplinary conventions held in recent years testify to this shared interest of scholars in different fields. See: *Storia della sanità in Italia. Metodo e indicazioni di recerca*, ed. CISO (Centro Italiano di Storia Ospedaliera) (Roma: Il Pensiero Scientifico, 1978); 'L'Emarginazione psichiatrica nella storia e nella società', *Rivista sperimentale di freniatria*, fasc. 2, (1980); L. Del Pistoia, and F. Bellato (eds), *Curare e ideologia del curare* (Lucca: Maria Pacini Fazzi, 1980); A. De Bernardi (ed.), *Psichiatria manicomio, classi sociali* (Milano: F. Angeli, 1982). In this study I will refer mainly to the Italian literature on the subject. Italian psychiatry in fact has not attracted the attention of British and French historians. For non-Italian-speaking readers I can suggest: G. Mora, 'Italy', in J. G. Howells (ed.), *World History of Psychiatry* (New York: Brunner/Mazel, 1975), pp. 39–89; L. Del Pistoia, G.B. Giordano, 'L'Italie' in J. Postel, C. Quetel, *Nouvelle histoire de la psychiatrie* (Toulouse: Privat, 1983), pp. 267–73, M. Beluffi, 'Les rapports entre la psychiatrie lombarde et la psychiatrie française cours de la deuxième moitié au XIXe siècle à travers les pages de *Archivio Italiano per le malattie nervose* édité à Milan entre 1864 et 1891 par A. Verga, C. Castiglioni, S. Biffi', *Annales de thérapeutique psychiatrique*, 4 (1969): 66–79.

2 I have discussed the most important studies in a review, see V.P. Babini, M. Cotti, F. Minuz, and A. Tagliavini, 'La Storia della psichiatria nell'Ottocento: i contributi italiani nell'ultimo decennio (1968–1978)', *Storia e critica della psicologia* 1 (2) (1980): 177–96.

3 For an excellent reconstruction of the history of psychiatric institutions in Italy, see R. Canosa, *Storia del manicomio in Italia dall'Unità ad oggi* (Milano: Feltrinelli, 1979); for a history of asylums in Milan, see A. De Bernardi, F. De Peri, and L. Panzeri, *Tempo e catene. Manicomio, psichiatria e classi subalterne* (Milano: F. Angeli, 1980).

4 The definition is that of R. Castel, *L'Ordre psychiatrique. L'age d'or de l'aliénisme* (Paris: Editions de Minuit, 1976).

5 On this subject, see F. Graziosi, 'Delinquenti su misura', *Expresso colore* 32 (1972): 21–3; the introduction to the modern edition of C. Lombroso, *L'Uomo delinquente in rapporto all'antropologia, alla giurisprudenza e alle discipline carcerarie* (Roma: Napoleone, 1971), and A. Pirella, Introduction to C. Lombroso, *L'Uomo di genio* (Roma: Napoleone, 1971).

6 As well as the now classic study by L. Bulferetti, *Cesare Lombroso* (Torino: UTET, 1975); F. Silvani, 'Recenti lavori su Lombroso', *La Questione criminale* 1 (1976): 194–205; the introduction by F. Giacanelli to G. Colombo, *La Scienza infelice. Il museo di antropologia criminale di Cesare Lombroso* (Torino: Boringhieri, 1975); E. De Bernart and M. Tricarico, 'Per una rilettura dell'opera di Cesare Lombroso', *Physis* 18 (1976): 179–84: R. Villa, 'Lettura recente di Lombroso', *Studi storici* 2 (1977): 243–52; R. Villa, 'Scienza medica e criminalità nell'Italia unita', in F. Della Peruta (ed.), *Storia d'Italia. Malattia e medicina* Annali 7, (Torino: Einaudi, 1984), pp. 1145–168.

7 Cf. V.P. Babini, 'La responsabilità nelle malattie mentali', in V.P. Babini, M.

Cotti, F. Minuz, and A. Tagliavini, *Tra sapere e potere. La psichiatria italiana nella seconda metà dell'Ottocento* (Bologna: Il Mulino, 1982); R. Villa, 'Pazzi e criminali: strutture istituzionali e pratica psichiatrica nei manicomi criminali italiani (1876–1915)', *Movimento operaio e socialista Crimine e follia. Le istituzioni segreganti nell'Italia liberale 4, a.* III (1980): 369–93.

8 For the most important aspects of the Italian history of the period see A. Asor Rosa, 'La Cultura', in R. Romano and C. Vivanti (eds.), *Storia d'Italia*, vol. 4 (Torino: Einaudi, 1975), vol. 4 (pp. 821–979; and E. Ragionieri, 'La Storia politica e sociale', *Storia d'Italia* (Torino: Einaudi 1976) vol. 4, pp. 1668–743.

9 For the most important aspects of the history of Italian psychiatry see F. Stok, *La Formazione della psichiatria* (Roma: Il Pensiero Scientifico, 1981) and F. De Peri, 'Il Medico e il folle: istituzione psichiatrica, sapere scientifico e pensiero medico fra Otto e Novecento', in F. Della Peruta (ed.), *Storia d'Italia. Malattia e medicina*, Annali 7 (Torino: Einaudi, 1984), pp. 1060–140.

10 Notices on the lunatic asylums in Italy can be found in G. Antonini, G.C. Ferrari, and A. Tamburini, *L'Assistenza degli alienati in Italia e nelle varie nazioni* (Torino: UTET, 1918); F. Ugolotti, 'Panorama storico dell'assistenza ai malati di mente in Italia', *Note e riviste di psichiatria* 75 (1949): 73–148; P. Sérieux, *L'Assistance des aliénés en France, en Allemagne, en Italie et en Suisse* (Paris: Imprimerie Municipale, 1903); Canosa, *Storia del manicomio.*

11 Cf. L. Passerini, *Storia degli stabilimenti di beneficienza e di istruzione elementare gratuita della città di Firenze* (Firenze: Le Monnier, 1853); O. Andreucci, *Della carità pubblica in Toscana* (Firenze: Le Monnier, 1864).

12 Cf. E. Coturri, 'Le Sostanziali innovazioni introdotte in psichiatria da Vincenzo Chiarugi', *Episteme* 6 (1972): 252–65; A. Palmerini, 'Chiarugi Vincenzo', *Enciclopedia Italiana*, vol. 9 (Milano: Edizioni della enciclopedia italiana: 1931). The most important work of Chiarugi is the treatise *Della Pazzia in genere e in specie. Trattato medico-analitico con una centuria di osservazioni*, 2 vols (Firenze, 1793–95).

13 Cf. *Il Regio manicomio di Torino nel suo secondo centenario (1728–1928)* (Torino Bocca: 1928).

14 See L. Panzeri, 'Il Manicomio a Milano: la Pia Casa della Senavra (1781–1878)', in De Bernardi, De Peri, and Panzeri, *Tempo e catene*, pp. 109–62.

15 Cf. L. Pelt, *Cenni storico-medici intorno al Manicomio Femminile di Venezia* (Venezia: 1847); 'Follia come crimine. I manicomi nel Veneti', *Materiali Veneti 7* (1977); pp. 289–320; H. Terzian and M. Galzigna, *Archivio della follia* (Venezia: Marsilio, 1981).

16 Cf. Stok, *La formazione.*

17 See V.D. Catapano, 'Appunti per una storia dei movimenti psichiatrici in Campania', *Gionale Storico di Psichologia Dinamica* 1 (1977): 207–38.

18 In particular see De Peri, 'Il Medico e il folle'.

19 'In common usage the word Risorgimento refers to the movement which led to the formation of the Italian national unitary state', the definition is by G. Candeloro, *Storia dell'Italia moderna*, 2 vols (Milano: Feltrinelli, 1956), vol. 1, p. 14, quoted in D. Beales, *The Risorgimento and the Unification of Italy* (London: Longman, 1981); see also D.M. Smith, *The Making of Italy, 1796–1870* (London: Macmillan, 1968).

20 See A. Tamburini, 'La Società freniatrica e la psichiatria italiana. Discorso inaugurale al XIV congresso freniatrico italiano', *Rivista sperimentale di freniatria* XXXVIII (1911) 11–18; on this new role of psychiatrists cf. F. Giacanelli,

'Un Nuovo quadro professionale della borghesia nel secolo diciannovesimo: il personaggio dello psichiatra tra filantropia medica e controllo sociale', *Rivista sperimentale di freniatria* 4 (1980): 915–28.

21 Cf. 'Movimento dei pazzi ricoverati nei manicomi d'Italia durante l'anno 1866', *Archivio Italiano per le malattie nervose* (1867): 270–71. For a more recent study see G. Gorni, 'Malattia mentale e sistema. L'istituzione manicomiale italiana dalla fine del Settecento agli inizi del Novecento', *Classe. Quaderni sulla condizione e sulla lotta operaia* 15 (June 1978): 193–222.

22 Antonini, Ferrari, and Tamburini, *L'Assistenza agli alienati.*

23 Cf. M. Cotti, 'L'istituzione manicomiale nel nuovo stato unitario. Regime amministrativo, regime sanitario e armonia istituzionale', in V.P. Babini, M. Cotti, F. Minuz, and A. Tagliavini, *Tra sapere e potere*, pp. 199–243.

24 A. Verga, 'Prime linedi'una statistica pei manicomi d'Italia', *Archivio Italiano per le malattie nervose* (1867): 270–71; F. Minuz, *Le sedi di formazione degli psichiatri italiani. Psichiatria negli stati pontifici e psichiatria italiana*, in *Sanità, società e storia*, 1985 (1), in press.

25 For a biography of Andrea Verga see A. Tamburini, 'Andrea Verga, commemorazione', *Rivista sperimentale di freniatria*, (1896): i–xx. His most important work is A. Verga, *Studi anatomici sul cranio e sull'encefalo, psicologici e freniatrici* (Milano: Manini-Wiget, 1897).

26 For details on specialist publications of the period cf. G. Padovani, *La Stampa periodica italiana di neuropsichiatria e scienze affini nel primo centenario di sua vita, 1843–1943* (Milano: Hoepli, 1946).

27 On the different characteristics of the two 'schools', the one of Milan more interested in the practical aspects of the profession, the one of Reggio Emilia in the anatomical and physiological study of the nervous system, see De Peri, 'Il Medico e il folle', pp. 1080–092.

28 The announcement of the foundation of the Società di Freniatria is to be found in 'I Medici alienisti all'undecimo congresso degli scienziati in Roma, 1873', (Anonymous) *Archivio Italiano per le malattie nervose* (1874): 41–63.

29 On the use of 'scientific naturalism' in British psychiatry see M. Clark, 'The Data of Alienism: Evolutionary Neurology, Physiological Psychology and the Reconstruction of British Psychiatric Theory, 1850–1900' (PhD thesis, University of Oxford, 1982), in particular ch. 7, 'The Natural Laws of Man and Society: Evolutionary Physiological Psychology, Mental Hygiene and Social Order in Late Victorian Britain', pp. 229–98; R. Smith, *Trial by Medicine* (Edinburgh: Edinburgh University Press, 1981).

30 The Association's statute was approved in 1873 during the first meeting, see 'I Medici alienisti'.

31 The need for central government legislation to regulate the asylum was a constant interest of psychiatrists, but a law was passed only on 12 February, 1904, as no. 36 in *Atti parlamentari, Camera dei Deputati*, Legislatura XXI, II sessione, p. 10551. The history of psychiatric legislation is discussed in Canosa, *Storia del manicomio*; Stok, *La Formazione della psichiatria.*

32 On the relationship between science and politics in nineteenth-century Italy, see G.C. Marino, *La Formazione dello spirito borghese* (Firenze: La Nuova Italia, 1974); *Scienza e tecnica nella cultura e nella società dal Rinascimento ad oggi*, ed. G. Micheli, *Storia d'Italia*, Annali 3 (Torino: Einaudi, 1980); G. Pancaldi (ed.), *I Congressi degli scienziati italiani nell'età del positivismo* (Bologna: Clueb, 1983).

33 On this subject and for further information on the psychiatric profession cf. F.

Minuz, 'Gli psichiatri italiani e l'immagine della loro scienza', in Babini *et al., Tra sapere e potere*, pp. 27–75.

34 C. Gallini, *La Sonnambula meravigliosa. Magnetismo e ipnotismo nell'Ottocento italiano* (Milano: Feltrinelli, 1984).

35 Cf. S. Biffi, 'Le Suore di carità nei manicomi', *Archivio Italiano per le malattie nervose* (1866): 129–41, and the debate on this subject in 'I Medici alienisti'.

36 On the conservative attitude of Italian psychiatry at the end of the century see L. Bulferetti, *Cesare Lombroso* (Torino: UTET, 1975); Stok, *La Formazione della psichiatria*; Canosa, *Storia del manicomio*.

37 Cf. 'Atti del I Congresso della Società di Freniatria (Imola, 1874)', *Archivio Italiano per le malattie nervose* (1874): and Stok, *La Formazione della psichiatria*. pp. 92–105.

38 G. Seppilli, 'La Terapeutica suggestiva nelle malattie mentali', *Archivio Italiano per le malattie nervose* (1890): 231–60.

39 G. Virgilio, 'Relazione della visita fatta al Manicomio di S. Lazzaro', *Archivio Italiano per le malattie nervose* (1881): 279–89; A. Tamburini, *Il Frenocomio di Reggio Emilia* (Reggio Emilia: Calderini, 1900).

40 E. Fornasari di Verce, 'Sui metodi di rilevazione nella statistica dei pazzi', *Rivista sperimentale di freniatria* (1907): 288–97; A. Tamburini, 'Sulla statistica degli alienati in Italia nel 1907', *Rivista sperimentale di freniatria* (1909): 343–52; *Statistica dei ricoverati in ospedali e altri istituti di assistenza pubblica e privata* (Roma: Società Editrice Libreria, 1909).

41 Cf. M. Figurelli, 'L'Alcool e la classe. Cenni per una storia dell'alcoolismo in Italia', *Classe. Quaderni sulla condizione e sulla lotta operaia*, 15 (June 1978): 93–137; R. Finzi, 'La Pellagra, una gloria capitalistica', *Classe. Quaderni sulla condizione e sulla lotta operaia*, 15 (June 1978): 137–65.

42 A. Tamburini, 'Un Biennio di esperimento di no-restraint', *Archivio Italiano per le malattie nervose* (1890): 405–15.

43 The organicist constitution of Italian psychiatry of the nineteenth century has been clearly pointed out by the most recent studies that I have mentioned; I have also discussed this aspect in 'La Scienza psichiatrica. La costruzione del sapere nei congressi della Società Italiana di Freniatria (1874–1907)', in Babini *et al., Tra sapere e potere*.

44 C. Livi, 'Del Metodo sperimentale in freniatria e medicina legale', *Rivista sperimentale di freniatria* (1875), i–xx; the same ideas are expressed in A. Tamburini, 'Del Concetto odierno della fisiologia normale e patologica della mente', *Lo Sperimentale* (extract, Firenze: Celliniana, 1877); and A. Verga, 'Se e come si possa definire la pazzia', *Archivio Italiano per le malattie nervose* (1874): 3–22, 73–83.

45 Cf. *Rivista di Patologia Nervosa e Mentale* 1 (1896): 1.

46 See the inaugural address by L. Bianchi to the first congress of the Società di Neurologia, 'I Congresso Italiano di Neurologia', *Rivista Sperimentale di Freniatria* (1908): p. 310.

47 Cf. E. Morselli, 'Psichiatria e neuropatologia', *Rivista sperimentale di freniatria* (1905): 15–43.

48 Cf. E. Lugaro, 'I Recenti progressi della anatomia del sistema nervoso in rapporto alla psicologia e alla psichiatria', *Rivista sperimentale di freniatria* (1900): 92–147.

49 I have discussed this problem in a paper 'La Mente femminile nella psichiatria italiana dell'Ottocento' given at the conference *L'Eta del positivismo: il caso di Reggio Emilia* (Reggio Emilia, 9/10/11 May, 1984) whose proceedings are now

being published by Il Mulino Press.

50 On the history of hysteria see I. Veith, *Hysteria. The History of a Disease* (Chicago: University of Chicago Press, 1965).

51 Two interesting studies on hysteria in Italy are A. Morselli, 'Sulla Natura dell'isterismo', *Rivista sperimentale di freniatria* (1912): 134–201; and M. Levi-Bianchini, *L'Isterismo dalle antiche alle moderne dottrine* (Padova: Durker, 1913).

52 Cf. G. Seppilli and D. Maragliano, 'Contributo allo studio dell'isteroepilessia', *Rivista sperimentale di freniatria* (1878); 345–61, esp. 356.

53 Seppilli and Maragliano, 'Contributo allo studio', p. 357.

54 Cf. A. Tamburini and G. Seppilli, 'Contribuzioni allo studio sperimentale dell'ipnotismo', *Rivista sperimentale di freniatria* (1881): 261–300.

55 The dissemination of Freud's work in Italy had been discussed in M. David, *La Psicoanalisi nella cultura italiana* (Torino: Boringhieri, 1965) and also in A. Carotenuto, *Jung e la cultura italiana* (Roma: Astrolabio, 1977). Both the authors agree on the hypothesis of an early reading of Freud's work but the first systematic study must be considered: E. Morselli, *La Psicoanalisi*, 2 vols (Torino: Bocca, 1926) In 1921 the *Archivio generale di neurologia e di psichiatria* added to his title 'e di Psicoanalisi', the editor, Marco Levi-Bianchini, supervisor of the asylum in Teramo, also published the Biblioteca Psicoanalitica Italiana with the most important translations. Not until 1932 was the *Rivista Italiana di psicoanalisi* founded, becoming the official organ of the Società Psicoanalitica Italiana.

56 Cf. A. Verga, 'Proposta di una classificazione uniforme delle malattie mentali a scopo particolarmente statistico', *Archivio Italiano per le malattie nervose* (1874): 217–41.

57 Cf. C. Bonfigli, 'Sulla Classificazione delle malattie nervose con alienazione mentale', *Archivio Italiano per le malattie nervose* (1874): 312–20.

58 See S. De Santis, 'Sulla Classificazione delle psicopatie', *Rivista sperimentale di freniatria* (1902): 184–254.

59 Camillo Golgi, professor of histology in Pavia (1875) and of general pathology (1881) made important studies on the tissues of the nervous system and on the grey matter. See his *Studi sulla fine anatomia degli organi centrali del sistema nervoso* (Pavia: 1874). His studies on the histology of the encephalus and spinal cord were for the most part published in the *Rivista sperimentale di freniatria* in 1882, 1883, 1885; cf. C. Golgi, *Opera omnia* (Milano: Hoepli, 1903).

60 Luigi Luciani, physiologist, professor of general pathology in Parma (1875) and of physiology in Siena (1880–82), then in Florence (1882–93), and in Rome (1897–1917). He made important studies on cerebral localizations, on the cortical pathology of epilepsy (1878), and on cerebral physiology (1891). His most important book *Fisiologia dell'uomo* (1898–1901) has been translated into English (1911–21).

61 On the relationship between psychiatry and positivism see F. Giacanelli and G. Campoli, 'La Costituzione positivistica della psichiatria italiana', *Psicoterapia e scienze umane* 3 (1977): 1–16; on positivism in Italy see E. Garin, *Storia della filosofia italiana*, 3 vols (Torino: Einaudi, 1966); A. Santucci (ed.), *Scienza e filosofia nella cultura positivistica* (Milano: Feltrinelli, 1982); AAVV, *Studi sulla cultura filosofica italiana tra Ottocento e Novecento*, (Bologna: Clueb, 1982).

62 Cf. M. Costenaro, 'La Rivista di filosofia scientifica e il positivismo italiano', *Giornale critico della filosofia italiana* (1972): 92–117; M. Costenaro, 'Scienza, filosofia e metafisica nella Rivista di Filosofia Scientifica', *Giornale critico della*

filosofia italiana (1975): 263–301.

63 On evolutionism in Italy see G. Landucci, *Darwinism a Firenze. Tra scienza e ideologia (1860–1900)* (Firenze: Olschki, 1977); G. Pancaldi, *Charles Darwin: 'storia' ed 'economia' della natura* (Firenze: La Nuova Italia, 1977).

64 Cf. G. Pancaldi, *Darwin in Italia* (Bologna: II Mulino, 1983).

65 Cf. F. Del Greco, 'Sul Duplice indirizzo in cui tende a differenziarsi il movimento psichiatrico in Italia', *Rivista sperimentale di freniatria* (1897): 226–27.

66 See G. Genil-Perrin, *Histoire des origines et de l'évolution de l'idée de dégénérescence en médecine mentale* (Paris: Leclerc, 1913); H. Werlinder, *Psychopathy: A History of the Concepts, Analysis of the origin and development of a Family of Concepts in Psychopathology* (Uppsala: Almguist and Wiksell International, 1978).

67 Cf. S. Nicasi, 'Il Germe della follia. Modelli di malattia mentale nella psichiatria italiana di fine Ottocento', pre-circulated paper at the conference, *L'età del positivismo: il caso di Reggio Emilia* (Reggio Emilia, 9/10/11 May 1984).

68 Cf. R. Villa, 'Scienza medica e criminalità nell'Italia unita', in Della Peruta, *Storia d'Italia*, pp. 1145–168; Pancaldi, *Darwin in Italia*.

69 Cf. Nicasi, 'Il Germe della follia'.

70 Cf. S. Tonnini, 'Degenerazione e primitività', *Archivio Italiano per le malattie nervose* (1890): 99–161.

71 In Tonnini, 'Degenerazione e primitività'.

72 E. Morselli, Preface to R. Brugia, *I Problemi della degenerazione* (Bologna: Zanichelli, 1906), pp. xx–xxi.

73 S. Nicasi, 'Il Germe della follia'; R. Villa, 'Scienza medica'.

74 See Clark 'The data of alienism'.

CHAPTER TEN

Murder under hypnosis in the case of Gabrielle Bompard: psychiatry in the Courtroom in Belle Époque Paris

Ruth Harris

IN DECEMBER 1890, a 22-year-old woman named Gabrielle Bompard was accused of complicity in the brutal murder and robbery of a Parisian bailiff. The prosecution's case was that Bompard, in association with her middle-aged lover Michel Eyraud, had willingly allowed herself to be used as a sexual bait to lure Alexandre-Toussaint Gouffé to a flat in the 8th arrondissement, where the two then hanged and robbed their victim. The crime and the trial that followed inflamed public opinion to a remarkable degree, despite the banal and sordid nature of a murder that had won the perpetrators cash and valuables worth only a few francs. The novelty of using a trunk to dispose of their victim generated lurid excitement, so much so, that some 20,000 people reportedly filed past this criminal relic in the Paris morgue.[1] This fervent interest in the crime – the details of which were recounted daily in the popular press for months – reached its pitch when Gabrielle Bompard deserted her lover in California and inexplicably though willingly returned to Paris and gave herself up to the police. Eyraud's ultimate capture in Havana after a search across North and South America added a final touch for a sensational trial.

After her return, Bompard turned against her accomplice and sought to exculpate herself by placing the entire blame for the crime on Eyraud. Her defence against the charge of murder brought against her rested on the extraordinary claim put forward through her lawyer that she had acted under a post-hypnotic suggestion implanted by her former partner. This system of defence, which required medical intervention to determine Bompard's state of mind, pitted two opposing schools of psychiatry against one another, and in so doing revealed a medical and philosophical controversy over the nature of individual liberty and unconscious mental activity which brought the profession and its academic precepts into the full light of public scrutiny.

The audacious view that Bompard had been completely unconscious of her acts was advanced by Jules Liégeois, Professor of Administrative Law at Nancy and the most outspoken disciple of the psychiatrist Hippolyte Bernheim. Throughout the trial, Liégeois ardently and tirelessly promoted the major precepts of both his *maître* and his fellow-disciples. The school, called the Ecole de Nancy,[2] maintained as its central tenet the view that anyone with a sufficiently impressionable nature could be prevailed upon to act unconsciously under the influence and power of external suggestion. Starting from this point, and the belief that Bompard had indeed been hypnotized, Liégeois's intervention in the case therefore asserted the defendant's lack of responsibility for her deeds, a claim made despite the fact that he had been prevented by the judge from testing his hypothesis by practising hypnotic experiments upon her.

To rebuff the assertion, the three most eminent Parisian forensic psychiatrists rose in steadfast opposition and sought to portray Liégeois and the Nancy School as both unscientific and socially irresponsible. In accordance with the doctrines of Jean-Martin Charcot and the Ecole Salpêtrière,[3] they argued that susceptibility to hypnosis was not, as Liégeois claimed, a general phenomenon requiring only a fairly impressionable nature, but was a tendency only apparent among hysterics. As ample evidence confirmed that Gabrielle Bompard was hypnotizable, even if not by Eyraud, they accordingly diagnosed the presence of hysteria in her. Concluding, however, that her symptoms were not acute, they saw in her only a *petite hystérie* which was not seen to affect her judgement seriously and consequently was not a justification for a verdict of diminished responsibility. They concluded instead that she was simply vicious and had acted in full conscience.

The case reveals, however, not only another episode in the history of French psychiatry and psychotherapeutics into which these opposing positions were telescoped into the public forum of the courtroom, but also demonstrates the way in which hypnotism and the discussion it aroused gave expression to some of the most central bourgeois anxieties of the *fin-de-siècle* period, providing a focus for a free-ranging moral, social, and political commentary. A murder committed by the youthful daughter of a prosperous tradesman under the possible influence of hypnosis demonstrated most frighteningly the ease with which individual liberty could be abolished and, with it, a whole series of cherished conventions, values, and beliefs. Moreover, as the trial was to show,[4] hypnotism in unscrupulous hands was also consciously regarded as a degenerative influence on, and powerful weapon against, genteel womanhood. Women and young girls, it was argued, might be raped in a state of complete unconsciousness, and hypnotism was accordingly perceived as a threat not only to decent family life but also to the stability of society in general.

The dangerous powers imputed to hypnotism were not, however, confined to the realm of private domesticity, but also expanded outwards into the public domain where popular magnetizers in the 1880s drew large crowds to their theatrical performances, expounding the benefits of the technique for the healing of both spiritual and physical maladies. Although hypnosis h'ad been practised by amateurs throughout the nineteenth century, it had been steadfastly condemned by the medical establishment as mere charlatanry until Charcot's 'scientific rediscovery' of it instantly transformed the subject into an area worthy of academic investigation. Charcot and his school attempted to dissociate hypnotism as much as possible from this marginal and unofficial past and indeed tended to blame the amateurs for keeping the procedure within the unhealthy confines of mysticism. Accordingly, medical men influenced by the Salpêtrière took a dim view of magnetizing performances, maintaining that this popular entertainment was responsible for producing uncontrollable psychic epidemics in which rape, suicide, and madness inevitably followed. This venomous campaign[5] against the amateurs ultimately resulted in their mesmeric performances being outlawed in many western European cities and was part of a campaign for state control of medical practice which was ultimately enacted in France with the 30 November law of 1892.

This medical discussion of mysticism and spiritualism also had implications for the case of Gabrielle Bompard. For example, in attacking Liégeois during the proceedings, Paul Brouardel, the head of the Parisian panel, made derogatory reference to the charlatanry of the occult and coupled the doctrine of the Nancy School with these 'unscientific practices'.[6] The facts that Liégeois and his associates had paid muted homage to the amateurs, had learned some of their procedures from them and, indeed, shared some of the same philosophical and therapeutic principles, were all emphasized in order to tarnish their reputation, and to demonstrate, by comparison, the Parisians' own unimpeachable scientific credentials.

Not only was hypnotism seen as a potential catalyst for unspeakable crimes, the motor of social degradation and a contributing factor to the psychic degeneration of a gullible and uninformed public, it was also viewed as a crucial element in the explanation of the politics of mass democracy in republican France. In early 1890, for example, when Bernheim made clear his view that Gabrielle Bompard had acted unconsciously under Eyraud's suggestible influence, he made a striking comparison between her slavish adherence to her lover's commands and the suggestibility shown to be operating in the frenzied political demonstrations of *boulangisme* during the previous year.[7] As the example of Gabrielle Bompard was to show, social theorists interested in mass behaviour drew their most powerful analyses for explaining the mechanisms of crowd action from the investigation of hypnotism's effects, and readily transposed the apparent abolition of consciousness observed in individual cases to qualitatively different instances of mass behaviour.[8]

When Gabrielle Bompard came to court in December, 1890, therefore, the appeal of the defence to hypnotism made the case resonate with significance that apparently had little bearing on her particular fate. The details of cold-blooded murder, hardened vice, and romantic adventure which the pre-trial investigation had brought to light became the context for a struggle between two schools of academic psychiatry in which the murderers' characters provided a fertile soil for the extrapolation of their analyses. At the confluence of these currents stood the personage of Gabrielle Bompard who, for a brief period, crystallized these anxieties and gave them an alarmingly tangible form.

The murderers and the murder: the judicial perspective

If Gabrielle Bompard maintained that she had been subjugated by her lover Michel Eyraud, it was perhaps not surprising that her partner in crime asserted that he too had acted without free will, having been subjected – through Bompard's youth, beauty, and insatiable appetites – to a domineering and irresistible influence that had induced him to murder.[9] In deciding between these contradictory versions of the murderers' moral responsibility, the judiciary undertook a year-long pre-trial enquiry into the character not only of the two depraved individuals, but also the entire milieu of shady businessmen and petit-bourgeois mistresses who accompanied them on lunchtime promenades along the Boulevards Montmartre and Poissonière. The detailed unveiling of this illicit financial world where fraudulent transactions were made in the cafés and brasseries near the Bourse was partly the judiciary's way of serving a warning to the public of the criminal results that such moral corruption would inevitably produce.

Michel Eyraud epitomized the dregs even of this society, and was presented in the popular press as someone who had arrived there through a career of unrestrained prodigality, debauchery, and vice. The fact that Eyraud was of middle-class origins, the son of a provincial merchant near Narbonne, educated to continue the life of an industrious and respectable bourgeois, meant that his fall from grace received more attention than, for example, that of a working-class criminal whose milieu often seemed to direct him towards crime. Because of the advantages of his position, therefore, Eyraud was denounced even more vehemently for squandering both his patrimony as well as his wife's dowry, his cowardly desertion from a military expedition in Mexico, his dismissal for dishonesty during his youthful business career in South America, and the life of swindling and deceit he had enjoyed since his return to France.[10] Wherever he went he was noted for his insatiable taste for women, upon whom he bestowed his money and attentions, leaving little for his legitimate wife and daughter. He was even said to have threatened his mother's life when she refused to give him money, and was obviously so hated by former business associates that during the trial one even accused him of necrophilia.

Despite a character sketch that portrayed him thus a coward, libertine, and matricidal monster, for the Parisian press Eyraud was more than just a moral degenerate, thug, and murderer. While his ruthlessness was acknowledged, he was none the less admired as a picaresque bandit who laughingly evaded the authorities in a year-long flight through North and Central America. This journey, which frustrated the efforts of the police to apprehend him,[11] ended only when one of his former employees recognized him in Havana, whence he was ultimately extradited and sent back to be welcomed by a reportedly bloodthirsty crowd at the Gare St Lazare in Paris.[12] The length of the police's mission and the frustrations they encountered in trying to ferret out the resourceful Eyraud indeed testify to the murderer's talents as wily impersonator, disguise artist, and polyglot. This personal versatility and charm, which enabled him to switch identities and countries with such apparent ease, was also regarded as the primary ingredient in his purported success with women along his course, despite the chagrin of being abandoned by Bompard and the physical drawbacks of his bulky frame and menacing appearance. The ceaseless womanizing magnified his reputation and contributed to his myth of invincibility,[13] so that whether as corpulent cavalier or as the decaying 46-year-old who fell prey to imperious youth, Eyraud did at least earn himself a well-deserved and unquestionable notoriety in the annals of Belle Epoque crime.

Despite his apparent bravado, Eyraud did not escape the vengeance of the state and was summarily guillotined in 1891, shortly after the trial. Bompard, however, was regarded more leniently, particularly since she had 'cracked' the case by willingly giving herself up to the police, after abandoning Eyraud and the fugitive's life to return to Paris with another shady entrepreneur named Garanger. She seemed perhaps a bit less evil than her accomplice since she had frustrated Eyraud's attempts to swindle her new lover in a fraudulent scheme that involved Garanger's extending credit to a fictitious enterprise in the Californian vineyards.[14] On 23 January, after reading the accounts of her exploits in the newspapers and admiring herself in full-page engravings, she volunteered to go to M. Lozé at the Paris Sûreté and tell her version of the murder,[15] undoubtedly hoping to profit from her current celebrity, and perhaps thinking that such a brave act might ensure her impunity.

She laid the moral responsibility for the crime on Eyraud at every opportunity that presented itself, admitting her part only in a piecemeal and contradictory fashion. Often caught in the act of uttering brazen lies, she none the less remained steadfast to her central claim that it had been Eyraud, not herself, who had masterminded the murder plan. The judicial dossier reveals a deceitful, coquettish, and histrionic personality,[16] and the unusual patience shown by the investigating judge to his lying charge was undoubtedly due to his professional interest in not laying himself open to the accusation of miscarried justice. There was also the probability that Eyraud had benefited from Bompard's prostitution,[17] hastening her degeneration, and hence lessening her moral responsibility.

In the attempt to decide who had subjugated whom, Bompard's past history was seen as crucial evidence for both the medical diagnosis and the judicial verdict. Like her co-defendant, she was the daughter of a provincial merchant, a widower and metal dealer whose prospering fortune in Lille had earned him the respect of the community, despite rumours that he had illicit relations with his housekeeper.[18] Bompard nurtured a particular hatred for this woman whom she held responsible for her exile to the nunneries to which she had been sent to eradicate early manifestations of unladylike behaviour. She had spent her adolescence being sent from one convent to another, the nuns testifying to the incorrigibility of her habits, the lewdness of her tongue, and the pernicious effect she had had on her schoolmates.[19] Her return to the paternal home in Lille in 1886 only worsened the situation since she had reacted rebelliously when confronted with her father's illicit romance. She began an affair with a local merchant, was notably indecorous in the streets of her native town, and wore extravagant clothes, all activities which aroused disapproving comment among Lille's respectable inhabitants. Her father's watchfulness and the chagrin caused by the collapse of her passing romance finally prompted her to leave for Paris where, in 1886, she became the mistress of Michel Eyraud. Even in the world in which the two moved, Bompard was noticed for being particularly vicious and *détraquée*. The more charitable of her acquaintances, however, explained away her character as being affected by an incipient hysteria that was accentuated by Eyraud's evil designs;[20] others in contrast maintained that her developing wickedness was the result of reason and effort, and that her evil nature was only strengthened by her quick intelligence and native wit.[21]

Throughout Bompard's career, the issue of hypnotism occurs repeatedly, and for this reason became a starting point for the elaboration of her defence. Shortly after her return to her father's home from the convent, for example, the family physician in Lille was summoned in a desperate effort to improve her wayward behaviour. During the trial, Dr Sacreste acknowledged that one of the expedients he employed had been to hypnotize her, although he was compelled to confess that his influence had not been sufficient to elicit the desired change in character. This failure was explained by the fact that her lover in Lille was simultaneously practising experiments on Bompard, and that his negative influence unhappily counteracted the doctor's own.[22] Finally, as an *habituée* of hypnotic evenings in the salons of the less-than-brilliant Parisian *demi-monde*, Bompard had often been subjected to these fashionable manoeuvres[23] – and only Eyraud among all the hypnotizers had been unsuccessful – a point which was to prove crucial during the courtroom proceedings.[24]

Gabrielle Bompard was thus presented as a figure of contradictions and polarities, the portrait testifying to her viciousness, but also partly excusing it because of the moral abuse she had experienced under the influence of her father and his mistress. Not only could she, therefore, serve in the judicial portrayal as a prime example of fallen womanhood, but her father and his irregular household became a case-study in parental shortcomings and a warning to other respectable families who might wish to imitate them. The photographs and engravings of the young, almost androgyne, Bompard, only 4 feet 11 inches high, could be interpreted as showing either a waif who was, as she herself maintained, pitilessly seduced and subjugated by brute male force, or a Parisian *gavroche* who lied, cheated, and stole to satisfy her sensual appetites. These extreme aspects of the image, which embodied a dichotomized appraisal of woman's behaviour,[25] were thus the two axes around which this morality piece of murder under hypnosis was enacted.

The murder itself, as reconstructed by testimony in the pre-trial investigation, undoubtedly confirmed the second version of her personality. In mid-1889, the pair found themselves once again without resources and with Eyraud under indictment for fraud. Having investigated the financial resources of their acquaintances, they decided that Gouffé was the most auspicious source of funds and laid an elaborate plan to kill and rob him, using Bompard as the sexual lure.[26] As Gouffé was a hopeless womanizer, he easily fell into the trap, arriving at the apartment previously fitted out to facilitate the murderers' plans. During the ensuing amorous exchanges, the pair worked their way over to a conveniently placed couch, while Bompard playfully showed off a wool peignoir and the thick silk cord that she sported around her waist. Bragging of one of her fictitious rich *amants*, she coquettishly put the rope around Gouffé's neck, while he was kissing her throat. Then she attached it to a snap hook on the bottom of the chaise longue that had been fitted by Eyraud who was then hiding behind a curtain, and he promptly pulled hard and suspended the surprised and unfortunate lover in the alcove, hanged and dead within an instant. As Eyraud remarked in conclusion, 'Gouffé did not struggle. I would never have believed a hanged man could die so quickly.'[27] Finding virtually no booty on the body,[28] the pair were obliged to flee the following day with their *malle funèbre* where the hapless victim was deposited in a forest outside Millery, a town near Lyons.

The Paris–Nancy debate and its medico-legal implications

That this sordid and banal murder aroused such a furore, and engaged some of the most eminent medical men of the period in vitriolic debate, tends to suggest that a good deal more was at stake than Gabrielle Bompard's neck. In fact, it was the very notoriety of the case that converted the trial into a worthy setting for the effective propagation of the conflicting views on hypnotism held by the rival Paris and Nancy Schools. The overtly sexual nature of Gouffé's entrapment – in which Gabrielle Bompard's soft caresses and playful words had become lethal murder weapons – provided, therefore, a seemingly endless fund of titillating details to which academic commentary could be profitably attached, thereby assuring it a wider audience.

The argument between the two schools had been raging for eight years before Liégeois and Paul Brouardel, Dean of the Faculty of Medicine, Professor of Legal Medicine and a personal friend of Charcot, met in the Cour d'Assises de la Seine. Like all sectarian arguments, the violence of the altercations ironically overshadowed shared perspectives, since both schools had laboured ardently and indeed successfully to promote hypnotism as a subject worthy of medical investigation. In sum, both Charcot and Bernheim had staked their respective reputations on laying claim to the true scientific study of the subject, with each accusing the other of fraud and misrepresentation.

The controversy revolved around three intermingling concerns. From arguments that concentrated on opposing views of the physiological and psychological nature of hypnosis, the debate extended into the realm of medical therapeutics, and culminated with diverging systems of hypnosis's medico-legal implications. The first level of debate concerned what contemporaries considered to be a further exploration of the relationship between mind and body. For example, in early 1891 in the *Revue des deux mondes*, the philosopher Alfred Fouillé discussed the Paris–Nancy controversy in the following way:

> 'From the point of view of philosophical trends, the rivalry between the Paris and Nancy Schools is only an application to a particular case of the great problem concerning the physical and the mental. The Paris School only considers the phenomena of consciousness as indicators of organic movements, without their own action. "An idea," says Mr Binet for example, "is nothing but an *appearance*, and behind it hides the energy developed by a previous physical excitation ..." The Nancy School, on the other hand, attaches much more importance to the mental; it has even contributed to demonstrating the action of ideas in hypnotism, and by extension, in the phenomena of normal life.'[29]

The implications of the debate are thus clear: in a century of psychiatric advance posited on a somatic interpretation of mental disorder, the philosophical implications drawn from the experimental technique of hypnotism were beginning to widen the crevices in the psychiatric edifice that had existed for fifty years. As a challenge to the view of insanity which tended to see it as ultimately a mental disequilibrium arising from organic and neurological malfunctions, the interpretation which grew up through the debate on hypnotism introduced a more complicated and diverse causality connecting the physical and mental state. Through their clinical studies, Bernheim and the Nancy School reappraised the nature of the connections between the two by asserting that causal influences could travel in the opposite direction also; that, in other words, ideas could affect the physical state. This concept of ideodynamism was at the core of a fundamental reorientation of psychological analysis and ultimately provided the central impetus behind the re-evaluation of orthodox views on mental processes.

The controversy in this early period can best be crudely summed up by describing it in terms of a conflict between the rival medical and philosophical perspectives of epiphenominalism and ideodynamism. The most influential advocate of the former tradition developed in relation to affective psychology under the leadership of Théodule Ribot, a philosopher by training,[30] who left the speculative halls at the Sorbonne to migrate to the experimental laboratory at the Collège de France. With a view to investigating maladies of volition, memory, and emotions,[31] he intended in the early 1880s to redirect traditional philosophical concerns related to associative psychology[32] onto a new and wholly positivist basis. The inspiration for this approach emerged from Ribot's familiarity with Spencerian evolutionary theories[33] and German neurophysiological work on reflex action,[34] both of which led him to concentrate on the underlying organic, hereditarian, and automatic elements of human behaviour.

Accordingly, his investigation was primarily concerned with exploring the human personality from the perspective of unconscious drives and irrational desires. Taking an evolutionary perspective on the development of the human personality, he maintained that the higher intellectual faculties were the last to develop, the least well established, and were constantly threatened by more ancient and primitive tendencies. It was through the investigation of the 'dissolution' of the human personality in the insane, where conscious choices and wilful action were overwhelmed by unconscious drives and savage impulses, that Ribot sought to show the frightening fragility of the state of balance which constituted and regulated the normal rational human being. As he described the two opposing forces which comprised human mental development:

'Two groups of opposing tendencies struggle to supplant each other. In fact, as everyone knows, this struggle takes place between inferior tendencies in which the ability to adapt is limited, and superior tendencies in which this ability is complex. The former are always the most naturally strong; the second are so by artificial means (*contrivance*). The first represent a power embedded in the organism, the others are a superficial (*défraîchissante*) acquisition.'[35]

The tenuousness of this delicate equilibrium was demonstrated not only by a great quantity of work on the effects of alcohol and drugs on the nervous system[36] – which disturbed and incapacitated the controlling intellectual faculties and replaced them with automatic ones – but also by the maladies of volition, a category of ailment in which hysteria played a crucial role. A healthy volitional capacity was made possible in this analysis not only by the co-ordination of the higher intellectual faculties, which enabled the individual to take rational and decisive action, but also by the inhibition of irrational qualities, which were subordinated to volition's sound influence. Among hysterics, however, this ability was notably lacking, with moodiness, chronic indecisiveness, lying, and a morbid need for attention, all epitomizing the mercurial and involuntary nature of the malady. As Charles Richet described the patients under his care, 'their characters change like the views of a kaleidoscope',[37] with volition's salutary regulation playing little or no role. Hysteria thus provided a perfect opportunity to observe the 'dissolution' of the human personality, a phenomenon the experimenters generally attributed to hereditarian degeneration in conjunction with a faulty education failing to rein in these destructive tendencies.

Charcot, like most practising alienists, was an epiphenominalist whose earlier investigations into paralyses, epilepsy, muscular atrophies, and spinal affections strikingly demonstrate his strong early neurophysiological bias.[38]

Such work had won him substantial acclaim as well as the creation of the Special Chair in the Diseases of the Nervous System in 1882.[39] With his scientific reputation solidly established by these respectable scientific endeavours, Charcot then began the exploration of the murkier terrain of hysteria in which he demonstrated the role of disturbed emotions and disintegrating volitional capacity in the production of the disease, and differentiated it as a functional disorder distinct from neurological disorders. Although acknowledging, therefore, the role of emotional disturbance in producing disease, he none the less defined hysteria not by the psychological symptoms of the disorder, but rather by the physiological stigmata of the malady, be they the classic four stages of hysterio-epilepsy, contractures, anaesthesias, or hypnosis itself.[40]

The much-discussed emotional manifestations – such as lying, a morbid need for attention, foul language, excessive coquettishness in the female patients, and 'femininity' in the male ones – were therefore regarded as behavioural symptoms of a more generalized psychophysiological disequilibrium, and in themselves not susceptible to rational scientific explanation.[41] The clinical context of this study of the 'irrational' led the Paris School, therefore, to emphasize the inherent morbidity of the unconscious side of the personality. Patients' dreams, hallucinations, fantasies, and behavioural disorders were regarded as nothing more than indicators of illness and as guides to marking out the malady's precise station in the nosological tables which grew up towards the end of the century.

It was this perspective on the nature and causality of mental illness that not only determined the Parisian approach to hypnotism but also fuelled the debate between Paris and Nancy. In opposition to Charcot, Bernheim argued that hypnotism was not a disease, but rather a state akin to sleep which could be induced in many normal individuals. For the Parisians, however, it was nothing more than a symptom of illness so that Charcot and his associates argued that it had therapeutic benefit only for hysterics. Among individuals who showed no morbid symptoms, however, its indiscriminate employment would incite insanity in people with latent susceptibilities, unleashing automatic urges and bestial tendencies that were better kept dormant. The number of hypnotizable individuals simply indicated that a high proportion of the population were in fact latent hysterics, and therefore the widespread use of hypnotism would release these diseased proclivities and greatly augment the sum of nervous disease.

The details of Charcot's discussion of hypnosis had important medicolegal implications. According to him and his disciples, hypnosis manifested itself in three distinct states – catalepsy, lethargy, and somnambulism – which were demonstrated by the *grandes hypnotiques* of the Salpêtrière.[42] In the first state, the subject was deemed to be completely at the mercy of the experimenter, who could induce an abolition of sensibility (that is, the operator could hit or pinch the subject with no sensation of pain), and a heightening of muscular rigidity which enabled some to stand with outstretched and unflinching arms for twenty-five minutes, thereby defying the laws of normal physiology. In this state, however, it was impossible to perpetrate a criminal action on the subject because its prolongation induced a generalized contracture or hysterical fit which would prevent, for example, a rapist from consummating his offence. Not so, however, in the lethargic state in which the subject was like a 'cadaver before rigor mortis',[43] with a muscular tonicity that invited sexual violation, and it was this state that was considered to be the most dangerous for unsuspecting females. The final state of somnambulism, however, was the one which had the most important implications for the trial of Gabrielle Bompard, as it was in this instance that the subject obeyed all the commands of the magnetizer and would execute acts upon waking without any conscious awareness or subsequent memory. Nevertheless, despite the striking display of automatism that the subject demonstrated while in a somnambulic trance, the Paris School asserted that deep inside this human marionette a consciousness of 'self' continued to subsist, so that a truly pure hypnotic subject would fail to realize commands that were repugnant to his or her inner nature.[44]

Hypnosis, therefore, could only induce passive acquiescence in crime in the form of a rape, not active participation. The reasoning behind this stance was that a simple abolition of feminine free will could allow sexual violation – an area in which women's control was explicitly recognized as being frighteningly unreliable anyway – without any need for a transfer of another's will.[45] The Paris School insisted that to reach any other conclusion led to the medico-legal absurdity of destroying the possibility of punishing any crimes at all by making all offences the possible result of hypnotic suggestibility.[46] Charcot and his disciples found themselves, therefore, in the rather ironic role of confirming with vehemence the existence of individual liberty and moral choice, a position completely at odds not only with the performances of the *grandes hypnotiques* at the Salpêtrière who slavishly obeyed Charcot's commands at the expense of their human dignity, but also with the psychiatrists' own scientific ethos based almost exclusively on neurophysiological theories and hereditarian ideas.

This entire system came under increasing attack by Hippolyte Bernheim and the Ecole de Nancy after 1882, when the provincial investigators developed their own perspective of hypnosis which was completely opposed to the Parisian School, not only in its broadest theoretical perspective but also in their view of its clinical applications and medico-legal implications. Like most physicians, Bernheim first became acquainted with hypnosis through Charcot's work at the Salpêtrière; initially the latter's doctrine, as he wrote in 1906, 'was for me, as for all physicians, a dogma shored up by the authority of a great man'[47] whose position he had not sought to question. Bernheim himself emerged out of a clinical tradition in which mental disorder played an insignificant role. An *agrégé* at the Strasbourg Faculty of Medicine, he had been repatriated after the Franco-Prussian War to Nancy, which replaced the Alsatian town as a French centre of medical teaching and research. As a general clinician who had done research into pneumonia, typhoid, rheumatism, and heart disease, Bernheim was primarily concerned with medical therapeutics, and was acquainted with nervous diseases only through his wide-ranging practice.[48] His personal interest in hypnotic therapy began when one of his own patients whom he had released from the hospital with an uncured sciatica was successfully treated by a philanthropist-practitioner named Ambroise Liébault, who had been ministering to his impoverished clientele with hypnosis with neither fees nor medical recognition for at least twenty years. After attending some of Liébault's sessions, Bernheim became convinced that this healer, scorned by the medical establishment, who had written a book on his technique as early as 1866, was in fact the true pioneer and scientific discoverer of hypnosis and its applications.[49]

During the course of their careers, Bernheim and Liébault hypnotized over 10,000 patients, using the method to treat not only psychological disorders but also such diverse phenomena as neuralgias, ulcers, menstrual cramps, rheumatism, as well as morphine and alcohol addiction.[50] Starting from a practical appreciation of the potentialities of hypnotism which was sometimes imbued with an evangelical ardour, they developed a theoretical perspective which differed completely from that of Charcot. Rather than seeing hypnotism as being necessarily linked to hysteria, they viewed it as a universal and powerful therapeutic tool, and for this reason wished to popularize rather than limit its usage. Hysteria was in fact perceived as having no bearing on the issue whatsoever, and consequently Bernheim accused Charcot and his followers of having greatly exaggerated the number of hysterics in order to account for the frequency of hypnotic suggestibility. Not only did he maintain that the Paris School had thereby created a completely fictitious hysterical epidemic, he also asserted that the four-stage syndrome of *grande hystérie* observed at the Salpêtrière was a chimera as well, for nowhere else in France or abroad was it reproduced. Bernheim deduced that its existence in Charcot's hospital was to be attributed to a mutual suggestibility between hypnotizer and hypnotized, rather than to a virtually invariable pathological formula that followed the clear-cut lines laid out so dramatically by the maître. In sum, Bernheim vociferously proclaimed that Charcot's disease was 'une hystérie de culture', produced by the physician's awesome powers of suggestion on his patients and his self-deluded willingness to be duped by his own authority and doctrine. To underscore this more concretely, he pointedly demonstrated that under hypnosis he could duplicate these symptoms in his own subjects.[51]

To counter the theoretical propositions of Charcot and to give a rationale for hypnotic therapy, Bernheim, who called his approach to the subject 'ideodynamism', maintained that suggestions administered by the hypnotizer 'activated the brain'. This procedure caused changes in the organic state of the subject, if the disorder was somatic, or provoked a gradual transformation in the emotional state which set off, for example, an hysterical contracture. The state of automatism induced by hypnosis therefore allowed the subject to unleash concentrated energy from the brain, 'to concentrate this force on the organs of animal and vegetable life, to sharpen the senses and faculties, to modify the tissues.'[52] This emphasis on the power of the mental apparatus to transform physical states was in clear contrast to the epiphenominalist perspective, which viewed the mind's faculties as being impoverished rather than heightened during hypnosis.

For the Nancians, the universality of this conception of the power of ideas was such that there was no logical or clinical reason why only the hysterical should be susceptible to them. Consequently, they maintained that anyone could be hypnotized, although certain subjects – for example, soldiers accustomed to the rigours of military discipline or the docile subjects of the lower orders – were perhaps better suited than others.[53] Accordingly, they concluded from their clinical observations that hypnosis was not a neurosis linked to hysteria, as the Paris School maintained, but an artificially induced normal condition corresponding to the naturally induced state of sleep. During hypnosis, however, there existed a rapport based on suggestibility between the subject and the hypnotizer who had provoked the hypnotic state which enhanced the patient's receptivity to external ideas. These psychological observations were extended in Bernheim's famous pamphlet, *De la Suggestion dans l'état hypnotique et dans l'état de veille* (1884), a work which put forward the audacious view that an hypnotic state was indeed not necessary to procure similar suggestible effects. Later, as his experience with psychotherapeutics grew, Bernheim relied increasingly on this procedure, since unlike hypnosis it sought to involve the conscious side of the patient's personality to procure more effective and long-lasting therapeutic results. If such unconventional procedures increased the wrath of the Paris School in the 1880s, they were none the less a crucial contribution to developing psychoanalytical therapy, of which Freud was the most famous exponent.

From these theoretical propositions, Liégeois championed a medico-legal doctrine in complete opposition to that of the Parisians, a system which he had developed alongside Bernheim and Liébault through conducting experiments on hypnosis in the Nancy clinics. Of the four leading lights in the Ecole de Nancy, he was by far the most unconventional, his legal background and occupation as Professor of Administrative Law at the University of Nancy supplying him with no previous medical preparation for the investigation of hypnosis and its effects. The lawyer's interest in the subject emerged from his conviction that the practice of hypnotism in unscrupulous hands threatened the basis of society founded on freedom of contract, a notion which fundamentally rested on mutual and voluntary consent. Under the influence of hypnosis, however, women might contravene their marriage vows, sign over their inheritance to the undeserving, and individuals be punished for crimes they had committed unconsciously under the commands of an evil and rapacious experimenter.[54] His fears were such that he wrote articles that discussed hypnotism as imperilling 'national defence and civil society',[55] in which he demonstrated the tenuousness of bourgeois institutions, and advocated defensive measures of combating this ubiquitous menace, as the case of Gabrielle Bompard was to demonstrate. He elaborated this doctrine replete with prophecies of doom undoubtedly because of his own extreme reaction to the Commune, against which he wrote earnest polemics demonstrating how socialism and the irrational destruction it had produced had undermined and virtually destroyed 'the eternal principles on which societies are based: *Religion, Family, Property, Justice, Liberty*'.[56] The Commune and its revolutionary impulses had demonstrated the dangers facing society and Liégeois remained dedicated to uprooting these evil influences in the aftermath of the civil war. In hypnotism and the elaboration of its medico-legal implications he found a perfect vehicle for bringing these views before the wider public.

In accordance with Bernheim's view that any individual was susceptible to hypnotic suggestion, Liégeois maintained that any criminal act, even murder, could be successfully induced in any individual hypnotized by someone with criminal aims. Necessarily, therefore, it was this doubly iniquitous evil-doer who should be punished, not his innocent agent, the latter being morally no more guilty than the pistol used by a murderer to shoot his victim. Considering the Nancians' almost visionary characterization of the therapeutic possibilities of hypnosis – a view that Liégeois ardently shared and promoted in a proposal for an International Psychic Institute that would treat indigent sufferers with hypnotic therapy free of charge[57] – this medico-legal doctrine had sinister implications that ironically contradicted the central thrust of the Ecole de Nancy's medical programme. On the one hand arguing that hypnotism had enormous potential to ameliorate previously intractable conditions, and on the other regarding it as the possible motor for the committal of unspeakable crimes, the Nancian characterization of hypnotism was full of unresolved tensions and ambiguities that were to mark every aspect of the debate. Despite these contradictions, Bernheim largely adhered to Liégeois's judicial interpretation of hypnotism's effects and confirmed the rigorous nature of the lawyer's experiments. Repeatedly, Liégeois sought to prove how free will in the most respectable subjects could be easily erased by the injunctions of a hypnotizer.[58] To these brazen assertions whose implications were said to have greatly troubled public sentiment, the Paris School responded with all the aloofness scientific scepticism could muster, remarking that Liégeois's experiments were poorly controlled and did not reflect actions taken outside the Nancy laboratory where moral choices were experienced more dramatically. With such finely marked-out positions, which were at odds not only with the medico-legal perspectives but also with widely divergent philosophical positions and clinical programmes, the ferocity of the medico-legal debate which surrounded the case of Gabrielle Bompard was not, therefore, especially surprising.

Medico-legal evidence in the courtroom

When the panel of Parisian psychiatrists opposed Liégeois in the Cour d'Assises de la Seine in December, 1890, the hold of Charcot's doctrine was weakening already, his insistence that hysteria and hypnosis were part of the same disorder contested by numerous other experimenters who shared Bernheim's view of hypnosis's healing power.[59] Not only was Charcot dismayed by murmurings of dissent within his own ranks, but also disinterested foreigners made pilgrimages to Bernheim's clinic and returned impressed and often persuaded by the Nancian approach. Having made such strides, the provincial school was jealous to guard its advances, and when the Bompard affair absorbed public attention, Bernheim sought to profit from the publicity by giving press interviews during which he made some general reflections on the role of suggestion in producing crime. Charcot, on the other hand, adopted the tactic of aloof disregard, dismissing Bompard as an 'être pervers et détraqué' whose banal criminality did not merit further academic reflection.[60]

If behind-the-scene discussions among the four members of the Ecole de Nancy demonstrated unanimity regarding Bompard's suggestibility to Eyraud's evil designs and hence her attenuated responsibility, there was none the less a disagreement over how best to present their views to the public. Bernheim was wary of making the case even more of a *cause célèbre*, fearing that an excessive intervention would tarnish the school's scientific integrity. Despite these doubts he was none the less determined to go before the court and present his views on suggestion in a brief, sober discourse, deleting any mention of either hypnosis or the fissure between the two schools.[61] He thus hoped to gain satisfaction by challenging the Paris School on its home ground by instructing the public on the superiority of his system. As he later wrote to the last member of the Ecole de Nancy, Etienne Beaunis, in private correspondence: 'Ordinary people and even many scholars just don't know what is going on; they take Charcot and Brouardel's word that we are involved in mysticism and the supernatural, while in Paris everything is clear, lucid and scientific.'[62]

However, Bernheim fell ill and these conservative plans were abandoned; in place of the master, Liégeois elected himself to go to Paris, believing that such an opportunity would sound the death knell on Charcot's system and usher in an era of Nancian supremacy. Despite his colleagues' advice on the need for caution, which they reiterated often before his departure, Liégeois threw discretion to the winds and passed four long uninterrupted hours in the courtroom exposing 'the doctrines of Nancy as comprehensively and unfortunately as tediously as a professor at the lectern'.[63] To banish this loquacious legal interloper from the inner sanctum of medical debate, the Parisian psychiatrists used the judiciary with dexterity and found eager allies in Jules Quesnay de Beaurepaire, the prosecuting attorney, and the officiating judge, who unequivocally repulsed Liégeois's attempts to examine Bompard and who visibly suffered the provincial lawyer's intervention with the greatest difficulty. The proceedings involved a remarkable degree of legal manoeuvring in which medical opinion was undisguisedly put forward to reinforce the prosecution's case. Meant to act as disinterested expert witnesses who simply replied to the questions posed to them by the investigating magistrate, the physicians generally sought a unanimous appraisal which they would then dispassionately present to the court. The doctors' testimony could, however, be challenged by either counsel who had the right to ask for another investigation into the defendant's state of mind. Bompard's lawyer, Henri Robert, accordingly made this request on the basis of Liégeois's opposing testimony. The judge simply refused to countenance another delay in the proceedings, remarking that Paris's three most eminent medico-legal experts had pronounced and that their judgement was more than sufficient.

During the five months in which Paul Brouardel, Auguste Motet and Gilbert Ballet[64] had examined Bompard and considered their opinion of her state of mind, they had endeavoured to decide between the two images of her character – the docile waif or the sensual and avaricious slut – and clearly had had no difficulties in concluding in favour of the latter. This moral assessment was one which could readily have been made by laymen, but the physicians imbued it with scientific rigour. With measurements that would have satisfied the most fastidious Lombrosian, they showed that she presented neither cranial asymmetries nor other identifying abnormalities, pointing out that her 'little well-curved ears' had lobes unattached to her neck (attached ones were considered by some criminal anthropologists as evidence of a degenerate predisposition to criminal behaviour). Nor did her ancestry present a family tree blossoming with crooks, prostitutes, or deranged individuals of any kind. In sum, she seemed remarkably free of the hereditary taints so commonly found in criminals of her calibre. With a medical history which presented nothing unusual, they cited only her precocious sexual maturity, evidenced by early menstruation, which had encouraged vicious tastes and habits in a girl whose youthful and rudimentary moral development could not hope to control such powerful instincts.[65]

After these 'scientific' prerequisites, the doctors proceeded to address psychological questions. They hoped to confirm or deny her claims to having been subjugated by Eyraud, an assertion that was the main pillar of the defence, which held up the belief that she was suggestible and easily led astray.[66] Their interviews did not, however, reveal a docile waif, but instead an eminently intelligent and wily woman who was alternately seductive, co-operative or meek according to her interests and interrogators[67] and hence they gave little credence to her purported terror of Eyraud. Basing their conclusions on her past behaviour, they developed a character analysis which showed all the dimensions of her moral depravity. Instead of ascribing her youthful vagaries in the convents of the Nord and in the streets of Lille to the innocuous rebelliousness of adolescence, they condemned her with the full weight of late nineteenth-century disapproval for her departure from the norms of the *bien-élevée*, and maintained that such comportment presaged her later criminal career.

Their conclusions, therefore, were that Gabrielle Bompard was an *aveugle moral*, a being to whom moral categories remained intellectual abstractions rather than experienced values which affected her actions. Perversion of the moral faculties could be viewed by doctors as a means of attenuating responsibility, when patients for some inexplicable reason exhibited a marked moral decline after a life of rectitude, leading the experts to surmise the onset of somatic illness, such as general paralysis, to explain the break with past behaviour. Occasionally, it was asserted that the offender had been congenitally deprived of the capacity to feel the difference between right and wrong (as it seemed with Gabrielle Bompard), but such an argument was deemed provable only by the revelation of stigmata.[68] Moreover, even in these cases doctors rarely advocated a conclusion of irresponsibility since they perceived them to be dangerous degenerates who needed to be locked up in order to safeguard society's security.

Since in their view Gabrielle Bompard resolutely did not fit into either category, her past life exhibiting no virtue and her family tree no knaves, the term *aveugle moral* was used merely to highlight a striking portrait of degraded character in which cerebral acuity was made to service vicious desires. With the medical terminology removed from their analysis, the doctors concluded – and Motet even asserted during the trial – that the only thing wrong with Gabrielle Bompard was that she was a seasoned prostitute.[69]

This simple declaration that she was a whore, however, did not mean that the doctors gave her a completely clean bill of health. By acknowledging her susceptibility to hypnosis, they were forced to conclude that she demonstrated a small number of hysterical symptoms, the occasional *crise de nerfs* and a little sensory anaesthesia – but refused to say that such symptoms should justify a claim of diminished responsibility.[70] They implicitly argued, therefore, that she had encouraged her neurosis because of a debased character, making her, as it were, responsible for her irresponsibility. By thus imputing blame for her instability to the murderess herself, they argued that the very lightness of Bompard's illness distinguished her from truly irresponsible *malades*, but none the less explained her susceptibility to hypnosis and consequently upheld a crucial element of the doctrine of the Paris School. Despite their adherence to Parisian dogma in diagnosis, the doctors diverged from it radically in their legal recommendations.

In fact one physician[71] familiar with the debate even remarked that any other person with similar symptoms, probably would have been consigned to the Salpêtrière, particularly since the doctors had described the frightening hallucinations and an attack of contractures that they had induced in Bompard. The fact that the Parisians laboured to have the defendant condemned with a vehemence which matched the prosecution's tends to suggest that moral and social issues outside the realm of medical doctrine alone influenced the position they upheld so rigidly in the courtroom.

Despite the strength of the moral indictment produced by the expert testimony, Liégeois was undaunted, and instead of defending the defendant, whose unsavory past could only hinder his cause, he counterattacked by concentrating his fire on the analysis of her accusers, emphasizing always evidence of her hypnotizability and therefore her probable suggestibility to

Eyraud's evil influence. Employing the most sensational experiments to drive home his point, he revealed how individual liberty could be completely abolished among some subjects and how he had made them realize several horrendous, albeit fictitious, crimes. He remarked during the trial that 'the subject, in induced somnambulism, loses all spontaneity; volition is effectively abolished; . . . and in this state, suggestions are completely accepted by the subject and carried out.'[72]

He underscored the point with an example to the court: 'I once had an uncle poisoned by his nephew, to whom I gave sugar rather than arsenic, his aunt was so afraid that I never saw the nephew again [laughter].'[73] Not only did Liégeois cite these contemporary examples in Nancy, he also went deep into the annals of medico-legal history, demonstrating how justice had been miscarried due to an inadequate understanding of hypnotism and its effects. He strengthened his case by submitting the striking visual evidence of photographs of women with *vésicatoires,* who through a process of internal suggestion had branded flaming red marks – of names and words – on their shoulders and backs.[74] Finally, he pointed to specific cases in which Motet and Brouardel had played active roles in convincing the court of the reality and medico-legal implications of hypnosis. The cases involved rape[75] and a violation of public decency,[76] and showed how these Parisian practitioners had made large claims for the power of hypnosis when it had suited them. He implied, therefore, that there was some inconsistency in their rejection of Gabrielle Bompard's claims and that this was based on a doctrinaire refusal to come to grips with the possibility of a murder induced by hypnosis.

These general remarks were the long prelude to his elaboration of his hypothesis concerning Gabrielle Bompard's state of mind during the crime. He argued that she had been hypnotized into an extended *état second* at the time of the murder preparations and during its execution, acting throughout under the influence of Eyraud's suggestion. The notion of *état second*[77] added a new element to his developing medico-legal assessment of Bompard's responsibility; making a strength of the defendant's perpetual prevarications under interrogation, Liégeois stoutly maintained that the reasons for her manifest duplicity were not an attempt on her part to evade justice, but rather a necessary outcome of her having been in a 'second state' when Gouffé was murdered and thus unable to remember clearly what had happened. Her convenient forgetfulness thus became the result of this induced state of which her conscious mind necessarily had no clear recollection.[78]

This detailed and at times garbled assessment of the defendant's state of mind was received with outraged indignation by the panel of physicians, who proceeded to outflank the lawyer and ridicule him mercilessly. He was particularly susceptible to such assaults because several witnesses had testified that Eyraud had never successfully hypnotized Bompard. With renewed vigour and despite this evidence, Liégeois countered by maintaining that Eyraud had produced an amnesia in his subject. Finally, to explain her collaboration in executing the most complicated procedures – renting an apartment, making and keeping various rendezvous, meeting Eyraud in London to purchase items for the murder – he asserted yet again that she had acted unconsciously under Eyraud's direction.

Making the best of the occasion, Brouardel and his associates replied to these long-winded assertions with utter disdain, claiming that Liégeois was fooled not only by the unconfirmed hysterics upon whom he was practising his experiments in Nancy, but also by the illusory power he had imputed to suggestibility. Suggestibility, Brouardel asserted, was doing something that one was inclined to do, under an influence that was not totally disagreeable, as he explained to the court in the following way:

> 'The truth is that when two people live together one has a certain influence on the other. Mr Liégeois is surprised that Gabrielle Bompard stayed with Eyraud who is not alluring and hasn't any money. But this is like something which we see every day ... It's like three schoolboys who commit some foolishness. The father of each will say, "My son was led along." (laughter).'[79]

In describing thus the often mischievous and pernicious influence exerted by lovers and adolescents on each other, Brouardel had characterized well Bernheim's notion of suggestibility, while ignoring the conclusions that the Nancian had drawn from such examples. What separated the two physicians was a fine distinction over the role imputed to volition in human behaviour: whereas Brouardel implied that a capacity for wilful action was always retained except among the mentally ill, Bernheim asseted that any susceptible subject could receive suggestions that would prove irresistible. In an article published after the trial,[80] Bernheim stressed this subtle point and concluded that the fact of Bompard's total lack of a moral sense meant that her resistance to nefarious suggestions was virtually non-existent and thus had justified a verdict of diminished responsibility. The potenital universality of suggestibility which Liégeois had posited, and which Bernheim had seconded in more sober tones, carried within it the dangerous implication that the establishment of the degree of intent for any act, criminal or not, was impossible to determine. Such a psychological observation left the Nancians open to charges of moral nihilism, in which all previous laws deemed to rule human behaviour were swept away by the dictates of the unconscious and its impulses. What Liégeois argued was that anyone's moral responsibility could be abolished no matter what his social class or physical constitution with nefarious suggestions acting as a permanent sword of Damocles threatening to descend on even the most upright of citizens.

The Paris School, in contrast, did not challenge moral absolutes to the same degree as their opponents, their belief that Bompard was a willing accomplice rather than a slave to Eyraud's evil designs reinforcing the judicial appraisal of her personality. Their legal-psychiatric report had carefully stayed within the traditional domain of alienists following a corpus of medico-legal guidelines in which the limitations placed on moral responsibility by both hereditarian and environmental factors were first demonstrated and then dispassionately analysed. Those, like Gabrielle Bompard, who had exhibited some pathological symptoms in conjunction with a degree of moral depravity which far exceeded their somatic-psychic disorder, were not to be excused by respectable physicians. Accordingly, they stood apart from Nancian claims and refused to sanction the moral anarchy implicit in Liégeois's arguments. The Parisians' evaluation of Gabrielle Bompard's state of mind was the more satisfactory in the eyes of the court and she received a sentence of twenty years, an extravagant penalty for a woman during this period. Their view that a hidden *moi* subsisted which could ward off evil impulses if it so desired was affirmed by the jurors who exhibited a lay scepticism of Nancian doctrine which mirrored the medical one of Charcot's school.[81]

While the Paris School visibly enjoyed the spoils of its victory in articles in learned journals,[82] and Bernheim desperately sought to temper Liégeois's extremism in defensive responses, the Nancian attorney disappeared from public view, apparently humiliated by his poor performance in the courtroom. One local Nancian newspaper mockingly wrote that his students were saddened by his absence at the law faculty: 'One demands with terror whether the illustrious professor has become the victim of a new Eyraud who has well and truly hypnotized him.'[83] Bernheim, in a private letter to Beaunis, wrote of his distress and dismay over the outcome of the trial:

'In Nancy, there is a general *outcry* against the unfortunate Liégeois; I even fear that the students will create a rumpus [*chari-vari*] at the beginning of term. I was afraid that he was clumsy, but I didn't believe that he was so to such a point. He has hidden himself away because he had hoped to strike a great blow and exploit the occasion to proclaim loudly and firmly the doctrine of the Nancy School and he only ended up seeming ridiculous; he compromised us.'[84]

These early doomsday predictions of the effects of Liégeois's intervention were not, however, to prove long-lasting. With his presentation to the court, the lawyer had expanded the context of the debate to such an extent that it became part of the general currency of public discussion, and even provoked an exchange in the senate in which one angry member demanded that Liégeois's doctrines be outlawed from the law faculties for destabilizing the French nation. Despite the initial setback which Liégeois's ardour had caused, Beaunis in his unpublished memoirs summed up the lawyer's role in the Bompard case in the following uncompromising way:

'At the time the outcome was appalling, but in the end, since he was basically right, and Parisian mockery, even when orchestrated by a professor of legal medicine and a state prosecutor is [sic] as short-lived as a soap bubble, good sense regained the upper hand and for good or bad Liégeois's ideas mattered in jurisprudence.'[85]

Before long, Liégeois had resumed his professional activities and steadfastly clung to his views, something which kept him in the limelight if not out of controversy. In 1903, on her early parole, he even had the personal satisfaction of reportedly hypnotizing Gabrielle Bompard who apparently relived Gouffé's murder with paroxysms of fear and loathing worthy indeed of the time and trouble the lawyer had invested in her cause.[86]

Hypnotism and its moral and social implications

The case of Gabrielle Bompard was one dramatic episode in a long-standing debate on the nature of hypnotism and its moral and social implications. Her trial – which revealed stark intra-professional rivalry in the courtroom and in the popular press – was, therefore, only one aspect of a broader debate in which hypnotism became a vehicle for analysing free will, the threat to the sanctity of the bourgeois family, issues relating to social hygiene and mysticism, as well as fear of mass insurrection. These anxieties were probed before and during the trial as well as in its aftermath, with the Paris/Nancy debate providing a focus for the discussion of these broader issues.

Liégeois expounded most volubly on the extra-medical realm of hypnosis as early as 1884 when he presented a memoir on its medico-legal implications to the Académie des Sciences Morales et Politiques before an audience of philosophers, publicists, social reformers, and medical men. In this statement of doctrine, Liégeois demonstrated how hypnotism revealed the weak links of genteel society, exposing the chinks in the armour of social and moral absolutes. The cherished objects and ideas most susceptible to this sort of manipulation were propriety, property, and the family, with the third category emphasizing in particular what was perceived as the most vulnerable pillar of bourgeois life, sexual fidelity. Indeed, Liégeois maintained that the more extreme the reversal of normal behaviour, the greater the likelihood of hypnotic manipulation having taken place. As he explained: 'Ideas developed spontaneously or acquired through education, sentiments or propensities, sympathy or repulsion, love or hate, prejudices or passions: all of these can in a moment be modified, transposed, upset!'[87]

While these bold assertions were far from achieving universal acceptance, there was none the less agreement over his warning about the possibility of rape under hypnosis, an anxiety which concerned medico-legists and moralists of whatever affiliation. The fear of being seduced without truly knowing it was the basic cause of alarm and constituted the refined focus for the fear surrounding this practice. This discussion revolved around not only the notion of feminine suggestibility – since women were acknowledged in both the lay and medical discourse as being weak-willed and fickle – but also the subjectibility of the feminine population who required protection from rapacious and unscrupulous sexual violators.

One striking example of the possibility of rape under hypnosis had been investigated by Paul Brouardel as early as 1878, in a bizarre case tried in Rouen, to which Liégeois had made reference during Gabrielle Bompard's trial. The prosecution maintained that an itinerant Jewish dentist named Paul

Lévy had cynically and violently abused an innocent Christian virgin who had come to him to improve her decaying teeth. The details of the encounter were even more outlandish than the charge, since the girl asserted that Lévy had executed his lascivious designs while she was in a near-horizontal position in the dentist chair, and when her mother was present in the room. At first denying the accusations, Lévy was later compelled to admit to having had sexual relations with *fille* Braquehais, but maintained that this had occurred with the girl's full consent, and in his opinion in order to oblige a marriage which would drastically improve Berthe Braquehais's humble situation. Only when they found out that he already had a wife and two children did the mother and daughter cease their dental visits and register their complaint with the courts.[88]

Despite this damning circumstantial evidence, the victim had arguments in her favour. Of an apparently impeccable character, Berthe lived quietly *en famille* and went regularly to confess her sins to the priest. All men who visited the household were rigidly inspected by the mother and father, and two marriage candidates had already been dismissed for trifling inadequacies. Moreover, *fille* Braquehais was universally acknowledged to be both flighty and naive to the point of simpleness, and her unprepossessing appearance made Lévy's claim that she had seduced him with provocative *allures* hard to believe. She insisted that she had been attacked in a state of torpor without any conscious knowledge of it. Her suspicions were aroused by pains in the lower back and genitals, and confirmed by a visit to the doctor.[89]

The first explanation for the 'rape' was that she had been abused when Lévy had administered a dose of chloroform. The medical ethics surrounding the administration of anaesthetics had long been at issue, first since their improper usage might result in death, and second because the state of submission they produced in the subject might tempt an unscrupulous practitioner to violate the slumbering patient. As a Jew and a womanizer, who was said to profit sexually from the bourgeois ladies who required his professional advice, as well as from his female servants, Lévy was particularly vulnerable to such an accusation. Unfortunately for the judge who put forward this hypothesis, no anaesthetics of any strength were found in Lévy's pharmacopoeia, and it was Paul Brouardel who suggested the possibility of hypnosis in facilitating the presumed rape. After an examination of the girl and a lengthy report, the professor of legal medicine concluded that Berthe Braquehais's undeniably hysterical and susceptible disposition had left her open to the possible manipulation of Lévy's magnetizing talents, although there was nothing in the dentist's past to suggest he had ever practised such arts. After a trial conducted in *huis clos*, which thereby prevented the legal arguments in court ever coming to light, Lévy was condemned to ten years' imprisonment.[90]

Brouardel's careful elaboration of his hypothetical case against Lévy reveals the Paris School's early willingness to stake its reputation on such a possibility, since the dean's apparently impartial intervention as an academic dignitary from the capital undoubtedly contributed greatly to the trial's final outcome. In the case of Lévy the dentist, Brouardel's intervention had the effect of blending a native anti-semitism with the fear of sexual violation: it thus not only gave frightening credence to the phantasm of racial hatred in the form of a lustful and evil Jew, but also underscored the necessity of protecting pure and genteel femininity from the attacks of such enterprising magnetizers. In speaking of the social peril and sexual havoc hypnotism promised to bring in its wake, Liégeois proclaimed: 'In a state of induced or spontaneous somnambulism, or in a *secondary state*, women or young girls could be raped without knowing or feeling it, having only the slightest memory of what had happened upon waking.'[91]

According to the lawyer, such disastrous results could occur with frightening ease because of the unhappy fact of women's suggestibility. This was an important element in his defence of Gabrielle Bompard, whose submission to masculine commands, he argued, epitomized the overly supple nature of woman's will. Liégeois went so far as to suggest that women should neither travel alone, nor stare at strangers, his reasoning being that extended eye-contact between a suggestible woman and a predatory male would be sufficient to lead a susceptible victim astray. As an illustration of his belief the following interchange in the trial occurred between the state attorney and Liégeois:

> '*The state attorney*: Doesn't the Nancy School go so far as to advise nervous women never to travel alone since a man, simply through mental suggestion . . .
> *Mr Liégeois* (sharply): Simply through mental suggestion . . . no, but just from a steady gaze, yes.'[92]

In 1892, Liégeois advocated a practical programme to guard against this peril by giving every nervous woman a 'moral vaccination'.[93] This meant that the women would be required to be hypnotized by a competent and trustworthy practitioner who would insert a permanent suggestion into her unconscious to thwart the aims of any nefarious magnetizer. He therefore earnestly searched for a means of shoring up flagging values by the implantation of suitable moral qualities by men of irreproachable character, thereby helping the feminine mind to cope appropriately with all eventualities.

This shared anxiety about the purity of womanhood was directly linked to fears about the lower orders and the threat they posed for the sanctity of the bourgeois family. These sexual interlopers were portrayed as insidious agents, lurking about and preying upon the *foyer familial* from within. No household, be it 'rich, opulent, princely, royal even' would be 'out of danger, because there is no place where women and young girls are not sometimes exposed to the occasionally prolonged contact or presence of people of doubtful morality: servants, *valets de chambre*, coachmen, etc.'[94] As the hypnotic state eradicated consciousness, it enabled these plebeian and bestial

schemers to infiltrate the minds and violate the bodies of refined womanhood, creating evil inclinations which, once seeded, could be difficult to
uproot. This fear was magnified by the impossibility of finding and
punishing the culprit because of the amnesia induced in his victim. Consequently, a gentleman could do little to protect his treasured family circle
from the spectre of the working-class hypnotizer-rapist who could potentially transform every loving and devoted wife into an unknowing adultress
and the mother of bastard children.

It can be argued that hypnosis was seen as promoting a mystical
proletarianization of the bourgeoisie, both spiritually and in terms of its
heredity,[95] through which their separateness from the lower orders was
being secretly undermined by the hidden power of the latter's sexual urges.
This fear undoubtedly arose from the ideal and dichotomized view of the
feminine personality, in which refinement and purity could not peacefully
coexist with voracious sensuality. It was presumed, therefore, that the
working-class man, who was characterized by his lack of intellectual
faculties and his superabundance of instinctual drives, would awaken these
animal tendencies in the unconscious and suggestible side of bourgeois
womanhood, with the result that such sexual energy might meet with the
appropriate, and moreover uncomplaining, response from the victim.

This remarkable obsession by the doctors and other bourgeois commentators with the sexual appetites of the working classes and their purported
assault on middle-class womanhood seems scarcely justified by the degree of
threat actually posed. The only possible explanation for it, therefore, would
appear to be a psychological one, that is the interpretation of a projection of
fears and desires. It is not perhaps surprising that the fears concerning rape
concentrated on servants, considering that the large class of underpaid
domestics had the privileged position of observing at close proximity the
supposed ideal of the bourgeois lifestyle. Animosity towards these under-
lings appears in medical advice manuals as early as the eighteenth century,
with nurses in particular coming under attack for their loathsome treatment
of the children of the middle and upper classes.[96] This discourse continued
throughout the nineteenth century, with repeated warnings to keep a steady
surveillance on these untrustworthy individuals, who would rob valuables,
poison children out of vengeance, and even perpetrate acts of lewdness on
unsuspecting minors.[97]

The vehemence and pervasiveness of these warnings may perhaps be
attributed to the less well-documented historical reality of the sexual
exploitation of female servants by bourgeois masters. It is, of course,
impossible to gauge how widespread this practice was, but Gabrielle
Bompard's father and Paul Lévy were examples which have already been
mentioned here, and occasionally an abused maidservant would come before
the Cour d'assises for an attempted murder against a master who had taken
advantage of her, made her his mistress, and then later evicted her.[98] Such
cases of desertion not only occurred within the *foyer*, but also more
frequently on its periphery, when a working-class mistress in her own

quartier was abandoned to her previous penury after the bourgeois man's marriage.[99] The two supposedly separate spheres of working-class and bourgeois life were thus intermingled through the latter's sexual predations. Recognizing that such incursions took place, bourgeois commentators necessarily worried lest the sexual contacts ceased to flow only in one direction.

Equally the interposition of the figure of the physician into the marital relationship created new possibilities for sexual tension. Popular and medical writing from the middle of the nineteenth century onwards stressed the expanding domain that medical men were carving out for themselves within the bourgeois *foyer*, replacing the priest as a resurrected secular confessor privy to the intimacies of respectable womanhood. The doctors, therefore, had to tread a fine line between reinforcing patriarchial authority through their medical knowledge, which confirmed the innate physical, mental, and emotional inferiority of women on the one hand, while on the other trying to enhance their own status and practice through their privileged role as confidant and medical adviser whose learned statements on childbirth, child-rearing, and women's health solidified the alliance with the wife. This intimacy was widely criticized, and the problem of medical hypnosis added another dimension to the issue, since middle-class women could potentially be made to confess secrets that would wreak havoc on the tranquillity of the conjugal home.[100]

Because of their own ambiguous status in regard to bourgeois femininity, therefore, the physicians were most sensitive to the issue of rape, undoubtedly projecting many of their own desires onto the working classes and sometimes onto women as well. In one frequently cited case, for example, the doctors acknowledged how an unnamed physician had carried out a passionate romance with his beautiful, aristocratic – but unfortunately married – patient during prolonged somnambulic trances in which she declared undying love for him. However, she ardently denied the illicit love-making in her conscious state so that when she became pregnant she went insane, lost the baby, and spent the rest of her life in an asylum. In the aftermath of the scandal the compromised physician was obliged to emigrate, his reputation irretrievably sullied.[101] This long and tragic story thus warned practitioners of the baleful consequences of such lustful but, in the author's view, completely understandable proceedings, and also demonstrates the acute temptation hypnotic therapy presented. An example of the type of projection involved is illustrated by Brouardel's advice on procedures of medical ethics over the administration of chloroform to women. Unlike the majority who saw anaesthetics as a way for unscrupulous practitioners to rape the subject, Brouardel reversed the argument and insisted that the doctor himself was endangered during such operations since the woman's state of unconsciousness might lead her to leap off the table and seduce the physician.[102]

The constant concern which the question of the relationship of women to their sexuality provoked also stimulated discussants to seek scientific explanations for why respectable wives broke their marriage vows to pursue brutal lovers. In one of his clinical lectures, for example, Charcot described the case of a 38-year-old woman who, because of her degenerate susceptibilities, craved to be hypnotized by a popular magnetizer during the 1887 festival in Aubervilliers. Not daring to submit herself to such manoeuvres in the presence of her husband, she returned unaccompanied to the magnetizer who purportedly dominated her to such an extent that 'she was tormented by the desire to leave her home and find the one whom she considered to be her master'.[103] Subjugated in this way, she left the conjugal home, only to be retrieved by her husband with the aid of a police order. Her condition, however, did not improve, despite the salutary influence of her spouse's presence, and by the time she had been entrusted to Charcot's care she was in a state of complete mutism. Thus silenced by the shamefulness of her deed, Charcot saw fit to subject her to the prying eyes of his bourgeois audience and to present her case as a pointed example of the widespread danger facing society.

More than such a case which involved a woman of humble background, episodes of widely publicized crimes of passion posed the difficult problem of assessing why bourgeois women often refused to return to their husbands and sometimes preferred suicide or even more dramatically a *suicide à deux* to the comfort and security of their former lives. In order to explain such apparently deviant behaviour, psychiatrists, moralists, and social commentators repeatedly pointed to the effects of a domineering or mutual suggestibility in order to neutralize the implied criticism of bourgeois norms such behaviour offered. Such a discussion surrounded the celebrated Chambige affair of 1888[104] when Mme Grille, a 30-year-old wife and mother of impeccable character, was found naked and dead in a villa in Sadi-Mabrouk, Algeria, beside her wounded companion, the 22-year-old Henri Chambige. Rather than disowning his wife, M. Grille, a prominent member of the colonial notables, maintained that his wife had been 'fascinated' by Chambige, who had lured her to the isolated villa in order to rape and then murder her, thereby escaping from the damning revelation he claimed she undoubtedly would have made. For those who believed this version of the story, the defence of Mme Grille became a central element in the defence of pure wifehood and motherhood everywhere. In contrast to the prosecution's case, Chambige asserted that the highly strung wife had herself proposed the double suicide, unable to reconcile her passionate love for the younger man with the cruel abandonment of her adored children. The case was further complicated by the fact that Chambige was a promising new member of the decadent school of literature who had written an article on 'les Goncourt et l'exotisme' and whose perverted propensity for such nihilistic work,[105] the prosecution maintained, had 'suggested' the idea of enacting the murder in order to desecrate the values of duty and honour that this *famille modèle*[106] were deemed to represent. It cannot be known whether either love or literature was in fact the ultimate cause of the crime, but the suggestible powers of both were used as a means of explaining the murder and of underscoring the destructive excesses which the extreme nature of such passions produced.

With such cases as the Chambige affair, the discussion of hypnotism, and more precisely suggestibility, intensified and gave an added dimension to the much broader contemporaneous discussion on the decline of the family, and by implication depopulation and racial degeneration. The standard account of these perceived social problems stressed the dangers of an effete stock and the bad effects caused by decadent values, especially in women such as Mme Grille who consciously or not shirked their duties as loyal wives and mothers.[107] Such gloomy prognoses for the future of the French nation, were voiced almost universally because of the relative decline in population, especially *vis-à-vis* its teutonic neighbour.[108]

These vague anxieties found a more concrete political focus during the 1890s when the anarchist and educational reformer, Paul Robin, and the radical feminist movement were advocating a massive programme of birth control education, particularly for the working poor. Anarchist agitation (the early 1890s was also the period of terrorist bombings) was thus directly linked to the *grève du ventre*, seen by some as a revolutionary movement dedicated to increasing feminine sexual promiscuity, under the banner of personal liberty, and with it the further degeneration of the family.[109]

By being regarded in this way as an exacerbating factor of France's social problems, hypnotism escaped the confines of medical debate and became a means, through the medium of the family, of linking marital infidelity with revolutionary political protest.[110] These explicit linkages made in the minds of social commentators explain the repercussions that the nature of the defence of Gabrielle Bompard triggered off. Because she epitomized the inversion of all decent bourgeois morality, she symbolized the possibility of decline and decadence produced by the whimsical dictates of suggestion. If hypnotism and its effects were a metaphorical vessel in which were contained a mixture of the most deeply seated worries and anxieties of the French bourgeoisie, above all the males of that species, the person of Gabrielle Bompard became for a brief period the literal personification of them.

Anxiety over the nature of feminine sexuality and its threat to the family was only one aspect of the developing debate over hypnosis which sharpened the edges of controversy during Bompard's trial. Hypnotism had increasingly captured public attention when a wave of mesmeric performances swept through France during the 1880s with Bompard herself attending such public entertainments in Lille. The supposedly reckless dissemination of the practice by quacks and mountebanks on such individuals as Bompard was, as will be shown, a crucial component of a more far-reaching campaign among doctors to achieve state control of medical practice which they ultimately won in November 1892;[111] moreover, it gave an added level of significance to the debate both in and out of court between the Ecole de Paris and the followers of Bernheim.

One of the major themes running throughout the court case was the

Parisian emphasis on its own scientific exactitude in contrast to the purportedly amateurish, if not ridiculous, nature of Nancian research. During the proceedings, Brouardel made mocking comparisons between the lawyer's gullible faith in suggestibility and the views and practices of spiritualists, mystics, and mediums who believed in turning tables and talking hats.[112] Although a mere rhetorical gibe, it was true that the Ecole de Nancy had definite contact with popular magnetizers, with whom they shared a belief in the healing power of hypnosis, thereby bringing some amateurs and the Nancians into some accord. On the whole, whereas the Nancy School took a *laissez-faire* attitude over the practice of hypnotism in which amateurs and medical men should have equal right to experiment, the Paris School and like-minded practitioners in Switzerland, Austria, Italy, Belgium, Germany, and Denmark launched a vicious assault on these non-medical healers so that, by 1890, their performances were legally banned in these countries.[113] It seems clear, however, that this did not always stop the magnetizers from practising their art,[114] nor did it prevent large crowds from flocking to their demonstrations.

Parisians' disapproval of the magnetizers was ostensibly based on the harmful effects theatrical presentations were supposed to have on a suggestible and gullible public. On the microcosmic level of the individual this concern was once more imbued with the question of sexuality. The rapport between the magnetizer and his usually female subject was frequently described in sexual terminology as a relationship between a prostitute and her pimp and once more gave rise to the alarm over the possibilities of rape that this opened up. Dr Gilles de la Tourette, a fanatical disciple of Charcot and Brouardel, was the main advocate of banning these performances and spoke in the expert capacity as alienist, medico-legist, and official mouthpiece for the Paris School on the subject. In this muck-raking volume,[115] Gilles de la Tourette demonstrated the seamier side of *spiritisme*, how young girls were lured into seances by the blandishments of the operator and by the applause of a vulgar and stupid audience.

On the macroscopic level of the general public, the doctors were alarmed at the possible consequences such performances might have for audiences which, in their view, threw caution to the winds in the foolish search for titillation by dabbling in the supposedly supernatural. Responsible French physicians who agreed with Charcot called for the banning of such popular entertainments, and cited blood-curdling examples of magnetizing's nefarious results. For example, an accident which occurred when a circus passed through the town of Béziers was blamed on amateur abuse of the practice. A young girl, magnetized into a cataleptic trance, was introduced into the lions' cage, where the wild beasts, rather than peacefully sniffing the sleeping subject, became enraged and tore her thigh to shreds.[116] In another case, Bérillon accused a performing magnetizer of suggesting to his audience outside of Paris that a fire was rapidly spreading throughout the theatre, with the result that the crowd stampeded out of the building, treading women and children mercilessly underfoot in a blind panic.[117] Such

Zola-esque images of savage violence were employed to waken the public to the dangers facing them, and to imply by contrast how medical men with their standards of professional ethics would not be found taking similar advantages.

This attitude toward popular performances followed from the Parisians' general view that hypnotism was an *agent révélateur* of latent hysterical and pathological symptoms which destroyed the capacity for proper moral and intellectual activity. In the hands of enterprising mountebanks this danger was increased, with hypnotism promising to trigger off mass explosions of hysteria in a public that was eminently susceptible because of deficient psychic constitutions. The fact that the crowds who came to these stage events were composed of the popular classes and of adolescents attracted by the miraculous claims of the performers meant that the danger of psychic accidents was enhanced, and to prove their point medical men cited numerous cases of instant insanity and rape in the wake of these stage events. One worthy physician from Bordeaux, for example, where the performances were outlawed in 1888, described in undoubtedly exaggerated terms the impishly immoral scene which occurred in the city after a performance by Alfred D'hont, called Donato, the most renowned magnetizer of the day:

'Disorder and profound trouble result from hypnotic procedures falling into unqualified hands. Pimps put girls to sleep in brothels; tradesmen, rakes, and dandies of every sort were hypnotizing their mistresses. It had become an absolute mania, and I approved of the measures taken by the municipality of Bordeaux to forbid the continuation of Donato's performances, because I believe ... that it is not good to store dangerous poisons and arms in everyone's hands.'[118]

This picture of magnetizing mania in which working-class sexuality was portrayed as an hypnotic embrace embellished the description of the plebeian crowds whose pathologcal tendencies led them to seek out these performances and to enjoy them with a reckless abandon that medical men could only condemn. Those physicians who accepted Charcot's pronouncements on the subject denounced unequivocally not only this 'unwholesome curiosity of an idle and impudent public, to put it mildly',[119] but also the emotionally charged attitude of the audience which 'recalls from the past ... the great mental epidemics of the middle ages with their convulsionaries, their sorcerers, and their superstitions'.[120] A Swiss physician named Ladame, tireless in his warnings against theatrical presentations, described the debasement of the subject on the stage in the following way:

'The hypnotized subject made a spectacle of to the crowd bubbling up with unwholesome emotion, publicly held up to ridicule, brutally held in thrall, made to hallucinate to the point of raging madness, reduced to the last extremity by the hideous criminal suggestions the magnetizer orders him to perform ... the hypnotized subject of public performances is truly a victim.'[121]

In the name, therefore, of social order, mental hygiene, and human dignity, the Parisian School and its followers called for an end to this public outrage. This apparently humanitarian campaign was part and parcel, however, of a broader movement to monopolize hypnotism as an aspect of medical practice alone, a programme that was ironic indeed considering official medicine's complete contempt for such therapeutic procedures during the previous fifty years. Doctors suddenly began to maintain, in the course of the 1880s, that hypnotism was like a powerful drug, something to be administered with medical care and precision. 'The law,' wrote Ladame, 'is very severe when it comes to the sale of a few drops of laudanum, while allowing somnambulists and magnetizers to practise with impunity.'[122] His view were overwhelmingly endorsed by the 1889 conference held in Paris on hypnotism and attended chiefly by physicians. They also called for the outlawing of theatrical performances,[123] after a stormy and undignified session during which the few supporters of the magnetizers were shouted down by a clique purportedly under the leadership of Gilles de la Tourette.[124]

The vituperative nature of this campaign, in which often questionable evidence of crime and madness were used to strengthen the Paris School's case[125] suggests that behind this assault deeper interests were at stake, striking at the heart of Charcot's doctrine. First, the rhetoric of the struggle reveals a pressing concern to dissociate completely the new 'scientific' age of hypnotism from its disreputable beginnings in magnetism, so much so that the latter was compared to alchemy and the former to chemistry. Charcot had built his reputation on his dedication to positivism, and his disciples repeatedly compared him to Pasteur to give a measure of his scientific calibre. Moreover, he had received the special creation of the Chair of Nervous Diseases in 1882 under Republican anti-clerical auspices, and it was while under this patronage that much of his early work on hysteria showed how the ecstasies of saints and the demons of past ages were nothing more than a disease which could now be treated by France's premier physician.[126]

It was not, however, only because of a dedication to scientistic precepts that his school reacted so violently against the amateurs. This display of anger was also due to the charges that the amateurs brought against Charcot himself, accusing him of precisely the same charlatanry that the psychiatrist levelled against them. The most powerful demonstration of the unity of the opposition took place during the 1889 Congress of Human Magnetism,[127] held at virtually the same time as the scientific gathering on experimental hypnotism in which Ladame and Gilles de la Tourette had hurled their abuse against the amateurs. The doctors' sinister portrait of money-grubbing sensationalists seems hardly confirmed by the magnetizers themselves, many of whom were pastors, retired army officers, or itinerant healers, and who practised their art sometimes free of charge. Although the magnetizers disagreed among themselves about the theories concerning hypnosis and their relationship to healing – some attributing it to a mesmeric fluid, or animal electricity, others to an unspecified *force neurique rayonnante* or suggestion – they were unanimous in decrying Charcot's coupling of hysteria and hypnosis and the implication drawn from this analysis that the latter had only limited therapeutic applications. In fact, many were vehemently opposed to Charcot's practice of producing somnambulistic trances and cataleptic states, since their own magnetic techniques did not rely on the inducement of artificial sleep which they maintained produced hysteria and mental congestion and resulted in madness and debility. Moreover, there was a consensus over the pitiful and deplorable nature of the maître's extravagant performances at the Salpêtrière which they asserted were more pernicious and socially destructive than theatrical presentations which informed the masses of powers that official medicine wished to keep hidden. Charcot's entire system – the four states of hysterio-epilepsy which erupted so conveniently, the dispassionate way in which madwomen's woes were used to regale a curious bourgeois public during his clinical lectures, the use of bright objects, loud noises, and theatrical gestures to induce hypnotic sleep – was totally condemned as a sadistic game devised by a devil in the name of official science and materialism.[128]

The most interesting figure in this 'fringe' community was the famous magnetizer Donato, whose travels throughout Europe had earned him an extensive reputation. Unlike many of his colleagues, Donato employed techniques very similar to those introduced to the medical world by the Ecole de Nancy, with suggestion rather than manipulation of magnetic fluid providing a theoretical basis for his therapeutic and theatrical practice.[129] His impact on the academic world was substantial, with Enrico Morselli of Turin dedicating a chapter in his *Magnetismo animale* to Donato's techniques, in which he accused official science of plagiarizing the amateur's discoveries.[130] Donato was supposed to have introduced Ladame himself to the wonders of hypnosis, and claimed to have suffered profoundly from the Swiss physician's relentless attacks. Joseph Delboeuf, a Belgian philosopher-psychologist who wrote extensively on topics related to both the psychology and politics of hypnosis, never tired to praising Donato's knowledge and candour, and defended all amateurs with a vigour that matched the venom of Gilles de la Tourette's assaults.[131] One of the undoubted reasons for the attack against Donato was his early, unrestrained, and perceptive criticism of Charcot's studies on hysteria. Mirroring Bernheim's assessment of the Parisian psychiatrist's work, Donato claimed in 1882 that Charcot had unwittingly suggested the hysterical crises in his patients who preferred to have their fits conform 'to his ingenious predictions'.[132] Strongly criticizing the errors of medical traditionalism, in which students were forced to accept and promote the fallacious doctrines of their maîtres to assure advancement in the professional hierarchy, Donato championed the masses as the ultimate arbiter in determining scientific truth:

'But the humble magnetizers, professional hypnotizers, tired of being repulsed by the academies, appealed to the crowds, showing them that the official scholars were denying the evidence. The crowd acclaimed the independent apostles of a misunderstood truth and forced the princes of official science to bow before the irrefutable facts.'[133]

His assertion that 'the academies too often hinder (*émasculent*) progress'[134] was seconded by sympathetic journalists in the popular press who reported on the 1889 magnetizing conference, one remarking that 'without doubt, this scarcely tallies with the academic dogmas under which the mandarins of scientific orthopaedics claim to discipline all new ideas under threat of heresy.'[135] In accordance with their criticism of the nature and structure of official science, Donato and other 'experimental spiritualists' called for the end to medical professionalism, maintaining that if the doors of the dissecting chamber and the clinic were flung open, a revolution in therapeutic procedures would be quickly realized by plebeian practitioners. They claimed that these amateur healers, concerned only with the alleviation of suffering and uncompromised by state subsidies and the dictates of official dogma, would not be duped by the type of fraud and trickery that Charcot's system contained. 'Doctoralism', as one indignant spiritualist called medical power, 'is a hundred times more intolerant, more monopolistic, more despotic than clericalism and militarism together.'[136]

However, although deprecatory of the Salpêtrière, the magnetizers were more laudatory of Liébault, Bernheim, and Liégeois. Some saw them as allies in the struggle for the survival of their fugitive knowledge and regarded the Nancians' work as more congenial to their own because of the latter's emphasis on the therapeutic possibilities of hypnosis. Liégeois's stance was perhaps peculiarly inconsistent as he disagreed with the Parisian view that the magnetizers implanted criminal suggestions in their audiences, a position completely at odds with his medico-legal system. In this instance, however, his own belief in the pure motivations of the magnetizers (Liégeois himself had received valuable lessons in hypnotic techniques from a famous amateur named Hansen, whom he described as a 'man of completely good faith and absolute integrity who did not pronounce a single word which in any way at all could be accused of charlatanism')[137] led him to support their struggle, because like himself they were unqualified and refused to accept that a medical training was necessary to practise hypnosis successfully.

By thus dismissing the danger of mesmeric performances and indeed sometimes agreeing with the amateurs themselves, Liégeois and the Nancy case in general were, in the example of Gabrielle Bompard, tainted by accusations of supporting charlatanry, mysticism, and professional irresponsibility. It was through his questioning of the doctor's unique role to perform hypnotic experiments that Liégeois could be cast by his opponents in the part of the misguided, if not dangerous, amateur, a tactic which in the courtroom helped the Paris School press its case.

The looming portrait of mass hysteria and social unrest that doctors painted in their discussion of mesmeric performances synchronized with developing theories of crowd behaviour which emphasized the same irrational, pathological, and criminal tendencies. If the example of Gabrielle

Bompard and the 'unhealthy' forces unleashed by popular magnetism were not enough to alarm the public, then criminologists and crowd theorists were eager to forge the links with mass insurrection, using analytical tools in which hypnotism, once again, was to play an important role.

Recent work[138] exhibits the extent to which the development of crowd psychology reflected the crises of mass democracy in France during the Third Republic. These academic speculations on the crowd emerged in part as a response to the terrors of the Commune and the perceived irrational reactions of the Parisian crowds, portrayed as drunken, frenzied rioters, hypnotized by unscrupulous leaders and bent on destruction. These phantasmagoric images were hardly restricted to social theorists, however, but in fact found their first vivid expression in the historical studies of Hippolyte Taine on the origins of contemporary France (in which the recent Commune was made to mirror the horrors of the Terror during the French Revolution) and in the work of Emile Zola, particularly in his view of striking miners in *Germinal*. As important to crowd theorists as the increasingly distant memory of the Commune was the Boulanger affair of 1886–89, which had swept across France, catching in its populist net such unlikely political allies as *revanchiste* Catholics and the miners of Decazeville (Avéyron). Boulanger's success with the masses was seen as a result of the influence he had on an irrational, suggestible mob who were impressed by this regal (if not very intelligent) military man astride a horse. Such a figure resonated with images of Napoleonic Caesarism, the man of action so dear to the French national *âme*,[139] as Gustave LeBon, the most renowned and influential popularizer of crowd psychology, would call the repository of national visions. In the view of crowd theorists, the mythological magnification of Boulanger touched, electrified and finally set into motion unconscious passions. France, it was claimed, hoped that Boulanger might provide a panacea to the faltering democracy of the Third Republic, beleaguered by scandal, corruption, and the political anarchy of revolving door ministries.

In the spring of 1890, during a press interview in which he maintained that Gabrielle Bompard had acted under suggestion, Bernheim had found it fit to explain her case and the Boulanger affair in similar terms. He explicitly used the same analytic concepts to connect his view of the abolition of liberty in susceptible individuals to the mechanisms by which large groups could be dominated and manipulated:

> 'Gabrielle Bompard is an excellent suggestible subject ... There are several stages within human beings. Those possessed of a solid moral sense are more impervious to suggestion. On another level, the epidemic of *boulangisme* which struck the calm and reasonable department of Meurthe-et-Moselle last summer was due to suggestion. Naive people had their eyes and ears filled with images of Boulanger and adulation of him, and you know that no reasoning could prevail against their fancy.'[140]

While a psychiatrist like Bernheim could make passing reference to hypnotism as an important factor in political analysis, it was the new discipline of criminal anthropology[141] elaborated primarily by French and Italian theorists during the period which used the clinical work of psychiatrists on suggestion and applied it to particular research interests. This work grew out of concerns with the legal responsibility of individuals involved in crowd violence, an issue which was brought into view by 'crimes' committed by striking workers.[142] Scipio Sighele of Italy, a disciple of Cesare Lombroso, was the first to discuss the politics of hypnosis in *La Foule criminelle* (1892),[143] in which he adapted Charcot's theory of hypnotic suggestibility and its view of mental disorder to explain crowd behaviour. For him, only degenerate individuals were susceptible to this sort of manipulation, which unleashed bestial primitive impulses, and which allowed the leader and the crowd to dance in a sort of frenzied and dangerous sexual communion.

Frenchmen such as Gabriel Tarde,[144] Henri Fournial,[145] and Gustave LeBon[146] further developed these ideas, having at their disposal a string of useful concepts developed by French psychiatric clinicians during the course of the nineteenth century. Emphasizing the idea of 'collective hallucination', they gave an explanation of why crowds acted as if in a dream state, unrestrained by rational thought processes.[147] Another important conception was 'mental contagion', an old notion continually refurbished with reference to psychiatric theory and clinical case-studies. This owed much to a well-documented pathology developed by Prosper Despine called *folie à deux*, in which one insane partner in a pair, usually of sexual intimacy, infected the other with his or her mental disorder.[148] The notion of mental contagion often blurred into another concept, that of imitation, which Tarde developed in his seminal work, *Les Lois d'imitation* (1890), as the basis of his social philosophy. The central focus of this book was his demonstration of how the production of cultural norms was a result of suggestibility.

These social theorists, therefore, found powerful analytical tools for their view of mass behaviour in individual cases of mental disease and criminal behaviour. Hypnotism, suggestibility and related concepts were therefore potent weapons in the arsenal of the social theorists, the more so because they were given scientific credibility by the research interests of psychiatrists in the early 1880s. Using a combination of precepts borrowed eclectically from both Nancy and Paris, these theoreticians regarded the mob as an unconscious beast whose lack of intellectual capacity did not diminish its destructiveness when directed by its leader. Such far-reaching analyses were made possible by the useful theoretical links hypnotism forged for the crowd theorists, for as Tarde remarked as early as 1884, when he stressed the wider implications to be drawn from hypnosis:

'I believe that I am adhering ... to the most rigorous scientific method in trying to elucidate the complex by the simple, the compound by the element, and by explaining the most tangled and complex social relationships by one which is at the same time very pure and reduced to its simplest expression. From the sociologist's point of view, this is showed up most strikingly in the somnambulic state ... *Society is imitation and imitation is a type of somnambulism.*[149]

The mention of the development of crowd psychology and the crucial centrality of hypnotism as the key means of its analyses underscores my point that Gabrielle Bompard's trial resonated with meaning beyond the establishment of her guilt or innocence, crystallizing anxieties over individual morality, the degeneration of the family, social hygiene, and, finally, the perceived threat of social revolution. What united these diverse levels of anxiety was the fear that rational, moral, and social processes were to be potentially bypassed through the ease with which hypnotism could open the Pandora's Box of the unconscious and its drives.

Clearly, in terms of the two schools it was the Parisian which seemed resolutely dedicated to keeping these forces under lock and key as much as possible. The desire to contain such urges ironically contradicted the thrust of their research programme, which had been to move the 'irrational' out of the confines of mysticism, eccentricity, and literature into the domain of science, with all the legitimation that that conferred. Their focusing of the 'clinical gaze' onto such areas had therefore the effect of heightening, rather than diminishing, the interest in and attraction of the unconscious side of the human personality, whose inherent morbidity the Parisian School never ceased to demonstrate. Accordingly, they linked hypnosis to hysteria and this combination was seen to have dire pathological import for both individuals and society. It was for these reasons that they saw their role in the courtroom as that of physicians who marked out boundaries between disease and vice, and as moralists who warned against the promotion of social degeneration.

They extended this dual role during their assault against the amateurs who had impugned their scientific integrity by pointing out their contradictions in doctrine. The war with the magnetizers was not, however, restricted to the level of abstracted intellectual debate, but took strength from the more profound struggle caused by the physicians' campaign to monopolize hypnotic practice and to outlaw the 'charlatanry' popularized by the performers. At first glance, the Nancy School's position was more ambiguous than that of their opponents. Having recognized and even promoted the notion of the possibility of murder under hypnosis in individuals and groups, and having alerted the public to the dangers of hypnotism through Liégeois's medico-legal system, they none the less advocated its continual unveiling for the sake of the advancement of medical knowledge and therapeutics, and consequently sanctioned its popularization by amateurs whom they thought to be imbued with the same visionary ideals.

Despite the differences between the two schools, which in the social realm concentrated on public mesmeric performances, both Nancians and Parisians shared a common perspective on the prophylactic measures to be taken *vis-à-vis* hypnosis. From the perspective of social unrest, it did not make much difference if, as the Paris School claimed, there was a large number of potential hysterics with latent susceptibilities or, as the Nancians maintained, everyone was more or less suggestible and, therefore, prey to sexual assaults and political demagoguery. Both views implied that hypnotism was extremely efficacious and potentially very dangerous, and that its practice ought, therefore, to be strictly confined to men of impeccable integrity and probity. The essential difference between the two in this regard was that, although the Nancians were as eager as the Parisians to keep hypnosis out of the hands of the unscrupulous, they did not accept that a medical degree necessarily doubled up as a certificate of good behaviour, nor that its absence was an instant indicator of moral turpitude.

It has been the contention of this essay that the trial of Gabrielle Bompard served as a major focus in the debate on the nature of hypnotism and revealed a far-reaching philosophical argument over the relationship of the mental and the physical. This provided an entry through which medical theorizing could examine moral, social, and political issues that were the perceived frayed spots in the fabric of Belle Epoque society, particularly among its middle-class members. The heat and acerbity of this sectarian debate in which each school envisioned alternative uses for hypnosis none the less revealed common strands of anxiety, chief among which was alarm over the inability of liberal values to withstand the lowering tendencies of unconscious drives. This pervasive fear took strength and grew with each crisis that the French experiment in mass democracy encountered – be that the Commune, the Boulanger affair, syndicalist strikes, or anarchist bombings – all political demonstrations which were described by social commentators as the confluence of criminal suggestions and the evil assertion of the unconscious.

Bompard's case served to bring into sharp focus this supposed moral and social decline, serving as an allegory of the impetus behind this frightening process. Despite the fact that many of the assertions that Liégeois put forward in his testimony for Gabrielle Bompard were instantly perceived by judges and jurors alike as being far-fetched and ludicrous, the extreme nature of his defence of a highly unsatisfactory person none the less served to publicize the Nancian case in the wider sphere which the lawyer was primarily addressing. As woman, slut, murderess, and bourgeois outcast, Bompard was a reification of the dangers facing society, and what she symbolized could not be ignored. Simply by introducing the possibility that hypnotism may have played a role in her descent to the position of social danger, Liégeois imbued the topic with a significance that captured the public imagination. Bompard was condemned, but the arguments put forward on her behalf continued and grew in power in areas unassociated with her case. Her trial destroyed the possibility of containing hypnotism to a strictly medical domain, and forced it more overtly into the consciousness of medico-legal experts, political theorists, and the public alike.

Notes

The details of this murder trial were discovered in the judicial dossier at the Archives de la Seine (henceforth AS) D2U8 263, which contains over 2,000 pieces of manuscript material. Unfortunately, approximately 400 of these are missing, but many may be found in printed form in journals and will be cited as such in the following notes. I wish to thank Michael Clark, Ludmilla Jordanova, and particularly Neil McWilliam and Iain Pears for their help in the preparation of this article.

1 For press coverage of morgue viewing, cf. Archives de la Préfecture de la Seine (APS) B-A/85/; *Petit journal*, 24 November, 1889; *Le Figaro*, 28 November, 1889.

2 The Ecole de Nancy was in fact a very small group, consisting of Hippolyte Bernheim, an internist by training; Ambroise Liébault, a local practitioner-philanthropist; Henri-Etienne Beaunis, physiologist and forensic expert; and the lawyer and professor of administrative law at Nancy, Jules Liégeois. The greatest influence of Bernheim's doctrine was in fact felt abroad; cf. Henri F. Ellenberger, *The Discovery of the Unconscious: The History and Evolution of Dynamic Psychiatry* (New York: Basic Books, 1970), pp. 85–9.

3 For Charcot and his school, cf. the following introductory biographies: Pearce Bailey, *J.-M. Charcot 1825–1893, His Life – His Work* (London: Pitman Medical, 1959); A.R.G. Owen, *Hysteria, Hypnosis and Healing: The Work of J.-M. Charcot* (London: Denis Dobson, 1971). For a general introduction to debates on hypnosis in France: Dominique Barrucand, *Histoire de l'hypnose en France* (Paris: Presses Universitaires de France, 1967). For the first statement of doctrine on hysteria, cf. Paul Richer, *Etudes cliniques sur la grande hystérie* (Paris: A. Delahaye et E. Lecrosnier, 1881); Georges Didi-Huberman, *Invention de l'hystérie: Charcot et l'Iconographie photographique de la Salpêtrière* (Paris: Les Editions Macula, 1982).

4 *Affaire Gouffe: Procès Eyraud-Bompard*, published in Paris by the *Gazette des tribunaux*, 1890, p. 128.

5 For an account of the debate over the magnetizers showing the passionate interests at stake for both sides, see Joseph Delboeuf, *Magnétiseurs et medecins* (Paris: F. Alcan, 1890).

6 *Affaire Gouffé*, p. 130. In mocking tones Paul Brouardel equated the lack of experimental rigour of the Nancians with spiritualist mumbo-jumbo.

7 André Pressat, 'L'Hypnotisme et la presse', *Rev. hypno.* 4 (1890): 230.

8 See Robert A. Nye, *The Origins of Crowd Psychology, Gustave LeBon and the Crisis of Mass Democracy in the Third Republic* (London: Sage Publications, 1975); Susanna Barrows, *Distorting Mirrors: Visions of the Crowd in Late Nineteenth Century France* (New Haven, Conn.: Yale University Press, 1981); and Serge Moscovici, *L'Âge des foules, un traité historique de psychologie des masses* (Paris: Fayard, 1982).

9 For the eloquent summation defence see the lawyer's pronouncements in *Affaire Gouffé*, pp. 161–71. The defence largely rested on his moral incapacity because of the weakness induced by love.

10 For the details of Eyraud's disreputable life, cf. 'L'Affaire Gouffé', *Archives d'anthropologie criminelle* 6 (1891): 4–8.

11 Some of the most amusing accounts of Eyraud's exploits came from the Parisian inspectors sent to apprehend the famous murderer. They followed him from New York to Canada, returning whining despatches to their superior head of the

Sûreté, M. Goron. AS D2U8 263, in particular pieces 1583, 1585, 1590.

12 Cf. *Le Figaro*, 21 July, 1890.

13 Anonymous, *Un Crime célèbre, mémoires secrets de Michel Eyraud* (Paris: Librarie Populaire Illustré, 1890), p. 9.

14 For Garanger's reaction to the extortion attempt, cf. AS D2U8 263, piece 1596.

15 In the psychiatrists' report, the doctors asserted that Gabrielle Bompard herself was prompted to go to the police after reading about the murder in the *Petit Journal*. For them this illustrated the enormity of her vanity, not mental incapacity. Cf. *Archives d'anthropologie criminelle* 6 (1891): 76–83.

16 During the pre-trial investigation she invented two other accomplices and then retracted her statement, cf. AS D2U8 263, piece 590.

17 For discussion of this possibility, cf. AS D2U8 263, piece 625.

18 For the police investigation into the parental home in Lille cf. AS D2U8 263, piece 707e.

19 AS D2US, piece 707e; for the nuns' depositions cf. pieces 711e and 713.

20 Adrien R., *rentier*, hypnotized Bompard frequently and maintained that she was unbalanced, cf. AS D2US, piece 613, for Dr Sacreste's description of her neuropathic state, cf. 'Affaire Gouffé', pp. 72–3.

21 AS D2US, piece 654 for Marie Félicie M . . . 's appreciation of Bompard's sanity and wicked nature.

22 *Affaire Gouffé*, pp. 104–07.

23 AS D2U8 263, pieces 653, 654, 659.

24 AS D2U8 263, piece 653.

25 Cf. James F. McMillan, *Housewife or Harlot: The Place of Women in French Society, 1870–1914* (London: Harvester Press, 1981) for a survey of the role of women in France and the dichotomized appraisal of their roles. For an overview of medical appreciations of women and their contribution to furthering and upholding these dichotomies cf. Yvonne Knibiehler and Catherine Fouquet, *La Femme et les médecins: analyse historique* (Paris: Hachette, 1982); also Stéphane Michaud, 'Science, droit, religion: trois contes sur les deux natures,' *Romantisme* 13 (1976): 23–40.

26 For the elaborate murder preparations, cf. AS D2U8 263 *passim*, in particular pieces 1660–1780.

27 For Eyraud's description of the murder cf. piece 1782. Throughout the trial both Gabrielle Bompard and Eyraud maintained that they had not intended to kill their victim, wishing only to steal his money. Premeditation, however, was established by the elaborate murder preparations made in the apartment before the crime, so this claim was quickly dismissed by the court. Also Bompard denied ever putting the silk cord around Gouffé's neck, asserting throughout that Eyraud had strangled Gouffé with his bare hands. This testimony was also largely disregarded because of the evidence of her willing collaboration in the crime, but there was never positive proof from the autopsy that Gouffé had been hanged since the cadaver was in an advanced state of putrefaction when found.

28 'Affaire Gouffé', p. 12. Their booty included a gold piece of 100 francs, a bank note of 50 francs, a watch and chain, a ring with two little diamonds, and a tortoise-shell pince-nez.

29 Alfred Fouillé, 'Le Physique et le mental à propos de l'hypnotisme', *Revue des Deux Mondes* 101 (1891): 437.

30 For Ribot's evaluation of the bankruptcy of philosophy in France until the 1870s and why he began the *Revue philosophique* (first edition in 1876), cf.

'Philosophy in France', *Mind* 2 (1877): 366–86.

31 These classic monographs of the 1880s include *Les Maladies de la mémoire* (Paris: G. Baillière, 1881), *Les Maladies de la volonté*, 2nd edn. (Paris: F. Alcan, 1884), and *Les Maladies de la personnalité* (Paris, F. Alcan, 1885).

32 For Ribot's early interest in English associationist psychology, see *La Psychologie anglaise contemporaine*, 2nd edn. (Paris: G. Baillière, 1875).

33 H. Spencer, *Principes de psychologie*, trans. T. Ribot and A. Espinas (Paris: 1876).

34 For Ribot's introduction to the work of Gustav Fechner, Wilhelm Wundt, and Hermann Helmholtz, cf. *La Psychologie allemande contemporaine* (Paris: G. Baillière, 1879).

35 Ribot, *Les Maladies de la volonté*, p. 66.

36 The most famous clinical pamphlet on this issue was Valentin Magnan's *Leçons cliniques sur la dipsomanie* (Paris: A. Delhaye and Lecrosnier, 1884). All examples of this type of work stressed the uncontrollable and bestial effects of alcohol, in particular absinthe, and what it did to mental and neurological functioning. For work on drugs cf., for example, H. Guimball, *Le Morphino-manes* (Paris: J.B. Ballière, 1891).

37 Ribot, *Les Maladies de la volonté*, quoting Richet, p. 113.

38 Charcot began his medical career with work on chronic rheumatism and diseases of the aged in the 1850s and 1860s. Cf. his *Oeuvres complètes*: vol. *7 Maladies des vieillards, goutte et rheumatisme* (Paris: Lecrosnier et Babé, 1890). He made his reputation with his famous neurological work, vol. *4 Leçons sur les localisations dans les maladies du cerveau et de la moelle épinière* (Paris: Félix Alcan, 1893), and vol. *2 Leçons sur les maladies du système nerveux* (Paris: Félix Alcan, 1894).

39 For a discussion of the relationship of psychiatry to politics cf. Jan Goldstein, 'The Hysteria Diagnosis and the Politics of Anticlericalism in Late-nineteenth-century France', *Journal of Modern History* 54 (1982): 209–39.

40 For Charcot's discussion of hysteria in the *Oeuvres complètes*, cf. vol. 1 *Leçons sur les maladies du système nerveux* (Paris: Louis Bataille, 1892), pp. 276–448, and all of vol. 3 of the same title (Paris: Lecrosnier et Babé, 1890). In these works Charcot concentrated on the physiological and clinical aspects of hysteria and rarely discussed the psychological manifestations of the disease. Once in lesson 16, vol. 3, he did describe a case of spiritualist infection among a family of children, for which he prescribed separation to prevent further 'mental contagion' (pp. 229–38). In *Hémorraghie et ramollissement du cerveau, métallothérapie et hypnotisme, électrothérapie* (Paris, Lecrosnier et Babé, 1890), Charcot described hypnotism, and emphasized the neurological and physiological aspects of the condition, that is cutaneous insensibility, neuromuscular hyperexcitability, transference of contractures, and the diverse stages of *grand et petit hypnotisme*. These works clearly demonstrate his 'epiphenominalist' approach when discussing hypnotism and hysteria; the difficulty, however, is that only a part of Charcot's research has ever been published, and it is possible that less strictly 'scientific' observation on the cultural, psychological, and emotional aspects of hysteria were not included by the disciples who compiled his notes and lectures.

The last area which must be taken into account in assessing Charcot's epiphenominalism is his work on traumatic paralyses. Charcot conceded that these were the result of ideas 'blocking' normal motor functioning, cf. *Oeuvres complètes*, vol. 3, pp. 335–37. Given this view, it is difficult to understand his profound hostility to the more far-reaching 'ideodynamism' of the Nancy School, except by explaining it by his insistence that such phenomena were related only to morbid states.

41 For an illuminating discussion of similar developments in England cf. Michael J. Clark, 'The Rejection of Psychological Approaches to Mental Disorder in Late-Nineteenth-Century British Psychiatry', in Andrew Scull (ed.), *Madhouses, Mad-doctors, and Madmen: The Social History of Psychiatry in the Victorian Era* (London: Athlone Press, 1981).

42 For a full and comprehensive discussion of the medico-legal doctrine of the Paris School, cf. Georges Gilles de la Tourette, *L'Hypnotisme et les états analogues au point de vue médico légal*' (Paris: E. Plon, 1887).

43 De la Tourette, *L'Hypnotisme*, p. 91.

44 *Affaire Gouffé*, 99. During the trial Brouardel forcefully made this point by citing the following hypnotic experiment: two hysterics were requested to remove their clothes, but only one realized the command, the other hesitating out of a sense of modesty. For an examination of similar ideas and experiments in Britain, cf., Perry Williams's article in the companion Volume 1 as well as his 1983 Cambridge PhD dissertation. The Making of Victorian Psychical Research: An Intellectual Elite's Approach to the Spiritual World', particularly pp. 183–96.

45 De la Tourette, *L'Hypnotisme*' pp. 321–82 for the Paris Schools' views on crime and hypnotism.

46 *Affaire Gouffé*, pp. 130–32, for Brouardel's tirade against Nancian doctrine and its leniency towards crime.

47 Hippolyte Bernheim, *Le Docteur Liébault et la doctrine de la suggestion*, Conférence faite sous les auspices de la Société des Amis de l'Université de Nancy, 12 December, 1906, p. 1.

48 See P. Kissel, 'L'École neuro-psychiatrique de Nancy: Le professeur Bernheim', *Médecine de France*, 68 (1960) pp. 11–13.

49 Bernheim, *Le Docteur Liébault*, pp. 1–13.

50 Hippolyte Bernheim, *Hypnotisme, suggestion et psychothérapie*, (Paris: Octave Doin, 1891), in particular pp. 239–497.

51 Hippolyte Bernheim, pp. 165–202. For Bernheim's specific remarks on the illusory nature of Charcot's hysteria, and the three stages of hypnotism cf. pp. 167, 169.

52 Bernheim, *Le Docteur Liébault*, p. 12

53 Hippolyte Bernheim, *De la Suggestion dans l'état hypnotique et dans l'état de veille* (Paris: Octave Doin, 1884), p. 6.

54 Jules Liégeois, 'De la Suggestion hypnotique dans ses rapports avec le droit civil et le droit criminel', *Séances et travaux de l'académie des sciences morales et politiques* 120 (1884): 220.

55 Jules Liégeois, 'L'Hypnotisme, la défense nationale et la société', *Revue de l'hypnotisme* 6 (1892): 298–304.

56 Jules Liégeois, *Origines et théories économiques de l'association des travailleurs* (Nancy: Imprimerie de l'Académie de Stanislas, 1872), p. 54.

57 Jules Liégeois, *Projet de Fondation à Paris d'un Institut psychique international: psychologie expérimentale-hypnologie* (Nancy: Imprimerie de Kreis, n.d.).

58 His system was developed further in Jules Liégeois, *De la suggestion et du somnambulisme dans leurs rapports avec la jurisprudence* (Paris: Octave Doin, 1889).

59 For an analysis of Charcot's loosening hold on French practitioners, cf. J.-J. Déjérine, 'Hypnotisme et suggestion', *Revue de l'hypnotisme* 5 (1891): 224–31.

60 Pressat, 'L'Hypnotisme et la presse', pp. 227–30.

61 Unpublished manuscript cited through the permission of Madame Tridon, Nancy, *Les Souvenirs inédits de Henri-Etienne Beaunis* (1830–1921), pp. 424–27.

62 Tridon, *Les Souvenirs Beaunis*.

63 Tridon, *Les Souvenirs Beaunis*.

64 Auguste Motet was a frequent psychiatric expert in the *cour d'assise* in the last two decades of the nineteenth century. Head of the *maison d'éducation corectionnelle* in Paris, he was also a frequent contributor to the *Annales d'hygiène publique et de médecine légale* and was a specialist in matters relating to crime and insanity. Gilbert Ballet was a *professeur agrégé* at the Faculty of Medicine at the time of the trial, and was to write a book with A. Proust called *L'Hygiène neurasthénique*. By 1900, he was one of France's most important alienists, an expert not only in the treatment of 'neuroses', but also a leading spokesman on all institutional, professional and theoretical problems connected with the insane.

65 'Rapport de MM. Brouardel, Motet and Ballet, Affaire Gouffé', *Archives d'anthropologie criminelle* 6 (1891): 68–72.

66 'Rapport de MM. Brouardel', p. 80, she described her subjugation to Eyraud.

67 'Rapport de MM. Brouardel', p. 77.

68 For a contemporary analysis of the difficult philosophical and moral questions raised by the notion of 'moral blindness' cf. L. Lévy-Bruhl, 'La Responsibilité des criminels', *Revue politique et littéraire*, 3rd series, 45 (1890): 643–48.

69 *Affaire Gouffé*, p. 100.

70 'Rapports de MM. Brouardel', pp. 78–80 for their discussion of her nervous condition and hysteria.

71 Edgar Bérillon in 'Bulletin: l'hypnotisme à la Cour d'assises', *Revue de l'hypnotisme* 5 (1891): 194–95, pointed out the contradictions of the Parisian stance.

72 *Affaire Gouffé*, p. 114.

73 *Affaire Gouffé*, p. 115.

74 U.A.E. Mesnet, 'Autographisme et stigmates', *Revue de l'hypnotisme* 4 (1890): 320–35.

75 *Affaire Gouffé*, p. 121. This case will be discussed in detail in the following section.

76 *Affaire Gouffé*, p. 116. In this instance Liégeois was referring to the famous case of a certain Didier that had occupied Motet in 1880–81. On 26 January, the *Chambres des Appels de Police Correctionnelle* revoked the judgement condemning Didier for *'le délit d'outrage public à la pudeur'* after an experiment was carried out by Motet. The physician had claimed that this *pauvre diable* had been in a spontaneous *condition second* when the police had arrested him for masturbating in a public urinal. Motet had the man relive the scene of the crime by inducing a somnambulic trance, without, however, having Didier repeat his indecent act. Cf. Motet's article, 'Accès de somnambulisme spontané et provoqué', *Annales d'hygiène publique et de médecine légale*, 3rd series, 5 (1881): 214–25.

77 *Affaire Gouffé*, pp. 122–3.

78 For Liégeois's extended interpretation of Gabrielle Bompard's state of mind and behaviour cf. *Affaire Gouffé* pp. 124–27.

79 *Affaire Gouffé* p. 131.

80 Hippolyte Bernheim, 'Discussions et polémique: l'épilogue d'un procès célèbre', *Revue de l'hypnotisme* 5 (1891): 270–72.

81 Cf. Roger Smith, *Trial by Medicine: Insanity and Responsibility in Victorian Trials* (Edinburgh: Edinburgh University Press, 1981), particularly pp. 124–42 for examples of Victorian trials in which evidence of moral depravity was often considered insufficient grounds by jurors for a plea of insanity.

82 The most virulent attack came from Gilles de la Tourette, 'Discussions et polémique: l'épilogue d'un procès célèbre', *Revue de l'hypnotisme* no. 5 (1891): 241–49.

83 'Où est-il?', *L'Est républican*, 25–26 December, 1890.

84 Tridon, *Les Souvenirs Beaunis*, p. 426.

85 Tridon, *Les Souvenirs Beaunis*, p. 427.

86 'Les Drames vécus, la confession de Gabrielle Bompard', *Le Journal*, 8 December, 1903.

87 Liégeois, 'De la suggestion hypnotique', p. 173.

88 Archives de la Seine Inférieure, Cour d'assises, U11, pieces 61, 63, 64.

89 Archives de Seine Inférieure, Cour d'assises, U11, *passim*.

90 Paul Brouardel, 'Accusation de viol accompli pendant le sommeil', *Annales d'hygiène publique et de médecine légale*, 3rd series, 1 (1879): 39–57. For details of the trial, cf. *Journal de Rouen*, 20 August, 1878, pp. 1–2.

91 Jules Liégeois, 'L'Hypnotisme et les suggestions criminelles', in Dr. Croz fils (ed.) *Congrès international de neurologie, de psychiatrie, d'électricité médicale et d'hypnologie* (Paris: Félix Alcan, 1898).

92 *Affaire Gouffé*, p. 128.

93 Jules Liégeois, 'Hypnotisme et criminalité', *Revue Philosophique* 33 (1892): 233–72; cf. in particular pp. 272–73.

94 Liégeois, *Congrès international de neurologie*, p. 208.

95 For a suggestive discussion of the perception of the working-class character, its base urges and lifestyle from the 'scientific perspective', see Jean Borie, *Mythologies de l'heredité au XIXe siècle* (Paris: Editions Galilée, 1981); cf., also Peter Gay, *The Bourgeois Experience: Victoria to Freud, Education of the Senses* (Oxford: Oxford University Press, 1984) for a recent interpretive account of sexual morality in nineteenth-century bourgeois society.

96 For the idea of servants as having a pernicious effect on the respectability, health, and sanctity of the *foyer familiale* in the eighteenth century cf. Jacques Donzelot, trans. Robert Hurley, *The Policing of Families: Welfare* vs *the State* (London: Hutchinson, 1979), pp. 9–20.

97 Cf. the case of Fille C., June, 1885, AS D2U8 178, who actually did try to poison the infant entrusted to her care because of the bad treatment she had suffered at the hands of her employers.

98 Cf. Fille C.'s case, April, 1886, AS D2U8 195, who, after having been evicted by her master when his brother moved into the house, tried to murder her former employer because of the venereal disease she had contracted from their relations.

99 There were countless cases of such abandonments, the most striking being that of Veuve B., July 1887, AS D2U8 217. After her lover married a respectable wife, she not only harassed the spouse in the street, but ultimately vitriolized and murdered the husband, disfiguring him beyond recognition. She received a penalty of life with hard labour.

100 Cf. Angus McLaren, *Sexuality and Social Order: The Debate over the Fertility of Women and Workers in France, 1770–1920* (New York: Holmes and Meier, 1983), pp. 44–64.

101 A.R. Bellanger, *Le Magnétisme: vérités et chimères de cette science occulte; un*

drame dans le somnambulisme, épisode historique, les tables tournantes, etc.
(Paris: Chez Guilhermet, 1852), pp. 207–90; the date of this event is not cited.

102 Paul Brouardel, 'Une Femme, peut-elle avoir rapports inconscients pendant le sommeil', *Annales d'hygiène publique et de médecine légale* 43 (1900): 46–7.

103 Jean-Martin Charcot, 'Accidents hystériques graves survenus chez une femme à la suite d'hypnotisations pratiquées par un magnétiseur dans une baraque de fête', *Revue de l'hypnotisme* 4 (1890): 8.

104 'L'Affaire Chambige', *Revue des grands procès contemporains* (Paris: Chevalier-Mareq, 1889), G. Lèbre (ed.) pp. 21–101.

105 'L'Affaire Chambige', pp. 76–8.

106 'L'Affaire Chambige', p. 22.

107 Liégeois, *Congrès international de neurologie*, p. 208. 'Through suggestion, the [women] could be inspired towards the lowest sentiments, the vilest propensities, the most shameful acts.'

108 Cf. A. Armengaud, *La Population française au XIX siècle* (Paris: Press Universitaires de France, 1971), pp. 47–61. Between 1872 and 1911, the French population grew from 36,103,000 to 39,605,000, an increase of 3.5 million in 39 years, with an average annual rise of 89,700. At the same time the German empire gained a yearly average of about 600,000 people with a population of 41,058,792 in 1871 and 64,925,993 in 1910. France in this period was the European country with the slowest population growth.

109 Angus McLaren, *Sexuality and Social Order*, in particular pp. 93–168.

110 Gabriel Tarde, the crowd theorist and 'interpsychologist', was fascinated by the connections between the 'hypnotic' and dangerous effect of love and sexuality in couples as well as in crowds. For examples of this cf. his 'Affaire Chambige' in *Archives d'anthropologie criminelles* 4 (1859): 92–108. Cf. also Tarde's 'L'Amour morbide', *Archives d'anthropologie criminelles* 5 (1890): 585–95, in which he wrote, 'What is love if not a malady'. Finally cf. Tarde's, 'Les Crimes des foules', *Archives d'anthropologie criminelles* 7 (1892): 353–86, which he stressed the same hypnotic and sexual link that made crowds lose control over their actions as well as their duties as good citizens.

111 For the background to this law and its significance cf. J. Léonard, *La Médecine entre les pouvoirs et les savoirs: histoire intellectuelle et politique de la médecine française au XIXe siècle* (Paris: Aubier Montaigne, 1981), pp. 275–302.

112 *Affaire Gouffé*, p. 130.

113 Pressat, 'L'Hypnotisme et la presse', p. 226.

114 Brouardel explained how the proposal to outlaw magnetizers jeopardized the passage of the 30 November, 1892 law on medical practice so that, in the end, the article on amateur hypnotic healing was left purposely vague in order to push the bill through without further delay; their right to heal was later upheld in Mans, but in 1892, magnetizers were successfully prosecuted in Lille and Paris. Cf. P. Brouardel, *La Profession médicale au commencement du XXe siècle* (Paris: G. Baillière, 1903) p. 96.

115 Gilles de la Tourette, *L'Hypnotisme et les états analogues*, pp. 298–383 and in particular pp. 383–450. For Charcot's anti-magnetizer position cf. *Oeuvres complètes*, vol. 9, pp. 479–80.

116 André Pressat, 'L'Hypnotisme et la presse', p. 225.

117 Edgar Bérillon, 'Hypnotisme utile et hypnotisme dangereux', *Revue de l'hypnotisme* 3 (1888): 2.

118 'Correspondence et chronique: les dangers de l'hypnotisme – une lettre de A.

Pitres de Bordeaux', *Revue de l'hypnotisme* 3 (1888): 65.

119 Dr Guérmonprez, *Congrès international de l'hypnotisme expérimental et théra-peutique, tenu à Paris du 8 au 12 août 1889, arguments présentés* (Lille: L. Quarre, 1889), p. 16.

120 *Premier congrès international de l'hypnotisme*, 8–12 août, *Paris 1889*, 'Rapport de M. le docteur Ladame', p. 30.

121 *Premier congrès international de l'hypnotisme*, 8–12 août, Paris 1889, 'Rapport de M. le docteur Ladame'.

122 Gilles de la Tourette, citing Ladame, *L'Hypnotisme et les états analogues*, p. 450.

123 *Premier congrès international*, p. 44.

124 Delboeuf, *Magnétiseurs et médécins*, p. 31.

125 One of the most extensively cited cases was of a supposed rape in Switzerland after a mesmeric performance. Cf. 'La Névrose hypnotique devant la médecine légale. Du viol pendant le sommeil hypnotique', *Ann. hyg. pub. med. leg.*, 3rd series, 7 (1882): 518–33. The accused, however, was released due to lack of evidence. For a passionate defence of Donato and an accusation of fabricated cases of insanity and crime in the wake of theatrical presentations, see *Premier congrès international*, 'Rapport de M. Delboeuf', p. 56.

126 Goldstein, 'The Hysteria Diagnosis and the Politics of Anti-Clericalism'.

127 *Congrès International de 1889, Le Magnétisme humain appliqué au soulagement et à la guérison des maladies: Rapport général d'après le compte rendu des séances du congrès* (Paris: Georges Carré, 1890).

128 For an example of the tirade fired by the amateurs at Charcot's School see Rouxel, *Rapports de magnétisme et du spiritualisme* (Paris: Librairie des Sciences Psychologiques, 1892), pp. 257–313.

129 Cf, Edouard Cavilhon, *Le Fascinateur magnétique* (Paris: Dentu, 1882), with a preface by Donato; Professeur Donato, *Cours pratique d'hypnotisme et de magnétisme* (Paris: Librairie Illustré, Jules Tallandier, n.d.). For the best summary of Donato's theory and technique see 'Discours de Donato', *Congrès international de magnétisme humain*, pp. 427–42.

130 Enrico Morselli, *Il Magnetismo animale. La fascinazione e gli ipnotici* (Turin: Roux and Farale, 1886).

131 See Delboeuf, *Magnétiseurs et médecins*.

132 Cavilhon, *Le Fascinateur magnétique*, p. xxxii.

133 *Congrès international … le magnétisme humain*, 'Discours de Donato', p. 431.

134 *Congrès international … le magnétisme humain*, 'Discours de Donato', p. 432.

135 Emile Gautier, 'Chronique', *Le Figaro*, 5 September, 1889.

136 Rouxel, *Rapports de magnétisme et du spiritisme*, p. 297. The word *doctoralisme* pertains both to an academic degree and the attitude of pomposity assumed to go with it.

137 Delboeuf, *Magnétiseurs et médecins*, quoting Ladame, p. 16.

138 Nye, *The Origins of Crowd Psychology*; Barrows, *Distorting Mirrors*; Moscovici, *L'Âge des foules*.

139 Nye, *The Origins of Crowd Psychology*, pp. 61–3.

140 Pressat, 'L'hypnotisme et la presse', p. 230.

141 For an introduction to the beginnings of criminal anthropology and its formulation in France cf. Robert Nye, 'Heredity or Milieu: The Foundations of European Criminological Theory', *Isis* 67 (1976): 335–55.

142 For an example of this cf. Tarde, 'Les Crimes des foules', 353–86.

143 *La Foule criminelle, essai de psychologie collective*, trans. from the Italian by Paul

Vigny (Paris: Felix Alcan, 1892).

144 *Les Lois d'imitation* (Paris: Félix Alcan, 1890), and for his later work on the public, popular opinion and mass communication, see *L'Opinion et la foule* (Paris: Félix Alcan, 1901).

145 Henry Fournial, *Essai sur la psychologie des foules: considérations médico-judiciaires sur les responsabilités collectives* (Paris: G. Masson, 1892).

146 Gustave LeBon's most famous and influential work is *La Psychologie des foules*, (Paris: Félix Alcan, 1895).

147 For the classic work done on hallucinations cf. A. Brierre de Boismont, *Des Hallucinations*, 3rd edn (Paris: G. Baillière, 1862).

148 For an excellent contemporary history of these ideas cf. George Dumas, 'Contagion mentale: épidémies mentales – folies collectives – folies grégaires', *Revue philosophique* 71 (1911): 225–44, 384–407.

149 Gabriel Tarde, 'Qu'est-ce qu'une société', *Revue philosophique* 18 (1884): 501; 'Je crois me conformer ... à la méthode scientifique la plus rigoreuse en cherchant à éclairer le complexe par le simple, la combinaison par l'élément, et expliquer le lien social mélangé et compliqué ... par le lien social à la fois très pur et tres réduit à sa plus simple expression, lequel, pour l'instruction du sociologiste, est réalisé si heureusement, dans l'état somnambulique ... *La société, c'est l'imitation, et l'imitation c'est une éspèce de somnambulisme.*'

CHAPTER ELEVEN

Shellshock and the psychologists

Martin Stone

Introduction: The Legacy of Shellshock

THIS ESSAY HAS two basic aims: first, to retell the story of shellshock and
its treatment and second, to explore its social construction as an illness. I
shall look at the problems shellshock presented to the British army and its
doctors, examining some of the arguments it provoked in military and
medical circles. I shall then go on to investigate the ways in which the clinical
phenomena it encompassed were constituted by military social relations –
paying particular attention to the organization of life and work in the
trenches and in the army hospitals.

I want to begin, however, by trying to find a place for shellshock within
our current picture of the development of psychological medicine in Britain
during the first half of this century. Although Lynch[1] has provided us with a
detailed study of the wartime treatment of shellshock, there have been no
serious attempts to relate this episode to subsequent developments in civilian
psychiatry. Indeed, with the exception of Clark,[2] who has noted its importance with regard to the spread of psychoanalytical doctrines in Britain,
shellshock has remained conspicuously absent from recent histories of
psychiatry, psychotherapy, and the mental health services. This is, I think,
an important omission in terms of our understanding of the changes which
occurred in British psychological medicine during the 1920s and 1930s, in
particular the ways in which British doctors became involved in the study
and treatment of the neuroses. I would argue that shellshock had a
considerable effect on the field of psychological medicine and that it
provides a key to understanding the reforms and innovations which
occurred during the inter-war years.

In order to get an idea of the upheavals caused by shellshock one could
begin by looking at the changing fortunes of psychotherapy following the
First World War. Before 1914 there were only a handful of British doctors
using psychological methods to treat nervous disorders. Most of these were
on the fringes of established psychiatry and were based in private practice in
and around London. Hugh Crichton Miller was using hypnotic suggestion
on his patients at Bowden House near Harrow. James Glover was single-

handedly running psychotherapy sessions at the Medico-Psychological Clinic of London set up in 1913 by Jessie Murray with support from the psychologist Charles Spearman. There were three doctors using psychoanalytic techniques – David Forsyth, David Eder, and Ernest Jones. When Jones and Eder set up the London Society for Psychoanalysis in 1913 it attracted around a dozen members of whom only four were interested in becoming practising analysts.[3] As far as the mainstream of British psychological medicine was concerned, a few neurologists and asylum doctors had developed an active interest in the new medical psychology that had grown up on the continent during the 1880s and 1890s.[4] Psychoanalysis had by 1914 established a toehold in Britain and could count on the critical support of several respectable medical figures, like Wilfred Trotter, Bernard Hart, and C. Stanford Read. The fact remains, however, that the vast majority of British neurologists and asylum doctors took no practical interest in psychotherapy. The amount of coverage given to the work of the continental medical psychologists in the neurology journal *Brain* and in the *Journal of Mental Science* was minimal. Freud's writings did achieve a certain notoriety in the years leading up to the war, but this did not mean that his ideas were greeted with clinical enthusiasm. Far from it; Jones and Eder faced an extensive boycott campaign orchestrated by the eminent psychiatrist Charles Mercier who took every opportunity to condemn psychoanalysis as morally corrupting and to urge respectable physicians to have nothing to do with it. Such was the official opposition faced by the Freudians that when Jones and Eder presented papers to the neurological section of the BMA, their audiences rose and left the room en masse before discussions of their papers were due to commence.[5]

By the end of the war this situation had changed dramatically. At Maghull military hospital near Liverpool, squads of fifty RAMC officers were being given three-month courses on the techniques of 'abreactive' psychotherapy – including dream analysis'.[6] A consultant psychologist working with the BEF in France had spent two years promoting the use of psychotherapy in the army hospitals in France. The Ministry of Pensions was publishing statements in the medical journals imploring GPs to hand over patients suffering from war-related nervous disorders to specialist psychotherapists, and civilian doctors were being trained as psychotherapists to work in the numerous clinics that had been set up by the Ministry of Pensions to deal with a flood of shellshocked ex-servicemen requiring treatment.[7] Forsyth and Eder began in one of these clinics handling the case-work by themselves but in a short space of time the number of staff had increased to around seventy.[8]

Many British doctors received their first practical introductions to the new medical psychology whilst working in army hospitals where shellshock cases had been sent. They subsequently gained a considerable expertise in handling and treating nervous disorders and were responsible for a prodigious volume of books and articles on psychotherapy and psychopathology published during the early 1920s. For some neurologists, their wartime work was clearly an eye-opening experience – one which explains why, as Armstrong notes, several of the standard neurology textbooks were revised following the war, sections devoted to the neuroses enlarged and references to psychoanalysis added.[9] As we shall see a number of shellshock doctors drew extensively on Freud's ideas, and it was largely because of this that the Freudians managed to secure a foothold in British psychiatry. Shellshock, by virtue of its sheer scale, demonstrated that the subject matter of psychoanalysis was by no means unimportant. Moreover, both as theory and as therapy psychoanalysis was proven to be of practical utility where conventional approaches failed. Following the war it was certainly more difficult for established psychological medicine to ignore Freud's writings and when the newly formed British Psychoanalytical Association held its first open meeting in 1919, a number of respected medical figures attended, several of whom joined as associate members.[10]

If the psychoanalysts made a a dramatic entry onto the medical stage during the war so too did the British psychologists. W.H. Rivers, William McDougall, and William Brown all made important contributions to the study of shellshock and established medical reputations on the basis of their wartime work. In fact, for most of the war, official responsibility for dealing with the problem of shellshock was shouldered by C.S. Myers, an experimentalist from the Cambridge Psychological Laboratory. Their subsequent contribution to the advancement of medical psychology in Britain was considerable. In 1919 a medical section of the British Psychological Society was set up to act as a forum for debate in psychopathology and psychotherapy. In the corresponding medical section of the society's journal a high proportion of the articles published during the early 1920s concerned the pathology and treatment of shellshock.[11] Similarly, Rivers's *Instinct and the Unconscious* (1920)[12] and McDougall's *An Outline of Abnormal Psychology* (1926),[13] two classic psychological texts both highly regarded in medical circles during the 1920s and 1930s, owe much to the psychotherapeutic activities of their authors during the war. McDougall based his book on over thirty volumes of case-notes he had collected while working in army hospitals at Netley and Oxford and Rivers declared that the aim of his book had been 'to put into a biological setting the system of psychotherapy that came to be adopted in Britain in the treatment of the psychoneuroses of war'.[14]

It was a significant achievement of the British psychologists during the 1920s that they provided the British medical readership with potted versions of Freud's theories at a time when psychotherapy was just beginning to get established there. However, although they took on board several of the central concepts of psychoanalysis, both in their theoretical writings and in their 'applied' work, they did not agree with a number of Freud's claims. Their major criticism of psychoanalysis was that Freud had been wrong in asserting that sexual factors played an all-important role in the aetiology of neurotic disorders. This of course was nothing new. The important point about this 'revisionist' approach to Freud's original theory, is that it was based to a large extent on the wartime experiences of British psychologists with cases of shellshock. As we shall see, there was a widespread feeling among British doctors after the First World War that shellshock had effectively 'disproved' Freud's theory of sexuality.

I have so far described the emergence of two new groups onto the mental medicine scene following the wartime episode of shellshock. This development was only part of a broader shake-up which beset the professional structure of British psychiatry during the early 1920s. The orthodoxies of the psychiatric establishment came under increasing pressure during this period. Certainly, psychiatry's performance during the war could not be relied upon as a source of comfort. Shellshock exposed an area of mental medicine about which many asylum doctors knew little. Moreover, when it came to the question of who was responsible for treating the mass epidemic of shellshock cases, such was the professional organization of the RAMC that they found themselves taking a back seat to the neurologists. In spite of the fact that asylum psychiatry remained out of the limelight during the war, shellshock nevertheless threatened the very foundations of its approach to mental pathology. The monolithic theory of hereditary degeneration upon which Victorian psychiatry had based its social and scientific vision was significantly dented as young men of respectable and proven character were reduced to mental wrecks after a few months in the trenches. Cyril Burt, while not a disinterested commentator, pointed this out in 1935:

'It was perhaps the First World War that most effectively brought home the artificiality of the distinction between the normal mind on the one hand and its abnormal conditions on the other. In the military hospitals the study of so-called shellshock revealed that symptoms quite as serious as the well-defined psychoses might arise through simple stress and strain and yet prove quickly curable by psychotherapeutic means. And thus it gradually became apparent that much of what had been considered abnormal might be discovered in the mind of the average man.'[15]

The psychiatric establishment lost a great deal of credibility over shellshock, not only in the eyes of the rest of the medical profession, but also in the eyes of the public and those government authorities who had become involved in the episode. If the psychotherapists had been the heroes of the piece, the asylum doctors had been its villains. It was certainly difficult for them to argue that the wartime episode was largely irrelevant to civilian practice and that the kinds of cases dealt with in the army hospitals had little to do with the types of patients seen by asylum doctors in their everyday line of work. Not only had shellshock effectively blurred the distinction between the 'neuroses' and 'insanity', but many chronically 'war-strained' ex-servicemen were, by the early 1920s, being transferred to asylums as in-patients.[16]

In a very real sense then, the existing medical and institutional structure of psychiatry was under threat during the years after the First World War. The assault on the orthodoxies of asylum-based psychiatry was led by a small but

vociferous group of former shellshock doctors referred to by C.S. Myers as a
'new breed of medical man' and given a scientific christening by McDougall
in the *Journal of Mental Science* (1919) as 'The School of Integral
Psychology'.[17] In a number of ways the novel 'front-line' approach to the
treatment of mental disorders they promoted during the early 1920s was
directly propelled by the epidemological legacy of shellshock. Indeed this
link was concretely symbolized by the appointment of Field Marshal Haig
and Admiral Beatty as honorary vice-presidents of the Tavistock Clinic
when it opened in 1920. More importantly, historians of psychiatry have
tended to overlook the fact that the boom in out-patient facilities after the
First World War began as an attempt to deal with over 100,000 'neurasthenic' ex-servicemen suffering from the after effects of shellshock – a flood of
cases which reached its peak only in 1922. The Ministry of Pensions was
forced to set up over 100 treatment centres in an effort to cope with this
situation and many of these began to take on civilian day patients soon after
the war had ended.[18]

It was not just the radicals in the Ministry of Pensions clinics who were
pressurizing the psychiatric establishment during the early 1920s. Following
the war there was a widespread feeling in British medical circles that the
asylum system was in need of reform. A number of physicians who had
previously not been 'experts' in mental disorders but who had long
suspected that asylum doctors ran a rather sinister closed shop gained
considerable experience in treating such cases in the army hospitals. They
now felt qualified to speak out – particularly on the question of the lunacy
laws and voluntary treatment. The Professor of Anatomy at Manchester
University, Grafton Elliot Smith, claimed that the need for early treatment
had been one of shellshock's major 'lessons' to civilian psychiatry. Furthermore, the treatment of shellshock patients in the army hospitals without
recourse to certification and often on open wards was seen as an experiment
that had successfully demonstrated the feasibility of asylum reform.[19]

A number of eminent psychiatrists tried to dismiss this outside interference as a case of 'preaching to the converted'.[20] Certainly there were asylum
doctors who had for some time supported a reform in the lunacy laws. Still
more in the wake of the upheavals caused by shellshock they saw a change in
the legislation as both a timely innovation and one which would ensure a
saving of psychiatry's professional face. However, from the articles published in the *Journal of Mental Science* during the years that followed the
war, it is evident that for many asylum doctors, the return to peacetime was
a question of 'business as usual'. It is perhaps a measure of this entrench-
ment, that, as Armstrong has noted, no asylum doctors were chosen to serve
on the committee of the 1924 Royal Commission on Lunacy and Mental
Disorder.[21]

If, following the war, there were still asylum doctors who opposed a
change in the lunacy laws there was also a substantial contingent in the
Medico-Psychological Association who had no time for the new-fangled psy-
chotherapies. This attitude had in fact crystallized during the war. The psycho-

therapeutically minded shellshock doctors had encountered substantial op-position to their work in the army hospitals. C.S. Myers had quit his job as consultant psychologist to the BEF in France in 1917 in a state of utter disillusionment with the medical authorities and he subsequently refused to give evidence before the War Office Committee of Enquiry into Shellshock when it was convened in 1919. Likewise, David Eder gave up his post in a shellshock hospital in Malta in 1916 claiming that 'The Institutes of medicine have remained unshaken by the war.'[22] Sir Robert Armstrong Jones, a pillar of the psychiatric establishment, clearly saw himself as Mercier's successor in the campaign against the Freudians. Speaking at a meeting of the Medico-Psychological Society in 1920 he declared his belief that 'Freudism was dead in England today'. Showing that the patriotic spirit was still very much alive in psychiatric circles he added that psychoanalysis was 'probably applicable to people on the Austrian and German frontiers, but not to virile, sport-loving, open-air people like the British.'[23] Spoken at a time when the British government was actually employing several self-confessed Freudians to work in the Ministry of Pensions clinics and when Freud's ideas were just becoming popular this statement bears all the hallmarks of a rearguard action.

What can we conclude from the account of the upheavals caused by shellshock that I have just given? Shellshock does, I think, tell us some important things about the kinds of changes occurring in British psycholo-gical medicine during the inter-war years, and moreover how these changes came about. The major innovations of this period – psychotherapy and the 1930 Mental Treatment Act which promoted out-patient clinics and 'volun-tary' treatment – have often been portrayed by historians as part and parcel of a psychiatric 'self-enlightenment' and as a triumph of the medical convictions of asylum doctors over their legal constraints. In fact, it took the exigencies of a war and a mass epidemic of mental disorders to set the mechanism of psychiatric change in motion. Asylum 'reform' was initiated under a compromising set of circumstances in which psychiatry's aegis over the field of mental disorder had been seriously undermined from outside.

The 'reform' of the asylum during the inter-war years was accom-panied by a more profound transformation of psychiatry's role in society. This entailed an expansion of the field of mental medicine, a broadening of the concept of mental disorder, the incorporation of other professions under psychiatry's medical umbrella, and the opening up of new sites of practice outside the asylum. I would argue that shellshock has an important historical bearing on this process too. Quite apart from the psychotherapy clinic, the shellshock episode furnished the modern psychiatric enterprise with a number of its rudimentary components. The study of the occupational neuroses and the 'clinical' approach to personnel selection and problems of industrial productivity pioneered in Britain during the 1920s drew heavily from the wartime work on shellshock. In the United States, shellshock gave a massive impetus to the mental hygiene movement with its ideas about prophylactic mental health care, and was largely responsible for establishing psychiatric social work as a professional discipline. It is seldom pointed out that Elton Mayo, founder of the 'human relations' movement and championed by the Tavistock during the 1930s, had himself begun his career working as a shellshock doctor with the Australian army.[24]

More importantly, the upheavals caused by shellshock have a direct bearing on our understanding of how and why psychiatry developed into its modern expanded format. Armstrong has suggested that this process entailed a 'medicalisation of the mind' characterized by the 'invention of the neuroses' at the level of medical discourse.[25] I would argue that this process was in fact propelled by a very concrete problem over which doctors found themselves presiding – namely shellshock. This problem did not go away when the war ended but remained in the form of a large number of 'neurasthenic' ex-servicemen who besides requiring expensive medical treatment and being unfit for work were responsible for an enormous pensions bill. Indeed, as late as 1939, the government was still paying out £2,000,000 per annum to the victims of shellshock.

Shellshock and the war

Having established that shellshock was of some importance for the development of inter-war British psychiatry, I want now to turn to the wartime episode itself. I shall attempt to tell the 'story' of shellshock from the standpoint of the bureaucratic machineries of the British army and its medical services who found themselves having to deal with a mass epidemic of mental disorders of an extent hitherto unknown in war. In this respect the problematic nature of shellshock related directly to a modern industrial mode of warfare that entailed on the one hand mass production in munitions factories and on the other, the deployment of barely trained civilian armies on the battlefield. The managerial strategy pursued by Haig on the Western Front – his celebrated 'cricket score' approach to the expenditure of troops and his tactic of 'the wearing out fight' – was one which made the availability of manpower crucial.[26] This particular point of relevance would therefore seem to be a suitable place to begin the story.

During the first two months of the war, mental breakdown on the battlefield does not seem to have presented a significant problem to Army High Command. But in December, 1914, a report reached the Director General of the Army Medical Services in London which indicated that 7–10 per cent of all officers and 3–4 per cent of all other ranks in hospitals in the Boulogne area were suffering from nervous or mental breakdowns. This prompted the AMS to send the Queen's Square neurologist William Aldren Turner, out to France to investigate what was happening.[27] During the early battles around Ypres the problem got worse and by late 1916 it had become acute. One observer claimed that at this stage in the war, shellshock cases constituted up to 40 per cent of the casualties from heavy fighting zones and William Brown, testifying before the War Office Enquiry into Shellshock, later claimed that at one time he had 'most of the officers and men of a certain regiment' under his care at the 4th and 5th Army Advanced Neurological Centre.[28]

While the official medical statistics throw some light on the extent of shellshock, they are incomplete and as their compilers profess, present formidable difficulties of interpretation. According to these figures, about 80,000 shellshock cases passed through army hospitals of which approximately 30,000 ended up in institutions in the UK.[29] Sir John Collie, who was appointed to run the pensions arrangements for shellshock cases, claimed that it was responsible for around 200,000 discharges from active service and there are a number of reasons for believing that the official figures do not realistically reflect the extent to which shellshock was a drain on manpower.[30] First, there was diagnostic confusion: hysterical symptoms were often mistaken for signs of organic disease and these cases ended up in the medical wards of base hospitals. An important group in this respect were those suffering from so-called 'Disordered Action of the Heart'. The heart specialist Sir Thomas Lewis later estimated that only 10 per cent of 'cardiac' cases in British hospitals were suffering from bona fide organic complaints.[31] Second, medical officers in the line were often reluctant to give a psychiatric diagnosis because of the stigma attached, preferring to use the label 'sick' or 'debility'. These cases frequently ended up getting 'lost in the system'.[32] Finally, it was not as if a 'normal' state of mind prevailed in the trenches. Feelings of unbearable terror and anxiety were an accepted feature of daily life. If the onset of shellshock was for some clearly demarcated by an acute trauma, for others it was a process of gradual breakdown. The point at which an individual would be sent off to the casualty clearing station of field hospital was to a large measure subject to the discretion of the regimental medical officer. In 1917, with the collapse of the French army and British manpower stretched to its limits many of those who were 'done for' just had to 'stick it out'.[33]

Quite apart from the sheer scale of shellshock casualties, two characteristics associated with the condition made it particularly pernicious in the eyes of the military bureaucracy and set it apart from other categories of disability. First, officers seemed to be especially prone to it. Army statistics revealed that officers were more than twice as likely to suffer from mental breakdown on the battlefield than men of the ranks.[34] This presented difficulties with regard to the command of troops and it was a situation made worse by the decimation of regular army officers during the early campaigns of the war. However, more importantly, shellshock was found to have a serious effect on morale. Line and medical officers were in agreement that it undermined unit discipline, 'esprit de corps' and the army's honoured 'code of conduct'. Furthermore some claimed that it was a highly infectious condition that was responsible for setting off mass panics.[35]

Military experts had long recognized that a high level of morale among fighting troops was one of the keys to success in warfare. The level of morale in the volunteer regiments of the British army during the early stages of the war was particularily high. In his recruitment campaign Kitchener had found himself dealing with a patriotic working class. Moreover it had been his masterstroke to employ the so-called 'Pal System' whereby friends and workmates from offices and factories joined up together to form the rank and file of the volunteer regiments.[36] The British army had therefore been provided with a pre-formed fabric of friendships and allegiances out of which to fashion 'esprit de corps' and with it the emotional bonds on which morale in the line so heavily depended. However by 1917 this situation had taken a dramatic turn for the worse. The 'Pal System' had been largely broken when the volunteer regiments had sustained massive casualties on the Somme. Lord Derby's conscripted troops were being brought in and a general air of cynicism and despair had come to prevail in the trenches. It was during this latter stage of the war that shellshock really emerged as a major problem.[37]

Besides constituting a significant drain on manpower, shellshock was also seen as a disciplinary problem and this not surprisingly had an effect on military attitudes to those who broke down on the battlefield. The official medical history of the First World War states that military thought had it that shellshock and malingering were impossible to separate and that both should be dealt with in army prisons.[38] The psychiatrist Henry Yellowlees who was working in an army hospital in France claimed that during the early stages of the war, 'Many highly placed officials in the War Office made no secret of their belief that the whole thing was humbug from beginning to end.'[39] According to C.S. Myers, a more polarized view prevailed among senior army officers in France: namely that shellshock cases were 'mad' and should be locked away in asylums, or were responsible and should be court-martialled and shot.[40] Many senior army officers retained these attitudes throughout the duration of the war. However, in their approach to the problem, the military authorities did after a while come around to the idea that shellshock was not merely a question of cowardice and malingering and that it was to some extent a 'medical' condition. In any case, by 1917, shellshock rates were running so high that it would have been a rather difficult, and in manpower terms, inefficient bureaucratic enterprise to court-martial all those concerned.[41]

If the War Office and the staff at GHQ on the Western Front had been caught totally unprepared for shellshock, so too had the army medical services in France and Flanders. Shellshock first confronted RAMC officers at the field and base hospitals behind lines rather than specialists in the treatment of mental disorders and one can get an idea of what they were faced with by looking at the early case-studies which appeared in the medical journals. Victims displayed a bewildering range of physical and mental disabilities: paralyses and muscular contractures of the arms, legs, hands, and feet, loss of sight, speech and hearing, choreas, palsies and tics, mental fugues, catatonia and obsessive behaviour, amnesia, severe sleeplessness, and terrifying nightmares.

With some notable exceptions, medical officers at the Front did not know what had hit them. The apparent severity of symptoms prompted many to employ the diagnosis 'delusional insanity'[42] and the main way of dealing with shellshock cases in the early years of the war was to send them back to the UK via the base hospitals in France. To begin with they went to the Royal Victoria Hospital at Netley and to the civilian neurological hospitals in London. However, in the spring of 1915, the War Office commandeered Moss Side asylum from the Board of Control, renaming it Maghull War Hospital. By the end of the war there were over twenty army hospitals in the UK handling shellshock cases along with numerous convalescent centres and small charitable homes mainly for officers.

The vast majority of the medical specialists approached the clinical problems associated with shellshock in a manner which relied heavily on traditional neurological and psychiatric doctrines. It was evident that some shellshock victims displayed symptoms akin to the condition known to doctors as 'hysteria'. Others appeared to be suffering from severe forms of 'neurasthenia'. These were two conditions which at the time were held in low medical esteem. According to McDougall, they were 'neglected and despised' by neurologists and psychiatrists alike.[43] In so far as specialists in the study of mental disorder took an interest in hysteria and neurasthenia, approaches to the question of pathology and treatment were, in the main, 'physicalist' in orientation. British neurology was, as Hearnshaw notes, 'brutally materialistic'[44] and the vast majority of practitioners in the field had little time for the new-fangled psychological approach to nervous disorders which had been developed on the Continent.[45]

In light of their pre-war approach to hysteria and neurasthenia, it is unsurprising that the 'experts' back home in the hospitals in the UK rapidly came up with an 'organic' interpretation of shellshock's pathology. This involved a model which was promoted by the famous continental neurologists Sarbo and Oppenheim, and by Sir Frederick Mott in Britain.[46] The common thesis of this model was that the debilities associated with shellshock were caused by the commotional effects of exploding shells. These, it was claimed, caused physical damage to the central nervous system – either through micropuncture and haemorrhage in the cerebral tissues or by inducing tears in the spinal pathways. Mott, carrying out an experiment of the kind he had frequently performed before the war as pathologist at Claybury asylum, based his explanation on an autopsy examination of the brains of two soldiers who had been blown up and had died without any external signs of injury. There was however a rather shaky logic operating when he generalized his evidence: shellstock victims had not died as a result of being blown up by shells, furthermore, such incidents were a common occurrence on the front and many of those who escaped shrapnel wounds had emerged unscathed. Anyway, it soon became apparent that symptoms of shellshock were occurring in soldiers who had not been directly exposed to shellblast.[47]

After the war, medical experts agreed that only a minute proportion of shellshock victims had suffered organic damage to the central nervous system.[48] During the war, however, the organic model of shellshock was not in any way 'disproved' by either circumstantial or medical evidence. Indeed, Mott and many other neurologists stuck to it throughout the war. The French neurologist, Ravaut, cited in the *Lancet* (1915) circumvented the apparent falsification of the theory by putting forward the view that the bullet-wind of machine-guns caused similar effects to shellblast.[49] A number of psychiatrists changed tack from the traditional 'lesion' theory to another of their pre-war themes. They began assembling family pedigrees that purported to show that those who had broken down had done so because of their 'tainted' heredities.[50]

This was openly contested by a number of medical commentators who believed that even the best of characters were prone to shellshock. Of course, it must be remembered that the 'volunteers' were considered to be the best of characters: the shellshock doctors were not dealing with pauper lunatics, but with 'England's finest blood'. Heredity, the ubiquitous explanatory tool of the psychiatric profession was in deep water here – the ideological tables had been turned. This was apparent when the eminent psychiatrist Sir Robert Armstrong Jones launched a predictable attack on G. Elliot Smith and T.H. Pear's book on shellshock in *Nature* (1917), criticizing them for their 'environmentalist' tendencies and claiming that tainted heredity lay behind the pathology of shellshock. Smith and Pear were able to reply that this was 'a slur on the noblest of our race'.[51]

Orthodox mental medicine was not just in theoretical trouble over shellshock. Conventional remedies for nervous disorders were found to be of limited value as far as treatment itself was concerned. Most of the early batch of cases that had arrived back in England after the retreat from Mons were given the standard Weir Mitchell cure of isolation, rest, massage, and milk diet. The psychiatrist R.D. Gillespie later claimed that most of these cases had remained ill throughout the duration of the war.[52] It was evident that shellshock patients had traumatic memories of their experiences in the trenches and as an accompaniment to 'physical' treatments many medical officers tried to keep patients distracted and to encourage them not to think about their times in the trenches. This rudimentary psychotherapeutic approach proved to be similarly ineffective in terms of bringing about permanent cure. However, one method that did seem to produce results was electricity – indeed electrical 'faradization' came to be one of the most popular ways of treating hysterical shellshock cases. If the rationale behind this form of treatment was initially physiological, by 1916 it was being openly used for its psychological effects and a number of army neurologists had come round to the view that mental factors were involved in the aetiology of shellshock.

These doctors were not interested in Freud's explanation of hysteria or in psychoanalytic techniques. Instead they took their inspiration from the writings of French neurologists like Babinski, Leri, Dejerine, and Pierre Marie. Their approach to treatment centred on the use of suggestion – and what Babinski referred to as 'persuasion' – to remove symptoms. Sometimes this was carried out using hypnosis or 're-education'. Other methods included painful lumbar punctures and retinal examinations.[53] However more often than not the preferred method was electrical faradization. Adrian and Yealland furnish us with a description of their electrical treatment of aphonia at Aldershot Military Hospital. Patients would be made to queue in the treatment room and watch the first in line receive painful electric shocks to his larynx. Faradization would continue until the subject emitted a noise (presumably a scream) – whereupon the doctor would inform him that he had recovered his voice.[54]

By 1917 the treatment of shellshock by methods of suggestion and persuasion had made some headway in RAMC circles. One hospital at Seale Hayne in Devon run by the neurologist Arthur Hurst had emerged as a specialist centre in this form of treatment.[55] Whilst these methods seemed to produce some rapid and dramatic cures when used with patients suffering from hysterical disorders, they proved to be of limited value when used with the mounting influx of 'neurasthenic' cases. Furthermore the efficacy of suggestion was often found to be short-lived and many of those who had supposedly been cured would promptly break down again as soon as they heard the noise of gunfire or exploding shells.[56]

Despite the fact that methods of treating shellshock based on suggestion came to be used more frequently as the war progressed, as Millais Culpin noted, a psychological approach was still 'anathema' to most army neurologists.[57] Indeed the opinion of many RAMC officers was not significantly different from that of the conventional military view on shellshock. Jones recalled serving on medical boards where neurologists claimed that if there were no signs of organic disease then the patient was obviously faking his symptoms.[58] McDougall remembered hearing a fellow medical officer declare that if there was no evidence of organic damage to the central nervous system the individual concerned should be shot.[59] As Lynch pointed out, before the war patients suffering from hysteria were considered by many neurologists as 'malingerers' who 'shammed' their disabilities.[60] If Hurst and his group introduced army neurologists to the notion that there was a certain morbidity involved in the malingering of shellshock patients, they did not explain this morbidity in terms of unconscious motives. Shellshock could still therefore be seen as some sort of more or less conscious, wilful malingering on the part of the patient. In this respect as late as 1922 when the War Office report on shellshock was published, a *Lancet* editorial criticized the investigating committee for failing adequately to distinguish shellshock from 'cowardice'.[61]

In striking contrast to prevailing military and medical attitudes to shellshock were those of parliament, the newspapers and the public at large.

Private charities were set up to help shellshock victims. Both in parliament and in the newspapers they were treated sympathetically and concern was expressed as to what was being done for them.[62] The Under-Secretary of State for war delegated a committee of the Royal College of Physicians to investigate how the 'regiments of broken men' were being dealt with.[63] The MP, Athelstan Rendell, voiced his worries about the treatment of shellshock cases by asylum doctors and in asylums.[64] Although Rendell was given an assurance that army hospitals were not under the aegis of the Board of Control, another anxious MP – Cecil Harmsworth – put a mental health bill before parliament in 1915 that was designed to exempt shellshocked servicemen from certification under the 1890 lunacy laws.[65] Shellshock had it seemed caught both the sympathy and the imagination of the public who, in the words of the official medical history of the war, had 'raised the psychoneuroses to the dignity of a new war disease before which doctors seemed well nigh helpless'.[66]

There were, however, a number of doctors in army hospitals in France and back in the UK who were developing what they themselves saw as a radically effective approach to the treatment of shellshock. These doctors disagreed with the organic model of shellshock's pathology that had been put forward by orthodox neurologists. They also claimed that treatment by 'suggestion' was by no means the best way of bringing about a permanent improvement in the condition of shellshock cases – particularly those who had been ill for some time. It was C.S. Myers who first took up this theme with two case-studies of shellshock victims suffering from aphonia published in the *Lancet* in February, 1915.[67] In these studies Myers demonstrated that his patients' aphonia was hysterical rather than concussive in origin and went on to describe the restoration of their hearing using hypnosis. Myers impressed William Aldren Turner – the man the AMS had sent out to investigate shellshock – with his understanding of the problem and in May, 1916 he was appointed consultant psychologist to the BEF in France. From then on he put considerable energy into promoting the use of psychotherapy and carrying out administrative reforms of the way shellshock cases were dealt with by the AMS – the most important of these being the setting up of special treatment centres close to the front.[68]

Around the same time back in the UK, two groups of psychotherapeutically minded RAMC doctors began to assemble at Maghull under Ronald Rows and at Netley under C. Stanford Read – two psychiatrists sympathetic to the new medical psychology. These places soon became talking shops where devotees of psychotherapy could discuss the ins and outs of theory and could develop their technique. By 1916, dotted around the army shellshock hospitals both in the UK and abroad, there were quite a few doctors using methods of psychotherapy – including the Freudians Jones and Eder, the Jungian analyst Maurice Nicoll, the psychologists Rivers, McDougall and Brown, and several other early pioneers of medical psychology in Britain like T.W. Mitchell, Bernard Hart, and Hugh Crichton Miller.[69] By 1917 a whole string of articles had appeared in the medical journals expounding on the psychological nature of shellshock and the use of psychotherapy in its treatment along with two books on the subject: Eder's *War Shock* and Elliot-Smith and Pear's *Shellshock and Its Lessons*.[70]

The psychotherapists at Maghull and Netley developed an approach to the treatment of shellshock based on various 'abreactive' or 'cathartic' techniques designed to get patients to re-live and re-experience painful 'emotional memories' which had been buried from consciousness. The choice of a particular method depended very much on the nature of the patient's disabilities and on the length of time since the onset of shellshock. Hysterical cases could often be successfully 'abreacted' in one treatment session using hypnosis or recall under the effects of ether. 'Neurasthenic' shellshock cases generally required a more complex and lengthy treatment programme with a greater emphasis on discussions of the patient's feelings about the traumas of his past.[71] Although a number of the psychotherapeutically minded shellshock doctors subscribed to Janet's views on the pathology and treatment of hysteria, and few supported the use of lengthy psychoanalytic procedures,[72] most nevertheless drew heavily on Freud's ideas – in particular his psychodynamic insights into the aetiology of the neuroses. This brought them into confrontation with several leading psychiatrists who bitterly condemned the use of psychoanalytic techniques in the treatment of shellshock on patriotic grounds – reviling Freudian theory as 'Teutonic Science'. Opposition to the psychotherapists at Maghull and Netley was led by the ageing Charles Mercier, a self-confessed Freud-hater who had 'for more than twenty years been demonstrating the rottenness of German teaching in mental disease'.[73] In spite of the fact that just before his death in 1916, Mercier confidently proclaimed that psychoanalysis was 'past its perihelion and rapidly retreating into the dark and silent depths from which it emerged',[74] Freud's theories did manage to establish a foothold in RAMC circles. This was largely thanks to an article by Rivers entitled 'Freud's Psychology of the Unconscious' which appeared in the *Lancet* in 1917.[75] The article impressed quite a few neurologists as a 'level-headed' account of a topic which had hitherto been associated with scientific doctrinairism, angry arguments and heated tempers on all sides.[76]

The account Rivers gave in his article was in fact a substantially moderated version of Freud's views. Plundering psychoanalysis for its psychodynamic concepts like repression, the unconscious, and the notion of mental conflict, he dispensed with the prime role accorded to the sexual life and its drives in the formation of neurotic illnesses. Rather than tracing the origins of the hysterical and anxiety states associated with shellshock back to the patient's infantile sexual impulses, Rivers centred his aetiological account on the emotional world of the battlefield. Not only Rivers, but also Myers, McDougall, and Brown all claimed that sex – in any meaning of the word – had little to do with shellshock.[77] Instead their accounts of shellshock's aetiology concentrated almost exclusively on the conflict between 'fear' and 'duty' as it manifested itself in the soldier's mind. It was this conflict which, as they saw it, caused the Freudian 'flight into illness'.[78]

Borrowing from McDougall, Rivers claimed that 'fear' was the affective aspect of an instinct of self-preservation – a mental function which in Freudian terms was not associated with the libidinous drives of the unconscious. Ernest Jones, Freud's faithful standard-bearer in Britain, was not surprisingly sceptical of Rivers's model. As he saw it the aetiology of shellshock didn't involve fear as such, but morbid anxiety – and this bore no simple functional relation to a supposed instinct of self-preservation. According to Jones, the replacement of the ideals of civilian life by the 'barbaric' attitudes necessary in warfare served to bring about the return of previously repressed and long-buried sadistic impulses. In other words, the trauma of battle had merely served to open a can of libidinous worms and to reconstitute the patient's infantile emotional war with the members of his family.[79]

Arguments between the representatives of orthodox psychoanalysis and the army psychotherapists over the question of shellshock's aetiology and what it had proved and had not proved went on well into the 1920's.[80] They are interesting from several standpoints – not least in terms of the modification of Freud's views after the First World War and the various revisionist adaptations of psychoanalysis promoted by the early pioneers of psychotherapy in Britain. These debates are however far too complex and convoluted to go into in this essay. Instead I want to end this central section with a brief investigation of the nature of the psychological 'fix' on shellshock developed by Rivers and Myers and its significance as a bureaucratic intervention.

What characterized the psychological 'fix' on shellshock was that it combined both military and medical concerns in a manner which valorized the importance of bureaucratic efficiency. Thus it incorporated a notion of discipline on the one hand and therapy on the other. In theoretical terms this was accomplished through the use of a dynamic psychopathology. By using the psychoanalytical concept of unconscious mental conflict, Rivers and his colleagues were able to avoid the simple distinction between malingering and disease. At the same time however they did see shellshock as a disciplinary problem – Myers in fact claimed that the frequency of shellshock cases in combatant troops could be taken as 'an index of unit discipline'.[81] If the polarity between malingering and disease had served to separate off the army's disciplinary and medical machineries, Myers and Rivers sought to bring them together – both from the point of view of prevention and cure.

A good example of this is Myers's reforms of the way shellshock cases were being handled by the AMS in France. One of the first things Myers did was to press for the banning of the informally used diagnosis 'shellshock' or any other medical term by medical officers at the front. The plethora of different labels applied to shellshock cases was replaced by a single standardized bureaucratic term NYDN – Not Yet Diagnosed (Nervous?). Such cases were to be kept apart from soldiers suffering from severe psychoses and from court-martial cases under medical observation. His major contribution was to persuade the military authorities to set up four

Advanced Neurological Centres only a few miles behind the Front to deal with shellshock casualties coming off the battlefields and out of the trenches. Rather than being hospitals or disciplinary training camps, these centres were a combination of the two. Treatment was supplemented by army drill and route marches where possible. NCOs remained in charge of the ranks and patients had to report sick on parade if they wanted to see a medical officer. A standardized bureaucratic form filled out by a medical officer at the casualty clearing station or field ambulance detailed the incidents related to the onset of disabilities. This not only helped in the detection of cases who were wilfully faking symptoms but also aided an informed decision as to whether or not the case in hand was one of 'wound' or 'sickness' – an important factor in the subsequent determination of pension awards. The whole system was designed to bring about the rapid return of soldiers to the line before they were 'lost in the system' and to enable early treatment before their disorders became chronically fixated.[82]

The social construction of shellshock

Throughout this essay I have referred to the range of mental disabilities contracted by soldiers serving in the trenches during the First World War as 'shellshock'. I have done so in order to avoid, as far as possible, any kinds of assumptions about what these disabilities 'actually' were and what it was that caused them. In keeping with this approach, I shall begin this investigation into the social construction of shellshock by examining it as a 'labelling' phenomenon. The word 'shellshock' was coined by C.S. Myers in early 1915 and it soon became a popular expression among soldiers at the front. Its widespread usage testifies to the fact that it was an expression which, at the level of immediate experience, grasped the essentials of the situation. However, as a medical and bureaucratic term it was almost immediately found lacking. Some medical commentators thought it meaningless and others thought it implied too much. The physician Farquhar Buzzard condemned it as a 'bungling' term and the neurologist W.M. Turrell deplored its usage as a 'quasi-legal' diagnosis.[83] The latter criticism was in essence true since 'shellshock' served informally both as an attribution of illness and as an administrative and disciplinary status. If it displeased army doctors and bureaucrats on both these counts, part of this displeasure derived from its popular usage by those over whom the army was attempting to exert control. Many soldiers at the front would literally have given their right arm to get out of the trenches and one can see why some army officers thought that by merely admitting the existence of a non-combatant mental condition a flood of such cases would result and that to do so would provide a ready opportunity for malingerers to avoid their duties.[84] One army lawyer in fact claimed that by the end of the war, 'shellshock' had become a 'parrot-cry' at court-martial hearings.[85]

Indeed, part of the problematic nature of shellshock was seen as stemming from the word itself and it was officially banned as a medical term by the AMS in 1917.[86] Such however was the confusion that the word had created that the Report of the War Office Committee of Enquiry into Shellshock began with a lengthy discussion of just what exactly the word was supposed to mean. Shellshock was certainly an eclectic label – one which during the early stages of the war acted as a makeshift umbrella covering a varied set of administrative, disciplinary, and medical problems the army and its doctors were trying to sort out. The particular medical label a patient would end up with was subject to considerable variation according to the numerous diagnostic schema and theories about shellshock's pathology circulating in the army hospitals in France and the UK. Medical boards concerned with pension awards for shellshock employed their own classificatory scheme. In this respect the diagnostic label pinned to a particular patient had, as far as the patient was concerned, very real consequences. If a conventionally minded neurologist considered that he wasn't suffering from a recognized organic complaint it could mean appearing before an army tribunal. If a medical officer judged that a patient's shellshock was a case of 'wound' rather than 'sickness' this made a significant difference to the size of the pension the patient subsequently received.[87]

In a very real sense then shellshock was a labelling phenomenon. However behind the plethora of diagnostic labels it more often than not entailed equally real – indeed crippling – disabilities. If one looks away from the medical boards and concentrates instead on the battlefield, the formation of a set of pathologies is clearly visible and I now want to look at some of the more concrete aspects of the social construction of shellshock.

Shellshock was, by its very nature, a highly personal emotional drama for those afflicted. But although for each individual it was a private and intimate encounter with the horrors of trench warfare it was an encounter common to many and reproduced thousands of times over. By the end of the war it had become a routine bureaucratic and medical event. It is a somewhat banal observation that shellshock was 'caused' by war. While substantial numbers of soldiers were temporarily or permanently scarred by their experiences in the trenches, still more emerged from this encounter relatively mentally unscathed. One could view the reason why this should be so as a question of personal attitude and individual emotional make-up. Such a 'romantic' view of shellshock does however fail to take into account the systematic nature of its reproduction as a set of illnesses. As the War Office investigators made clear in their report particular 'objective' conditions governed the morbidity of shellshock and these were related to specific features of the organization of life in the trenches. From a clinical standpoint these conditions were immersed within the psychological fabric of military life, work, and training.

It was the psychologists who, more than any other group of medical experts, grasped that the aetiology of shellshock was intrinsic to the organization of army life and work and to the peculiar nature of trench warfare. Their writings on the relation of shellshock's aetiology to army morale and military duties provide a suitable starting-point for a critique of shellshock's social construction. Psychologists like Rivers and Myers saw themselves as providing a critique of shellshock but as a critique their writings are 'reformist' rather than 'radical'. Indeed, their vantage point was still very much from within the military machine and as we shall see this bounded their approach both to the 'prevention' of shellshock and to its 'cure'. I will endeavour to examine shellshock from a broader perspective: its social construction in relation to the industrial mode of warfare which characterized the First World War. Two features of this industrial mode of warfare and its ideological and political framework have an important bearing on the social construction of shellshock – the 'deskilled' nature of military work in the trenches and the ignorance on the part of the public back home in Britain about what life on the Western Front was actually like. The first of these two features deserves discussion in some detail.

In his book *The Face of Battle*, the military historian John Keegan points out that the work of the average British infantryman at the Battle of the Somme was of a highly 'deskilled' variety compared to that of a foot soldier serving in Wellington's army at Waterloo.[88] This was in spite of the fact that since the early nineteenth century there had been a number of major developments in the technology of warfare. At first glance such a state of affairs may seem paradoxical. One must remember however that the First World War was characterized by a particular mode of industrial warfare which set it apart from several other wars in modern history. The basic features of this particular mode of warfare were in keeping with the kinds of developments occurring in European and American industry during the early decades of this century. Indeed, Britain's involvement in the First World War bears several hallmarks of the 'Taylorized' industrial enterprise – the most important of these being the use of mass production techniques and a large deskilled workforce. In the context of the war effort this entailed the mass production of shells in the munitions factories and the use of a vast army of barely trained civilian recruits on the battlefields. The managerial strategy of Britain's war leaders was geared up to this configuration – Lloyd George's production drive at the Ministry of Munitions was complemented on the Western Front by Haig's 'cricket-score' approach to the expenditure of manpower.

This mode of industrial warfare had important consequences for the troops serving in the trenches. Such was the deskilled nature of military craft that it was stripped down to a basic disciplinary function. Moreover, the mass deployment of high-explosives and the use of a manpower strategy which accommodated for vast casualties put the whole disciplinary framework of military duties under a particularly intense stress. I have noted that military and medical experts agreed that a pernicious effect of shellshock was the effect it had on unit discipline. One can see then why it was considered such a profoundly disruptive problem by the military authorities, but also why at the same time the sheer size of the problem had a lot to do with the peculiar nature of work in the trenches.[89] A closer examination of the different duties of officers and men of the ranks enables one to understand a more specific relation between the nature of military work in the trenches and the aetiology of shellshock.

In the trenches, the rank-and-file soldier's duties were valorized primarily as an ability to maintain a physical presence and to act on orders. The mental application required to load the standard issue Lee-Enfield rifle was as nothing compared to the 'nerve' required when going 'over the top' or when sitting out a long bombardment. The military training given to recruits reflected this state of affairs, consisting almost exclusively of drill. Haig thought it a waste of time to teach the volunteer regiments the skilled 'fire and cover' tactics of the regular army and the amount of technical instruction given to recruits was minimal.[90]

If the work of the rank-and-file soldier had been pared down to the basic requirement of being able to respond to orders, the work of line officers had, for the most part, been reduced to the ability to give them. As the brief period of open campaigning at the beginning of the war gave way to the static situation on the Western Front, the operational skills traditionally associated with junior officers were largely taken over by army GHQ. Line officers were left with the basic, but increasingly difficult task of maintaining unit discipline. This was a job which, more than anything, required 'strength of character'.

In an article on shellshock and military training, Rivers examined the two major kinds of shellshock disorder from the point of view of the different duties of officers and men of the ranks. I mentioned earlier that the model of shellshock used by the psychologists was based on a mental conflict between fear and 'duty'. This conflict was not of course in itself extraordinary and was to varying degrees experienced by most soldiers under fire. However, in certain instances it could lead to a 'flight into illness' accompanied by the morbid symptomology of shellshock. Rivers saw the key mechanism precipitating this flight into illness as 'repression'.[91] For him this mechanism provided an insight into the distinction doctors had noted between the way officers and men of the ranks were liable to break down – namely, that shellshocked officers tended to suffer from chronic anxiety states while men in the ranks generally suffered from acute hysterical disorders.

Rivers claimed that this was so because officers, by virtue of their class background – (in particular their experiences in the public school system) were highly capable of dealing with fear. Indeed, many of them having undergone a 'character-building' education were all too capable and continued bottling-up their fears and repressing their anxieties until they finally broke down. On the other hand, most men of the ranks with less previous experience in the 'systematic' handling of fear and without the responsibilities of command shouldered by their officers were, under conditions of acute stress, liable to depart rapidly on the flight into illness.[92]

This distinction between the aetiologies of the two major kinds of shellshock disorders in relation to differences between the duties of officers and men of the ranks may appear common-sensical but it was nevertheless an incisive analysis. Such was the deskilled nature of work in the trenches and the extent to which it had pared down to its basic disciplinary framework that Rivers wasn't just looking at one particular aspect of military duties but was looking at the whole picture.

In this investigation of the social construction of shellshock I have so far concentrated on relating the aetiology of shellshock to the objective determinants of 'duty'. For many the impossible choice precipitating a flight into illness may have been one of 'stay and be shot by the enemy or desert and be shot by your own side'. However there was more to the socialization of the volunteers into a working life in the trenches than a mental representation of the firing squad. In this respect Rivers and the other psychotherapists made it clear that it was often a highly subjective and internalized notion of duty that lay behind the pathology of shellshock.[93] A key phenomenon mediating the internalization of duty was morale.

I have already mentioned that morale in the British army was at a notably high level during the early stages of the war, but that this initial high level dissipated considerably during the latter stages of the war and it was then that the shellshock problem became acute. To understand this it is necessary to look at two methods used in the recruitment of the volunteers both of which have an important bearing on shellshock's aetiology. First, what Lynch has referred to as the 'exploitation of courage'. As Lynch points out the exploitation of courage was, and for that matter still is, one of the prime methods used in the socialization of the soldier.[94] In the First World War it certainly played an important part in a recruitment campaign famous for its appeals to the manly virtues of true-born Britons and for the stigma of the white feather. This systematic exploitation of traditional masculine virtues did however lean on a more well-defined image of wartime self-fulfilment – an image not only promoted by recruitment propaganda but also one firmly grounded in the minds of many would-be recruits before the outbreak of the war itself. 'Empire' patriotism and jingoist teachings were strong among the British working classes before the First World War – a credence fuelled by the events of the Boer War.[95] Among the public schoolboys who made up the backbone of officer recruits to the volunteer regiments, patriotic ideals were buttressed by a military mysticism of the kind evident in the poetry of Rupert Brooke.[96]

This image of wartime self-fulfilment and of a test of personal qualities held by the volunteers bore little relation to the reality of life on the Western Front. Indeed, from a psychological standpoint it was positively dysfunctional. Such was the nature of trench warfare that by 1917, gung-ho jingoists and Hun-haters had come to be regarded by seasoned troops as a dangerous liability, and a profound cynicism was seen as necessary for both physical and mental survival. For many this revelation was a deeply personal disenchantment as it was for the poet Ivor Gurney who after being shellshocked in 1917 wrote to his confidante Marion Scott:

'Do you know my dear friend, the thing that shocks a soldier most is [something] that not many civilians guess at. The fact that men at last do things not for courage or their country but because of discipline (as I was told in 1914, and more still in 1915 but refused to believe).'[97]

The disenchantment described by Gurney was at the heart of many a case of shellshock. Typical 'neurasthenic' patients experienced profound feelings of personal failure in spite of the fact that most had never shirked their duty.

In an important sense then, the systematic exploitation of courage by the government recruitment authorities was implicated in the aetiology of shellshock. A second kind of exploitation involved in the recruitment of the volunteer armies also had an important bearing on the aetiology of shellshock and it could be described as the systematic 'exploitation of friendship' in the form of Kitchener's famous 'Pal System'.

I have already mentioned that the 'Pal System' was effectively destroyed on the battlefields of the Somme in 1916. However, long after this time, the public in Britain still gave widespread credence to the idea that the rank and file of the British army on the Western Front constituted a self-disciplined and self-motivated fighting force. This myth was still supported by the *Manchester Guardian* in 1917 which objected to the drilling of the volunteer regiments claiming that 'moral discipline' was already present.[98] If the *Manchester Guardian* along with many of the leaders of the labour movement in Britain thought that an independently spirited army of working-class patriots could manage their own morale in the trenches, the army's general staff clearly thought otherwise. The remnants of the volunteer regiments discovered this at the notorious Etaples 'bull-ring'. Before the battle of Passchendaele in 1917, preparatory drilling at this training camp was so severe that it provoked a mutiny.[99]

During the latter stages of the war, then, when shellshock became a serious problem, the constitution of morale in the trenches bore little real relation to the mythology of the Pals. Rather it revolved around conventional army discipline. Rivers highlights this point in a study of the prevention of shellshock and military training. In a discussion of the promotion of morale among army recruits he makes use of the concept of 'suggestion' – a concept I have already referred to in the context of medical treatments of shellshock. Rivers claims that 'suggestion' had a direct bearing on the problem of maintaining morale and preventing shellshock. Moreover, he cites a comment by the psychoanalyst Ferenczi that 'prestige' suggestion could be likened to the command of an officer – a comment which aptly summarizes the constitution of morale in the trenches.[100] Rivers was however dealing with suggestion operating in accordance with the army command structure. In this fashion suggestion would maintain morale, internalize the notion of duty in the rank-and-file soldier and prevent outbreaks of shellshock. Suggestion could however operate differently and undermine morale and unit discipline. An eye-witness account of a mass-turnaround of a battalion

of the Royal Scots on the Western Front in March 1918 provides an example
of just such a situation. 'On every face there was a kind of hopeless look. It
seemed everyone's aim was to get as far away as possible from the battle, and
it was surprising how soon after being amongst this crowd, we appeared to
be obsessed by the same idea.'[101]

The psychoanalyst, A.A. Brill, while having no truck with the concept of
suggestion, also saw morale as being dominated by the army command
structure. According to Brill, morale was an essentially libidinous phenomenon whereby the soldier's sergeant would become his older brother,
his junior officer would become his father and his senior regimental officer
would take on the guise of the more 'powerful' and 'distant' infantile
father.[102] It was this regressive scenario of familial relationships that
dominated the emotional life of the soldier in the trenches. At the same time
it constituted the emotional substrate on which shellshock thrived –
furnishing the soldier under stress with a cast of characters from his infantile
past, and according to the psychoanalysts involved in the treatment of
shellshock, with a repertoire of sadistic and homosexual impulses which he
was unable to cope with mentally.[103]

If one examines the psychoanalytical case-studies of shellshock from a
broader sociological perspective it is apparent that the pathology of shellshock was in a number of ways actively engineered and cultivated by the
military ethos of army life. The soldier was encouraged to kill at the expense
of unleashing infantile sadistic impulses that had previously been successfully repressed. He was encouraged to form close emotional bonds with other
men and yet homosexuality was forbidden. Moreover the whole lopsidedly
masculine scenario described by Brill was reinforced by wartime ideology
and propaganda – by the mythology that sprung up around the 'Pals' and by
a recruitment drive that amongst other things promised the fulfilment of
masculinity on the battlefield.

So far I have looked at the social construction of shellshock from the
standpoint of its genesis in the trenches. I now want to concentrate on the
army hospitals where shellshock cases were sent, looking at three different
kinds of 'psychological' approach to the treatment of shellshock which came
into use as the war progressed.

First, the 'put it out of your mind old boy and try and forget all about it'
approach employed by conventionally minded medical officers as a concomitant to their physical treatments. I have showed how Rivers used the
concept of repression to explain the aetiology of shellshock in the trenches.
He also used this concept as a critique of the conventional psychological
approach to treatment – lampooning the standard talking-to that many
shellshock patients received from their medical officers as actually responsible for perpetuating and fixating their neurotic disabilities. Furthermore, as
Rivers indicated, this 'repressive' approach to shellshock was not merely a
question of old-fashioned or ill-informed therapeutics but had a firm
grounding in the procedures by which the staff of army hospitals managed
their patients. In many of these institutions patients were forbidden to

discuss their experiences in the trenches either amongst themselves or with visitors. Thus they remained permanently 'bottled-up'.[104]

Rivers was suggesting that far from curing shellshock, conventional treatments cultivated it. However, what his account failed to acknowledge was the functional nature of this managerial approach to shellshock patients in terms of the basic ideological framework of the war. This ideological framework articulated around two principal sites – the Western Front and the home front. The successful conduct of the war depended, amongst other things, on the maintenance of morale and discipline in the army in the trenches. It also depended on the support of the civilian population back home that provided the industrial back-up to the army on the Western Front in the form of a steady supply of munitions and new recruits. This situation made it important that soldiers serving in the army should stay within the 'exploitation of courage' equation and see the grim realities of trench warfare as a test of personal qualities. It also made it important that the population at home should know as little as possible about what life in the trenches was actually like and keep supporting the war effort and its propaganda. Military hospitals of the kind Rivers was talking about carried out both these tasks admirably. The repression of war experience in these places both maintained the format of army discipline by keeping up the impression in the patient's mind that his problem was one of personal failure and at the same time helped to maintain the credibility of home front propaganda.

If the second kind of approach to treatment – methods based on 'suggestion' – at least managed to return patients to the line and not merely sacrifice their illnesses to the war effort, this was to a large degree due to the face that the medical techniques involved were reinforced by the basic fabric of military social relations. Sir James Kingston Fowler, addressing the neurological section of the Royal Society of Medicine, summarized the suggestion approach to the treatment of shellshock as the 'domination of a strong mind over a weak one'.[105] I have already noted Ferenczi's comment that the therapeutic act of suggestion could be likened to the command of an officer. In this respect one has to remember that in the shellshock hospitals, the doctors treating rank-and-file patients were in fact army officers. In other words, in this therapeutic setting military and medical prestige were inseparable.[106]

The third approach to the treatment of shellshock that came into use during the war – one based on methods of 'abreaction' was presented as, in therapeutic terms, a radical departure from conventional methods. However, it still incorporated a notion of cure fixed within the framework of military social relations – not only in the formal sense of seeing fitness for duty as the criterion of therapeutic success but also in terms of the process of treatment itself.[107] Rivers was regarded as a rebel in RAMC circles but the example of his treatment of the poet Siegfried Sassoon at Craiglockhart War Hospital in 1917 – related in his autobiographical *The Memoirs of George Sherston* – demonstrates that he was still operating very much within the basic framework of military social relations.[108] Sassoon came to Craiglockhart via a trumped-up medical board arranged by his friend Robert Graves after he had declared his support for the pacifist movement. Shaken by his experiences in the trenches and disenchanted with himself in spite of the fact that he had been decorated for bravery on the battlefield, Sassoon was none the less in a relatively stable mental condition. Rivers told Sassoon on his arrival at Craiglockhart, not without a touch of humour, that he was suffering from an 'anti-war complex'. However, the fact remains that he convinced Sassoon that the only way he could mend his sense of personal disenchantment was by returning to the trenches. Rivers may have been a rebel in RAMC circles but he had not escaped the exploitation of courage equation. Moreover his own 'abreactive' approach to shellshock, though presented as a radical critique of existing treatments, also had its problems with the institutionalized repression of war experience. At Maghull where he and Rows had developed an abreactive technique involving dream analysis, the word got around the wards that medical officers were using these sessions to determine whether or not patients were fit to go back to the front. The doctors at Maghull subsequently found it extremely difficult to get their patients to divulge the contents of their dreams.[109] Clearly then there was another side to the repression of war experience.

Conclusion

I hope to have shown in this essay that shellshock and its treatment constituted an important and dynamic episode in the development of psychological medicine in Britain. Traditional approaches to mental disorder were challenged and new ones adopted and adapted in a medical setting dominated by military social relations and by a particular mode of industrial warfare. The criteria governing this reformulation of psychiatry did not revolve around a set of scientific judgements of an 'abstract' ideological kind but around a set of practical problems. These were related to undermining of army discipline, the existence of a large number of servicemen unfit for any kind of work – military or otherwise – and the accumulation of a substantial pensions bill.

By way of conclusion I want to return to a theme I have already touched on in this essay – namely the emergence of the modern psychiatric enterprise. Examining what happened in the US, Castel, Castel, and Lovell have traced the origins of this enterprise back to Freud's writings – in particular his extension of the concept of mental pathology to the non-hospitalized population.[110] Certainly the expansion of the field of mental medicine during the first half of this century incorporated, at the level of medical discourse, a redefinition of the boundary of the 'pathological'. However, I would argue that if we want to understand the historical relation between the redefining of this boundary and the nature of the modern psychiatric enterprise in Britain, we should look not to Freud's writings but to shellshock. No matter how important Freud's writings now seem to us when we look back on the history of psychiatry, the fact remains that before shellshock their influence on the mainstream of British psychiatry was marginal. Freud's redefinition of the pathological remained for all intents and purposes a literary event and the psychoanalytic study of the neuroses took place on the fringes of the medical world where it involved a handful of private practitioners dealing with a small number of upper- and middle-class patients. The wartime episode of shellshock and its treatment stands in dramatic contrast to the heroic intellectual endeavours associated with this scenario. Here the boundary of the pathological was redefined at all its constitutive levels within the social and economic framework of warfare. Shellshock demonstrated that the neuroses could be a widespread working-class health problem that amongst other things was extremely expensive. It brought the neuroses into the mainstream of mental medicine and economic life and set psychiatry's field of practice squarely within the social fabric of industrial society.

Notes

1 P.J. Lynch, 'The Exploitation of Courage' (unpublished MPhil thesis, University of London, 1977). Copy lodged in Senate House Library.

2 R.W. Clark, *Freud: The Man and the Cause* (London: Granada Books, 1982).

3 See E. Jones, *Free Associations* (London: Hogarth, 1959), pp. 228–29.

4 See W.F. Bynum's essay in the companion volume.

5 J.B. Hobman, *David Eder: Memoirs of a Modern Pioneer* (London: Gollancz, 1945), p. 89; E. Jones, *The Life and Works of Sigmund Freud*, ed. and abridged by L. Trilling and S. Marcus (Harmondsworth: Pelican, 1974), p. 365.

6 See M. Culpin, *Recent Advances in the Study of the Psychoneuroses* (London: Churchill, 1931), p. 20.

7 See J.J. Mitchell and G.M. Smith, *History of the Great War Medical Services: Casualty and Medical Statistics of the Great War [HGWMS]* (London: HMSO, 1931), p. 310; also notice in *BMJ* 1 (1920): 36.

8 Hobman, *David Eder*, pp. 5, 99.

9 D. Armstrong, 'Madness and Coping', *Sociology of Health and Illness* 2 (2) November, 1980): 296.

10 See *International Journal of Psychoanalysis* 1 (1920): 115–16.

11 These articles include several about the on-going problem of chronically ill shellshock victims still undergoing treatment in Ministry of Pensions Clinics. See for instance M. Culpin, 'The Problem of the Neurasthenic Pensioner', *British Journal of Medical Psychology* 1 (1920–21): 316–26.

12 W.H. Rivers, *Instinct and the Unconscious* (Cambridge: Cambridge University Press, 1920).

13 W. McDougall, *An Outline of Abnormal Psychology* (London: Methuen, 1926).

14 Rivers, *Instinct and the Unconscious*, p. 12.

15 C. Burt, *The Subnormal Mind*, 3rd edn reprint (Oxford: Oxford University Press, 1977), p. 5.

16 McDougall makes the point that many shellshock cases displayed symptoms severe enough for them to be certified with a diagnosis of grave psychosis had they been civilians. See McDougall, *An Outline of Abnormal Psychology*, p. 34. A far greater number of shellshocked servicemen ended up in asylums than the

authorities seem to suggest. Indeed this group of patients was largely forgotten about. C. Stanford Read informs us that 20.5 per cent of the patients that went through 'D' block Netley – one of the major UK shellshock hospitals – ended up in asylums. See C. Stanford Read, *Military Psychiatry in Peace and War* (London: H.K. Lewis, 1920), p. 52. Here they initially enjoyed certain privileges and were granted a special 'Service Patient' status.

17 C.S. Myers, *Present Day Applications of Psychology: With Special Reference to Industry, Education and Nervous Breakdown* (London: Methuen, 1918, 4th edn 1919), p. 44; W. McDougall, 'The Present Position in Clinical Psychology', *Journal of Mental Science* 65 (1919): 148.

18 Shellshock was second only to wounds in the pensions awards list for the First World War. Many shellshocked servicemen received only a £20–£30 gratuity payment. In 1939 the Ministry of Pensions was still handing out over £2,000,000 per annum to ex-servicemen suffering from chronic neurasthenia. Between April 1919 and March 1929, altogether some 114,000 ex-servicemen passed through Ministry of Pensions facilities dealing with the treatment of war-related neurasthenia. There was a permanent shortage of beds and trained staff, and a considerable backlog of patients requiring treatment throughout this period. For further references to the 'problem of the neurasthenic pensioner' see:

  1 *HGWMSs*, vol. 7 *Casualties and Medical Statistics of the Great War* (London: HMSO, 1931), p. 310.

  2 Ministry of Pensions files on the treatment of war neurasthenia lodged in the Public Records Office, Kew, London. PRO PIN 15/54–55.

19 See G. Elliot-Smith and T.H. Pear, *Shellshock and Its Lessons*, 4th edn (London: Longman, Green, 1919), pp. 78–82, 108.

20 See R. Armstrong Jones, *Nature* 100 (September, 1917): 1–3.

21 D. Armstrong, 'Madness and Coping', p. 298.

22 M.D. Eder, *War Shock* (London: Heinemann, 1917), p. i; also Hobman, *David Eder*, p. 99.

23 Sir Robert Armstrong Jones cited in *Lancet* (2) (1920): 402–04. For evidence of the reactions of leading British psychiatrists to the wartime episode of shellshock, see T.S. Good, 'The Oxford Clinic', *Journal of Mental Science* 68 (1922): 17–23 and the discussion of Good's paper in *Journal of Mental Science* 67 (1921): 525–34. Also see *Journal of Mental Science* 67 (1921): 405–49.

24 For information of the effect of shellshock on the mental hygiene movement and psychiatric social work in the United States, see N. Fenton, *Shellshock and Its Aftermath* (London: Henry Kimpton, 1926); M. Levine, *The History and Politics of Community Mental Health* (Oxford: Oxford University Press, 1981), pp. 33–4.

25 See Armstrong, 'Madness and Coping', p. 293.

26 These themes are discussed in J. Terraine, *White Heat: The New Warfare 1914–1918* (London: Sidgwick and Jackson, 1982), p. 92; J. Keegan, *The Face of Battle* (London: Jonathan Cape, 1976, 1977 reprint), especially pp. 270–72.

27 *HGWMS* vol. 2 *Diseases of the War* (London: HMSO, 1923), p. 2. Also see W. Aldren Turner, 'Arrangements for the care of cases of nervous and mental shock coming from overseas', *Lancet* 1 (1916): 1073–75.

28 E. Wittkower and J. Spillane in *The Neuroses in War*, ed. E. Miller (London: Macmillan, 1940), pp. 18–19. William Brown's testimony before the War Office Committee of Enquiry into Shellshock in the *Report of the War Office Committee of Inquiry into Shellshock* (London: HMSO, 1922), p. 43.

29 *HGWMS*, vol. 2, p. 7.

30 Collie cited in N. Fenton, *Shellshock and Its Aftermath*, p. 166. Also see Miller *The Neuroses in War*, p. 169.

31 See Miller, *The Neuroses in War*, pp. 18–19. Also see M. Culpin, *Recent Advances*, pp. 16–17 and T. Lewis, *Soldier's Heart and the Effort Syndrome* (London: 1918).

32 *HGWMS: Casualty and Medical Statistics*, p. 115. *HGWMS*, vol. 2, p. 13.

33 See Keegan, *The Face of Battle*, p. 271. For a good discussion of life in the trenches and its everyday stresses see J. Ellis, *Eye Deep in Hell* (London: Purnell Book Services, 1976).

34 See Miller, *The Neuroses in War*, p. 15; also *HGWMS*, vol. 2, p. 17.

35 See the *Report of the WOCIS*, p. 28 *et passim*. Also see C.S. Myers, *Shellshock in France* (Cambridge: Cambridge University Press, 1940), p. 40.

36 See Keegan, *The Face of Battle*, p. 215.

37 See Ellis, *Eye Deep in Hell*, pp. 160–80.

38 *HGWMS*, vol. 2, p. 10.

39 H. Yellowlees, *Frames of Mind* (London: William Kimber, 1957), p. 154.

40 Myers, *Shellshock in France*, p. 83.

41 According to J.R. Rees, many shellshock cases found wandering behind lines at the beginning of the war were court-martialled and shot; see R. Ahrenfeld, *Psychiatry in the British Army in the Second World War* (London: Routledge and Kegan Paul, 1958), p. 7.

42 See Elliot Smith and Pear, *Shellshock and Its Lessons*, p. 11.

43 McDougall, *An Outline of Abnormal Psychology*, p. 33.

44 L. Hearnshaw, *A Short History of British Psychology* (London: Methuen, 1964), p. 71.

45 For references to the fact that the study of the neuroses was a neglected field, see A. Lewis, *The State of Psychiatry* (London: Routledge and Kegan Paul, 1967), ch. 8, especially pp. 115–18. A. Hurst, *A 20th Century Physician* (London: Edward Arnold, 1949), p. 103. Hurst claimed that before the war, when neurologists at Guy's examined a patient and no signs of organic disease could be found, there was 'no further interest in cause or cure'. For the neglect in psychological study among psychiatrists and neurologists see W. McDougall, *An Outline of Abnormal Psychology*, pp. 32–3. Ernest Jones makes the basic point that neurologists didn't listen to their patients: see E. Jones, *Free Associations*, pp. 85, 158.

46 See A. von Sarbo in *Neurologische Zentralblatt* 36 (1917): 360; H. Oppenheim, *Berlin Klinische Wirtschaft*, 52 (1915): 257. F.W. Mott, 'A Microscopic Examination of the Brains of Two Men Dead of Commotio-Cerebri (Shellshock)' *Journal of the Royal Army Medical Corps* 26 (1916): 612–15. Oppenheim's theory had been in circulation (*vis-à-vis* the pathology of hysteria) before the war.

47 McDougall picks upon the faulty logic of Mott's argument. See McDougall, *An Outline of Abnormal Psychology*, p. 2. Also see Jones, *Free Associations*, p. 246.

48 The official estimate was around 2.5 per cent. See *HGWMS*, vol. 2, p. 182. Also see *Report of the WOCIS*, pp. 4, 394.

49 M. Ravant cited in *Lancet* 2 (1915): 348, 766.

50 See F.W. Mott, 'War Psychoneurosis', *Lancet* 1 (1918): 127–29; J.M. Wolfsohn, 'The Predisposing Factors of War Psychoneurosis', *Lancet* 1 (1918): 177–80.

51 R. Armstrong Jones, *Nature* 100 (6 September, 1917): 1–3. See Smith and Pear's reply in *Nature* 100 (27 September, 1917): 65.

52 R.D. Gillespie, *The Psychological Effects of War on Citizen and Soldier* (New York: Norton, 1942), p. 21.

53 See H. Cushing, *From a Surgeon's Journal* (Boston, n.p., 1938), p. 388; E.E. Southard, *Shellshock and Other Neuropsychiatric Problems*, (Boston: Arno Press, 1973) p. 693, D.W. Carmalt Jones, 'War Neurasthemia: Acute and Chronic', *Brain* 40 (1919): 205.

54 E.D. Adrian and L.R. Yealland, 'The Treatment of Some Common War Neuroses', *Lancet* 1 (1917): 870. Also see W.J. Turrell, 'Electrotherapy at a Base Hospital', *Lancet* 1 (1915): 229–33. Electrical treatment of shellshock became a favourite method not only in Britain, but in France, Germany, and Austria too. Sigmund Freud gave evidence on the abuse of electrical treatment to an official inquiry carried out in Austria after the war. See S. Freud, 'A Memorandum on Electrical Treatment', in *The Complete Psychological Works of Sigmund Freud*, ed. A. and J. Strachey (London: Hogarth Press, 1955), vol. 17, 211–15.

55 For examples of the methods used at Seale Hayner, see A.F. Hurst and J.L. Symms, 'The Rapid Cure of Hysterical Symptoms in Soldiers', *Lancet* 2 (1918): 139–41.

56 Hurst and Symms, 'Rapid Cure of Hysterical Symptoms', p. 140. Also see Miller, *The Neuroses in War*, pp. 40–1.

57 M. Culpin, *Recent Advances*, p. 24. Also see Miller, *The Neuroses in War*, p. 85.

58 Jones, *Free Associations*, p. 246.

59 McDougall, *An Outline of Abnormal Psychology*, p. 2.

60 Lynch, *The Exploitation of Courage*, p. 28.

61 'Shellshock and Cowardice' (editorial), *Lancet* 2 (1922): 330–40.

62 E.g. see *Manchester Guardian*, 17 March, 1917, p. 6; 24 May, 1917, p. 4.

63 See *Parliamentary Debates of the Commons*, vol. 74 (1915), p. 490.

64 See *Lancet* 1 (1915): 632, 1377.

65 See *Lancet* 1 (1915): 352, 922.

66 See *HGWMS*, vol. 2, p. 9.

67 C.S. Myers, 'A Contribution to the Study of Shellshock', *Lancet* 1 (1915): 316, 320.

68 Myers in fact became the effective 'boss' of shellshock treatment in France as early as March 1915. For a detailed account of Myers's activities see his book *Shellshock in France* which was based on a diary he kept during the war.

69 Ernest Jones was refused a job at Palace Green but ended up doing some work at Maghull. See Jones, *Free Associations*, p. 246.

70 Eder, *War Shock*; Elliot-Smith and Pear, *Shellshock and Its Lessons*. Both these books sold well. Elliot-Smith's and Pear's book went through three editions before the end of the war. Also see Rows, *British Medical Journal* 1 (1916): 441; G. Elliot-Smith, 'Shellshock and the Soldier', *Lancet* 1 (1916): 813–17; C.S. Myers, *Lancet* 1 (1916): 65–9.

71 For accounts of 'abreaction' in theory and practice as used with shellshock, see Smith and Pear, *Shellshock and Its Lessons*; McDougall, *An Outline of Abnormal Psychology*. For the various different positions of the British psychologists on the theory of abreaction see 'The Revival of Emotional Memories and Its Therapeutic Value'. A mini-symposium in four parts with contributions by C.S. Myers, W. McDougall, and W. Brown, *British Journal of Medical Psychology* 1 (1920–21): 20–9.

72 McDougall and Myers both gave partial support to Janet's ideas. See McDougall's *An Outline of Abnormal Psychology*, pp. 11–13, 234–45; C.S. Myers's contribution (II) to the mini-symposium on 'The Revival of Emotional Memories', pp. 20–2.

73 See Clark, *Freud: The Man and the Cause*, p. 375.

74 Mercier, *British Medical Journal* 2 (1916): 900.

75 Mercier, *British Medical Journal* 2 (1916): 900.

76 W.H. Rivers, 'Freud's Psychology of the Unconscious', *Lancet* 1 (1917): 912–14.

77 See Rivers, 'Freud's Psychology of the Unconscious', p. 913; W. Brown, *Psychological Methods of Healing* (London: University of London Press, 1938), p. 11; Myers, *Shellshock in France*, p. 59.

78 After the war some of the psychologists took a more complex view of the aetiology of shellshock – particularly shellshock cases where chronic illness had set in. As far as these kinds of cases were concerned, they acknowledged the importance of 'domestic' causes in the fixation of the illness. E.g. Myers, *Shellshock in France*, p. 132.

79 See E. Jones, *Papers on Psychoanalysis* (London: Ballière, Tyndall, and Cox, 1923 edn), ch. 32, 'War Shock and Freud's Theory of the Neuroses' (Paper read before the RSM Psychiatry Section, April 1918), pp. 577–94.

80 For the various arguments and opinions on the question of whether or not shellshock had 'disproved' Freud's theory of the neuroses, see Jones, *Free Associations*, p. 242; T.W. Mitchell, *Problems in Psychopathology* (London: Kegan Paul, Trench and Trubner, 1927), p. 174 *et passim*; S. Freud, 'Introduction to Psychoanalysis and the War Neuroses', *Complete Works*, vol. 7, pp. 205–10; K. Abraham, 'Psychoanalysis and the War Neuroses', *Clinical Papers and Essays on Psychoanalysis* (London: Hogarth Press, 1955), ch. 14, pp. 59–62. Although the orthodox Freudians claimed that Freud's theory had not been 'disproved' by shellshock, the study of shellshock did reveal weak spots in psychoanalytical theory. Indeed, this work played an important role in the revision of psychoanalytical theory following the war, notably with regard to the nature of 'anxiety', the relation between libido and the ego, the question of primary narcissism, the principle of compulsion-repetition, and Freud's concept of the 'death instinct'.

81 Myers, *Shellshock in France*, p. 39.

82 For accounts of Myers's activities in reforming the medical bureaucracy involved in handling shellshock cases and for accounts of the way the advanced neurological centres were run, see Myers, *Shellshock in France*, pp. 78–84; Miller, *The Neuroses in War*, p. 172; *HGWMS*, vol. 2, pp. 11–12; W. Brown, *Psychology and Psychotherapy* (London: Edward Arnold, 1923), ch. 12.

83 E. Farquhar Buzzard, *Lancet* 1 (1917): 34; W. Turrell cited in the *Report of the WOCIS*, p. 36.

84 See Miller, *The Neuroses in War*, p. 171. Some medical officers agreed – see the *Report of the WOCIS*, pp. 32, 36, 38.

85 See *Lancet* 2 (1922): 339–40.

86 See Myers, *Shellshock in France*, p. 100.

87 See *HGWMS, Casualties and Medical Statistics of the War*, pp. 331–34.

88 Keegan, *The Face of Battle*, ch. 5, pp. 290–342.

89 Several of the psychologists touch on this point. See Elliot-Smith and Pear, *Shellshock and Its Lessons*, pp. 9–10; Rivers, *Instinct and the Unconscious*, pp. 52–60, 241–47. It also came out strongly in the *Report of the WOCIS*. See J.F.C. Fuller's testimony pp. 28–9.

90 See Keegan, *The Face of Battle* p. 226; *Report of the WOCIS*, p. 42.

91 See W.H. Rivers, 'War Neurosis and Military Training', *Mental Hygiene* 2 (4) (October, 1918): 513–33. Monograph Reprint (New York: National Committee of Mental Hygiene, 1918).

92 Rivers, 'War Neurosis and Military Training', p. 5.

93 See for instance McDougall, *An Outline of Abnormal Psychology*, p. 2.
94 Lynch, 'The Exploitation of Courage'. See the conclusion of the thesis.
95 For a discussion of British working-class patriotism before the First World War, see L. Cunningham, 'The Language of Patriotism: 1750–1914', *History Workshop* 12 (1981): 8–33.
96 A good account of this public school, poetic, military mysticism is to be found in P. Fussell, *The Great War and Modern Memory* (Oxford: Oxford University Press, 1977), p. 60.
97 R.K.R. Thornton (ed.), *The War Letters of Ivor Gurney* (London: Coronet Books, 1983), pp. 233–34.
98 *Manchester Guardian*, 27 January, 1917, p. 5.
99 The best account of what life was like at the Bullring is given in W. Allison and J. Farley, *The Monocled Mutineer* (London: Quartet Books, 1978).
100 Rivers, 'War Neurosis and Military Training', pp. 6–7.
101 Eye-witness accounts of Frank Dunham cited in Ellis, *Eye Deep in Hell*, p. 187.
102 A.A. Brill, *Freud's Contribution to Psychiatry* (New York: William Norton, 1944), p. 210.
103 For an account of these themes in the psychoanalytic writings on shellshock, see *Psychoanalysis in the War Neuroses* (London: International Psychoanalytic Press, 1921), contributions by S. Ferenczi, K. Abraham, E. Simnel, E. Jones. The theme of homoeroticism in relation to male comradeship in the trenches is dealt with, from a literary viewpoint, in Fussell, 'Soldier Boys', *The Great War and Modern Memory*, ch. 8, pp. 270–309.
104 See Rivers, *Instinct and the Unconscious*, pp. 187–89; W.H. Rivers, 'The Repression of War Experience', *Lancet* 1 (1918): 173–77. Also see W.H. Rivers's testimony before the WOCIS in the *Report of the WOCIS*, P. 58. E. Wittkower and J.P. Spillane refer to the conventional 'covering' psychotherapeutic approach. See Miller, *The Neuroses of War*, p. 24. Also see Culpin, *Recent Advances*, p. 37.
105 H.G. Fowler, *Lancet* 1 (1918): 438.
106 It is interesting that Ellenberger relates Bernheim's dictum about the power of suggestive therapeutics – namely that hypnosis was easier to induce in people accustomed to passive obedience such as old soldiers and factory workers. H. Ellenberger, *The Discovery of the Unconscious* (New York: Basic Books, 1970), p. 87.
107 See for instance Myers, *Shellshock in France*, p. 50.
108 S. Sassoon, *The Complete Memoirs of George Sherston* (London: Faber and Faber, 1972), ch. 1 'Sherston's Progress'; 'Rivers', pp. 517–57.
109 W.H. Rivers, *Conflict and Dream* (London: Kegan Paul, 1922, 2nd edn 1932), p. 6.
110 F. Castel, R. Castel, and A. Lovell, *The Psychiatric Society* (New York: Columbia University Press, 1982).

Name index

Subject index

abreactive psychotherapy 243, 255, 264–65

Acomb House (York) 111–12

acquittal rates (insanity trials) 40–42, 45, 46–7

admissions 4, 7, 19, 21, 30–31, 134–41, 143; Ticehurst 147–63

aetiology 44, 186, 187, 189; of shellshock 244, 252, 255–56, 258, 260–62, 263

agriculture 63, 64, 88

alcohol 65, 66, 104, 205

alcoholism 54, 140, 141, 142, 182, 208

Aldershot Military Hospital 253

alienism 106, 108, 115, 205, 215; Italian 176, 178–80, 182, 184, 189

Alleged Lunatics Friends Society 161

America 5, 6–9, 247–48

Anabaptists 77

anaesthesia 169, 206, 213

anarchy, hypnosis and 223, 229

animality 27, 54

anthropology 94, 176; criminal 176, 187, 188–9, 230

Anti-Corn Law League 138

antimony (in treatments) 65, 91

antipsychiatry movement 1, 2, 3

antisepsis 169

aperients (treatments) 65

aphonia 253, 254

Appendage (York Retreat) 64

Appendice psichiatrica (journal) 179

army hospitals 242–51, 253–55, 263–65

associationism 53

Asylum Officers Association 112, 113, 115

asylums 3–4, 5–7, 9, 100; admissions *see* admissions; discharges *see* discharges; Hanwell 58, 61, 103, 118; Haydock Lodge 107, 108; inspection *see* Lunacy

Commission; Italian 175–83, 190; Kent County 109, 111–12; Lincoln 61, 109–10; private 12, 102–03, 105–06, 113–19, 147–69; reform (inter-war) 245–47, 251, 254; single patient *see* lodging system; staff-patient ratios 58; Swedish 12–13, 87–96 *passim*; York 53, 58, 99; *see also* Bethlem Royal Hospital; Ticehurst Asylum; West Riding Asylum; York Retreat

Asylums Act (1845) 148

atavism 188–89

authority (medical) 221

automatism 207, 208

autopsy 38, 251

Bastilles of England, The (Lowe) 162–63

bed confinement (treatment) 94

Bedlam on the Jacobean Stage (Reed) 22–3

behaviour, certifiable 140–41, 148

Bethlem Royal Hospital 37, 44, 99–100; administration/finance 20–24, 117; curability in 19–20, 29–31, 65; rules 27–9; stereotype image 11, 17–27, 29, 32, 110; visitors 21–4

birth control education 223

Blackburn workhouse 139

bleeding (treatment) 65, 117

blistering (treatment), 65, 91

Bonifacio Hospital, 177

brain 94, 142, 181, 183; lesions 44, 184–85, 186

Brain 243

Bridewell Hospital 17, 20, 24, 28, 32

bringing back *see* discharges

Brislington House Asylum 58, 100

Britain 5, 7–8; criminal intent (history)

RAMC 243, 245, 250, 253, 254–55, 264–65
rape 198, 214, 217–21
rational recreation campaign 134
recreation 63–4, 110, 134
reflex action 205
Reformation 77
reforms 5–6, 74
refuge (Bethlem's role) 19
religion/religious: at Bethlem 28, 30, 32; delusion 138, 141, 155–56; enthusiasm 76–81; at York 53, 55–8, 62, 68–9, 75; *see also* Catholics; evangelicals; Quakers
Renaissance 2
Representative Government (Mill) 118
repression 255, 260–61, 263, 265
Restoration 79, 81
restraint 112, 115, 117, 181, 183; chemical 3, 11, 65–7; coercive 54–5, 66, 75, 101, 111, 135, 138, 143; at York 53–5, 58–61, 65–7, 69; *see also* non-restraint
revolving chair treatment 87, 91
Revue des deux mondes 204
'Risorgimento' 178, 180
Rivista di filosofia scientifica 187
Rivista di patologia nervosa e mentale 183–84
Rivista superimentale di freniatria 179, 183
Romantics 90
Royal College of Physicians 254
Royal Commission on Lunacy and Mental Disorder 246
Royal Victoria Hospital 251, 254–55

St Elizabeth's Hospital (USA) 2
St Luke's 20, 43
Salpêtrière Asylum 2, 10, 198–99, 206–08, 213, 227, 228
San Lazzaro Asylum 179, 182–83
San Servolo Hospital 177
scarifications 65
schizophrenia 3–4, 44
science 1, 93–6, 104, 119, 180, 183–86
scientific naturalism 179, 190
seances 224
seclusion 54, 59, 61, 91, 109–10, 164
second state 214, 219–20
secularization 79
sedation 92, 94, 139, 165, 181, 218
Select Committees 98, 99–100, 104

self-control 53–4, 57–62, 68–9, 73; *see also* discipline
sensationism 61
servants 220
sexuality 140, 141: Freudian theory 244–45, 255–56; hypnosis and 223–24, 225, 232; infidelity 217, 222–23; rape 198, 214, 217–21
shellshock 10, 242–62: interwar psychiatry and 242–48; social construction of 257–67; wartime treatment 248–57
Shellshock and Its Lessons (Pear) 255
single patients *see* lodging system
skin irritants 65, 91
skull malformations 44, 94
social class 5, 12, 24, 105, 135–36, 140, 153, 159; in Italy 175, 182; *see also* working class
social conditions 34, 38, 45–7, 57, 92–3, 96
social control 116, 159; in Italy 176, 177, 181; as therapy 4–6, 12, 73–4, 88, 132–43; at York 53, 54, 67–8, 69
Social Control and the State (Scull and Cohen) 5
social Darwinism 94
social marginalization 175, 177
social therapy 62–5
Società Italiana di Freniatria 176, 179–82, 186, 187, 188
Society of Friends 53, 55–6, 58, 60, 61, 62, 68; *see also* Quakers
Society of Neurology (Italy) 181, 184
Society for the Protection of the Insane 115
Society of Public Asylum Physicians (Italy) 181
'soldier's heart' 10, 249
solitary confinement 54, 59, 61, 91, 109–10, 164
somatic disorders 93, 94
somnambulism 206, 207, 214, 219, 226, 227, 231
Southall Park Asylum 116
Sozialeinrichtungen 1
spade husbandry 63
spiritualism 199, 228
stimulants 92, 181
Story of Bethlem Hospital (O'Donoghue) 17
subscription hospitals 105, 110
suggestibility 215, 217, 219, 222–23,

229–30
suggestion (shellshock treatment) 253, 254, 262–63, 264
suicide 60, 140, 141, 154, 164, 167, 222
supervision, continuous (treatment) 94
Surrey Asylums 7, 111
Survey of London (Stow) 28
Sweden 12–13, 86–96
Swedish Society of Physicians 94, 95
syphilitic insanity 157, 158

Tavistock Clinic 246, 248
testimony, medical 34–8, 42–7, 50–51, 210–17
therapy 2–3; lay 54, 56–8, 67; moral *see* moral therapy; social 62–5; *see also* psychotherapy
Ticehurst Asylum 58; accommodation and policies 163–65; admissions 12, 147–63, 169; admissions (voluntary) 167–68; case histories 152–53; discharges 147–53, 162, 166–67; lunacy reform movement and 161–63, 165–66
Times, The 155, 169
total deprivation 36, 37, 41
'total institutions' 2, 4, 132
Traité des degenerescences (Morel) 188
Traité des maladies mentales (Morel) 188
trances 80, 224, 227; *see also* hypnosis
tranquillizers 92
Trattato di psichiatria (Bianchi) 185
Treatise concerning Enthusiasm (Casaubon) 79–80
trench warfare 242, 248–50, 255–63, 265
trials 8; Bompard case 10, 197–232; medical testimony 34–8, 42–7, 50–51, 210–17; Old Bailey 9, 34, 39–47, 78

unemployment, insanity and 140–41
Uppsala University 94, 95
Useful Architecture (Matthews) 26
'unsound mind' 35–6

Uomo delinquente studiato, L' 188

Vadstena Asylum (Sweden) 87, 89–92
Vagrancy Act (1714) 28
vagrants 28, 136, 138
violence: certifiable 140, 141, 154; restraint by 54–5, 66, 75, 101, 111, 135, 138, 143
volitional capacity 204, 205, 206, 214, 215
voluntary soldiers 250, 252, 260–62
voluntary treatment 167–68, 247

Wakefield Asylum 58, 63, 135
war, shellshock and 10, 242–57
War Office 247, 249, 258
War Shock (Eder) 255
Welfare State/welfarism 1
Wellcome seminars 22
West Malling Asylum 112
West Riding Asylum 58, 63, 135
'wild beast test' 37
witchcraft 2
womb (lesions) 80
women: in Bethlem 29, 32; fidelity 217, 222–23; rape under hypnosis 198, 214, 217–21; in York Retreat 57, 63, 64
work *see* occupational therapy
workhouses 12, 107, 132–35, 137–40, 142
working class 135–36, 140, 220–21; patriotism 250, 262
World, The (1753) 23

York Asylum 53, 58, 99
York Retreat 2, 100, 106; design/openness 54–6, 63–4, 67; lay therapy 52, 54, 56–8; moral therapy 65–9, 73–6; Quakers at 11, 53–6, 58–9, 60, 62, 68–9, 73, 75–6, 82; self-control or restraint 58–62; social therapy 62–5
Yorkshire Ripper (trial) 9